"I couldn't put my career on hold for two years, but I knew that an MBA would permit me to serve my clients more effectively. Steve Silbiger has placed these necessary skills within reach of all professionals in large and small firms. *The Ten-Day MBA* gave me the competitive edge many professionals seek."

—GARY BLEIBERG
Ten-Day MBA
Chief financial officer—High Yield, The Carlyle Group

"For professionals like me who frequently travel, plowing through night school was out of the question. Now I no longer feel like an outsider when my MBA friends talk. Someday I may need to get my MBA diploma; in the meantime, however, I feel more secure about my business knowledge with only this minimal investment of time and money."

—GREGORY R. RINGEL
Ten-Day MBA
Program manager, U.S. Department of Commerce

"After graduating I never took the time to go back over my notes, case studies, and texts to 'pull together' all that I learned during those two whirlwind years to give the entire experience some substance. *The Ten-Day MBA* did just that . . . well done! The condensed knowledge and fact-filled summaries make this book an excellent refresher course. This should be a must reading for MBAs every year."

—JIM ERNST
Northwestern MBA
Project engineer, United Engineers

"Let's face it. If you are lucky, you remember about 5 percent of what you learn at a top business school. That's where *The Ten-Day MBA* comes in. Silbiger provides an intensive, efficient review of all the important stuff that you've probably already forgotten, but frequently need to know."

—MISHO PROTIC
Wharton MBA
Equity trader, Donaldson, Lufkin & Jenrette

"The conventional two-year MBA is like drinking from a fire hose; *The Ten-Day MBA* is like sipping from a water fountain. You can sip at your own speed until your thirst is quenched."

—ARTHUR KLAUSNER
Stanford MBA
Director of research, Domain Associates (Venture Capital)

"Just like the case method used at most top schools, *The Ten-Day MBA* helps the reader internalize the lessons by using the subject material to solve real-life business situations. The book is a must as a B-school primer or as a stand-alone mini-MBA education."

—GREGORY D. SCHWARTZ
Harvard MBA
Senior consultant, Deloitte & Touche

"Possessing both a law degree and an MBA has been invaluable to me and my clients. Attorneys without an MBA should arm themselves with *The Ten-Day MBA*."

—LAWRENCE BROWN
Chicago MBA
Corporate attorney, Centecor, Inc. (Biotechnology)

"My medical education provided me substantial earning potential, but none of the necessary business skills. *The Ten-Day MBA* has quickly given me the detailed understanding of business that I require."

—DANIEL E. FLYNN, M.D.
Ten-Day MBA
Radiologist

"An attorney needs to have a working knowledge of both law and business. *The Ten-Day MBA* has given me the business tools to best manage my practice and represent my clients. Every lawyer should read *The Ten-Day MBA*."

—CAROL A. CINOTTI
Ten-Day MBA
Partner, McCausland, Keen & Buckman

"The book reminded me of the notes I took in school. It was comfortable to read and poked the appropriate amount of fun when needed."

—KEITH J. DAY
Dartmouth MBA
Real-estate executive

"*The Ten-Day MBA* offers both a comprehensive review for those of us who have completed business school and a great sneak preview for those readers who are contemplating the challenge. The only thing missing from the book is the all-nighters."

—TIMOTHY L. KRONGARD
Virginia MBA
Chief financial officer, Quest Mark Partners (Venture Capital)

"How could you sell out our 'MBA Secrets' so cheaply? If just anyone can sling the jargon around, we won't be 'special' anymore. How will I pay off my student loans?"

—JOHN LEONARD
Virginia MBA
District sales manager, Engineered Assemblies and Components Corp.

"*The Ten-Day MBA* has helped me in countless situations, not only on the job but also in my personal life. Silbiger's tenacious and diligent coverage of all the core MBA courses has given me a more well-rounded understanding of the business world."

—JAMES T. MOONEY
Ten-Day MBA
Marketing manager, McDonald's Corp.

"In less than a week, I was able to refresh my memory on two years of coursework—this book will remain on my desk for the rest of my career."

—ANDREW CROWLEY
Virginia MBA
Consultant, Bain & Company

"*The Ten-Day MBA* has a terrific franchise, owing in no small part to Silbiger's gift for conveying complicated ideas straightforwardly and appealingly."

—ROBERT F. BRUNER
Harvard MBA
Dean, Darden Graduate School of Business, University of Virginia; coauthor of *The Portable MBA*

# *the*
# TEN-DAY
# *MBA*

## 5TH EDITION

# the
# TEN-DAY
# *MBA*

## 5TH EDITION

A Step-by-Step Guide to
Mastering the Skills Taught in
America's Top Business Schools

# Steven Silbiger

**HARPER
BUSINESS**

*An Imprint of HarperCollinsPublishers*

FIFTH EDITION

Designed by Nicola Ferguson

Library of Congress Cataloging-in-Publication Data has been applied for.

ISBN 978-0-06-330777-3

24 25 26 27 28 LBC 5 4 3 2 1

# Contents

Acknowledgments, vii

Introduction, ix

**DAY 1** Marketing, 1

**DAY 2** Ethics, 62

**DAY 3** Accounting, 75

**DAY 4** Organizational Behavior, 123

**DAY 5** Quantitative Analysis, 166

**DAY 6** Finance, 206

**DAY 7** Operations, 264

**DAY 8** Economics, 300

**DAY 9** Strategy, 339

**DAY 10** MBA Minicourses, 381

Research and Competitive Intelligence
Gathering, 381

Public Speaking, 386

Negotiating, 386

International Business, 387

MBA Movie Guide, 387

Business Law, 390

Business Writing, 402

Real Estate Investor, 403

Leadership Coach, 407

Financial Planner, 411

Ten-Day MBA Diploma, 416

Appendix: Quantitative Analysis Tables, 417

MBA Abbreviation Lexicon, 421

Permissions, 423

Index, 427

# *Acknowledgments*

I gratefully thank Rose Marie Morse and Sarah Zimmerman of William Morrow for all their diligent efforts to transform my MBA drafts into the original book. Thanks to Toni Sciarra at Quill, who championed the second edition; Herb Schaffner at HarperCollins, who led the third; Colleen Lawrie, the fourth; and Hollis Heimbouch with Kirby Sandmeyer, in this historic fifth edition.

I also thank Rafe Sagalyn at the Creative Artists Agency (CAA) for his extraordinary ability to see my book's potential and to place it with publishers around the world. The best always make it look easy.

Questions, comments? E-mail the author at tendaymba@gmail.com or visit our Web site at www.tendaymba.com.

# Introduction

After I earned my MBA, I had a chance to reflect on the two most exhausting and fulfilling years of my life. As I reviewed my course notes, I realized that the basics of an MBA education were quite simple and could easily be understood by a wider audience. Thousands of *Ten-Day MBA* readers have proven it! Readers are applying their MBA knowledge every day to their own business situations. Not only useful in the United States, *The Ten-Day MBA* has been translated into many languages around the world. So many people are curious about business education, including doctors, lawyers, businesspeople, and aspiring MBAs. This book answers their questions. *The Ten-Day MBA* really delivers useful information quickly and easily. Current MBA students have written me that they even use the book to review for exams. Ten-Day MBAs are "walking the walk and talking the talk" of MBAs every business day. Executive mini-MBA programs are designed around the book. It's proven that this book can work for you. Written for the impatient student, *The Ten-Day MBA* allows readers to really grasp the fundamentals of an MBA without losing two years' wages and incurring a $225,000 debt for tuition and expenses.

Prospective MBAs can use this book to see if a two-year investment is worth their while; those about to enter business school can get a *big* head start on the competition; and those of you who cannot find the time or the money can get at least $30,000 of MBA education at 99 percent off the list price. Unfortunately, this book cannot provide you with the friendships and lifelong business contacts that you can develop at an elite school. However, it can impart many of the skills that make MBAs successful.

*The Ten-Day MBA* summarizes the essentials of a Top Ten MBA education. The mystique and the livelihood of the Top Ten business schools are predicated on making their curriculum appear as unique and complex as possible. Companies pay thousands of dollars to send their executives to drink from these hallowed fountains of knowledge for a few days. I spent two years of my life not only drinking from the fountain but also bathing and washing my clothes in it.

Which schools are included in the Top Ten is a subject of considerable debate, as displayed by the recent rankings shown at the end of this introduction. The Top Ten actually refers to a group of fifteen nationally recognized schools that play musical chairs for Top Ten ranking. They distinguish themselves by long application forms, active alumni networks, long lists of recruiters, and the ability of their graduates to demand and receive outrageous starting salaries. The Top Ten schools require of candidates at least two years' work experience before admission. Experienced students can enrich class discussions and study groups. A great deal of my learning came from my classmates' work experiences. This was put to the test during the Covid pandemic's remote classes.

The Top Ten schools do not necessarily offer the best teaching, facilities, or curriculum. Reputation plays a great part in their status. A variety of rating books are available that give the "inside" story on those reputations. So many magazines and Web sites are now publishing rankings because they are among their best-selling issues.

My aim is to cut to the heart of the top MBA programs' subject matter clearly and concisely—the way only an MBA can, and the way academics would not dare. To cover the major concepts, I use examples and outlines and summarize wherever possible. I slice through the long-winded and self-serving academic readings that at times I had to trudge through. This book contains only the pearls of wisdom buried in my thirty-two binders of cases, course materials, and notes, and updated by current MBAs.

I have no vested interest in promoting any of the business theories presented in the book. Therefore, this book does not repeat the same idea over the course of two hundred pages as many popular business books tend to do. I crystallize the most important concepts in brief passages so you can learn and remember them without losing interest.

From my interviews with graduates from Wharton, Harvard, Northwestern, and other top schools, I learned that all of their programs serve up the same MBA meal. Only the spices and presentations of the business banquets vary.

The basics of MBA knowledge fall into nine disciplines. Some schools have carefully crafted their own exalted names for each subject, but their unglorified names are:

Marketing
Ethics
Accounting
Organizational Behavior
Quantitative Analysis
Finance
Operations
Economics
Strategy

The synthesis of knowledge from all of these disciplines is what makes the MBA valuable. In the case of a new product manager with an MBA, she can not only see her business challenges from a marketing perspective, but she can recognize and deal with the financial and manufacturing demands created by her new product. This coordinated, multidisciplinary approach is usually missing in undergraduate business curricula. By learning about all the MBA disciplines at once, in one book, you have the opportunity to synthesize MBA knowledge the way you would at the best schools.

When MBAs congregate, we tend to engage in "MBA babble." Our use of mystical abbreviations like NPV, SPC, and CRM is only a ruse to justify our lofty salaries and quick promotions. Please do not be intimidated. MBA jargon is easy to learn! As you read this book, you too will begin to think and talk like an MBA.

My goal is to make you familiar with the significant MBA tools and theories currently being taught at the leading business schools and to help you understand and develop the MBA mind-set. When you finish the ten days, please feel free to fill in your name on the diploma at the end of the book. It serves as evidence of your scholarship, and you should proudly display it for all your friends to see.

## CURRENT MBA SCHOOL RANKINGS

Below are the most current rankings of MBA programs. Although the rankings change from year to year, the same schools are consistently listed. School names listed in parentheses immortalize founders and major benefactors. International schools have become a force to be reckoned with.

### *TWO-YEAR MBA DEGREE PROGRAMS*

#### *U.S. News & World Report,* Top Business Schools, *2023*
Based on peer academic leaders, recruiter surveys, admission standards, and employment success
1. Chicago (Booth)
1. Pennsylvania (Wharton)
3. Northwestern (Kellogg)
3. Stanford
5. Harvard
5. MIT (Sloan)
7. Yale
8. Columbia
8. Berkeley (Haas)
10. Michigan (Ross)
11. Dartmouth (Tuck)
12. Duke (Fuqua)
12. NYU (Stern)

14. Virginia (Darden)
15. Cornell (Johnson)
(Several ties in the rankings)

## *Bloomberg Businessweek,* Top Business Schools, 2023–24

Based on employer, student, and alumni polls

*Top U.S. Schools*

1. Stanford
2. Chicago (Booth)
3. Virginia (Darden)
3. Dartmouth (Tuck)
5. Columbia
6. Harvard
7. Northwestern (Kellogg)
8. Pennsylvania (Wharton)
9. Michigan (Ross)
10. MIT (Sloan)
11. UC Berkeley (Haas)
12. NYU (Stern)
13. Cornell (Johnson)
14. Duke (Fuqua)
15. Yale
(Several ties in the rankings)

*Top European Schools*

1. SDA Bocconi (Italy)
2. IESE Business School (Spain)
3. IMD (Switzerland)
4. INSEAD (France / Singapore)
5. London Business School (UK)
6. IE (Spain)
7. Mannheim (Germany)
8. St. Gallen (Switzerland)
9. Cambridge (Judge) (UK)
10. Oxford (Said) (UK)
11. ESADE (Spain)
12. Cranfield (UK)

13. EDHEC (France)
14. ESIC (Spain)
15. Manchester (UK)

*Top Asian-Pacific Schools*

1. Hong Kong (HKUST)
2. Shanghai University of Finance and Economics (China)
3. China European International Business School (CEIBS)
4. Indian Institute of Management Bangalore
5. Indian School of Business
6. Shanghai University MBA Centre (China)
7. SP Jain (Singapore)

## *Financial Times,* Top Business Schools, *2023*

Based on student outcomes, alumni network, faculty quality, diversity, and carbon footprint

1. Columbia
2. INSEAD (France / Singapore)
3. IESE Business School (Spain)
4. Harvard
4. Stanford
6. SDA Bocconi (Italy)
7. Berkeley (Haas)
8. Cornell
9. Northwestern (Kellogg)
10. Yale
11. Duke (Fuqua)
11. MIT (Sloan)
11. Chicago (Booth)
14. UCLA (Andersen)
15. Dartmouth (Tuck)
16. London Business School
17. HEC Paris
17. University of Virginia (Darden)
19. NYU (Stern)
20. CEIBS (China)

(Several ties in the rankings)

## *The Economist,* 2022

Based on current and former student surveys

*Top MBA Programs in the U.S.*

1. Harvard
2. Stanford
3. Pennsylvania (Wharton)
4. Chicago (Booth)
5. MIT (Sloan)
6. NYU (Sloan)
7. Columbia
8. Dartmouth (Tuck)
9. Berkeley (Haas)
10. Virginia (Darden)

*Top Educational Experience, rated by students and alumni, world survey*

1. IMD (Switzerland)
2. Virginia (Darden)
3. Washington University St. Louis (Olin)
4. Michigan (Ross)
5. NYU (Stern)

*Best Faculty, rated by students and alumni, world survey*

1. Virginia (Darden)
2. Chicago (Booth)
3. MIT (Sloan)
4. Washington University St. Louis (Olin)
5. MD (Switzerland)

## *Fortune, Best MBA Programs,* 2022

Based on salaries, placement, brand reputation, C-suite alumni

1. Harvard
2. Chicago (Booth)
3. Northwestern (Kellogg)
4. Pennsylvania (Wharton)
5. Stanford
6. Columbia
7. NYU (Stern)
8. Duke (Fuqua)

9. MIT (Sloan)
10. Virginia (Darden)

### *Princeton Review,* "*The Top Ten of the Top Ten,*" *2023*

Poets&Quants Web site compilation of Princeton's Top Ten review categories

*Best Classroom Experience, Best Professors, Best Career Prospects, Best Campus Environment, etc., based on student surveys*

1. Virginia (Darden)
2. Michigan (Ross)
3. Duke (Fuqua)
4. Harvard
5. Stanford
5. Cornell (Johnson)
5. Rice (Jones)
8. Yale
8. North Carolina (Kenan-Flagler)
8. UCLA (Anderson)
8. NYU (Stern)

(Several ties in the rankings)

# *the*
# TEN-DAY
# *MBA*

## 5TH EDITION

## Day 1

# MARKETING

### *Marketing Topics*

The 7 Steps of Marketing Strategy Development

The Buying Process

Segmentation

Product Life Cycle

Perceptual Mapping

Margins

The Marketing Mix and the 4 P's

Positioning

Distribution Channels

Advertising

Promotions

Pricing

Marketing Economics

A scene from the boardroom of Acme Corporation:

DIRECTOR: Every time we do our annual review of our executives' salaries, I cringe when I think that we are paying more to Barbara Mooney, our vice president of marketing from Penn State, than to our company's president, Hank Bufford from Harvard. I just don't understand it.

"HOLD ALL CALLS. I'LL BE DOWN IN ACCOUNTING—FLEXING MY MUSCLES."

CHAIRMAN OF THE BOARD: What don't you understand? Without Barbara's sales we wouldn't need a president—or anyone else for that matter!

Marketers see the world like the chairman of Acme. As renowned professor Philip Kotler of the Kellogg School at Northwestern teaches, marketing comes first. Marketing integrates all the functions of a business and speaks directly to the customer through advertising, salespeople, and other marketing activities.

Marketing is a special blend of art and science. There is a great deal to be learned in marketing classes, but no amount of schooling can teach you the experience, the intuition, and the creativity to be a truly gifted marketer. That's why those with the gift are so highly paid. Formal education can only provide MBAs with a framework and a vocabulary to tackle marketing challenges. And that is the goal of this chapter and of the numerous expensive executive seminars conducted by the leading business schools.

The top schools prepare their students for executive marketing positions—in spite of the fact that their first jobs will likely be as lowly brand assistants at large food or soap companies. Therefore, the core curriculum stresses the development of full-fledged marketing strategies instead of the technical expertise needed on an entry-level job out of MBA school.

Numbers-oriented students tend to view marketing as one of the "soft" MBA disciplines. In fact, marketers use many quantitative or "scientific" techniques to develop and evaluate strategies. The "art" of marketing is trying to create and implement a winning marketing plan. There are literally an infinite number of possibilities that may work. McDonald's, Burger King, Wendy's, and Shake Shack successfully sell burgers, but they all do it in different ways. Because there are no "right" answers, marketing classes can provide students with either an opportunity to show their individual flair, or many hours of frustration as they try to come up with creative ideas. Marketing was my favorite subject. It was fun cooking up ideas for discussion. My B-school buddies still kid me about the time I proposed to the class that Frank Perdue introduce a gourmet chicken hot dog.

## THE MARKETING STRATEGY PROCESS

The marketing process is a circular function. Marketing plans undergo many changes until all the parts are *internally consistent* and *mutually supportive* of the objectives. All aspects of a proposal need to work together to make sense. It is easy to get one part right, but an internally consistent and mutually supportive marketing plan is a great accomplishment. It's a seven-part process.

1. Consumer Analysis
2. Market Analysis
3. Review of the Competition and Self
4. Review of the Distribution Channels
5. Development of a "Preliminary" Marketing Mix
6. Evaluation of the Economics
7. Revision and Extension of Steps 1–6 until a consistent plan emerges

Although there are seven steps, their order is not set in stone. Based on circumstances and your personal style, the order of the steps may be rearranged. This chapter could get bogged down in a morass of marketing theory, but to make it practical, I will outline the questions and areas that should be considered when developing a marketing plan. For expediency, I will concentrate on product marketing, but the same frameworks and vocabulary are also applicable to service marketing.

I will present the MBA models in the same seven-step order in which they are taught at the best schools. This chapter offers a generic structure to apply to whatever marketing issue you may encounter. I have not neglected to use the vocabulary taught at the schools, so you can pick up on the MBA jargon and speak like a real MBA marketer. Marketing is an area especially rich in specialized vocabulary. With the correct vocabulary, even your mediocre marketing ideas can appear brilliant. That may sound funny, but that's the way ad agencies market *their* product, advertising.

This seven-step marketing process is comprehensive, and MBAs will often refer to more abbreviated ones, such as STP (segment, target, position), or the four C's of marketing (consumer behavior, company analysis, competitor analysis, context), but the methodology presented here covers it all.

## 1. CONSUMER ANALYSIS

Consumer Analysis → Market → Competition → Distribution → Marketing Mix → Economics → Revise

All marketing plans should begin with a look at the all-important "consumer" and his or her needs. People do not have the same needs or desires. The objective of consumer analysis is to identify *segments* or groups within a population with similar needs so that marketing efforts can be directly targeted to them. Starting anywhere else tends to restrict your thinking and all subsequent analysis. Several important questions must be asked to find the market that will unlock untold marketing riches:

What is the *need category*?
Who is buying and who is using the product?
What is the *buying process*?
Is what I'm selling a high- or low-involvement product?
How can I *segment* the market?

*What is the need category? Who needs us and why?*

What is the need or use that your product addresses? The question may seem unnecessary, but in answering it you may uncover a potential market for the product that was previously overlooked. That is why this question has to be addressed first, before you begin to pollute your mind with conventional thoughts. The people at Arm & Hammer baking soda have done a great deal of this type of analysis. They have made use of their powder in their own brand of toothpaste, air freshener, and carpet freshener. In addition, they

MARKETING STRATEGY DEVELOPMENT

profitably recommend their raw baking-soda powder for hundreds of uses.

*Who is buying versus who is using the product?*

Buyers many times are different from users. Women, for example, make the majority of purchases of men's underwear and socks. If an advertising campaign wanted to target the buyer of men's socks, it would probably be inappropriate to send e-mails to men. Determining the buyer as well as the user provides the essential initial insights to create a marketing plan.

*What is the buying process?*

Once you have established the need, and who is making the purchases, you should try to form a hypothesis on *how* the product is bought. Marketing research is a prime source of information, but just as valid are your own observations, investigation, and intuition.

Understanding the *buying process* is critical because it will lead to the possible routes to reach buyers. The buying process includes all the steps that a person takes leading to a purchase. It is also called the *adoption process* and the *problem-solving process* by some academics. Some researchers call it a Learn/Feel/Do process. Others call it AIDA, for Attention/Interest/Desire/Action. I have read extensively on this topic and have boiled the theories down to five steps. For any particular product, the buying process can include one or all of the following steps:

**Awareness → Information Search → Evaluate Alternatives → Purchase → Evaluate**

In the instance of a soap purchase, the process would look like this:

Smell Body → What Should I Use? → Soap → Ask Wife for Advice → Make Trip to the Store → Read Labels → Buy Dial Soap → Bathe → Smell Body for Odor → Buy Dial Soap Next Time

The steps of the buying process explained:

Awareness. (Interest, Problem Recognition). "I might need something." At some point a person will realize a need, like the need to use soap. Advertising may trigger that need. Prestige products such as designer clothes and fragrances trigger desire. They meet emotional needs such as love and group acceptance. Head & Shoulders preys on the fear of a loss of love and group acceptance. You need to ask yourself, "How do consumers become aware of my product?" "Where are my targets likely to be exposed to my message?"

Information Search. "Sounds good, let me find out more about it." People involved in purchase decisions are confronted with information from a variety of sources: *Consumer Reports,* salespeople, blogs, specialty magazines, family, friends, and local experts. As a marketing manager, you want your target market to get as much favorable information as possible about your product when and where buyers make their buying decisions. For example, store displays play that role at the *point of purchase* (POP). Cover Girl Cosmetics has a display in drugstores to help buyers select colors. For the same purpose, Estée Lauder has its Clinique ladies in department stores to do its talking.

Evaluate the Alternatives. Which one is best for me? This includes not only products within a category, but substitutes as well. When confronted with the high prices of automobiles, a college student may end up buying a motorcycle, a longboard, or a bicycle. Depending on the importance of the product, consumers may seek additional information and advice. Car purchases often include a trip to the local mechanic or the neighborhood car buff. Placing positive information where your buyers are likely to look is one key to marketing success.

At this stage of the buying process the marketing manager would like to identify the *influencers* of his target's buying behavior. On the Internet, TikTok, Facebook, and Instagram celebrities spread the word. In the golf industry the club pro is a key influencer in the equipment-buying decision of golfers. If you can sell the pro, you can sell to the club's members.

Distribution is also crucial at the evaluation stage of the buying process. If a product is not readily available, a comparable substitute may be chosen just for convenience or immediacy of need. Coca-Cola's and Pepsi's wide distribution makes it tough for any new cola competitor to ever be any more than a fringe brand. Even if you crave Dr. Brown's creme soda, you will probably accept a Coke or a Pepsi when you're thirsty at the beach.

The Purchase Decision. This is the big sale. Even though the decision to buy could be yes, in certain instances the first purchase is only a *trial*. *Adoption* of "new and improved" Bounty paper towels as your regular brand occurs only after a successful test with those tough spills. With many big-ticket items, such as ocean cruises and appliances, a trial is not possible. In those instances the decision process is more time-consuming and difficult to make because there is more risk involved. It is very important for the marketer to understand risk. Through the use of a number of marketing tools, such as advertising, knowledgeable salespeople, warranties, printed materials, and Web sites, purchase risk can be reduced by offering the buyer information explaining what level of performance he or she can expect, as well as providing a basis of comparison with competing products.

Evaluate. (Postpurchase Behavior). Did I make a mistake? This conclusion can be reached either on a physical level by testing the product's efficacy or on a psychological level by checking for peer approval. *Buyer's remorse* and *postpurchase dissonance* are terms to describe the period of confusion that often follows a purchase. Automobile advertising, for example, is not only targeted at potential buyers, but also at recent buyers to reassure them that they didn't screw up when they bought a Toyota Sienna minivan instead of a Honda Odyssey.

In trying to understand the buying process, the first sparks of a marketing plan can be ignited into a tentative idea about advertising or promotion (to be considered later in Step 5 of the strategy development process).

*Research Can Help to Understand the Buying Process.* Consumer research is a major tool in helping make the buying process theory useful. Research can show a marketing director where he has succeeded and where his efforts need to be redirected. Research is valuable if it can be translated into tangible marketing actions. Before you embark on research, you *must* ask yourself:

"What specific question do I need answered?"

"How am I going to use the information once I have it?"

If you haven't thought through these two simple questions, you will probably waste your time and money. I can assure you that many marketing research companies will be glad to help you waste money.

*Is the product a high- or a low-involvement product?*

As the discussion of buyer behavior indicates, different products elicit different purchase behaviors because of their inherent importance to the buyer and user. If the consumer feels a high level of "risk" in buying a product, then it is considered a *high-involvement* product. There are several reasons for high-involvement purchase decisions:

**High price**

**The need for the product's benefit** (e.g., reliability, as in the case of a pacemaker)

**The need for the product's psychological reward** (e.g., status, love)

Clothing, cars, and professional services are examples of high-involvement purchases. They are usually higher priced and at times difficult to compare. Determining the differences between alternatives makes high-involvement purchases difficult, especially if the buyer is not an expert. Thus, the information search can be quite extensive. When litigating a damage claim, for example, usually there is no second chance to take the case to trial. Therefore, the choice of a lawyer is a high-involvement selection. With *low-involvement* products the decision is simpler. For example, if a candy bar isn't tasty, you can always pitch it and buy another one.

A helpful matrix below captures the possible behaviors resulting

CONSUMER BEHAVIOR MATRIX

|  | High Involvement | Low Involvement |
|---|---|---|
| Significant Differences | – Complex Process<br>– Brand Loyalty | – Experiment<br>– Random Behavior<br>– Variety Seeking |
| Few Differences | – Anxiety (Dissonance)<br>  Reduction<br>– Baseless Beliefs<br>  About the Product | – Buy Cheapest One<br>– Random Behavior<br>– Baseless Loyalty<br>– Inertia |

Adapted from Henry Assael, *Consumer Behavior and Marketing Action*, 4th ed. (Boston: PWS-Kent Publishing Co., 1992), p. 100.

from the interaction of the levels of involvement and product differences. By understanding the possible behaviors, you, as a marketer, may be able to take advantage of this knowledge to sell your product.

This academic model does have real-world implications for action. A high-involvement product, such as a Harley-Davidson motorcycle, would appear in the upper left-hand corner of the matrix. The model would suggest that Harley's marketing efforts should be geared toward demonstrating its technical superiority, but also include an emotional appeal—"buy an American classic"—to engender loyalty.

The marketer's magic is at work when he or she transforms a previously low-involvement product into a high-involvement one. Athletic shoes are a prime example. Once just functional shoes for gym class, sports shoes have become a status symbol for young people and valuable collectibles for speculators. The conversion of a low-involvement product to a high-involvement product can make a simple commodity product stand out against an undifferentiated field of competitors. There are four generic ways in which this can be accomplished.

Link Product to a High-Involvement Issue. Linking no-cholesterol cooking oil to a wife's fear of a husband's heart attack is a classic example of an advertising ploy.

Use Involving Advertising. If the advertising creates a *value-expressive* message about the product or service, then a product can become important. Such messages link values, such as social status and love, instead of promoting physical product attributes to differentiate the product from the competition. Pepsi tries to link being modern and youthful with its products by using singers in elaborate commercials to sell its soda.

Change the Importance of Product Benefits. Products as well as services provide a variety of benefits. If through marketing action a benefit can be raised to a heightened level of importance, buyers are likely to become more involved. The beer wars of the 1980s made calories an important competitive issue. An overlooked attribute—calories—made health-conscious drinkers more aware of their purchasing decisions, and consequently Miller Lite made out like a bandit. In the 2000s it was carbohydrates. In 2022 the "gluten-free" labels on baked goods were attractive to many, even to those with no gluten allergy.

Introduce Important Characteristic to Product. A marketer can also tinker with some of the elements of the product itself to distinguish it. When childproof caps were introduced on household cleaners, the involvement of parents in this purchase decision was heightened. The first products with protection caps stood out on the store shelves. But once all competitors copied the cap, new avenues of differentiation were needed and the purchase returned to its low-involvement status.

Truly low-involvement products often are that way because a minimum level of acceptable performance is required. A thumbtack, for example, does not have a difficult job to perform. No matter what the brand, you can't go too wrong. If the cost of trial is low, such as for a pack of gum, involvement is difficult to stimulate.

Related to involvement is the level of purchase planning. Is the purchase planned or an impulse buy? High-involvement products are usually planned, while impulse products are bought on the spur of the moment. If a purchase is planned, then a buyer is likely to seek information. If not, the proximity of the product to the need is important. Snack foods are an example of impulse buying. Midday hunger leads to the nearest junk food.

*Do I intend to segment the market? Why? How?*

I skirted around this issue in the buyer behavior section, but the question "Who is our consumer?" is central to the marketing task. If you think you have something that is for everyone, then a *mass market* strategy is appropriate. If your product satisfies the masses, then feed it to them. If not, you must choose a *segment* or segments of the market to target. Segments are homogeneous groups of similar consumers with similar needs and desires. For instance, Coca-Cola uses a mass-market approach to get everyone drinking the "real thing." Snapple, a specialty tea, appeals to a more narrowly defined market segment. It's priced higher and its bottle is shaped different. Snapple appeals to a special segment of the soft drink market.

*Segmentation* of the market serves the following functions:

To identify segments large enough to serve profitably.
To identify segments that can efficiently be reached by marketing efforts.
To help develop marketing programs.

By having a definite segment in mind, you can effectively aim and efficiently execute your marketing activities to yield the most sales and profits. Without a target, you risk wasting marketing dollars on disinterested people. There are four major variables used in segmenting consumer markets:

- Geographic
- Demographic
- Psychographic
- Behavioral

*Geographic Segmentation.* Divides the market by country, state, region, county, and city. The federal census lists 310 *Standard Metropolitan Statistical Areas* (SMSAs) to define the major geographic population centers of the United States. Arbitron, a large media research firm, has defined a similar measure to capture the 210 major television markets of the country, called *Areas of Dominant Influence* (ADIs). A. C. Nielsen, a competitor, has a similar measure called *Designated Market Areas* (DMAs). Geolocation by zip codes and GPS data from cell phones are used to target ads for hyperlocal advertising, both for online and mobile marketing.

*Demographic Segmentation.* Divides a population based on the following measurable variables to reach a homogeneous group of people:

*Age* — Different generations' different wants and needs
*Sex* — Gendered and non-binary use and buying patterns
*Income* — The ability to purchase
*Marital Status* — Family needs
*Family Life Cycle* — Starting out, empty nesters, etc.
*Education/Occupation* — An indication of the sophistication of the consumer
*Ethnicity, Religion, and Race* — Particular tastes and preferences

*Psychographic Segmentation.* Divides the market by psychological differences:

*Lifestyle* — Activities, interests, and opinions
*Personality* — Conservative, risk-taking, status-seeking, compulsive, ambitious, authoritarian, gregarious. (People may have different hot buttons that advertising can try to trigger.)

Psychographic segmentation is difficult. Personality variables are tougher to identify and quantify than demographics, but they can be valuable.

*Behavioral Segmentation.* Divides the market by observable purchase behaviors:

*Usage* — Amount of use, manner of use, benefits sought

*Purchase Occasion* — Gift, vacation, seasonal, etc.

*Brand Loyalty* — Loyalty to one product indicates receptiveness to others

*Responsiveness to Price and Promotion* — Some groups respond to special marketing efforts more than others.

Marketers must not only select the "right" group of variables but also decide how many to use. The correct number of "useful" variables will identify the most accessible and receptive target, not the most specific. For example, it is possible to describe a target segment for Corvettes as brown-haired, male, twenty-five to sixty-five years old, with income over $150,000. However, the ability to target just brown-haired men with effective advertising is limited and its usefulness would be dubious. Is brown hair a necessary segmentation variable? There are no magazines exclusively targeted to brown-haired males. Besides, blond and redheaded men may also be a reasonable market for Corvettes. You should use the following criteria to evaluate possible marketing segments:

*Measurability* — Can you identify the segment? Can you quantify its size?

*Accessibility* — Can you reach the segment through advertising, sales force or distributors, transportation, or warehousing?

*Substantiality* — Is the segment large enough to bother with? Is the segment shrinking, maturing, or growing?

*Profitability* — Are there enough potential profits to make targeting it worthwhile?

*Compatibility with Competition* — Are your competitors interested in this segment? Are competitors currently investigating it or is it not worth their trouble?

*Effectiveness* — Does your company have the capabilities to adequately service this segment?

*Defendability* — Can you defend yourself against a competitor's attack?

With that theoretical background, here's a sample demographic profile of gourmet coffee buyers that marketers actually use:

Twenty-five to fifty-four years old
College educated
Professional or business executive employment
Childless households
Household incomes greater than $100,000

This market segment is measurable, accessible, large, and profitable. Consequently, many large coffee companies continue to target it.

Even in markets that appear hopeless, there may be a segment that others overlook. Xerox controlled 88 percent of the copier market in the 1970s. The majority of its sales came from large and medium-sized units. But by 1985, Xerox had lost more than half of its market share. What happened? Xerox ignored the small-copier market. Thousands of small companies with light copy needs had to run to the local copy shop every time they had a copy job. Canon, Sharp, and Ricoh seized this market by selling a smaller and less expensive copier. With a foothold in small copiers, the Japanese competitors proceeded to topple Xerox in the large-copier segment of the market.

Consumer analysis serves to "prime the pump" when you need to form a comprehensive marketing strategy. Do it first so as not to stifle your creativity with the quantitative analysis you will perform as part of the strategy development framework. On a first pass, you can make an "intuitive" choice of a target segment. After the other steps are completed, it can be altered to fit an evolving marketing strategy.

## 2. MARKET ANALYSIS

Consumer → **Market Analysis** → Competition → Distribution → Marketing Mix → Economics → Revise

While segmentation analysis focuses on consumers as individuals, market analysis takes a broader view of potential consumers to include market sizes and trends. Market analysis also includes a review of the competitive and regulatory environment. By closely examining the market, a marketing manager can determine if the segment selected is worth the trouble of a targeted marketing effort. MBAs ask three important questions to evaluate a market:

What is the *relevant* market?
Where is the product in its *product life cycle*?
What are the *key competitive factors* in the industry?

*What is the relevant market?*
The easiest mistake to make is to believe that your *relevant* market includes the total sales of your product's category. In between the first and second years of my MBA education, I worked for an international trading company. I investigated the possibility of selling a Mexican gourmet ground coffee in U.S. grocery stores. It would have been misleading for me to assume that all coffee sales were in my relevant target market. Approximately $11 billion of coffee was sold in the United States at the time. However, 60 percent of that total was sold in stores, while the other 40 percent was sold to the institutional markets, including restaurants and vending machines. That left me with a retail market of $6.6 billion.

But within that larger coffee market there were additional submarkets to investigate before arriving at my final relevant market. The gourmet coffee market accounted for $750 million, or 11 percent of the retail market's sales. Within the gourmet coffee market, only 60 percent of the coffees sold had no artificial flavorings. My Mexican coffee had no additives and the producer refused to artificially flavor his coffee. Therefore, my relevant market was further reduced to $450 million. But of that market slice, only 55 percent was sold in supermarkets. That left me with a $248 million market. *That* was my relevant market.

Once a market segment is identified, you have to ask if it is large and accessible enough to justify your marketing effort. If the answer to that question is no, then you have what is called a "makable" product, but not a "marketable" one. Only marketable products make money.

These questions are difficult to answer and involve marketing research. If it is a new product, the answers will not be readily available. Test markets may have to be used to obtain that information. This step may lead to further segment investigation.

The growth and decline of consumer segments within a market should also be noted. When the market is growing, future sales growth can come from new users or existing customers. If the pie is shrinking, any sales growth has to come out of your competitors' hide, and they'll fight you for market share! Following the demographic trends to attract a growing senior citizen market, Pfizer, the manufacturer of Centrum vitamins, made a minor reformulation and successfully introduced its "Silver" formula.

*Where is the product in its product life cycle?*

Products can be characterized by the stage that they are at in their *product life cycles* (PLC). Instead of being merely a factor of time, the PLC describes how a product's sales grow as new segments become aware and begin buying it. Cellular phone service began in the early 1970s with fewer than ten thousand users. But it wasn't until the 1990s, when the prices dropped and many could afford a unit for their cars, that a multisegment market of over 6 million users emerged. Now everyone has a cell phone.

The PLC concept is important because the process of *diffusion* or adoption by the population has major implications for how a product is marketed. Each product develops its own unique PLC as it matures. Understanding the PLC can give you an MBA insight that your competitors may lack.

The four generic stages of the PLC and their implications for action are:

Stage 1: Introduction, "What is it?" Awareness and education are needed. If possible, a trial is important. High advertising costs may be incurred to get the word out. Some vendors opt for an *exclusive distribution* of their products in a few select outlets at first. Initially companies make frequent product changes as customers' needs become known. The first buyers are called the *innovators,* followed by the *early adopters*. They freely take purchase risks because their personalities or pocketbooks allow them to do so. When companies introduce new products, managers must make difficult pricing decisions because there is frequently no basis for comparison. The level of initial prices and profits has great implications regarding the outcome of future battles with competitors as well as your ability to perform additional research and development (as with products like couture fashion, new drugs, and AI products).

Stage 2: Growth, "Where can I get it?" Education is still important, but at this stage competition is intensified. The *early majority* becomes interested. As more consumers become familiar with a product, they examine the new models to decide *which* to buy, not *whether* they should buy. When buyers get to the store or investigate on the Internet, they start comparing features. To make the product more accessible, marketers often choose a *selective distribution* to gain a greater number and variety of outlets. At this "tipping point" it is important to boost your sales volume ahead of the competition in order to reduce costs through production and advertising efficiencies. This helps a company gain the competitive advantage in the next stage of the PLC (e.g., electric vehicles, virtual reality headsets, smart watches, and diabetic weight loss drugs).

Stage 3: Maturity, "Why this one?" At this stage the *late majority* of the mass market buys. Because people are accustomed to buying the product and the differences are few, brand loyalty plays a dominant role. Price competition often becomes heated in stable markets because additional market share comes directly from your competitors in this "shake-out" stage. The product's features that were so important in the growth stage have become standardized.

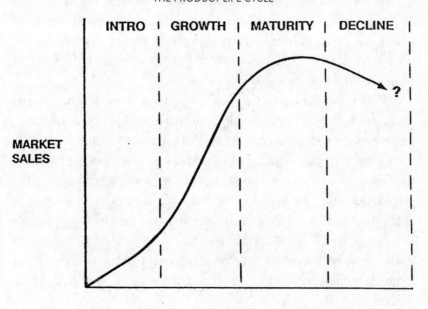

THE PRODUCT LIFE CYCLE

INTRO | GROWTH | MATURITY | DECLINE |

MARKET SALES

?

TIME

Because there is less differentiation on product attributes, advertising is used as a vehicle to differentiate products. Marketing managers try to segment their target market as much as possible to meet specific unmet consumer needs. In mature markets, competitors are ferreting out all possible segments. All possible channels of distribution are also considered using a *mass market* distribution strategy (e.g., cell phones, laptops, jeans, colas, vacuums, flat screen TVs).

Stage 4: Decline, "How much?" As a product ages in its PLC, it is likely that its competitors offer similar products. Even the most timid consumers, the *laggards,* find it safe to buy the product at this late stage. (If it does cause cancer, the FDA has usually found out by now.) Consumers turn a deaf ear to advertising because they know that all competing products are the same. At this stage many companies focus their efforts on reducing price if competition remains, or slowly increasing prices if the competitive field thins. Top rankings on Amazon and Internet searches are key. Trade relations are key to staying on the retail shelf at this point, because without the excitement of novelty, distributors and retailers would rather allocate space to newer and potentially more profitable products. The effort to sell the trade is popularly called *relationship marketing* (e.g., DVDs, digital cameras, GPS devices, cable TV).

With some products the maturity phase does not necessarily mean death. Products can be reinvigorated after a period of maturity, and a new growth phase can begin, like the surge in vinyl records.

In some cases, lingering death throes produce large profits for the last manufacturer. In the vacuum tube business, which supplies electronic tubes for imaging, communications, and other equipment, Richardson Electronics is the survivor in an industry once dominated by GE, RCA, Westinghouse, and Sylvania. Using an *end game strategy,* the remaining producers can extract large profits from customers since they have nowhere else to go for their replacement parts.

*What are the key competitive factors within the industry?*

The basis of competition in each industry or market tends to be different. It has a major impact on how a business attacks its market. There are five major *key competitive factors* that constitute the battleground in most industries:

· Quality
· Price
· Advertising
· Research and Development
· Service

In the fast food industry, for example, intensive advertising and promotion are key. In industries providing raw materials to others, price and service are key. In my investigation of the coffee industry, I found price and quality to be the basis of competition. When developing a marketing plan, you may want to try to change the basis of competition to one that favors your firm, but the key underlying competitive factors cannot be ignored.

## 3. ANALYSIS OF YOUR COMPANY VERSUS THE COMPETITION

Consumer → Market → **Competitive Analysis** → Distribution → Marketing Mix → Economics → Revise

By this stage the marketer has preliminarily chosen a consumer segment toward which to direct his or her efforts. Now, a plan to beat the competition must be developed. You need to look at yourself and at the competition with the same level of objectivity. What are your advantages? What things do you do well? (MBAs call them *core competencies*.) What are your weaknesses? How can your company capitalize on its strengths or exploit your competitors' weaknesses? The following questions help to flush that out.

*How does your SWOT Compare to Your*
*Competitor's SWOT*
SWOT is a related framework MBAs use to organize the previous questions about how your company stacks up versus the competition. SWOT stands for Strengths, Weaknesses, Opportunities, and Threats. Strengths and weaknesses are internal factors. Opportunities and threats are external. It is vitally important to perform this analysis on your own company as well as on your competitors. The following questions help to flush out the key points required for a SWOT analysis.

*What is your company good at and what is the competition good at?*
· Distribution (Frito-Lay)
· New Product Development and Introduction (Apple)
· Advertising (Geico)

*Who are we in the marketplace?*
· Market Size and *Relative* Market Share
· Financial Position
· Historical Performance and Reputation

*What are our resources versus those of the competition?*
· People
· Technology, Research
· Sales Forces
· Cash
· Trade Relations
· Manufacturing

*Barriers to entry* to new competitors in a market play an important role in assessing the competition. Barriers are conditions or hurdles that new competitors have to overcome before they can enter the market. The availability of cash and specialized knowledge are such barriers. The pharmaceutical industry, for example, is dominated by a few companies. To be a player, a company needs a large sales force, research labs, and a large bank account to pay for it all. Because of these barriers, most small companies team up with large ones if they have a promising new drug to peddle. In the online auction market, eBay has a huge advantage because of the size of its buyer audience, vendor base, and infrastructure. On the other hand, Google's Internet search competitors have a lower barrier to entry. Internet searchers can easily switch services, and competitors, such as Bing, can develop new AI-powered search technologies. Google is creating proprietary databases of information that competitors' searches can't access to create a barrier to entry as well as tying users to the service with Gmail. MySpace was the leading social platform until Facebook overwhelmed it in 2008 with a more user-friendly, open platform. Facebook was upended in 2012 by Instagram's photo-sharing capabilities, so Facebook acquired it. TikTok's video functionality upended them both in 2021.

If in an industry the barriers to entry are low, the playing field becomes crowded. Savvy marketers should plan for that eventuality by trying to form a marketing strategy that new competitors cannot easily copy. This is more fully discussed later in the book in the "Strategy" chapter.

During my coffee investigation, I looked at what my company had to offer. It didn't have much. It didn't have any experience in the United States. We lacked distribution, advertising expertise, a reputation, and cash. The only thing my Mexican employer had to offer was quality packaged coffee. What could a small competitor do against Folgers and Maxwell House coffees? After much questioning, and feeling a little ill, I hoped that there might be a large food company that would like to enter into a joint venture. We would supply the coffee and the partner would do the distribution and marketing. We could *piggyback,* not unlike what small pharmaceutical companies do, recognizing that some profit is better than none.

*What are the market shares of the industry players?*

Many tracking services are available for consumer products such as NPD Group and InfoScan. Checkout scanners and warehouse tracking collect supermarket sales data. Such details are called *granular* sales data. However, for industrial products, such as manufacturing equipment, the information is less accessible. Trade associations are a good source.

*Market share leverage* is a key concept to consider when examining market shares within an industry. The companies with larger market shares relative to their competition usually enjoy higher profits. Larger competitors can produce more cheaply per unit because they can spread their costs over more units. A smaller competitor cannot afford to spend as much on either research or more efficient equipment, because the smaller sales volume cannot support the burden. If I had been charged with a new instant coffee to sell, I would have had to reconsider entry into the declining instant-coffee market dominated by three bigger, lower-cost competitors: Kraft, Nestlé, and Folgers. Fortunately for my Mexican coffee's entry, 18 percent of the "ground" coffee market was controlled by smaller competitors. And that share had increased from 16 percent in the prior year. This constituted a far more favorable environment for a new entrant such as my Mexican ground coffee.

*How does my product perceptually map against the competition?*

The *perceptual mapping* technique is a graphic way to view and compare your product against the competitors'. A commonly used grid is *price* and *quality,* but many others are possible and useful.

Maps are another MBA technique to generate ideas for marketing for your product, and perceptual maps may highlight an unserved market segment by showing how the consumer perceives competing products, regardless of the physical reality of performance. Perceptions are paramount in marketing, just as they are in politics. In the paper towel industry, for example, towel strength and decorator appeal are important. As an example, using my own judgment, I have created a "hypothetical" map below. Notice that Bounty found itself a profitable market segment by providing strength and a pretty pattern.

By visualizing how your product maps versus the competition, you may gain an insight into how to market your existing product, make product changes, or add additional products in a comprehensive marketing strategy. Open areas of opportunity are called *white spaces*.

If your company has many products within a category, then you are said to have *depth* of line. In the paper towel market no one pro-

PERCEPTUAL MAPPING PAPER TOWEL BRANDS (HYPOTHETICAL)

ducer dominates the category. But over in the dog food aisle, Nestlé Purina depth chokes the shelves with Dog Chow, Puppy Chow, Pro Plan, O.N.E., Beneful, Alpo, and at least six other brands.

If your company has many products in a variety of product classes, you are said to have *breadth* of product line. Kimberly-Clark has a wide breadth of paper products in several categories: Viva paper towels, Kleenex and Scott tissue, Cottonelle toilet paper, Kotex sanitary napkins, and Huggies, Depend, and Pull-Ups diapers. Depth and breadth of product lines can be cleverly used in a *blocking strategy* to prevent competitors from gaining access to the channels of distribution. If they are not on the shelf, your competition can't make any sales.

In the dog food industry, competitors found other ways around Nestlé Purina to reach doggie owners. Hill's Pet Nutrition, a division of Colgate-Palmolive, pushed $3 billion worth of Science Diet pet food and other products through veterinarians' offices.

*How is my product positioned against the competition?*

In the 1950s, it was all about creating a "unique selling proposition" (USP) that focused on product features and customer benefits. In the 1960s and throughout the 1970s, the product's "image" was important. In 1972, Al Ries and Jack Trout developed the concept of "positioning" that has been popular ever since. They believed that the perception of your product in the minds of consumers is actually more important than the physical reality of the product's attributes. What consumers believe is their reality. They had ten rules for positioning that they believe can make a product or service stand above the competition.

1. Own a word in the consumer's mind. If you establish one benefit in the consumer's mind, the consumer may attribute other positives as well to your product. FedEx means "overnight delivery." Only one company can own a word, and it is tough to change it once it's established.

2. Positioning begins with the product's name. The name should be descriptive, to establish the main benefit in the consumer's mind. Draino opens clogged drains.

3. If you have a unique new product, use a new name. Owning a unique, simple URL also helps in top search results. Think the Tesla car, Hint Water, Ozempic drug, or Google search engine.

4. The easiest way to own a word is to be first. Consumers tend to stick with products that work for them. Kleenex cleans runny noses.

5. Don't stray from your message; "reinforce the original concept" in all marketing activities. "Coke Classic is the real thing!" Having *unity of message* across all media aids in "omnichannel marketing."

6. The best way to respond to a new competitor is to introduce a new brand, not blurring the original one. When bottled water became popular, Coke didn't call theirs Coke Water, rather, it chose Dasani.

7. The first option for a follower is to establish a new category. Established brands are tough to beat, but consumers will adopt a new category more easily. Charles Schwab established the discount brokerage category.

8. The second option of a follower is to find an open position in the consumer's mind. Starbucks became the premium quick-service coffee brand.

9. The third option for a follower is to reposition the competitor to undercut the leader's concept, product, or spokesperson. Tylenol said, "If your stomach is upset, check with your doctor before your take aspirin."

10. Stay consistent with the positioning you choose.

## 4. REVIEW OF THE DISTRIBUTION CHANNELS

Consumer → Market → Competition → **Distribution Analysis** → Marketing Mix → Economics → Revise

Marketers speak of the avenues to the consumer as the *channels of distribution*. There are often many ways of reaching your customers, as described with dog food sales. Distribution channel analysis is critical, because the choice of channel influences the price you can charge, and, consequently, the profit margins that you may enjoy. Three questions should be asked to provide you with a basis for your distribution decision:

How can my product reach the consumer?
How much do the players in each distribution channel profit?
Who holds the power in each distribution channel available?

*How can my product reach the consumer?*

In the case of many clothing mail-order catalogs, there is a direct link between the marketer and the final consumer. A catalog manufacturer of clothing has a direct pulse on sales, returns, pricing, and consumer tastes. As manufacturers of grocery items, brand managers are distanced from the buyer. Cereal, a consumer packaged good (CPG), must go through wholesalers and retailers before reaching the consumer. Those middlemen are called *channel intermediaries*. As a strategist, the marketing manager must outline all the paths to the consumer to develop a plan.

Commonly used channel intermediaries to the consumer are:

· Wholesalers
· Distributors
· Sales Representatives
· Sales Forces
· Retailers

*How do the players in each distribution channel profit?*

As I mentioned, it is helpful to understand all the paths to the consumer in order to know all the possible ways to market your product. Take the time to draw them out on paper. A channel sketch can also give you the insight into the retail price that must be charged to make a profit.

Everyone who touches the merchandise takes a cut, which is called their *margin*. Participants in the distribution chain are said to "take margin" from the manufacturer. As a manufacturer of a product, you do not "give" the channel margin; there is no charity involved. Channel participants in most industries calculate their cut as a *markup on selling price*. Canadian and some U.S. drug firms use a markup on cost, but they are the exceptions. The *selling price* is not the ultimate *retail* price, but the price at which one intermediary sells goods to the next intermediary in the chain. The retail price is what a consumer pays.

Because of my experience in the coffee industry, I will use coffee retailing to demonstrate the economics of the channels of distribution. At each level of the chain, the intermediary buys the coffee from the previous level and takes a margin based on the sales price to the next level. The margin is *not* based on cost.

$$\text{Percent Markup on Selling Price (SP)} = \left( \frac{\$ \text{ Markup}}{\$ \text{ Selling Price}} \right) \times 100$$

This is how one dollar's worth of coffee beans, in my example, can reach the consumer at a price of six dollars. At each level, the channel participant adds value and incurs costs by either roasting, grinding, and packaging the coffee beans; promoting the brand; or distributing and shelving the packaged coffee for the consumer. I have outlined on page 29 what I estimated were the channel economics for Maxwell House's gourmet coffee.

At each level in the distribution channel, the participant performs its function, takes its margin, and sells to the next participant closer to the consumer. If a coffee processor, such as Kraft Foods, believes that its gourmet Maxwell House coffee brand must retail at $4.00 per pound rather than $6.00, then the economics of the chain must change. Let's work backward through the chain to see its effect on the prices charged at each level.

CHANNEL OF DISTRIBUTION FOR MAXWELL HOUSE'S PRIVATE COLLECTION
COFFEE WITH CHANNEL MARGINS AND PRICES

| Channel Participant | Channel Function | Selling Price to Next Level | Margin (Markup on Selling Price) |
|---|---|---|---|
| Sr. Juan Valdez | Grower | $1.00 lb. | |
| Westway Merkuria | Coffee Broker | $1.05 lb. | 4.8% ($.05 / $1.05) |
| Kraft Foods | Processor | $4.20 lb. | 75% |
| Associated Grocers, Inc. | Grocery Wholesaler | $4.62 lb. | 9% |
| Bob's Market | Retailer | $6.00 lb. Retail Price | 23% |
| Mr. Mocca Java | Consumer | | |

Selling Price × (1 − Markup %)
= The Preceding Distribution Level's Selling Price

Working backward through the distribution chain:

$4.00 Retail Price to Consumer × (1 − .23 Retail Markup) =
$3.08
$3.08 Wholesaler Price to Retailer × (1 − .09 Wholesale
Markup) = $2.80

$2.80 would be Kraft Foods' (the Processor's) Price to
   Wholesalers

At the $4.00 price, Kraft Foods' brand manager must ask
if $1.75 ($2.80–$1.05) per pound is a sufficient margin to cover
costs and provide an adequate profit. If the answer is no, the brand
manager must reexamine the marketing plan's channel mathematics. Because marketing strategy is a circular process, another price,
manufacturing process, or cost may have to be altered. Such changes
could affect all the other elements of the plan.

The relative power of the channel participants can dictate pricing decisions based on the economics of the channel chosen. In Kraft
Foods' case, the brand manager could have opted for the lower
$4.00 retail price in the grocery store. However, he chose $6.00 to
yield his desired profits.

Kraft Foods decided to use an alternative channel in addition to
grocery stores. Kraft "bypassed" the grocery trade's middlemen and
sold its Gevalia coffee brand directly to coffee lovers by mail order
at a price over $10.00 per pound. With most products there are usu-
ally a variety of ways to reach the consumer. Each channel has its
own channel margin mathematics. By understanding the math you
are better able to make a choice of channel.

### Who has the power in the channels?

The question of channel power is crucial in selecting where to
sell. If your product is unique and in demand, then the manufacturer
generally has the power to outline the terms of the relationship. If
not, the channel's intermediaries will be able to dictate the terms to
take as much margin as possible.

In the grocery trade, the power of the channel has shifted from
the manufacturers to the supermarket chains. As smaller grocery
chains consolidated into larger superchains in the 1980s, the larger
chains' management realized that they held the prized real estate,
"shelf space." Each *stock keeping unit* (SKU) on the shelf takes
space. Each product must be tracked, shelved, and inventoried.
When Mazola cooking oil produces three sizes, it takes up three

SKUs. With a finite amount of store and warehouse space, the shelf real estate has become valuable, and retailers want to be paid for carrying each SKU. Marketers even diagram their shelves like architects in drawings called *planograms* and fight over best placement.

Packaged-goods companies, large and small, must often pay *slotting fees* to the chains to reserve "slots" on their shelves for both new and existing products. In the 1970s the packaged-goods giants could force their products on the trade. When there were many smaller grocery chains, Procter & Gamble and Kraft Foods could play one chain against another by threatening to withhold their popular products. That is no longer the case.

Unfortunately, slotting fees can run into millions of dollars for a new product introduction. Therefore, in practice, slotting fees bar smaller competitors from selling in the supermarket. A maker of an excellent pizza in the Midwest that I knew failed to get off the ground because it could not afford the bribes necessary for space. Slotting fees are a "hot topic" in retailing. Feel free to interject this topic into MBA conversation as often as you like.

*What is the Internet's role as a channel of distribution?*
The Internet can be a great way to sell product. The Internet has four functions as a channel of customer communication, called the *Four C's of Internet marketing.* The "commerce" function of a Web site allows for sales, but more importantly it provides a 24/7 storefront to fit the customer's schedule to shop, browse, and compare product offerings. The "content" of your Web site is an extension of the product. It can provide additional support and value, and if it is compelling, it can attract new prospects, from generic search and AdWords and convert leads to sales. Your site can provide "customer care" by allowing customers to access their accounts, check on deliveries, and get answers to frequently asked questions (FAQs). This pleases customers and also reduces a manufacturer's cost of live customer service. And lastly, Web sites also "convert leads" from your Internet and other marketing efforts, such as television, radio, sales promotions, and public relations.

## 5. DEVELOPMENT OF THE MARKETING MIX

Consumer → Market → Competition → Distribution → **Plan the Marketing Mix** → Economics → Revise

Based on judgments developed in the analysis of the consumer, the market, the competition, and the distribution channels, the marketing manager must make a set of tangible decisions. MBAs call it the *action plan*. Marketing managers choose what *mix* of marketing efforts should be made. The mix is commonly referred to as the *Four P's* of marketing.

The development of the *marketing mix* is an evolutionary process whose goal is an *internally consistent and mutually supportive* plan. That cannot be overemphasized. Tinkering with one P in the mix generally means the marketing strategist must alter all the other P's in some way, because one P affects the others.

| **Product** | Place | Promotion | Price |

### *PRODUCT DECISIONS*

How does my product fit with my other products?
How will I differentiate my product?
How does the product life cycle affect my plans?

*How does the product fit with my existing product line?*
This question tries to identify areas of synergy among your products, or uncover a constraint on your activities. For example, if "The Dependability People" at Maytag added dishwashers to their line of clothes washers and dryers, the product, the customers, and the retailers for the dishwashers would be shared with their existing line. There would be a fit with this *line extension*. But if Maytag wanted to sell personal hair dryers, the fit would be questionable.

THE MARKETING MIX

*How will I differentiate my product?*

*Differentiation* is a broad issue that includes any way that a marketer can distinguish his product from the field. Consequently there are many ways to do it.

- *Features* — Capabilities
- *Fit* — Tailoring
- *Styling* — Functional, visual
- *Reliability* — Warranties, return policies
- *Packaging* — Color, size, shape, protection
- *Sizes* — Clothing, appliance, computer, and luggage sizes
- *Service* — Timeliness, courtesy, accuracy
- *Brand Naming* — Labeling

If Ralph Lauren had used his real name, Ralph Lifshitz, he would have forgone the psychological benefits derived from his Ralph Lauren's Polo label on $6 billion in clothing, cologne, and bedding in 2022. Lifshitz somehow fails to convey the image of aristocracy.

In many cases the so-called *brand equity* of one product can be transferred to new products using a *brand* or *line extension* strategy that differentiates it from the pack. The Jell-O brand bestows upon the new products all the goodwill and brand recognition (brand equity) that Jell-O has earned over decades. It would take many years of expensive advertising to establish the brand equity of the Jell-O brand. Accordingly, almost 90 percent of the thousands of new product introductions since 1987 were line and brand extensions. If stretched too far, a brand's equity can be diluted and its effectiveness with consumers devalued.

The choice of any one of these product differentiation techniques affects the entire marketing process, as it lays the groundwork for your promotional efforts. A product can be differentiated from the competition by creative advertising and promotion, even if competing products are physically identical.

*Perceptual maps and positioning can help to differentiate the product.* All the product attributes mentioned affect the *positioning* of a product in the marketplace. The marketer can always call upon his company's product engineers to develop a product's physical characteristics if the profits justify it. As my perceptual map of paper towels indicated, consumers have specific needs within a product class, and they perceive each product differently. The marketer's job is to uniquely position the product (using a perceptual map as a guide if desired) to earn its place in the market. That place is often called a product's *niche* in the market. As pictured in the perceptual mapping of paper towels, Georgia Pacific's Brawny brand is positioned as the tough, durable towel for really dirty cleanups. Hopefully the brand manager will choose a niche that will yield the most sales and profits by targeting a market segment his product serves best. Positioning is inexorably tied to the market segment selected through your consumer and market analysis.

*How does the product life cycle affect my plans?*
Based on the point in the *product life cycle* (PLC), different aspects of the product become more important in the competitive battles. The previous discussion of the PLC noted that product features are extremely important to differentiate products in the growth

phase, while branding is increasingly more important in the maturity phase. The emphasis on multiple features on smartwatches, for example, currently indicates the growth phase of the PLC. Whatever the choices for the product, product decisions will have a definite effect on the other P's of the mix.

Product     **Place**     Promotion     Price

### *PLACE OF SALE DECISIONS: WHERE TO SELL?*

In your review of the distribution channels, the goal was to determine what avenues exist and what margins are available. At this stage, having made product decisions and a choice of target market, the marketer has to choose an appropriate channel to fit with the product and the intended buyers.

What distribution strategy should I use?
On what basis should I choose a channel of distribution?

*What type of distribution strategy should I select?*
- *Exclusive* — Sell in only one outlet in each market
- *Selective* — Sell in only a few outlets in each market
- *Mass or Intensive* — Sell in as many outlets as possible

The place of sale affects the perception of your product. The choice of distribution is an evolving process that matches the product's intended diffusion along the product life cycle, as described in the market analysis passage. A distribution strategy can differentiate your product from the crowd. For example, if a new designer chooses to sell *exclusively* at Neiman Marcus, it gives a certain cachet to the product. Consumers tend to perceive certain attributes in a product, such as style, quality, and price, based on the point of sale. The same designer may choose to *selectively* sell in only better department stores to provide greater initial sales volume. The California marketer of car-window sun shields had no such concern, and selected a *mass* distribution strategy. The company wanted to distribute the cardboard shade as widely and quickly as possible. That choice made sense since the shades, unlike designer clothing, did not have any status appeal and could easily be copied and manufactured.

Each of these distribution methods places certain responsibilities upon the manufacturer and the retailer. By choosing to be selective, the manufacturer may be "obligated" to provide high quality, good service, and possibly *cooperative payments* (co-ops) for promotional support. When manufacturers share the costs of advertising with retailers, that is called *cooperative advertising*.

In distribution relationships involving manufacturers' incentives, the retailer is also obligated. Retailers may be "obliged" to pay special attention to the product by giving it preferential placement, special promotion, display, and sales attention. If those obligations are not met, the contract is breached and the relationship can be severed. In Ralph Lauren's case he believed that his Polo clothing line was so unique that he became the first designer to demand separate boutique space in department stores. Ralph provided the image and the margins sought by retailers. The retailers were in turn obliged to provide Ralph Lauren with special placement and selling efforts.

*Which channels of distribution to choose?*

It depends . . . on a variety of factors. There is usually more than one choice. If a channel is integrated into a "mutually supportive and internally consistent" strategy, many choices can potentially be successful. Three factors should serve as a guide to make a selection.

Product Specifics. Another factor to consider is the level of attention needed for the sale. This is related to the level of complexity of the product, the newness, or the price. The product may indicate a need for your own sales force despite the costs. On the other hand, products such as candy and soft drinks are sold through a series of wholesalers and distributors before reaching the store shelves. These products are simple and do not require direct control by the manufacturer over the presentation and sale.

Need for Control. The ability to motivate the channels to carry your product effectively and appropriately enters into the placement decision. The further the manufacturer is removed from the consumer with distributors, wholesalers, and jobbers, the less control the manufacturer has over how a product is sold. Pharmaceutical companies usually have their own sales forces, also called *captive* sales forces, that are thoroughly trained to provide credible information to doctors. If Merck or Pfizer had to rely on an independent sales force, they would not have absolute control over their training or conduct in the field.

Margins Desired. The analysis of the channels of distribution helps to determine the potential profits available. Where are the margins taken at each level? Can your company deliver the product through the channels at a competitive price and still reserve enough margin for itself? Based on the available margins, channel decisions can be made. In the case of Bose premium priced headphones and earbuds, more selective marketing in corporate stores, print, and other forms of direct marketing allow for Bose to maintain their margins and control their brand's premium image.

| Product | Place | **Promotion** | Price |

## *PROMOTIONAL DECISIONS*

Promotion includes all the advertising and selling efforts of the marketing plan. Goal setting is paramount in developing a promotional campaign. You need to know the mission you want to accomplish before you can begin to draft or spend the promotion budget. The ultimate goal of promotion is to affect buyer behavior; therefore, the desired behavior must be defined. Different products, at different stages of the PLC, with different levels of involvement and complexity, require different promotional efforts to perform different missions. The promotional mission chosen for your product must be consistent with the buying process outlined in your *consumer analysis*.

| BUYING PROCESS | PROMOTIONAL MISSION |
| --- | --- |
| Awareness | Inform about product, prompt a need message |
| Interest | Provide compelling message, solve a need message |
| Trial | Motivate action |
| Repurchase | Cue to buy, increase usage |
| Loyalty | Reinforce brand or image, special promotions |

*Push or Pull Strategy?* As with distribution, promotional efforts should be guided by a strategy. *Pull* strategies are those efforts that pull buyers to the outlets that carry your product. TV pitches that instruct viewers "to ask for Perdue chicken by name at your local grocer" *pull* consumers to the stores that carry it. Another important mission of promotion is to encourage the distribution channels to stock and sell a product to consumers. Such efforts are a *push* strategy. Beer distributors, for instance, spend a great deal of their time trying to court bar owners to stock and promote their brew on tap. Most plans have an element of both push and pull strategies. In the beer industry they spend heavily to advertise the brand as well as to gain greater bar distribution.

To pull buyers to a store or to push the distribution channel to stock and sell, there are five general categories of promotional efforts:

Advertising
Personal Selling
Sales Promotion
Public Relations and Publicity
Direct Selling

*Advertising* Advertising takes many forms: television, radio, outdoor (billboard), magazines, keyword Internet search, banner ads, pop-ups, e-mail, streaming content ads, and newspaper. Two important things to keep in mind are your intended mission and the quantitative measurement of exposure required to accomplish it.

Please pay attention to the following measurement vocabulary. This is what you pay for when you buy advertising. The tendency for the uninitiated is to listen to the ad world's babble, not understand it, and buy their wares anyway. Buying advertising is just like buying marketing research—know what and why you are buying—buyer beware. You have to track your *key performance indicators* (KPIs), your goals, and success metrics you plan to measure.

*Reach* and *frequency* are key quantitative measurements of media goals. Reach is the percentage of the target market who see and hear your promotion or advertisement. Frequency is the number of times they saw or heard it. Marketers refer to the number of times a person is exposed to a message as the total *impressions* made on that audience. Because of the buying behavior associated with different products, different mixes of reach and frequency are required to induce purchase. When multiplied, Reach × Frequency equals a measure called *gross rating points* (GRPs). Add the GRPs together and you get *total rating points* (TRPs). GRP and TRP are the measures by which radio, TV, streaming TV, online, and outdoor advertising is sold and purchased.

The desired demographics and segmentation variables of the audiences delivered also enter prominently into the equation. A TV station's regional golf program that delivers active, middle-aged golfing males with incomes over $100,000 in the Southwest could efficiently be used to advertise a variety of products. A TV program that attracts a muddled mix of demographic audiences is less valuable per audience member. Even if you have the right media vehicle, scheduling is key in reaching your target.

High GRPs do not guarantee sales. The message delivered is also a key determinant. When advertising people refer to the message, copy (wording), or layout of advertising, they call it the *creative*, a noun. Ad agency people who develop the ideas are called *creatives*.

Online, magazine, and newspaper advertising is purchased based on the size and segmentation variables of their circulations. Magazines have a longer shelf life, but online and newspapers deliver a much more immediate and focused viewership, which is best for sale promotions.

TV viewership has changed. People continue to cut their cable cords. For the first time in 2022 more viewers watched streaming TV. Both of these TV audiences, linear TV (conventional live TV) and connected TV (CTV), also called over-the-top (OTT), are bought on a *cost per thousand basis* (CPM). Advertisers can target streaming audiences with *programmatic* ads with a precision unavailable in the past.

A competitive measure of media is *share of voice*. Using this measure, an advertiser can target a certain percentage of media spending by all competitors within a product category. Advertisers believe that to have an impact through the competitive *media clutter* and noise, the relative spending level is just as important as the absolute dollars spent.

Through the clutter, it would have been futile to run a TV ad to promote the tiny coffee brand that I managed during my summer internship. A small competitor had no chance against the likes of Procter & Gamble, Kraft Foods, and Nestlé, who together spent millions. Any affordable ad would have been drowned out by the giants.

Remember, each medium has its strengths in reaching people. Some are more selective than others. Marketers want to reach their intended targets as efficiently as possible to induce the desired buying behavior.

*Personal Selling.* Marketers choose *personal selling* when they need to make direct contact with the buyer. A salesperson can personalize your message to fit the buyer's needs and situation and can field objections and questions in this interactive process. This avenue is generally the most expensive element in any marketing mix because of the high cost of labor and commissions paid.

Managers of products that are new, complex, or expensive find that the benefits of personal selling often outweigh their high cost. Because some target markets are inaccessible by other media vehicles, personal selling is sometimes the only means to reach consumers. Solar electric and water purification systems, pharmaceuticals, copiers, and industrial products widely utilize personal selling in their marketing mixes. The use of telemarketers has greatly been reduced by the adoption of many do-not-call lists.

Current theory holds that personal selling is a *problem-solving* and *consultation* process. Professor Derek A. Newton of the Darden School at the University of Virginia saw personal selling as having evolved over the years in four stages: Music Man, Animated Catalog, Magic Formula, and Problem Solver. Before World War I it was believed that the "Music Man" approach to selling was the key to success. It was the salesperson's personality that enabled him to charm his customer into buying. After World War I, the "Animated Catalog" was considered the right way to sell. Vacuum cleaner salespeople knew all the facts about their products, and their sales presentations were rehearsed catalog readings. During the 1930s the slick pitch or "Magic Formula" was thought to be the best sales approach. Encyclopedia sales reps would control the presentation and lead the customer down a "mapped-out road" to a "sure sale." Many books currently on the bookstore shelves claim they hold the "secret" of how to close a sale. Today, academics agree that personal selling still requires some element of pizzazz and catalog-like product knowledge, but sales forces must also have extensive knowledge of the prospect's needs and buying processes to be successful. Salespeople should sell *benefits* that solve customers' problems, rather than simply peddling products.

*Sales Promotion.* Sales promotion is designed to elicit the desired behavior from the consumer, the sales force, and other channel participants. Sales promotions are designed to complement and reinforce other promotional efforts, especially advertising. Each type of promotion has its own associated vocabulary that you should be aware of. If you are not a marketer, knowing the vocabulary does not make you an expert, but it can sure help you to engage in intelligent marketing conversation, if need be. There are two types of promotions: those directed toward the consumer, and those directed at the distribution channels.

*Consumer sales promotions* techniques available are coupons, refund offers, samples, premiums, and contests.

*Coupons* are a direct way to pass a price reduction on to consumers. As a manufacturer, if you give retailers a discount in hopes that they will pass it along to consumers, you may be sadly disappointed. Marketers use coupons to encourage trial, brand switching, and brand loyalty. Grocery coupons are most often placed in a special coupon section of the Sunday paper called *freestanding inserts* (FSIs). Coupons can also be distributed on a corporate Web site at little cost or at the grocery store checkout register. Groupon, the social media couponing site, provides daily deals for a variety of services and products.

*Rebates* are also used for more expensive items, especially electronics, to reduce their perceived cost to the consumer. Rebates require buyers to complete paperwork, retain receipts, and mail them in. Because of the work involved, even rebates of $50 or more have low redemption rates. Marketers need to estimate the redemption rate and net cost and include the net cost in their marketing budgets.

*Refunds* are generally used to accelerate the normal consumer purchase cycles. Refunds are usually used to increase the quantity or frequency of purchase by encouraging buyers to stock up. Battery manufacturers frequently use refund offers. Such offers have been cleverly used to stock up consumers just before a competitor's promotion or product introduction.

*Samples* are a high-cost way of introducing a new product. Sampling requires a cash investment to produce and stock the smaller-sized packages. Samples are properly used for products whose benefits are "sensory in nature" and cannot be communicated effectively by advertising. Sampling may also be effective for products that consumers would view as risky in switching to a new brand, or that may have a high probability of generating *word of mouth* (WOM) activity after use. Many new shampoos use free or low-cost samples since their benefits are sensory. Consumers are reluctant to risk ten dollars to try a whole bottle. Sampling reduces the buyer's risk of trial.

*Premiums* are items offered at low or no cost to purchasers of a product. *Self-liquidating* premiums are those for which the price charged covers just costs. Hershey's has periodically offered watches and Christmas ornaments as premiums. To get the goodies, chocolate lovers have to send in wrappers as proof of purchase.

*Contests and sweepstakes* are a popular promotion and the most restricted legally, because they border on gambling. Many contests are conducted by inviting customers to corporate Web sites to play a game and enter contests. A thorough analysis of the game rules, security, and the laws must be conducted to avoid a disaster. State gambling laws must be investigated to ensure compliance. The game rules and odds of winning must also be scrutinized to ensure that the promotional budget will cover the forecasted costs. In 1984 McDonald's ran a summer Olympics medal game. Every time the United States won, game pieces could be redeemed for free food and other prizes. When the Communist bloc boycotted the games, the United States won most of the medals, and most of the game pieces became winners.

*Trade-directed sales promotions* tools include sales contests, point-of-purchase displays, dealer incentives, trade shows, and in-store demonstrations.

There are many variations on the *point-of-purchase display* (POP). To get them in the stores requires the cooperation of the trade. On the retail shelf a POP can be *a shelf talker,* a minibillboard attached to the end of the shelf with a little ad used to attract attention. Freestanding aisle displays and built-in shelf displays are other forms of POP. When a display is at the end of an aisle it is referred to as an *end cap.* To get those prime spots, the manufacturer must entice the retailer. A marketer can do it by providing a high markup per item or a high turnover on lower-margin items.

*Dealer and employee incentives.* Payments made to dealers for marketing support are called *spiffs.* They can take the form of slotting fees, case discounts, cash payments, free merchandise, or prizes. Spiffs enable the dealer to discount, promote, or justify carrying a product. A manufacturer can also give incentives to the dealer's employees to place store displays or award prizes for meeting sales targets.

*Trade shows* are a way to promote a new or existing product to the wholesalers, dealers, retailers, and distributors. This promotion tries to encourage the channel participants to carry your product. A fledgling start-up company making housewares, for example, would need to attend trade shows to develop the distribution contacts that might carry their products to retail. If you have no trade contacts, you have to develop them.

*In-store demonstrations.* Trained experts from the manufacturer are extensively used to promote products that would not otherwise generate consumer interest or be accepted by the trade. Small kitchen gadget hucksters set up demonstration platforms to bring inconspicuous blades to life by creating "beautiful" plate garnishes with ordinary vegetables. The Clinique ladies in their white smocks perform a similar mission for their boxes of "natural" beauty at the cosmetics counter. Many retailers use a DVD player to play a recorded demonstration when a live one is not practical.

Whatever the sales promotion you choose in a marketing mix, each element must have an explicit marketing mission to justify its cost in the marketing mix.

*Public Relations and Publicity.* Public relations (PR) is typically a promotional tool used to communicate to a broader audience. PR is intended to create a favorable climate for your product, not to directly sell it. The list of possible PR targets can include politicians as well as the communities in which a company operates. The PR message can be intended to create goodwill, correct a mistaken impression or factual situation, or to explain a firm's actions. Sponsorship of prestigious or charitable events or causes is often used to create a *halo effect* of positive feeling toward a corporation and its products.

Because the goals of PR are less defined than a sales target, the results are more difficult to measure. Opinion polls and legislative victories are often used to measure PR success.

Public relations also include *viral marketing*. By trying to reach opinion leaders, a marketer can create a buzz about its product without an ad on TV. Generating a positive discussion about your product on TikTok, blogs, vlogs, podcasts, YouTube, Instagram, and Twitter, and on college campuses can launch a product and propel sales. Online social media influencers and *user-generated content* (UGC) by others, both paid and organic, can quickly translate into direct measurable sales via links to Web sites.

*Publicity,* a form of public relations, is any *unpaid* form of mass media communication about a company or product. It can take the form of a news story or even the appearance of a product in the media. Publicity and public relations are a two-edged sword. It is judged as more credible by the public because it is not purchased; however, there is less control over the message. Press conferences, press releases, use by celebrities, and staged events are used to capture the media's attention. Using a PR agency allows you to tap into their media contacts to capture an audience and hopefully control the impression made about your company or products.

When a tennis star wears Nike shoes and sportswear at the U.S. Open, the TV can't help but flash Nike on the screen each time he or she serves and volleys. This network time has great value. If the athlete makes the national news the value of free media exposure can be great.

Accordingly, PR executives track their effectiveness by measuring the value of the media time or space captured. Tracking services report on their clients' PR and advertising media exposure across the country. You can also track competitors in the same way. Although it is often overlooked in the marketing mix, publicity can often create a tremendous impact if skillfully and creatively orchestrated.

***Direct Sales.*** Direct sales includes the realm of online, junk mail, catalogs, shopping networks, long-format TV *infomercials*, and short-form TV spots.

"I HAVE CREDIBILITY, AND FOR THE RIGHT PRICE I COULD BRING IT TO THIS COMPANY."

The nature of the direct mail game is to *segment, segment, segment.* Mailers target their market with a focused mailing list to directly reach those households with a compelling mail piece. Lists can be developed internally or purchased from vendors. The more defined, affluent, and focused the list is on a desired demographic composition, the higher cost per thousand (CPM) names. The results are tracked by *rate of return* (ROR) and *dollar amount per order.* Because TV audiences lack a list's selectivity, TV sales pitches cannot be as directly targeted as direct mail.

*Online Marketing.* Online marketing is the largest and a growing method of directly contacting the customer and receiving a direct response. In 2022 marketers spent over $500 billion internationally on online advertising. *Search engine marketing* (SEM) or *key word advertising* on Google's search engine is purchased on a cost-per-click (CPC) or pay-per-click (PPC) basis. You select your customers by their interest when they are interested. In a competitive bidding process, the most sought-after word is priced at a market price. Because the cost-per-click is well defined, the conversion of leads to sales and the resulting profit needs to be carefully calculated. If the customer has a continuing value, the lifetime value should be considered.

*Search Engine Optimization and Web Marketing.* Other online marketing techniques include *search engine optimization* (SEO), a way to make a Web site more visible to search engines. Key words grab the attention of search engines' web crawlers that try to match users' searches to relevant content. If you are doing it correctly, your page will be shown on all important *search engine results pages* (SERP). If that is not working well, you can always buy placement at the top of the page with *search engine marketing* (SEM) ads. Better yet, you can do both for relevant searches.

The same can be said for social media pages and posts on TikTok, YouTube, and Meta's Facebook and Instagram. Their algorithms are designed to serve the most attractive content to the users. By using compelling text and visual content combined with relevant hashtags, you can boost the visibility, the number of followers, platform interactions, and hopefully interactions with your external Web sites. User-generated content (UGC), both paid and unpaid, is powerful and impactful. It is so easy to test. Make a change to the content and get immediate feedback, then compare to your control. On Amazon, generating positive reviews are the key for high rankings on the SERP.

In addition to SEO, there are many other paid forms of SEM and web marketing that include banner ads, social media ads, paid influencers, text messages, annoying pop-ups, email solicitations, and retargeting ads. Use all or some of these in order to reach your desired audience profile.

***Search Engine Marketing Methods and Vocabulary.*** Marketing on the Internet cannot be simply defined. The Internet is a diverse place and advertising results are hard to track exactly. The content and ads on one platform influence the sales on the other. That is called the *sales funnel*. A comprehensive plan, with a spectrum of ads and content that can be strategically combined, will bring the best results. Google's AdWords and Amazon's "Sponsored Ads" are some of the many *search engine marketing* (SEM) tools available.

*Tracking Cookies* are the key marketing tools that track your Internet travels, determine your demographics, and provide valuable data about ad effectiveness. Prospects can be touched by various forms of digital media. Even if prospects do not act, knowing how they got to your Web site is all part of the sales funnel. Privacy restrictions imposed by users and platforms make the tracking job increasingly more difficult. Apple iPhone privacy changes in 2021 upended the advertising sales of Meta's Facebook.

Internet marketing is filled with jargon, acronyms, and measurement matrices. We already talked about CPC, SEM, and SEO, but there are other terms you should be familiar with in order to understand other ways ads can be purchased and evaluated. Which medium and method is best depends on the target, budget, and goals. Remember to always keep your goals in mind.

*Pay-Per-View* (PPV). Buying ads that are visible on a Web page for a specific amount of time. Often these and most online ads are purchased on a *demand side platform* (DSP), a marketplace to purchase placement on ad networks like Google.

*Cost-Per-Lead* (CPL). Paying for leads that hit your Web site but do not necessarily result in your *call to action* (CTA). Your request to order, donate, or watch is the CTA. It's your responsibility to convert the leads to sales. The platform does not share that risk for its payment.

*Cost Per Action* (CPA). This acquisition model pays the platform for a specific action by the lead, like a purchase, a donation, taking customer information, or answering a survey. This is more expensive than CPL, because the platform is sharing the risk, even if your Web site is not doing its job efficiently.

*Click-Through Rate* (CTR). This is an efficiency measure. The number of clicks divided by the times the ad is shown is the CTR. A high CTR shows the content is compelling, which is a great measure of effectiveness. It shows immediate interest but not necessarily a desire to purchase. Remember AIDA from the Marketing Chapter? (calculate Clicks/Views)

*View-Through Click* (VTC). This is a measure of the effectiveness of an ad campaign. A VTC would mean your customer saw your ad, did not click to the Web site, but "later" visited your Web site. (calculate Visits/Views)

*Effective Cost-Per-X* (eCPL, eCPA, eCPM). On an overall campaign basis, these "effective" rates are based on your total marketing budget for multiple campaigns to determine the overall effectiveness of your marketing strategy. Goals can be sales, impressions, donations, subscribers.

A specific measure of ad effectiveness widely used in the Amazon ecosystem is TACoS, not the food, *total (true) advertising cost of sales.* It measures ads $ / sales x 100. A low TACoS is good.

**Fulfillment.** The other component of both direct mail, Internet, and TV selling is *fulfillment.* Fulfillment is the process of order entry, order processing, inventory management, mailing, and customer service. The operation may be executed internally or subcontracted out to a *fulfillment house* that performs the duty for a per-order fee over certain volume minimums. It saves smaller companies the initial investment required to establish in-house fulfillment capabilities.

A thorny issue connected with direct selling methods is the backlash against the Big Brother effect of having *very* personal information captured that churns out personalized pitches. This topic, like slotting fees, is a "hot" one for MBA chatter.

Each method of promotion—advertising, personal selling, sales promotions, public relations, and direct selling—can accomplish a separate mission depending on the product, the place of sale, and the price. The gifted marketer goes to his or her palette of promotional options and combines them in a coordinated promotional strategy to sell the product efficiently.

Product        Place        Promotion        **Price**

### PRICING DECISIONS: WHAT SHOULD MY PRICE BE?

The pricing decision, like the product decisions, can dramatically affect the marketing mix by suggesting a channel of distribution or an advertising strategy. The pricing itself can differentiate your product from the competition. Both the Kia and the Rolls-Royce are differentiated at opposite ends of the automobile spectrum. There are many rationales behind pricing each product and service. Haven't you seen a pair of Nike cross-trainers for sale at $99.99 instead of $100 for some psychological advantage? Besides psychological pricing, there are eight major pricing methods and strategies suggested by research and case analyses.

*Cost Plus.* This is a simple method of taking your cost and adding a desired profit margin. Highway contractors often use this simple method; however, it is not the proper way to price.

*Perceived Value to the Consumer.* You can charge the customer the value provided, regardless of its cost. Replacement parts are a prime example—exorbitant prices are charged for a cheap but crucial custom nut or bolt. The owner of a bathroom fixture manufacturer confided to a group of my classmates during a school-sponsored plant visit that the majority of his company's profits were derived from the twenty-by-twenty-foot replacement-parts cage, not from the long assembly lines producing the fixtures. If the price charged for an item is commensurate with the benefits provided, then it will be considered a good *value* in the mind of the buyer. But remember, there are limits even in a monopolistic situation.

*Skimming.* Early in the introduction phase of the PLC, a company can opt to charge a high price and *skim* high margins from a new and novel product or service. The margins could be used to further R&D, as is done in high-tech industries, or to immediately reward the owners for fad product introductions. RCA used this strategy to charge high prices for color TVs when they were introduced in the 1960s, and large-screen TV manufacturers did it in the 1990s.

*Penetration.* This pricing can be used in the introductory phase or later in the PLC. A *penetration* strategy would use a low price to gain market share; the goal is primarily to lower costs per unit by producing many units in hopes of eventually controlling a market as the low-cost producer.

*The Price/Quality Relationship.* Because consumer perceptions are not necessarily based on just the physical attributes of a product, the "perceived" quality is often influenced by its price. Apparel, perfume, and jewelry are examples where the price itself affects the perception of product attributes. Consumers often *attribute* the characteristics of style and workmanship to a product just because of the high price charged.

*Meet Competition.* Strategies frequently decide to match or beat competitors' prices to gain or retain market share in a competitive market. This is especially the case in commodity products and services such as gasoline, steel, and airline tickets. The economics of pushing a product through the distribution chain, as explained in the discussion of distribution channels, has a great effect on what price a manufacturer can charge to sell his product to the distribution chain and still end up with a competitive retail price.

*Meet Profit Goals Based on the Size of the Market.* If a market is limited in size, then a price must be charged that will allow enough profit to justify the marketing and manufacturing effort. If the product cannot command a profitable price, then to lower costs investigate either other user markets or manufacturing improvements.

*Price Based on the Price Elasticity of the Buyer.* Price elasticity describes how a buyer's behavior changes due to a change in price. Buyers with *elastic* demand do not readily accept price hikes. Their demand is greater or smaller depending on the price. Buyers with *inelastic* demand behaviors don't care about price increases. They don't decrease their quantity or frequency of purchase depending on the price. Tobacco smokers, for example, have absorbed many price increases and continue to buy because their addiction makes their demand inelastic. If elastic, buyers will not pay more than a given *price point* and will stop buying or buy much less based on the intensity of their desires, their personal disposable income, or their psychological price thresholds. When airline ticket prices are low, they encourage tourist travel. When they are high, tourists take more car trips or stay at home.

Many avenues may be taken with any given product. In the case of my gourmet packaged coffee, a distinctive coffee "product" may require a distinctive package, a higher "price," a targeted promotion, and a selective "place" for distribution. But what really tells the story is the economics. Can I do it and make money?

## 6. WHAT ARE THE ECONOMICS OF MY PLAN?

Consumer → Market → Competition → Distribution → Marketing Mix → **Determine the Economics** → Revise

This may be the last step of marketing analysis. This step may also send the marketing manager directly back to Go without collecting two hundred dollars. By that I mean that the consumer analysis may be exemplary, the marketing mix masterful, but it just doesn't make money. The costs may be too high, the market price too low. Perhaps unrealistically high sales volume may be needed to break even. In those sad cases the entire circular process of marketing strategy must be restarted in an effort to find a profitable solution. To determine whether you have created a plan that is both profitable and reasonable, you must address several issues.

What are the costs?
What is the break even?
How long is the payback of my investment?

*What are my costs? Fixed or variable?*
The first cost question for a marketing manager should be, "Which of my costs are *variable* and which are *fixed*?" If this sounds like accounting, it is.

*Variable costs* are those that vary with the volume of products sold or manufactured. The costs of materials and labor are variable costs. As more units are sold or manufactured, the total costs of material and labor are higher. *Fixed costs* do not vary with volume even if no sales are made. As volume fluctuates neither rent nor supervisor salaries change—within a *relevant range*. By that I mean that if sales triple, a new factory may have to be leased, and thus fixed costs will go up. Promotional expenses such as advertising are also seen as a fixed cost of a marketing plan, because if the product is a flop, the advertising dollars are already spent. They are considered *sunk costs*—after a TV ad airs, the dollars are "sunk" in the ocean of TV land. Total costs are a combination of both variable and fixed costs.

Total Costs = Variable Costs Per Unit (VC) × Units Sold
  + Fixed Costs (FC)

They can also be shown graphically as on page 54.

What can be seen in the graphs is that regardless of unit volume, the fixed costs remain constant. When units are actually produced, variable costs are added on top of the fixed costs to equal total costs.

*What is my break even and is it reasonable?*

*Break even* is the point at which the fixed costs are recovered from the sale of goods but no profit is made. Promotion and manufacturing are expensive. A way must be found to recoup those investments. That's the whole point of marketing: to recover costs and make profits.

$$\text{Break Even Unit Volume} = \frac{\text{Fixed Costs}}{\text{Unit Contribution}}$$

(Unit Contribution = Your Selling Price – Variable Costs)

Using my data from the coffee industry, I have provided an example from the real world. I determined that the prices and costs of a proposed marketing plan for the Mexican gourmet coffee were:

|  | *COST* | *COST TYPE* |
|---|---|---|
| Retail Sales Price | $6.00 lb. |  |
| Selling Price to Distributors | 4.20 lb. |  |
| Coffee Beans Cost | 1.00 lb. | Variable |
| Roasting and Processing Cost | .44 lb. | Variable |
| Packaging Cost | .55 lb. | Variable |
| Shipping Cost | .25 lb. | Variable |
| Spiffs and Slotting Fees | 50,000 | Fixed |
| Production Equipment Rental | 12,000 | Fixed |
| Promotional Efforts | 150,000 | Fixed |

The corresponding break-even volume was calculated:

$$\frac{(\$50,000 + \$12,000 + \$150,000)}{[\$4.20 - (1.00 + .44 + .55 + .25)]}$$

= 108,163 lbs. break-even (BE) volume

WOODEN END TABLE PRODUCTION

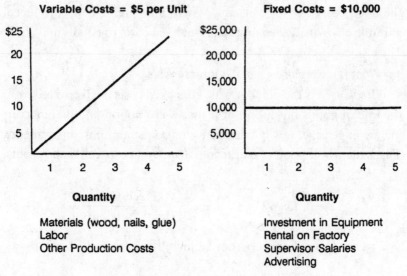

**Variable Costs = $5 per Unit**

Quantity

Materials (wood, nails, glue)
Labor
Other Production Costs

**Fixed Costs = $10,000**

Quantity

Investment in Equipment
Rental on Factory
Supervisor Salaries
Advertising

FIXED COSTS + VARIABLE COSTS = TOTAL COSTS

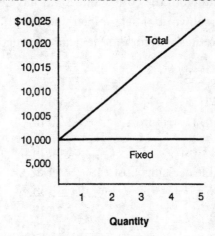

And the *break-even dollar sales* were:

108,163 lbs. × $6.00 lb. = $648,978 break-even retail sales

The same equation can be used to calculate a *target volume* to yield a desired profit.

$$\text{Target Volume} = \frac{(\text{Fixed Costs} + \text{Profit})}{\text{Unit Contribution}}$$

To return a $30,000 profit target, you just add the profit to the numerator with the fixed costs.

$$\frac{(212{,}000 + 30{,}000)}{(\$4.20 - \$2.24)} = 123{,}469 \text{ lbs. target volume}$$

123,469 lbs × $6.00 = $740,814 target retail sales

One *very* important aspect of this analysis is that it does not include the costs that were "sunk" in the development of the product or a past ad campaign if they have already been spent. The evaluation of past economics is always performed from the perspective of the present. There should not be any crying over spilled milk. You need to decide if you can make money on the proposed marketing spending in the future. For example, if the coffee blend was the product of millions of dollars of research, that would be irrelevant to the decision of whether I should spend additional money to market it. If I include the millions of research, it would be a definite "no go." However, with that money down the drain, it might be profitable to invest additional cash in a marketing effort.

The graphical representation of the marketing plan economics for the Mexican coffee looked like this:

GOURMET COFFEE MARKETING PLAN ECONOMICS

*Is my break even reasonable in relation to my relevant market?* Answering this question *must* be your next step. In the coffee example, $648,978 of break-even retail sales was a .26 percent share of the $248 million market for gourmet, nonflavored coffee sold through the supermarket channel as explained earlier in the chapter. The targeted retail sales of $740,814 equaled only a .3 percent share of the relevant market. On that level, the plan appeared reasonable if I believed $150,000 of promotion and $50,000 of dealer incentives could have produced $740,814 in sales. Imagine that—I could have reached my goal with only a .3 percent share of the market!

Unfortunately, a small target share can easily lead you to believe that it is easy to obtain. How fierce was the fight for the grocer's shelf? If my coffee got on the shelf, somebody else's had to be kicked off. How would they react? Once in the supermarket, would my company have been willing to continue to support the coffee when a competitor went after my shelf space? In my case, the company was not willing yet to make that kind of long-term commitment to coffee.

*What is the payback period on my investment?*
This is another hurdle frequently used by companies to evaluate marketing projects when they have many to choose from. Companies want to know how long it will take just to get their investment back. Forget about profit. The payback formula is:

$$\frac{\text{Initial Investment}}{\text{Annual Profit}}$$

In the coffee example, the calculation would be:

$$\frac{\$212,000}{\$30,000} = 7 \text{ years}$$

If the yearly profit is not the same each year, there is no formula. The break-even point is where the plan returns the initial investment.

Seven years is a bit long for a risky venture. This may indicate that the whole marketing development process should start again. And unfortunately for me it did.

## 7. GO BACK AND REVISE THE PLAN

Consumer → Market → Competition → Distribution → Marketing Mix → Economics → **Revise the Plan**

At this stage of disappointment, I revisited the *marketing strategy development process* outlined at the beginning of this chapter. In circumstances such as those I faced, you must either tweak or discard your plans entirely. You may have something that can be salvaged . . . if you're lucky. You have to start by asking yourself tough questions. In the case of the coffee project I tormented myself with:

Should I target another segment?
Is the mail order distribution channel an option?
Should I not advertise and rely on a cheap price to move my
    product?

As these questions indicate, the marketing process is not easily defined or executed. It can be frustrating because there are no "right" answers. Consumer reactions cannot easily be predicted. It takes creativity, experience, skill, and intuition to develop a plan that makes sense and works together (*internally consistent and mutually supportive*). Marketing also requires close attention to the numbers to be successful. With this chapter you are armed with the MBA problem-solving structure and the MBA vocabulary to attack the marketing challenges that you may encounter. You haven't even paid a dollar in tuition, sat through a class, or anted up for an expensive executive seminar. Figure the break even on that investment!

I include the following notes that we all passed among ourselves at school to guide our case discussions and tests (open notes). These are the key questions that must be addressed by a comprehensive marketing strategy.

## MARKETING STRATEGY OUTLINE

### 1. Consumer Analysis
- Makable or marketable product?
- Who's buying, who's using?
- What is the buying process?
- Who are the "influencers"?
- How important is it to the consumer?
- Who needs it and why?
- What is the value to the end user?
- Is it a planned or impulse buy?
- What are the perceptions of our product?
- Does it meet their needs?

### 2. Market Analysis
- What is the market's nature? Size, growth, segments, geography, PLC
- Competitive factors? Quality, price, advertising, R&D, service
- What are the trends?

### 3. Competitive Analysis
- What is your company good at? Poor at?
- What is your position in the market? Size, share, reputation, historical performance
- What are your resources? Trade relations, sales force, cash, technology, patents, R&D
- Who is gaining or losing share?

- What do they do well?
- Compare your resources to theirs.
- What are the barriers to entry?
- What are your objectives and strategy?
- Any contingency plans?
- Short- and long-term plans and goals?

## 4. Marketing Mix
- Who is the target?
- *Product* — Fit with other products? Differentiation, PLC, perception, packaging, features
- *Place* — How best to reach segment? Channel mathematics, draw channels
- Exclusive, selective, intensive distribution? Fit with product?
- Who has the power?
- How to motivate the channels?
- *Promotion* — What is the buying process? How are $'s targeted to buying-process goals?
- Push or pull strategy?
- Media — type, measure, message?
- Dealer incentives?
- Consumer promos — coupons, contests?
- *Price* — What strategy? Skim, penetrate?
- Seek volume or profits?
- Perceived value, cost-plus pricing?
- How does price relate to the market, size, product life cycle, competition?

## 5. Evaluate the Economics
- Break even in units.
- Fixed Cost/(Selling — Variable Cost). Include fixed marketing and promo costs in fixed costs of the plan!
- Relate break even to relevant market.
- What is the payback period? Exclude sunk costs!
- Are goals reasonable? Attainable?

# KEY MARKETING TAKEAWAYS

## *The 7 Steps of Market Strategy Development*

1. Consumer analysis
2. Market analysis
3. Competitive analysis
4. Distribution channel analysis
5. Develop the marketing mix
6. Determine the economics
7. Revise

*Need Categories* — All the possible uses of a product or service

*The Buying Process* — The stages of making a purchase

*Product Involvement* — The importance of a product to the consumer

*Segmentation Variables* — Ways to divide the population to find a profitable target

*Relevant Market* — The portion of the market that is interested in your product

*Product Life Cycle* — The birth-to-death (and possibly rebirth) life cycle of a product

*SWOT Analysis* — Competitive analysis of strengths, weaknesses, opportunities, and threats

*Perceptual Mapping* — A multivariable picture of a product and its competitors

*Channel Margin Mathematics* — Each level in the distribution takes a margin of the selling price it charges to the next level of distribution

*The Marketing Mix of the 4 P's* — Product, place, promotion, and price

*Distribution Strategies* — Exclusive, selective, and mass market

*Channel Power* — Who in the distribution chain dictates the terms of the relationships

*Advertising Measures* — Reach, frequency, GRP, TRP, share of voice. Buy wisely.

*Pricing Strategies* — Cost plus, penetration, value pricing, skimming

*Break Evens* — The volume of sales needed to recover the fixed cost of marketing plan

# Day 2

## ETHICS

### *Ethics Topics*

Relativism

Stakeholder Analysis

Environmental, Social, and Governance

Unlike most topics in the MBA curriculum, which have remained fairly consistent for decades, ethics is a new area. What appeared at first to be only a trendy elective course has now become institutionalized as part of the core MBA curriculum at Harvard, Wharton, and Darden. With the criminal convictions of insider traders in the 1980s, business schools took notice and jumped on the ethics bandwagon in the 1990s. In the new century, the collapses of Enron, WorldCom, and Arthur Andersen; Bernie Madoff's Ponzi scheme; the subprime mortgage frauds; the FTX crypto exchange case; and the revelations have kept ethics on the front burner.

Ethical dilemmas make for a lively classroom discussion. It was revealing to see my fellow students deal with controversial topics. Since ethical problems often have no definitive answers, the area will remain fertile academic ground for years to come.

The purpose of ethics in the MBA curriculum is not to make students model corporate citizens. Rather, the intention is to make students aware of the ethical implications of business decisions. Through casework and role-playing, students confront ethical dilemmas similar to those they will face in the workplace.

The top business schools train their future champions of industry to deal with any challenge. You name the "hot" topic, we thrashed out the issue in class:

"WELL, THE DISCUSSION HAS APPARENTLY TURNED TO BASIC BUSINESS ETHICS, AND I MUST CONFESS TO BEING OUT OF MY DEPTH."

Environmental issues — pollution, toxic waste dumping, animal rights, recycling, climate change

Corporate restructuring — layoffs

Employee privacy issues — AIDS, drug testing, genetic testing, vaccinations

Diversity issues — race, BLM, ethnicity, gender, sexual orientation, LGBT, and LGBTQIA

Sexual harassment — #MeToo

Conduct of multinational corporations (MNCs) — bribery

Other — antitrust actions, predatory pricing, insider trading, deceptive marketing

## THE SOCIAL RESPONSIBILITY OF BUSINESS

Talk about ethics rests on the assumption that businesses ought to adhere to a socially responsible approach to decision making called the *social responsibility* approach. Proponents of this approach believe that corporations have societal obligations that go beyond maximizing profits. It is argued that because corporations are so powerful, they have an obligation to assume social responsibilities. Corporations should be managed for the benefit of their *stakeholders:* their customers, suppliers, employees, and local communities, as well as their owners. Corporate leaders bear a fiduciary responsibility to all stakeholders.

Flying in the face of the corporate good citizen philosophy espoused at most institutions is a competing school of thought led by Milton Friedman of the University of Chicago. Friedman believes that business's sole duty is to make profits. "Businesses are in the business of maximizing shareholders' value by a prudent use of scarce organizational resources, as long as the activities of the business are within the letter of the law." In Friedman's view, it is up to government to determine what the laws should be. A profitable business benefits society by creating jobs, increasing the standard of living of its owners and its employees. Corporations pay the taxes that support government's social action. Although Friedman is exalted as one of the defenders of capitalism in economics courses, my school tended to discourage his views when it came to ethics class.

Two major topics are taught in the ethics curriculum: *relativism* and *stakeholder analysis*. Relativism examines why we often ignore ethics in our decision making, while stakeholder analysis provides a structure with which to confront ethical decisions.

## RELATIVISM

The proponents of relativism hold that we can't decide on matters of right and wrong, or good and evil. Things are rarely black or white. There are so many shades of gray. Relativism proposes that ethics are "relative" to the personal, social, and cultural circumstances in which one finds oneself. Relativists are not torn by ethical dilemmas since they do not believe that truth can be discovered through soul-searching. Professors teach relativism so that students may guard against it. To understand relativism, you need to recognize its four forms:

Naive Relativism
Role Relativism
Social Group Relativism
Cultural Relativism

*Naive relativism* holds that every person has his or her own standard that enables him or her to make choices. No one can make a moral judgment about another person's behavior. So many variables affect behavior that an outsider cannot possibly be privy to all the elements that went into making a decision. Therefore, a sales person of OxyContin is not equipped to make moral judgments regarding the actions of the president of Purdue Pharma, Richard Sackler, whose corporation was accused of selling harmful opioids. Neither were the McKinsey consultants equipped to make a judgment when they advised Purdue how to encourage addiction and increased prescriptions.

*Role relativism* distinguishes between our private selves and our public roles. These public roles call for a "special" morality that we separate from the individual making the choices. The president of a fishing company may personally dislike the incidental killing of dolphins in his company's tuna nets, but as an executive, he must not let his feelings interfere with the best interests of the company.

*Social relativism* is akin to naive relativism. People refer to social norms to render ethical judgments. "Industry practices," "club rules," "professional codes of conduct," and "accepted practices" are the cop-outs of the social relativist. In the produce industry, it is "industry practice" to ignore child labor laws and employ children to work in the field and miss school.

*Cultural relativism* holds that there is no universal moral code by which to judge another society's moral and ethical standards. If a whole culture holds certain beliefs, how can an outsider sit in judgment? "When in Rome . . ." The concept of cultural relativism becomes more important as companies compete globally. Multinational corporations often follow local laws and customs that may violate ethical standards in their home countries. Discussions about apartheid revolved around issues of cultural relativism. Adopting a cultural relativist philosophy, a multinational corporation might have justified its participation in South African gold and diamond mining activities despite the employment of "slave" labor in the mines.

In some instances U.S. corporations and citizens are barred from adopting the host country's business practices. In some countries it is ordinary business practice to pay bribes to get favorable treatment from businesses and government. The Foreign Corrupt Practices Act of 1977 outlaws overseas bribery.

The relativism concepts provide MBAs with an awareness of and a way to guard against inaction on ethical and moral issues. They provide a framework to go beyond currently held beliefs and patterns of behaviors. These concepts also make for great debates when MBAs get together on social occasions.

*Other Ethical Frameworks.* Relativism is not the only philosophical framework with which to approach ethical decisions. There is also *natural law, utilitarianism,* and *universalism.* Natural law serves as a guide to some who believe that the "right" thing to do is revealed in nature or the Bible. Utilitarianism holds that an action is justified if it provides the greatest benefit for the greatest number of people. Finally, universalism propounds that any action is condonable if the motive behind the action is good, since the results of a person's actions are so often not in his or her control.

*Guide to Help Avoid Rationalizations for Unethical Decisions.* There are many ways that managers try to rationalize poor ethical decisions. Here are three tests to consider when questioning oneself, taught by Professor R. Edward Freeman of the Darden School at the University of Virginia.

1. Could you defend the decision if it were made public? What if it appeared on the front page of the *Wall Street Journal*?
2. Reversibility. If you were the party negatively affected by a deci-

sion, could you respect the rationale for the decision, even if you didn't necessarily agree with it?

3. Generalizability. Could you defend the decision as a precedent for future decision makers in similar cases?

## STAKEHOLDER ANALYSIS

Although there are no magic formulas for solving ethical dilemmas, it is helpful to have a framework with which to organize your thoughts. *Stakeholder analysis* provides you with the tools for weighing various elements and reaching a decision.

As a first step a list should be made of all potentially affected parties, then an evaluation of all the *harms* and *benefits* that a particular action will have on those involved. The next level of analysis ought to determine each of the affected parties' *rights* and *responsibilities*. Employees, for instance, have the right to a fair wage and safe working conditions, but they also have the responsibility to be productive for the company. In a typical stakeholder analysis the list of potentially affected parties might look like this:

The Decision Maker

Executives, Board of Directors

Customers — and the industry in which they operate

Shareholders, Bondholders

Suppliers — and their industry

Employees — and their families

Government — federal, state, and local and their agencies

Special Interest Groups — industrial, consumer, environmental, political, unions

The Affected Community

The Environment — "sustainability"—plants, animals, natural resources

Future Generations (an MBA favorite)

Competitors

Lawyers and the Courts

Obviously, the list could be much longer. At the analysis stage the list is narrowed to the significant players, then a situational analysis is performed, and eventually a decision is reached. In order, these are the steps:

1. Get the main cast of characters.
2. Determine the harms and benefits to each player.
3. Determine their rights and responsibilities.
4. Consider the relative power of each.
5. Consider the short- and long-term consequences of your decision alternatives.
6. Formulate contingency plans for alternative scenarios.
7. Make a judgment.

If you are interested in walking through the steps outlined above, browse the headlines and pick a topic with an ethical aspect. With a piece of paper, jot down the main characters along the top, then along the side, place the words "Harms and Benefits" first, and below that "Rights and Responsibilities." Now you have the framework with which to attack the moral dilemmas of the day—MBA style.

As an example, you might choose the debate regarding the need to preserve the habitat of the spotted owl by reducing logging on federal lands. The stakeholder analysis grid would look like that on page 69.

You may disagree with the way in which I have framed this issue, but with ethics there is no "right" way. People can approach a situation differently and feel other stakeholders need to be represented. In this situation, at the very least, a timber company executive ought to consider the stakeholders before clear-cutting the owls' woods. With the tools of stakeholder analysis an MBA can tackle the issue of endangered owls as well as other ethical issues and make thoughtful and informed decisions. Corporations often do their own stakeholder analyses and publish them as corporate social responsibility (CSR) reports.

# THE SARBANES-OXLEY ACT OF 2002

As a result of the corporate scandals of the late 1990s and early 2000s, Congress was forced to legislate ethics in corporate America. The system of government regulation and private self-regulation was inadequate. The hall of shame includes Tyco, WorldCom, Adelphia, Enron, Credit Suisse First Boston, Arthur Andersen, and FTX. Other international scandals centered on rogue traders left alone to amass millions of dollars of trading losses. This rogues' gallery included Nick Leeson at Barings ($1.2 billion loss), Yasuo Hamanaka at Sumitomo ($1.8 billion loss), and John Rusnak at Allfirst ($750 million loss).

Where employees, accountants, and lawyers intend to do wrong, no amount of legislation will stop them, but Congress felt that it would at least make it more difficult and send a message to others

SPOTTED OWL ISSUE IN A STAKEHOLDER FRAMEWORK

**Stakeholders**

| | Lumber Companies | Loggers | Logging Communities | Owls & Trees |
|---|---|---|---|---|
| **Harms & Benefits** | • Higher Costs<br>• Lower Profits,<br>• Higher Value on Private Lands Owned | • Less Work More Free Time | • Lost Wages in Local Economy<br>• Business Failures | • Survival |
| **Rights & Responsibilities** | • Value Maximization for Owners Within the Law | • Reasonably Exploit Natural Resources<br>• Make a Living | • Reasonably Exploit Natural Resources | • Life |

| | Consuming Public | Politicians | Environmental Groups | EPA |
|---|---|---|---|---|
| **Harms & Benefits** | • Higher Costs<br>• More Recreational Areas | • New Campaign Issue | • Power<br>• Press Coverage | • Power & Influence |
| **Rights & Responsibilities** | • Benefit from Public Lands | • Public Good<br>• Constituent Desires | • Free Speech | • Protect Environment<br>• Regulate Industry |

to think twice. The new provisions of the Sarbanes-Oxley Act (SOX or SARBOX) and related agency regulations that became effective in 2005 include four broad categories of new rules:

### Financial Accounting Rules

- Audit committee must consist solely of independent directors and at least one financial expert.
- Chief executive officers (CEOs) and chief financial officers (CFOs) must certify that their financial statements fairly present the financial condition and results of the company.
- The SEC has the power to establish the new Public Company Accounting Oversight Board to end failed industry self-regulation.

### Internal Control Rules

- CEOs and CFOs must certify the working system of internal controls over financial reporting.
- Outside auditors must attest to and report on management's evaluation of the strength of its system of internal controls.
- Section 404 requires annual audits for larger corporations.

### Executive Ethical Conduct Rules

- Public companies must adopt a code of ethical conduct for their most senior executive and senior financial officers.
- Public companies cannot make loans to their executive officers or directors.
- CEOs and CFOs can be required to return compensation if financial statements are restated due to "material noncompliance" with reporting requirements.
- Officers, directors, and other "insiders" are prohibited from trading company stock during pension-fund blackout periods.
- New protection from executive retribution for whistle-blowers on corporate misdeeds.

### Ethical Conduct Rules for Related Parties

- New professional responsibilities for lawyers.
- New conflict-of-interest rules for financial analysts.

In addition to these rules, public companies listed on the New York Stock Exchange (NYSE) and the NASDAQ have many additional listing standards that address the lack of corporate governance standards that were not addressed by the Sarbanes-Oxley Act.

The internal controls systems to control fraud and corruption that the Sarbanes-Oxley Act requires are complex and expensive to audit. The Committee of Sponsoring Organizations of the Treadway Commission (COSO) prepared a comprehensive study of corporate internal controls called the "Internal Control-Integrated Framework." The Securities and Exchange Commission (SEC) accepts it as the approved framework for corporate officials, auditors, and compliance professionals to use to comply with Sarbanes-Oxley.

An excellent framework to implement a comprehensive system of internal controls is contained in Scott Green's *Manager's Guide to the Sarbanes-Oxley Act*. This book provides compliance officers a practical methodology called the Control Smart Approach to integrate the multivolume COSO framework into action:

1. Identify the possible threats from within and outside the organization.
2. Identify all the processes within your company.
3. Identify the vulnerable process gaps with control assessment tools.
4. Implement internal controls to fill gaps and fill them with strong control processes.
5. Monitor and test the controls with an early warning system of performance and management statistics.

All the efforts of Sarbanes-Oxley have not appeared to stem the tide. After implementation of Sarbanes-Oxley, other corporate scandals occurred: rapid mutual-fund trading in 2003 (Putnam, Invesco, and Janus), bid rigging in the insurance industry in 2004 (Marsh & McLennan), and egregious accounting at Fannie Mae in 2004. It did not end there: Lehman Brothers' lack of debt disclosures in 2008, Ernst & Young's ethics test cheating scandal in 2012 (imagine CPAs cheating on ethics training tests!), Luckin Coffee's fabrication of millions of phantom sales in 2020, and FTX's soured related party loans of customer assets to Alameda Research in 2022.

The subprime mortgage meltdown in 2008 was the grand-daddy lapse of ethics on the part of the bond rating agencies, mortgage brokers, bankers, investors, and home owners. In response Congress passed the *Dodd-Frank Wall Street Reform and Consumer Protection Act* in 2010 to prevent excessive risk-taking by banks and predatory lending. However, many of its provisions were repealed in 2017 and 2018. MBAs need to be aware of the ethical environment that they work in and the ones that they help to create.

## ENVIRONMENTAL, SOCIAL, AND GOVERNANCE (ESG)

One of the hottest ethics topics is evaluating companies based on their impact on the environment and society, and their responsiveness to all stakeholders. Companies are increasingly making ESG disclosures in their annual reports or in standalone sustainability reports. ESG rating agencies give ranking scorecards (0–10 or CCC–AAA), with a wide ratings dispersion between agencies on individual companies. ESG investing is more than *socially responsible investing* (SRI). ESG investors are looking for capital appreciation, not just support of a set of values.

### Environment—Conservation of the planet
- Climate change and carbon footprint, sustainability reporting
- Air pollution and water pollution and resource conservation
- Biodiversity, deforestation, animal welfare
- Energy efficiency and sources
- Waste management, Scope 3 upstream and downstream product impacts

### Social—consideration of people and relationships with stakeholders

- Customer satisfaction, product safety
- Supplier relationships and standards
- Data privacy and protection
- Gender, Diversity, and Inclusion (D&I), Diversity, Equity, and Inclusion (DE&I), and LGBTQIA+ equity and advancement
- Employee engagement, work/life balance
- Community relations
- Human rights, conflict minerals, firearms, tobacco
- Labor standards and safety

### Governance—standards and systems in place for operating a company

- Board members composition, practices, and accountability
- Audit committee structure, responsibilities, reporting transparency
- Bribery and corruption policies and monitoring systems
- Executive compensation equity, conflicts of interest
- Lobbying, political contributions
- Whistleblower processes

"The rapid growth of ESG investment funds has led to claims that companies have been insincere or even misleading in touting their ESG accomplishments," according to Investopedia. "The strongest argument for ESG is that society endows corporate shareholders with benefits like limited liability, that persons don't have," and "companies need to earn their social license every day," per the *Wall Street Journal* (September 2022).

## KEY ETHICS TAKEAWAYS

*Social Responsibility of Business* — Concept that businesses are accountable to more than their owners

*Relativism and Its Four Forms* — Reasons to avoid making ethical decisions

*Stakeholder Analysis* — A framework considering who is affected by a business decision

*Sarbanes-Oxley Act of 2002* — A federal law attempting to legislate ethics in corporate America

*Environmental, Social, and Governance (ESG)*—An assessment of corporate responsibility

# Day 3

## ACCOUNTING

### Accounting Topics

Accounting Rules

Accounting Concepts

The Financial Statements

Ratio Analysis

Managerial Accounting

Accounting is the language of business. Corporations need to communicate their results to the world. Their audience includes employees, investors, creditors, customers, suppliers, and communities. Within the company, accounting information provides a means to control, evaluate, and plan operations. Whatever the audience or function, accounting is *numbers*. Accountants (a-count-ants) "count the beans" so that business activity can be recorded, summarized, and analyzed. Accountants have been around from the beginning of time, and professors don't let you forget it.

In biblical times the accountants kept track of how much grain was stored in the community's silos. How do you think King Solomon knew that there was only a thirty-day supply of grain during a drought? It was from the accountants. Throughout the ages accountants have kept track with their fingers, abacuses, and calculators. In modern times accounting has gone beyond the physical

"THE PHOENICIANS, OF COURSE, WERE THE FIRST ACCOUNTANTS."

count of grain in storage. Accounting answers these basic questions about a business:

What does a company own?
How much does a company owe others?
How well did a company's operations perform?
How does the company get the cash to fund itself?

*All* corporate activities must eventually be measured in dollars, and that is where accounting comes in, like it or not. Although this area may appear tedious, you must have a working knowledge of accounting to function in the business world. Because knowledge is power, MBAs need to be literate in accounting to understand its function; more important, they must be able to ask for and use accounting information for decision-making purposes. Lawyers with accounting knowledge, for example, can interpret financial statements to get valuable information. In settlement negotiations, they become a force to be reckoned with. Because employee performance is often evaluated with accounting data, a knowledge of accounting is essential.

Having expert knowledge of complex accounting rules, however, is not the MBA's goal. Therefore, my aim here is to give you the basics, not to make you a CPA. Because every function of business, including finance, operations, and marketing, uses the numbers generated by the accountants, it is important to grasp the fundamentals and read this chapter carefully.

## GAAP RULES

Accounting has innumerable rules. You should not attempt to memorize them, but you should become sufficiently familiar with them to communicate with CPAs. Accounting rules set the standards so that financial reports of companies may be compared on an equal basis. Accounting's governing rules are called *Generally Accepted Accounting Principles* (GAAP). These "Gap" rules have been developed over the years and are analogous to the precedents in the legal profession.

As new areas of business activity developed, the *Financial Accounting Standards Board* (FASB) wrote additional rules to deal with these situations. This body had generated over a hundred "Fasbee" rules over the years, and accountants referred to them by number.

In 2009, after decades of pronouncements and hundreds of rules, the FASB finally created the *Accounting Standards Codification* (ASC). Although it did not change the rules, the ASC organized all the rules into topics for easier reference. Currently, the ASC is considered the single source of Generally Accepted Accounting Principles. Accountants still use the old FASB rule numbers for reference.

Accounting is also an international concern, especially for multinational corporations. The *International Accounting Standards Board* (IASB) has created its own set of guidelines, called the *International Financial Reporting Standards* (IFRS). Accountants consider it a less-detailed "principles-based" system of rules, which permits companies to use their judgment. In contrast, the GAAP rules in the United States are "rules based" and companies must adhere to well-defined rules.

In 2002, the FASB and IASB agreed to begin the process of "convergence" of their systems. To date neither the details of the system nor an implementation date have been agreed upon.

## THE FUNDAMENTAL CONCEPTS OF ACCOUNTING

To understand accounting, before you get into the numbers you first must become familiar with the underlying concepts. The rules do not tell the whole story. The following seven concepts and vocabulary are not a set of laws, but rather a guiding set of policies that underlie all accounting rules and reporting.

The Entity
Cash and Accrual Accounting
Objectivity
Conservatism
Going Concern
Consistency
Materiality

### THE ENTITY

Accounting reports communicate the activities of a specific *entity*. The parameters covered by an accountant's report must be clear. A reporting entity can be a single grocery store, a production plant, an entire business, or a conglomerate. For example, Darden Restaurants is a corporate entity. The Red Lobster and Olive Garden chains are also entities within it.

## CASH BASIS VERSUS ACCRUAL ACCOUNTING

How the beans are being counted is important. Using *cash basis* accounting, transactions are recorded only when cash changes hands. Very small businesses can get all the accounting information they need from their checking account register. If a store pays two years' rent in 2024, all the rent cost would be recorded as a cost in 2024, not over a period of two years. When a small machine shop purchases a power tool, its cost would be recorded when it was purchased, not over the useful life of the tool. Get the idea? Cash accounting tells you when and how much cash changed hands, but it doesn't try to match the costs of conducting business with their related sales.

Most companies of any significant size use the *accrual* accounting method. Accrual accounting recognizes the financial effect of an activity when the activity takes place without regard to the movement of cash. Target's rental costs are recorded each month with the benefits of occupancy. The cost of rivet guns at Boeing's aircraft factory is recorded over the useful life of the tools as workers use them on the factory floor. Due to the dollar magnitude of Boeing's purchases, cash accounting would distort its financial statements. Accrual accounting, as a consequence, raises two related issues, *allocation* and *matching,* because activity and cash movement most often do not occur at the same time.

*Allocations to Accounting Periods.* Because profit-and-loss statements reflect activities over a specific time, the period of recognition is *very* important. If IBM sold a large computer on credit to Ford Motor Company on December 31, 2024, accrual accounting would record the sale in 2024 when the binding contract was signed, not when Ford actually laid out the cash in 2025. The sale could be recorded at that point, because it was then that Ford became legally bound to take delivery of the computer. That was also the *period* in which IBM's accounting records would recognize the sale and its related costs and the profits. Ford, on the other hand, would recognize or *accrue* and *allocate* the cost of using the computer over its useful life.

*Matching.* Using the same logic as in allocation, sales made in one period are *matched* with their related selling costs or *cost of goods sold* (COGS) in the same accounting period. By matching sales dollars with their related costs, you can figure the profit a company has actually made. For example, when Safeway sells fresh produce on December 31, 2024, but doesn't pay the supplier's bill until 2025, accrual accounting will nevertheless record the costs related to those sales in 2024. Safeway's sales in 2024 caused the expense, and therefore, the sales should have the related costs allocated against them in the same year. Without established policies for *allocation* and *matching,* accountants could easily manipulate financial reports by choosing when to record sales or expenses in order to cover up or delay bad results.

## TRANSACTION DEFINITION AND OBJECTIVITY

Accounting records only contain transactions that have been "completed" and that have a "quantifiable" monetary value. Sales that have not been completed, but are thought of as "sure things," cannot be recorded. Even if a trustworthy salesman from John Deere swears that farmer Jones is a sure bet to buy a combine, the accountant would say no. For his accounting purposes, the sale has not taken place. John Deere has not delivered the machinery, nor has the farmer signed an enforceable contract.

Accountants also have an *objectivity* rule to guide them when in doubt. There must be *reasonable and verifiable* evidence to support the transaction, or else it does not get recorded.

For example, the goodwill generated by a public service campaign cannot be recorded on the books. What value could you put on it? Archer Daniels Midland (ADM) regularly runs TV propaganda telling consumers how cheap food is in America compared with the rest of the world. How could an accountant objectively put a dollar value on the "good feelings" directed toward the company in the hearts of grateful Americans or incumbent congressmen? Patents and inventions are also hard to value. If Du Pont purchases a patent on a new chemical from an inventor for $1,000,000, it would be recorded on the books at $1,000,000. The patent has quantifiable market value. However, if a Du Pont scientist developed a new process in the lab, the accountants could not record the innovation until it was sold. The accountant would need to have a contract and a canceled check to substantiate the entry in the books.

In the case of WorldCom's collapse in 2002, their telecommunications network assets were overvalued on the books by $3.3 billion and so were their reported profits. Accountants added the ongoing costs for local access to the value of their network when they should have been ordinary costs to place customers' long-distance calls through local carriers.

## *ACCOUNTING CONSERVATISM AND HISTORICAL COSTS*

When companies incur losses that are *probable* and that can *reasonably be estimated,* accountants record them, even if the losses have not actually been realized. When *gains* are expected, accountants postpone recording them until they are actually realized. If in 2024 the management of International Paper Company anticipated a big profit in 2026 on the sale of their Manhattan corporate headquarters, they could not record their profit until 2026. Their move was uncertain. Management could have changed their minds, or the real estate market could have tumbled. But for the sake of argument, let's assume that International Paper discovered in 2024 that in 2026 it would have to clean a toxic-waste pool beneath its building. Management would have to hire a consultant to estimate the cost of cleanup and record that cost in 2024. In this way, the financial-statement readers would be warned of dark clouds looming over the horizon in 2026. In the same way, the ongoing lawsuits related to asbestos that many companies battle are *contingent liabilities* that must be reviewed annually and disclosed to ensure readers understand their possible impairment of corporate assets. Accounting *conservatism* governs the preparation of financial statements. When in doubt, be conservative. Accounting records contain only measurable and verifiable properties, debts, sales, and costs.

Conservatism also dictates that transactions be recorded at their *historical costs*. International Paper's New York headquarters appreciated in value during the real estate boom, and yet this gain could not be recognized, even if the company had paid the Lenape a few trinkets for it in the 1600s. The records continue to value the real estate at the cost of the beads given in exchange for the property. In the accountant's mind, the value of the building may decline by the time it's sold.

If the value of an asset falls below the recorded cost, that's another story. Conservatism dictates that the loss be recognized *today*. To do otherwise could mislead the reader of a financial statement to believe that the assets represented are at least worth their historical cost. Only in the case of assets held for investment by a trading company, would the assets be "marketed to market" above and below cost, as that is their regular course of business.

The value of goods held in inventory is also stated at historical cost. Even if prices change, the *objective* price is that which the business paid historically. There must be verifiable purchase orders and bills to support the cost. For instance, if Staples Office Supplies carries notepaper produced by International Paper on its books, it would value the paper at cost. Even if reorder costs for the same inventory had gone up, the cost of the merchandise on hand would remain at Staples' historical cost on the books.

## GOING CONCERN

Financial statements describe businesses as *operating* entities. The values assigned to items in the accounting records assume that the business is a *going concern*. Accountants presume that companies will continue to operate in the foreseeable future; therefore, the values assigned in the financial statements are not "fire sale" prices. They use historical costs, as you already know. Steel-rolling equipment, for example, is expensive to purchase. It may have great value to an ongoing manufacturing company such as US Steel, but put up for sale at a bankruptcy auction, its value would be pennies on the dollar. Used industrial equipment has limited value to outsiders. Accordingly, accounting records use historical costs assuming that the company is using its machinery productively.

## CONSISTENCY

The *consistency* concept is crucial to readers of financial statements. Accounting rules demand that an entity use the same accounting rules year after year. That enables an analyst to compare past with current results. This rule, like the others presented earlier, tries to minimize the temptations of accounting monkey business that businessmen like to engage in to cover up bad results.

The consistency rule insists that companies value their inventory the same way from year to year. The major methods available are a *FIFO* (First In First Out) or *LIFO* (Last In First Out) basis. Using FIFO, the oldest purchase costs of goods are recognized as costs "first," leaving the most recently purchased cost of goods in the value of inventory held for sale. Using LIFO, the "last" costs of goods are recognized as costs first, leaving the oldest costs in the value of inventory. The accounting method is independent of the physical movement of inventory. It is just an *accounting method*. As you might imagine, if you could change accounting methods at will, a crafty accountant could manipulate the financial statements from year to year. Consistency requires that the same accounting method be used from year to year.

As an example of FIFO and LIFO methods, consider a coin dealer who has only two identical gold coins in his showcase. One he bought in 1965 for $50, and the other he purchased in 2024 for $500. A numismatist comes to his shop and buys one of the coins for $1,000. Using FIFO, the shop owner would record a sale of $1,000, a cost of $50, and a resulting profit of $950 in his accounting records. His remaining inventory would reflect one coin at a historical cost of $500. The cost of the first coin purchased was the first to be recorded as a cost of goods sold. Using the alternate LIFO method, the owner would record a cost of $500, and a profit of only $500. His inventory records would show a coin with a value of $50. The last cost was used first. Which coin was actually sold, the 1965 or the 2024 acquisition, does not matter. It's only an accounting method. But the method chosen dramatically affects the way a company calculates profits and values inventory. That *does* matter.

If a change of accounting method is necessary for a "substantial" reason, the financial statements must state the reason in the footnotes located at the end of the report. The footnotes must also state how the change affected the profits and asset values that year. You can run, but you cannot hide from the accountants.

## MATERIALITY

An important caveat of financial statements is that they are *not* exact to the penny, even though you would expect that tenacious accountants would produce such reports. In fact, they are only *materially* correct so that a reader can get a *fairly stated* view of where an entity stands. Financial statements give a materially accurate picture so that a reasonable person can make informed decisions based on the report. For a small snack kiosk's financial statements, a one-hundred-dollar error may materially distort the records, while a ten-dollar error may not. In contrast, huge multinational companies like Coca-Cola may have million-dollar errors in their reports and not materially distort the picture for decision making.

By now you can begin to develop an insight into how accountants think about businesses and possibly why they are, for the most part, conservative even as people. In my previous edition I showed a cartoon that poked fun at the conservatism of accountants. I'd found it on a bulletin board at Arthur Andersen LLP, where I had worked as an auditor. Arthur strayed in the years after I left and collapsed in 2001 in connection with its fraud involving the collapse of Enron. That left only the *Big Four* accounting firms: Pricewaterhouse-

Coopers LLP (PwC), KPMG LLP, Deloitte Touche Tohmatsu Ltd., and Ernst & Young LLP (EY). In keeping with the changes I have selected a different cartoon, below.

"NEW FROM ACCOUNTING, SIR. TWO AND TWO IS FOUR AGAIN."

## THE FINANCIAL STATEMENTS

MBAs are not trained to key transactions into a computer; rather they are schooled to interpret the information that accountants generate. The financial statements are the summary of all the individual transactions recorded during a period of time. Financial statements are the final product of the accounting function. They give interested users the opportunity to see in a neat summary what went on. To know a company, you must be able to read and understand three major financial statements:

The Balance Sheet
The Income Statement
The Statement of Cash Flows

### THE BALANCE SHEET

*Definitions*

To set the stage you need to know the basic vocabulary of the *balance sheet*. The balance sheet presents the *assets* owned by a company, the *liabilities* owed to others, and the accumulated investment of its owners. The balance sheet shows these *balances* as of a specific date. It is a snapshot of a company's holdings at a given time. The balance sheet is the foundation for all accounting records, and you must be familiar with it. The following are the components of balance sheets.

*Assets* are the resources that the company possesses for the future benefit of the business.

- Cash
- Inventory
- Customers receivables — *accounts receivable*
- Equipment
- Buildings

*Liabilities* are dollar-specific obligations to repay borrowing, debts, and other obligations to provide goods or services to others.

- Bank debt
- Amounts owed to suppliers — *accounts payable*
- Prepaid accounts or advances from customers to deliver goods and services
- Taxes owed
- Wages owed to employees

*Owners' equity* is the accumulated dollar measure of the owners' investment in the company. Their investment can be either in the form of cash, other assets, or the reinvestment of earnings of the company.

- Common stock — *investment by owners*
- Additional paid-in capital — *investment by owners*
- Retained earnings — *reinvestment of earnings by owners*

*The Fundamental Accounting Equation*

As the name implies, the balance sheet is a "balance" sheet. The fundamental equation that rules over accounting balance is:

$$\text{Assets (A)} = \text{Liabilities (L)} + \text{Owners' Equity (OE)}$$

What you own (assets) equals the total of what you borrowed (liabilities) and what you have invested (equity) to pay for it. This equation or "identity" explains *everything* that happens in the accounting records of a company over time. Remember it!

*Examples of the "Balancing" Act*

Using the example of a new local supermarket called Bob's Market, I will give you three examples of how the balancing act works.

1. When the market opened up for business, Bob purchased a cash register. Assets increased on the left side of the scale, while bank debt, a liability, was also increased on the right to pay for it. The asset increase was balanced by an increase in liability.
2. When Bob invested some of his own money and attracted some of his parent's to open the market, equity increased on the right side of the scale, and cash, an asset, increased on the left to balance the transaction.
3. When the store becomes successful, it will hopefully be able to pay off its bank debt for the register (liabilities reduced on the

right). The cash, an asset, would be reduced, thus balancing the transaction on the left.

*All* transactions adhere to this balancing concept. There is no way to affect one side of the balance sheet without a balancing entry. The accounting records are therefore said to be in "balance" when the assets equal the liabilities and owners' equity (A = L + OE). If the records do not balance, an accountant has made a mistake.

### The Accounting Process: The Double Entry System

As you may have heard, accountants make *journal entries* in their books to record each of a business's individual transactions. Accountants call their books the *general ledger.* The listing of the accounts is called the *chart of accounts.* Using the same balancing concept shown by accounting's *fundamental equation,* asset additions are placed on the left side, called a *debit.* Liabilities and owners' equity additions are placed on the right side, called a *credit.* In all cases, journal entries have at least two lines of data, a debit and a credit. Entries to reduce assets are placed on the right, a credit, and reductions of liabilities and equity are placed on the left, a debit. Because of this right-side/left-side method, the manual record keeping of each account's transactions resembles a *T,* and consequently these records are called *T accounts.*

RULES FOR ENTRIES INTO ACCOUNTS

| Asset Accounts | | Liability Accounts | |
|---|---|---|---|
| | | Debit<br>Decrease | Credit<br>Increase |
| Debit<br>Increase | Credit<br>Decrease | Owners' Equity Accounts | |
| | | Debit<br>Decrease | Credit<br>Increase |

To illustrate, at the beginning of the year Bob and his parent issued themselves one thousand shares of stock for their initial investment of $15,000 in their store. The journal entry to record the transaction looked like this:

### BALANCE SHEET JOURNAL ENTRY #1

| ACCOUNT TITLE | (TYPE) | DEBIT | CREDIT | EFFECT |
|---|---|---|---|---|
| Cash | (Asset) | 15,000 | | increase |
| Common Stock | (OE) | | 15,000 | increase |

Similarly a repayment of a debt would be *journalized* as:

### BALANCE SHEET JOURNAL ENTRY #2

| ACCOUNT TITLE | (TYPE) | DEBIT | CREDIT | EFFECT |
|---|---|---|---|---|
| Bank Debt | (Liability) | 15,000 | | decrease |
| Cash | (Asset) | | 15,000 | decrease |

Because each entry to the records balances, at the end of a period of time, the entire balance sheet that summarizes the individual "accounts" and their net ending balances also balances (A = L + OE).

### A Balance Sheet Example

Let's continue with the local grocery store example and see what balances appeared during its first year of operation.

Bob's statement on the next page resembles the typical balance sheet of many retail and manufacturing firms. Three things are worth noting. *The total of assets equals the total of liabilities and owners' equity.* Second, the *assets are on the left* and the *liabilities and OE are on the right,* just like the journal entries of debits and credits. The third noteworthy item is that the balance sheet is as of a *point certain in time,* December 31, 2024, a specific date. Even though a business is the result of buying and selling over time, the

## BOB'S MARKET, FAIRWAY, KANSAS
## BALANCE SHEET AS OF DECEMBER 31, 2024
### (the first year of operation)

| ASSETS | | LIABILITIES | |
|---|---|---|---|
| **Current Assets** | | **Current Liabilities** | |
| Cash | $ 5,000 | Accounts Payable | $80,000 |
| Accounts Receivable | 10,000 | Wages Payable | 5,000 |
| Store Inventory | 100,000 | Taxes Payable | 2,000 |
| Total Current Assets | $115,000 | Total Current Liabilities | $87,000 |
| | | | |
| **Long-Term (Noncurrent) Assets** | | **Long-Term (Noncurrent) Debts** | |
| Store Equipment | $30,000 | Bank Debt | $10,000 |
| less one year's | | Total Liabilities | $97,000 |
| *Accumulated* | | | |
| *Depreciation* | (3,000) | | |
| Net Long-Term Assets | $27,000 | **Owner's Equity** | |
| | | Common Stock issued | |
| | | (1,000 shares | |
| | | outstanding) | $15,000 |
| | | Retained Earnings | 30,000 |
| | | Total Owners' Equity | $45,000 |
| | | | |
| | | **Total Liablities and** | |
| Total Assets | $142,000 | Owners' Equity | $142,000 |

balance sheet is only a "snapshot" of what the company's resources and obligations are at a stated time.

### Liquidity: Current and Long-Term Classifications

An important aspect of the balance sheet statement is that the assets and liabilities are listed in order of their *liquidity*, from most liquid to least. Liquidity means the ability of an asset to be converted to cash. Cash, accounts receivable from customers, and inventory are labeled *current* and are listed first since they are easily transferred and converted into cash within the next operating period, typically in one year (i.e., they are liquid). Equipment is not easily sold; therefore, it is classified as *fixed, long-term,* or a *noncurrent* asset (NCA) and listed below the current items. Check out Bob's balance sheet to verify the placement of these items.

On the liabilities side, the accounts payable to suppliers, wages payable to employees, and taxes payable are current liabilities. They are short-term obligations that will have to be paid within a year. The bank debt is *long-term* or a *noncurrent* liability (NCL) because it will be paid off over a period of years.

### Working Capital

A commonly used term in accounting as well as finance is *working capital.* It refers to the assets and liabilities that a company constantly "works with" as part of its daily business. They are also most *liquid* assets, giving a financial statement reader a clue to a firm's solvency. Consequently, working capital items are the current assets *and* liabilities of the firm. *Net working capital,* a measure of solvency, is the total of current assets less the total of current liabilities.

Current Assets − Current Liabilities = Net Working Capital

At Bob's Market net working capital amounts to $28,000 ($115,000 − $87,000). That's Bob's excess of liquid assets to make good on its current obligations. From a banker's vantage point, a grocer with a large amount of net working capital may be considered a good credit risk because the business can make its debt payments. Conversely, it could also show a corporate raider or operations analyst that the store owner is mismanaging his inventory by holding too many goods on the shelves or too much cash in the registers. An astute operator would reduce inventory levels and the cash on hand to more efficient levels and pocket the difference as a dividend. The proper amount of working capital depends on the industry. However, in 2020 these stores with "lean" inventories were caught short when Covid supply chain disruptions prevented rapid resupply.

*How Owners' Equity Fits In*

Owners' equity represents the long-term obligation of a company to its owners. Companies are obligated to pay the owners a return on their investment based on the success of the firm. OE does not carry a set rate of interest or maturity like a bank loan, so it is segregated below the liabilities. Owners are paid only after all other debt payments are made. An owner's return is dependent on the success of the company. If debt repayments cannot be made, the firm can be forced into bankruptcy. The inability to pay a dividend to investors has no such penalty. If the company is highly profitable, the owners win. If not, they can lose all of their investment. That's the risk of ownership.

By reversing algebraically our accounting identity from $A = L + OE$ to $OE = A - L$, you can see that OE is the "residual" interest of the firm, assets less liabilities. OE is also called *net worth,* as it is the "net" value after all other obligations. In the case of Donald Trump, the notorious real estate magnate of the 1980s, he may have owned billions of dollars of property, but temporarily his net worth reportedly became negative in 1990 as his debts became even larger than the value of his properties in New York City and Atlantic City.

Owners' equity is increased by conducting business. Businesses buy and sell and provide and receive services. Hopefully after a period of time, the company has increased its wealth with those activities. If the net assets increased over time, then it must have increased its OE.

The OE captions on the balance sheet can be affected in two ways. Investors can contribute more funds or they may elect that the company "retain" its profits. The line "retained earnings" is on the balance sheet for that purpose. If owners want to take out earnings, they may elect to receive *dividends.* Dividends reduce their accumulated retained earnings.

Accountants sometimes prepare the *Statement of Owners' Equity* with the financial statements if the information is useful. These detailed statements outline the owners' investments, their stock transactions, and the dividends paid to them during the year. These transactions affect the owners' equity captions on the balance sheet. The Statement of Owners' Equity, also called the *Statement of Changes Shareholders' Equity*, is considered a minor statement. However, it may be important for companies that have a great deal of owner activity. Large companies always produce this statement because it reveals many transactions that interest the public. Take a moment and go back to Bob's balance sheet and review its presentation before you move on to the income statement.

## THE INCOME STATEMENT

As the balance sheet shows *balances* as of a specific date, the income statement shows the "flow" of activity and transactions over a specific "period." That period may be a month, a quarter, or a year. There are *revenues* from sales and *expenses* relating to those revenues. When revenues and expenses are properly *matched* using *accrual accounting*, the difference is "income."

$$\text{Revenue} - \text{Expenses} = \text{Income}$$

### An Income Statement Example

On page 94 we'll look at the income statement of Bob's Market to see how his operation performed during his first year of business.

### Income Statement Terminology

As with the balance sheet, the income statement has several noteworthy features. In the income statement, the classifications of expenses are extremely important because different types of income are calculated. Each offers a particular insight about Bob's operating results. Please refer to Bob's income statement as you read through this terminology section.

*Gross Margin.* The top part of the income statement calculates *gross margin*.

Gross Margin =
Sales – The "Direct" Cost of the Goods or Services Sold

## BOB'S MARKET, FAIRWAY, KANSAS
## INCOME STATEMENT FOR THE YEAR ENDING
## DECEMBER 31, 2024

| | | |
|---|---|---|
| Sales to Customers | | $5,200,000 |
| Cost of Goods Sold | | 3,900,000 |
| **Gross Margin** | | **$1,300,000** |
| | | |
| **Less Selling, General, and Administrative Expenses** | | |
| Payroll | $1,000,000 | |
| Rent | 150,000 | |
| Utilities | 75,000 | |
| Advertising | 18,000 | |
| Allocated Cost of Store Equipment (Depreciation) | 3,000 | |
| All Other | $10,000 | |
| | | $1,256,000 |
| | | |
| **Operating Income (EBIT)** | | **$44,000** |
| Less Interest Expense | | 1,000 |
| | | |
| **Income Before Taxes** | | **$43,000** |
| Less Federal and State Income Taxes | | 13,000 |
| | | |
| **Net Income** | | **$30,000** |
| Net Income per Share ($30,000/1,000 shares) | | 30.00 |

At this point, the reader can determine if the company is making a profit without considering the burden of corporate expenses. At Bob's Market gross margin was his sales less the cost of goods sold (COGS). COGS includes the cost of groceries and all costs "directly" related to making the groceries salable, such as the cost of shipment from the wholesaler. In a manufacturing company it includes the costs of production, materials, and labor. In a simple retail situation like Bob's, COGS is calculated by this formula:

Beginning Inventory + New Purchases − Ending Inventory =
Cost of Goods Sold

If a business has a negative gross margin, either costs are out of control, or the pricing structure of the industry does not afford the company a profit. A small electronics manufacturer would encounter this situation if it tried to compete with the Asian flat-screen TV manufacturers LG, Samsung, and TCL. A small U.S. manufacturer could not be as efficient and could not charge a higher price to cover its higher costs of production.

*Operating Profit.* The next part of the income statement relates to the *operating profit* of the company, the earnings before interest and taxes (EBIT). The further we move down the income statement, the more expenses that are deducted. At the operating level of profit measurement, all the other corporate expenses *directly* related to the revenue process are deducted. In Bob's case he has employee wages, rent, utilities, advertising, and many other smaller items.

Accrual accounting dictates that the *allocated cost of fixed assets,* also called *depreciation* or *amortization,* be charged to earnings. Using the principle of *matching,* the cost of providing the company's products is matched with its related revenues of the period. Accountants divide the cost of equipment, tools, buildings, and other fixed assets by their *useful lives* to estimate the cost of using up assets needed in the revenue-generating process. In Bob's case, he spent $30,000 for shelves, carts, and cash registers. Because he estimated that they will last ten years, Bob's income statement will show an expense of $3,000 ($30,000/10) each year *to match and allocate* the cost of using those assets with the period of sales benefited. A measure of profitability that many analysts calculate is EBITDA, earnings before interest, taxes, depreciation, and amortization. Other analysts use NOPAT, net operating profit after tax.

"Other expenses" is a catchall category for items not large enough to justify a separate line on the income statement. On Bob's income statement it includes fixing those annoying stuck wheels on his shopping carts and the losses on bad checks.

*Net Income.* Below the *operational* level of profit, items not directly linked to operations are deducted to calculate income. The first is the interest expense for the period. A case can be made that corporate borrowing is used to support the operation. However, the method of financing the company is separate from the operating activities of the business. Accountants do not include interest in operating income, because companies in similar businesses may have been funded by using differing proportions of bank borrowing and investors' money. Investors' dividends are not deducted. Owners pay dividends out of the net income at the bottom of the statement.

If interest were to be included in *operating income,* similar companies could have vastly differing operating incomes just by the way they funded their cash needs. A company under a different management could fund all its cash needs by additional investments from its owners. These funds would incur no interest charges, and, therefore, the company's operating income would be higher. If the same company borrowed for all its needs, its operating income would be reduced by the interest expenses. By segregating interest expenses, the operating income reflects only the costs of "operating" the company, rather than "financing" it.

Using the same logic that excluded interest from operating income, tax expenses are segregated to leave operating income free of nonoperating expenses. Different tax strategies can result in greatly different tax expenses. Because taxes are often the product of a skilled tax accountant's pen instead of operating results, tax expenses are put below operating results as a separate deduction, leaving *net income* as the *final* measure of income. Net income is the bottom-line profit of the company, and it is the figure that is reported in the media as the measure of success or failure.

### How Income Statement Journal Entries Are Made

In keeping with their age-old duty to count the beans, accountants make *journal entries* to the company's books to tally up net income during the year. Net income is the result of subtracting the expenses from the sales made during a defined period of time. Net income is also the net increase in assets for the same period of time.

Journal entries keep track of the total of all the revenues and expenses as well as their corresponding increases and decreases in assets. Accountants make the entries for the income statement at the same time as they prepare the balance sheet.

During the year, running totals are accumulated for each revenue and expense to calculate the final net income figure for the entire year. At year's end when the final tally is completed and net income is calculated, the running totals of revenues and expenses are set to zero for the new year, and the difference or net income or loss is recorded on the balance sheet as retained earnings. That accounting year, at times called a *fiscal year*, can begin in any month. It does not have to start in January.

The journal entries look the same as those that you have seen used for the balance sheet. To track the income statement, *revenues* are recorded as *credits* (on the right side), and *expenses* are recorded as *debits* (on the left).

Income statement entries are combined with balance sheet entries. A sale means that the business received something of value, an asset, in exchange for something else of value, an expense. At Bob's grocery store, sales meant that an inflow of cash came in exchange for grocery inventory. Bob's accountant made weekly entries to record his sales and their costs in the following way:

## INCOME STATEMENT JOURNAL ENTRY #1

| ACCOUNT TITLE | (TYPE) | DEBIT | CREDIT | EFFECT |
|---|---|---|---|---|
| Cash | (Asset) | 100,000 | | increase |
| Sales Revenue | (Income Statement) | | 100,000 | increase |

Similarly the accountant recorded the cost of those sales:

## INCOME STATEMENT JOURNAL ENTRY #2

| ACCOUNT TITLE | (TYPE) | DEBIT | CREDIT | EFFECT |
|---|---|---|---|---|
| Cost of Goods Sold | (Income Statement) | 95,000 | | decrease |
| Inventory | (Asset) | | 95,000 | decrease |

To illustrate a full year's income statement entries, assume that those two entries were the only sales and costs for the entire year. The net income for the year would have been the net of the total sales revenues of $100,000 less the total COGS of $95,000, or $5,000. That net income figure also mimicked the change in net assets recorded by those same entries. Cash increased $100,000 and groceries decreased $95,000, a net of $5,000.

At year's end the net increase of assets of $5,000 equals the net income for the year. Bob would have recorded that net change on the balance sheet as an increase to retained earnings. He would also *close out* or set to zero all the revenue and expense accounts for the year in preparation for recording the next year's activity in the following entry:

## INCOME STATEMENT YEAR END
## CLOSE OUT ENTRY

| ACCOUNT TITLE | (TYPE) | DEBIT | CREDIT | EFFECT |
|---|---|---|---|---|
| Sales Revenue | (Income Statement) | 100,000 | | reversal |
| Cost of Goods Sold | (Income Statement) | | 95,000 | reversal |
| Retained Earnings | (Owner's Equity on the Balance Sheet) | | 5,000 | increase |

Notice that the journal entry balances. The income statement entries reversed themselves, leaving the net income addition to retained earnings on the balance sheet. Where sales of $100,000 were entered on the right during the year, they are cleared at year end with a $100,000 entry on the left. The balance sheet's asset, liability, and owners' equity balances are permanent running totals that are carried forward to the next accounting year. There you have it. In a page you've witnessed an abbreviated version of an entire year's accounting cycle and hours of MBA classroom consternation.

### The Income Statement's Link to the Balance Sheet

From Bob's actual income statement, the reader can see that the store had a marginally profitable year. He had a *net income* of

$30,000. What is even more important than just the calculations of income is the understanding of how the income statement relates to the balance sheet. The income statement is the result of many activities during the year. Assets and liabilities are affected upward and downward during the year through many individual transactions. At year's end, the net assets of the firm, as totaled by the balance sheet, had changed because of operating activities. The net income, as calculated by the income statement, tells the story of the year's operations by showing *how* that change in net assets occurred. Because it was Bob's first year, retained earnings equaled $30,000, the first year's net income. In succeeding years it will be affected by the next year's earnings and dividends.

## THE STATEMENT OF CASH FLOWS

### The Importance of Cash

As the saying goes, "Cash is king." Without the green a business cannot function. For example, let's take a look at Amanda, Inc., who sold package-printing equipment to the food companies that supplied Bob's Market. If Amanda, Inc., sold three printing presses to Kraft Heinz at $5 million each and earned $2 million on each, Amanda's income statement would show $6 million in profits. However, Amanda manufactured the equipment during the summer and Kraft Heinz paid for it in the fall when it was delivered. The factory employees wouldn't be too happy if their July paychecks bounced while the company waited for the cash in October.

Because the cash is critical for operations, and—most important—in order to stay out of bankruptcy, all financial statements include the *Statement of Cash Flows* or *Cash Flow Statement*. Because knowing the "sources" and "uses" of cash is paramount for a business, the addition of the statement of cash flows has widely been seen as a great improvement by the financial community.

The inability to manage a company's cash needs is often the primary cause of the demise of many "profitable" enterprises. Many companies that measured their success by their net income have had a rude awakening when confronted with cash shortages and angry creditors.

Investors myopically looking at the income statement for a measure of health can be deceived. For example, Boeing's McDonnell Douglas, the defense contractor, had healthy earnings that masked an underlying corporate illness. *Forbes* reported it to its readers:

> On the surface, things don't look so bad for McDonnell Douglas. It will probably report over $10 a share in earnings . . . , versus $5.72 last year. But even a cursory glance examination of the numbers shows that earnings are shaky, if not ephemeral. Start with cash flow. It was negative $35 million by the third quarter . . . and the bleeding of cash could accelerate. . . .

The leveraged buyout (LBO) phenomenon of the 1980s used the principles of cash flow as its tool. A raider's ability to repay the money borrowed to acquire a target company was based in large part on the cash-flow-generating ability of the acquisition. Much of that information lies in the statement of cash flows. In 1989, Kohlberg Kravis Roberts (KKR) bought RJR Nabisco in the largest leveraged buyout up to that time with $26.4 billion in debt financing based on the cash-generating ability of the company to pay off the debt.

*The Cash Flow Statement's Link to the Balance Sheet*
The cash flow statement also follows the balancing-act principle of accounting. I will present the accounting math first so that you may understand the logic of what, at first glance, can be a confusing statement. With the math out of the way, the cash flow statement example can readily be understood. The equations that follow are not included to impress, merely to inform.

Using the golden *fundamental accounting equation* we have:

$$A = L + OE$$
$$\text{Assets} = \text{Liabilities} + \text{Owners' Equity}$$

Because assets and liabilities are composed of both current (short-term) and noncurrent (long-term) items, the equation can be expanded:

$$CA + NCA = CL + NCL + OE$$

Current Assets + Noncurrent Assets = Current Liabilities + Noncurrent Liabilities + Owners' Equity

To further break it down, the *current asset* class can be shown as its individual components:

Cash + Accounts Receivable (AR) + Inventory (INV) + NCA = CL + NCL + OE

Rearranging the equation algebraically, we can isolate cash:

$$Cash = CL + NCL + OE - AR - INV - NCA$$

As revealed by the equation, an increase in a current liability (CL) on the right of the equals sign would mean an increase in cash on the left. Increasing your debts to suppliers frees up a business's cash for other purposes. Conversely an increase in an asset such as inventory would mean a decrease in cash. It makes sense; buying inventory requires cash. Adding or subtracting on one side of the equals sign affects the total on the other side of the equation.

My study group at business school found cash flow statements to be the most confusing of the major topics in accounting. But if the former Peace Corps volunteer in my study group with no business training caught on, I have full confidence in your ability to pick it up also. With the preceding as foundation, I will illustrate the importance of the cash flow statement and use Bob's Market as an example to finish off the cash flow lesson.

*The Uses for the Cash Flow Statement*

The cash flow statement is a management tool to help avoid liquidity problems. Both the income statement and the balance sheet are used to form the cash flow picture of a company. The statement answers the following important questions:

What is the relationship between cash flow and earnings?
How are dividends financed?
How are debts paid off?
How is the cash generated by operations used?
Are management's stated financial policies reflected in the cash flow?

By using a statement of cash flows, managers can plan and manage their cash sources and needs from three types of business activities:

Operations Activities
Investing Activities
Financing Activities

These activities are shown clearly in the cash flow statements.

*A Cash Flow Statement Example*

Let's look at Bob's Market as a springboard from my theoretical discussion and get into an actual cash flow statement, found on page 103.

It is easy to get too wrapped up in the numbers and not really grasp the logic behind the preparation of the statement. Therefore, let's look at each entry separately and explain the logic behind it. The MBA's accounting education focuses on the logic behind the numbers, while undergraduate programs focus primarily on the accounting mechanics to turn out CPAs, not MBA managers.

## BOB'S MARKET
## STATEMENT OF CASH FLOWS FOR THE YEAR
## ENDING DECEMBER 31, 2024

*Operating Activities*

**Net Income** $30,000

**Add Back Expenses Not Using Cash**

Depreciation (Allocated Cost of Store Equipment) 3,000

$33,000

**Adjust for Changes in Working Capital**

Increases and Decreases During the Year

**Current Assets**

| | | |
|---|---|---|
| Customer Receivables (Increase) Decrease | $(10,000) | |
| Store Inventory (Increase) Decrease | (100,000) | |

**Current Liabilities**

| | | |
|---|---|---|
| Vendor Payable Increase (Decrease) | 80,000 | |
| Wages Payable Increase (Decrease) | 5,000 | |
| Taxes Payable Increase (Decrease) | 2,000 | |
| | | $(23,000) |

**Cash Flow from Operating Activities** $10,000

*Investing Activities*

| | | |
|---|---|---|
| Purchase of Store Equipment | $(30,000) | |
| **Cash Flow from Investing Activities** | | $(30,000) |

*Financing Activities*

| | | |
|---|---|---|
| Proceeds from Bank Borrowing | $10,000 | |
| Sale of Stock to Owners | 15,000 | |
| Payment of Dividends to Owners | 0 | |
| **Cash Flow from Financing Activities** | | $25,000 |

| | |
|---|---|
| *Increase in Cash for the Year* | $5,000 |
| Cash at Beginning of Year | 0 |
| Cash at End of Year | $5,000 |

Please refer to Bob's cash flow statement during the following discussion.

### Operating Activities

In the *Operating Activities* section, accountants calculate the cash generated from the day-to-day operating activities of a business. The income statement showed "accounting profit" of $30,000 for Bob, but it did not show how much *cash* was used or generated by his operations. As I explained earlier, most companies use *accrual basis accounting,* as Bob has, to determine his net income. The cash flow statement converts that accrual basis net income to a cash basis. To do that the net income has to be adjusted in two ways to get back to a cash basis.

*Step 1. Adjust Net Income for Noncash Expenses.* The first step to determine the flow of cash is to adjust the net income from the income statement. Operating items that did not use cash, but were deducted in the income statement as an expense, must be added back. *Depreciation,* as explained in the income statement section, does not actually take the company's cash "out the door." Only when Bob purchased the carts, registers, and displays was cash used. But over the life of these assets, depreciation is only an "accounting cost" that *matches* the original cash expenditure for these assets with the sales they benefit. Therefore, depreciation must be added back. It is not a use of cash. The purchases of the assets themselves are included later in the *Investing Activities* section.

*Step 2. Adjust Net Income for Changes in Working Capital.* Net income must also be adjusted for the changes in current assets and current liabilities that *operational activities* affected during the year. By adjusting net income for working capital increases and decreases, we can determine the effect on cash by using the fundamental accounting equation.

When Bob increased his current assets, such as his shelf inventory, he used cash because it took cash to buy groceries. This is shown as subtractions on the cash flow statement. When he extended credit to his customers, it delayed his receipt of cash, thus "using" cash that the store could have been using for other purposes. This is also shown as a subtraction on the statement. Conversely, reductions in inventory, i.e., sales, would have increased Bob's cash. If receivables had declined, i.e., customers' payments, cash would have been generated. *Point of Learning:* Increases in current assets use cash while decreases in current assets produce cash.

Current liabilities changes have the opposite effect on cash. In Bob's case his vendors advanced him $80,000. When Bob ran up a large debt with his vendors and employees, this meant that credit was extended to him, which in turn freed his cash for other purposes. In a sense, cash was created. If Bob had reduced his liabilities, that would have meant that he had made payments to reduce his debts, reducing cash. *Point of Learning:* Increases in current liabilities increase cash while decreases use up cash.

To calculate the net changes for the year, simply subtract the beginning of the period's balances of current assets and liabilities from the ending balances items. Because it was Bob's first year (and to make it simple), the beginning balances were all zero and the ending balances are equal to the account increases for the year. The increases in current assets are "uses" and the increases in current liabilities are "sources" of cash.

Convince yourself that Bob's cash flow statement is correct. Refer to his cash flow statement. Look back at the income statement to verify the net income. Review the balance sheet to check that the changes in the working capital items (CA + CL) equal the changes shown on the cash flow statement. It all fits together!

### Investing Activities

As the title explains, this area of the cash flow statement deals with cash use and generation by long-term "investments" by the company. Accordingly, the investment activities section reflects the cash effects of transactions in *long-term* (noncurrent) assets on the balance sheet. When a company buys or sells a long-term asset like a building or piece of equipment, the cash relating to the transaction is reflected in the *investing activities* section of the cash flow statement. In Bob's case, he invested $30,000 in store equipment as shown on his statement. If he had sold the equipment, the cash received would have been reflected. Review the balance sheet to verify how the change in his long-term assets was reflected in the investing section of the cash flow statement.

### Financing Activities

There are two ways a company can finance itself. Either managers borrow money or they raise money from investors. Borrowing would be reflected in changes in the long-term liabilities section of the balance sheet. The participation by investors would be reflected in changes in the owners' equity accounts of the balance sheet.

Bob borrowed $10,000 from the bank, which increased cash. On the balance sheet, "bank debt" increased from $0 to $10,000 and it was reflected as a source of cash. When the store repays the debt, it will be reflected as a use of cash in the *financing activities* section.

Referring back to Bob's Market's balance sheet, the owners' equity accounts are on the right side. The balance sheet shows that investors contributed $15,000 cash to start the business. That is shown on the balance sheet as "common stock" issued, and it is also reflected on the cash flow statement as a source of cash.

As we have already learned, the other component of the owners' equity section is *retained earnings* (RE). As explained, there will be changes in RE when net income is added during the year and if *dividends* are paid out to investors. Bob and his parent elected to continue to "finance" the business by having the company "retain" its earnings. The financing section, accordingly, does not show any dividend payments. If the owners elected to pay a dividend, it would have been shown as a use.

After a year of operations Bob had $5,000 more than when he started. With his cash flow statement he can understand how it happened!

### Once prepared, what does the cash flow statement mean?

Take a step back, or else you can get lost in the mechanics. This cash flow statement shows the net change in cash for the year. It appears at the bottom of the statement. Take a look. It sounds simple, but some newly minted CPAs I worked with never really understood that fact as they labored to prepare the report's details. You do. *Where* the changes in cash took place is of real importance to MBAs.

Was the company a seemingly profitable company, but must borrow heavily just to stay alive?

Did the company's operations throw off cash, even though it may be just marginally profitable according to the income statement?

Those are samples of the important questions that neither the balance sheet nor the income statement can tell a reader. That is why the cash flow statement exists.

When a company is healthy, operating activities will generate cash. That message is delivered by the net income adjusted for changes in working capital. That is the *operating activities* section's function.

Does the company require a great investment in fixed assets such as new equipment or technology? Is the company selling off its assets to fill an insatiable cash drain from operations? That type of information lies in the *investment activities* section.

Dying businesses stay alive by cannibalizing their assets to fund their unprofitable operations. Pan American Airlines, once the largest airline in the world, withered in 1991 when it sold its coveted European routes to its competitors to raise cash. Pan Am died in 1992.

Did the company borrow heavily or has the company gone to investors to fund its operational or investing activities? The *financing activities* section tells that important story. In Bob's case he borrowed from the bank and invested his own money.

Whatever the sources and uses of cash, the statement of cash flows tells a great deal about a business's health. To many financial analysts, it is the most important statement of all.

## ACCOUNTING'S BIG PICTURE

A knowledgeable person can always get back to the fundamental equation of accounting to make sense of any jumble of numbers making up any of the financial statements of a company: *Assets = Liabilities + Owners' Equity.*

With the statement of cash flows it was demonstrated that the changes during the year in the cash balance had to result from changes in assets, liabilities, and owners' equity. The assets and liabilities changes came from the balance sheet. The owners' equity changes were the result of changes in net income, provided in detail by the income statement. *The three basic financial statements are inextricably tied together.*

The fundamental accounting equation, the balance sheet, and each of the many journal entries made during the year *always* balance. That fundamental property allows for changes in any piece of the accounting puzzle to be explained by changes in the other parts. By grasping this basic concept of the interrelationships of the financial statements, you have learned the essence of accounting. Congratulations!

## READING THE FINANCIAL STATEMENTS USING RATIOS

With an understanding of how accountants create their financial statements, let me add some tools to interpret them: *ratios.* Absolute numbers in a financial statement in and of themselves often are of limited significance. The real information can be found in an analysis of the relationship of one number to another or of one company to another in the same industry—using ratios. In the grocery game, profits are usually low in relation to sales, so grocers must sell in large volume to make any real profit. A jewelry store survives on slower-paced sales but higher profits per item. That is why ratios are used to compare performances among companies within an industry and against a company's own historical performance.

There are four major categories of ratios:

*Liquidity* measures: How much is on hand that can be converted to cash to pay the bills?

*Capitalization* measures: Is a company heavily burdened with debt? Are its investors financing the company? How is the company funding itself?

*Activity* measures: How actively are the firm's assets being deployed? (MBAs deploy assets, rather than just use them.)

*Profitability* measures: How profitable is a company in relation to the assets and the sales that made its profits possible?

There are literally hundreds of possible ratios, but most have their origin in eight basic ratios from the four categories listed above. Using Bob's financial statements, I have calculated these eight ratios for his operation and have placed them below each of the ratio explanations.

## *LIQUIDITY RATIOS*

*1. Current Ratio = Current Assets / Current Liabilities*
Can the company pay its bills comfortably? A ratio greater than 1 shows liquidity. It shows that there is leeway in the current assets available to pay for current liabilities.

$$\left( \frac{\$115,000}{\$87,000} = 1.32 \right)$$

## CAPITALIZATION RATIOS

*2. Financial Leverage = (Total Liabilities + Owners' Equity)
/ OE*

$$\left( \frac{\$142,000}{\$45,000} = 3.155 \right)$$

When a company assumes a larger proportion of debt than the amount invested by its owners, it is said to be *leveraged*. In a profitable company, by using a higher level of debt, the return is much higher because a smaller amount appears in the denominator of the ratio. The "same" amount of earnings is divided by a smaller equity base. Ratios of greater than 2 show an extensive use of debt. I will explain leverage more fully when discussing the profitability ratios.

*3. Long-Term Debt to Capital = Long-Term Debt /
(Liabilities + OE)*

$$\left( \frac{\$10,000}{\$142,000} = .07 = 7\% \right)$$

Because debt payments are fixed obligations that *must* be paid while dividends to investors are not, the level of debt is an important measure of a company's riskiness. A ratio of greater than 50 percent shows a high level of debt. Depending on the timing and stability of a firm's cash flows, 50 percent could be considered risky. Stable electric utilities have predictable sales and cash flows; therefore, ratios over 50 percent are commonplace. Investment analysts on Wall Street consider those debt levels conservative.

## ACTIVITY RATIOS

4. Assets Turnover per Period = Sales / Total Assets

$$\left( \frac{\$5,200,000}{\$142,000} = 36.6 \text{ turns} \right)$$

This ratio tells the reader how actively the firm uses all of its assets. The firm that can generate more sales with a given set of assets is said to have managed its assets efficiently. Ratios are industry-specific. Thirty-six is a high turnover of assets for most industries, but for an antique shop a turnover of three may be considered high. One-of-a-kind antiques sit waiting for the right collector to come along. In the grocery trade 36.6 turns per year is normal because the shelf inventory of a supermarket is sold about every week. The produce, milk, and toilet paper inventory turn over several times a week, while the exotic spices take much longer to sell.

5. Inventory Turns per Period = Cost of Goods Sold / Average Inventory Held During the Period
(A simple way to calculate "average inventory" is by adding the beginning and ending inventory balances, then dividing by two.)

$$\left( \frac{\$3,900,000}{\$100,000} = 39 \text{ turns per year} \right)$$

6. Days Sales in Inventory = Ending Inventory / (Cost of Goods Sold / 365)

$$\left( \frac{\$100,000}{(\$3,900,000 \, / \, 365)} = 9.36 \text{ days} \right)$$

These two *activity* ratios show how actively a company's inventory is being deployed. Is inventory sitting around collecting dust or is it being sold as soon as it hits the shelf? In a high-turnover business, like the grocery trade, there are many turns of inventory during a year and only a few days of inventory on hand. Most grocery items are perishable and purchased frequently.

## PROFITABILITY RATIOS

*7. Return on Sales (ROS) = Net Income / Sales*

$$\left( \frac{\$30,000}{\$5,200,000} = .005769 = .58\% \right)$$

"Return" ratios are easy to calculate and investment analysts use them frequently. They calculate the return on just about any part of the balance sheet and income statement. Another common one is the return on assets (ROA).

*8. Return on Equity (ROE) = Net Income / Owners' Equity*

$$\left( \frac{\$30,000}{\$45,000} = .6667 = 67\% \right)$$

The mix of debt and equity can dramatically affect the ratios. If a company has a high level of debt and a small amount of equity, the return on equity (ROE) can be tremendously affected. That is called *financial leverage,* the term that I mentioned before in discussing capitalization ratios. To illustrate the point, Bob and his parent could have decided to leave very little equity in the company in 2024. They could have taken all of the $30,000 of net income made in 2024 out of the company as dividends and borrowed for their future cash needs. If that had happened, the balance sheet would have reflected a long-term debt balance of $40,000 ($10,000 + $30,000) and only $15,000 ($45,000 − $30,000) in equity. The resulting *debt to equity ratio* would increase from 7 percent to 28 percent, and the *return on equity* would have increased from 67 percent to 200 percent ($30,000/$15,000). As shown, ratios can be greatly affected by the financial leverage used. The choice of a lower equity level can "leverage" the ROE to extremely high levels.

ROE ratio is a widely accepted yardstick to measure success. If management's goal is to achieve a higher profitability ratio through leverage, there is a risk cost. Higher debt levels require higher interest payments that a company may not be able to service if operations do poorly. The corporate failures in the financial meltdown of 2008 of Lehman Brothers and Washington Mutual were cases in which management risked bankruptcy with high leverage and lost.

## THE DU PONT CHART

Academics have a tendency to give imposing names to simple concepts. Your MBA vocabulary would not be complete without including the *Du Pont Chart*. The chart shows how several of the most important financial statement ratios are related to one another by displaying their components.

By charting the interrelationships among ratios, one can see that changes in a component of one ratio affect the other ratios. The ratios share the same inputs. For example, when Total Assets is reduced, both the Asset Turnover and Return on Assets ratios increase

THE DU PONT CHART

| Profit Margin | | Asset Turnover | | Return on Assets (ROA) |
|---|---|---|---|---|
| $\dfrac{\text{Net Income}}{\text{Sales}}$ | X | $\dfrac{\text{Sales}}{\text{Total Assets}}$ | = | $\dfrac{\text{Net Income}}{\text{Total Assets}}$ |
| Return on Assets | | Financial Leverage | | Return on Equity (ROE) |
| $\dfrac{\text{Net Income}}{\text{Total Assets}}$ | X | $\dfrac{\text{Total Assets}}{\text{Owners' Equity}}$ | = | $\dfrac{\text{Net Income}}{\text{Owners' Equity}}$ |

because Total Assets are included in the calculation of both of those ratios as a denominator. Conversely, a reduction of Total Assets (equal to total liabilities and owners' equity) decreases Financial Leverage as it is used in that ratio's numerator.

## RATIOS ARE INDUSTRY-SPECIFIC

Profitability is, as in the case of all other ratios, industry-specific. Every industry has a profit level depending on the physical demands of the industry. Heavy manufacturers such as steel makers have a *return on assets* (ROA) of less than 10 percent. They have large steel mills and a great deal of factory equipment. Service businesses such as profitable headhunting firms may have ROAs over 100 percent. The only assets they need are cash, office furniture, and customer receivables. Their real asset is their staff's talent for seeking and persuading, which cannot be quantified on the balance sheet.

Profitability also depends on the level of competition. In the grocery business, intense competition keeps the *return on sales* to a low 1 percent. During Bob's first year he had a .58 percent return, which was below the industry average. Considering that it was his first year, any profit should be commended.

Any part of the financial statements can be compared to another with a ratio of some sort. Any calculator can divide one number by another. Only those ratios that can provide some insight into a business's performance are valuable. The true value of ratios is seen when one firm's ratios are compared to those of another in the same industry, or to that firm's historical performance. Alternatively the "attractiveness" of various industries as business opportunities may be explored by comparing their averages. Each firm and industry has its own key operating statistics that are meaningful.

For industry-specific references on all these ratios, RMA publishes its *Annual Statement Studies*. This valuable reference book, available in most libraries, includes financial and operating ratios for over three hundred manufacturers, wholesalers, retailers, services, contractors, and finance companies.

## MANAGERIAL ACCOUNTING

*Managerial accounting,* like ratio analysis, uses accounting data to manage and analyze operations. Managerial accounting focuses on operations. Instead of ratios, managerial accounting uses *standards, budgets,* and *variances* to run the business and explain operational results. The object of managerial accounting is to budget a company's activities for a period of time, and then to explain why the actual results "varied" from the projections. In most manufacturing settings, monthly budgeting and analysis are the norm so that management can take *timely* action.

To establish a yardstick for measuring performance, the factory team must set *standards* for comparison. This requires the input from more than just the accountants. In automobile manufacturing, the production manager establishes what he or she believes should be the standard costs for materials, labor, and other expenses. Industrial engineers help by performing studies to obtain the data. Factory managers work with sales managers to *budget* production volumes to meet forecasted demand and also to maintain assembly line efficiency. Sales managers set standard prices and quantities for their products. Using those standards as a yardstick, managerial accountants analyze actual results to explain the *variances* from those budgets and standards the company's team developed. Once completed, variance analysis highlights the source of positive or negative results for management decision making.

### *PRICE AND VOLUME VARIANCES*

There are two basic types of variances, *price* and *volume variances.* As with financial statement ratios, they are derived from simple mathematical formulas.

*Sales Price Variances.* The *price variance* tells the manager how much of the difference between budgeted sales revenue and actual sales revenues is due to changes in sales price changes.

$$(\text{Actual Sales Price} - \text{Standard Sales Price}) \times$$
$$(\text{Actual Quantity Sold}) = \text{Sales Price Variance}$$

*Sales Volume Variances.* The *volume variance* isolates the dollar effect of a different unit volume from what was budgeted assuming no price changes.

$$(\text{Standard Sales Price}) \times (\text{Actual Quantity Sold} -$$
$$\text{Standard Quantity Sold}) = \text{Sales Volume Variance}$$

Using a hypothetical example, Honda planned to sell 10,000 Odyssey minivans in July 2022 at a price of $30,000 each for a total of $300 million in sales. In August the analyst received accounting data showing that sales were actually $580 million in July. Honda actually sold 20,000 Odysseys at an average price of $29,000 due to a $1,000 rebate program. The total variance of sales was $280 million: $(20,000 \times \$29,000) - (10,000 \times \$30,000)$. How did that occur? Variances told the story.

The variance solely due to price, the *price variance,* was a negative $20 million $((\$29,000 - \$30,000) \times 20,000 \text{ units})$. But because 10,000 more units were sold than planned, the *volume variance* was positive $300 million $((20,000 - 10,000 \text{ units}) \times \$30,000)$. The two variances $(-\$20 + \$300 = +\$280)$ equaled the total variance from the total sales budget $(\$580 - \$300 = +\$280)$. The variance analysis told the Honda executive in charge of the Odyssey model that the overall increase in sales was due to a larger sales volume, rather than to a price increase. Conversely, the small negative price variance due to a rebate was more than made up for by a stronger sales volume. When you add together the price and the volume variances, they equal the "total" monthly sales variance from budget. The variance analysis enabled the Honda executive to explain why their results hit his division's targets.

## PURCHASE PRICE, EFFICIENCY, AND VOLUME VARIANCES

Using the same two basic formulas, *sales price* and *sales volume variances,* production departments also calculate variances for management control.

Purchases and usage of production materials have *purchase price variances.*

Purchase Price Variance = (Standard Price − Actual Price)
× (Actual Quantity Purchased or Used)

The amount of materials and labor used to produce products may also differ from the standard amount. Similar to sales volume variances, these differences are called *efficiency variances.* Shoe workers, for example, can be more efficient by using more leather from a hide than planned. Chemically dependent workers on the assembly line could take more labor hours than planned to produce their cars.

Material or Labor Efficiency Variance = (Standard Use Quantity − Actual Usage Quantity) × (Standard Cost of Material or Labor)

Using the Odyssey again as a hyphothetical example, the production foreman had budgeted in July that each Odyssey made should use a standard 8 gallons of paint at a cost of $10 per gallon. It actually took 7 gallons at a cost of $12 per gallon for the 20,000 minivans that were produced. The accountant calculated the following variances for the Honda executive:

Material Price Variance = ($10 − $12 price per gallon)
× (20,000 units × 7 gal.) = −$280,000 negative paint
price variance

This was the effect of paying more per gallon than planned. Instead of scratching one's head, the Honda executive could use this information to confront the purchasing agents and demand that they negotiate a better deal the following month.

$$\text{Material Efficiency Variance} = (8 \text{ gal.} - 7 \text{ gal.}) \times (20{,}000$$
$$\text{units}) \times \$10 \text{ per gallon} = \$200{,}000 \text{ positive variance}$$

This was the effect of using less paint than planned.

As with ratios, there are an infinite number of variances that can be cooked up to keep a department of accounting analysts busy from now until the next century. There are basically only two types of variances: *price* and *volume* variances. When you hear the words *managerial accounting*, think "variances."

## COST ACCOUNTING AND ACTIVITY-BASED COSTING

Cost accounting is the relatively straightforward process of determining the cost of producing goods and services. It is closely associated with managerial accounting, as all its "standards" are based on the data gathered by cost accountants. With manufactured goods, direct labor and direct materials are relatively simple to allocate to the cost of a product. However, allocating overhead is much more difficult. More important, if not done properly, it may falsely determine profitability of individual products and divisions of companies. Overhead must be allocated based on the actual usage of the overhead expenses; hence, it is called *activity-based costing* (ABC). Overhead should be allocated based on what it takes to create and deliver the product to the customer. In the past, overhead expenses were a relatively minor component in relation to materials and labor costs, but today expenses such as telephone, billing, consultants, and computer systems are huge.

For example, if a high-revenue division of a company makes sales to a few vendors with few orders, it should be allocated less of the cost of the billing department's cost than a lower-sales division that has many small customers ordering many times a year. If accountants allocate based on sales, not volume of transactions, the profit picture would be distorted. When a manufacturing process of a product is highly automated and that of another product is not, allocation of computer system expense based on direct labor hours would be misleading. What often happens in a company is that accountants, detached from the business, arbitrarily or mechanically allocate overhead expenses. That distorts the financial results that managers live or die by. Entire product lines and divisions can be shut down and or outsourced because of these relatively "unimportant" allocation decisions that neglect their ABC's.

## THE SKEPTICAL ACCOUNTING-INFORMATION CONSUMER

As described in the "Ethics" chapter, the Sarbanes-Oxley Act of 2002 tried to make accountants more honest. As a Ten-Day MBA you should be aware of the major ways that accountants can "cook the books." When big frauds or bankruptcies occur, "forensic" accountants try to discover how things went wrong and often find the problem in following areas:

### Ten Ways Accountants Can Misstate Earnings

1. Misclassify expenses as assets. WorldCom classified its ordinary cost of purchasing local phone access as an investment in their network.
2. Underestimate sales allowances for returns, discounts, and markdowns. Underestimating allowances raises profits.
3. Underestimate bad-debt allowances on sales made on credit. If you underestimate the allowance for bad-debt expense, profits are increased.
4. Create off-balance-sheet liabilities. Enron's "special purpose entities" that were off the balance sheet created billions in liabilities that caused the company's bankruptcy in 2002.
5. Recognize phantom revenues. Qwest Communications recognized $1.1 billion in revenues for selling fiber-network use that was contingent on purchasing fiber services from other telecommunications

firms. Both transactions never actually occurred, but both parties claimed revenues and the profits.

6. Depreciate assets too slowly. Waste Management was caught in 1998 stretching out the depreciable lives of its landfills and underreported by $3.5 billion its annual depreciation expense.

7. Modify adjustments to inventory. A company can underestimate how much inventory will become obsolete. Reducing obsolescence expense increases profits.

8. Forecast unusual gains or losses. By underestimating the cost of restructuring or overestimating the proceeds from assets sales, an accountant can inflate profits. Under certain circumstances these items are segregated in the income statement and may not affect "operating earnings."

9. Create special reserves by overestimating future expenses and boost profits by revising those estimates downward later. Using the same adjustments referred to above to boost profits, a company can overestimate expense allowances to dampen profits when profits are high. This creates a "cookie jar" reserve to open when profits sag to "smooth" the fluctuations in earnings year to year. When companies need extra profits, accountants revise the previous expense estimates downward and record profits. Jack Welch's General Electric conglomerate achieved an uncanny track record of consistent profitability through the use of income smoothing as revealed in a 2022 book, *The Man Who Broke Capitalism*. "Too good to be true, it was a rigged game."

10. Manipulate measures of performance that are tied to key executive bonus compensation. Depending on how bonuses are calculated, executives in collusion with financial accountants can manipulate the financial data to generate unearned bonuses and therefore reduce actual net income.

## ACCOUNTING OVERVIEW

I hope you have not struggled too hard through this chapter, but in a few pages I have tried to give you the essentials of accounting from both my CPA background and the MBA curriculum. If the material in this chapter was totally new for you, most probably you have not completely absorbed it. You should have remembered that:

- Assets = Liabilities + Owners' Equity
- There are three basic and interdependent financial statements: balance sheet, income statement, and cash flow statement.
- Accounting records and statements *always* balance.
- The statements can be interpreted by using ratios.
- Operating results can be analyzed and managed using variances.

That's the accounting game in a nutshell. At MBA school, accounting struck the most fear in the hearts of the liberal arts undergraduates. This chapter has given you, in a tidy predigested form, what kept them up late at night.

## KEY ACCOUNTING TAKEAWAYS

*Cash Basis Accounting* — The method of recording transactions only when cash changes hands

*Accrual Basis Accounting* — The method of recording transactions that matches revenues and expenses regardless of cash flow movements

*The Balance Sheet* — The listing of what a company owns and owes at a point in time

*The Fundamental Accounting Equation* — Assets = Liabilities + Owners' Equity

*Net Working Capital* — Short-term assets less short-term liabilities

*The Income Statement* — The summary of profit-generating activities during a period of time

*Gross Margin* — Revenues less the direct cost of goods sold

*The Statement of Cash Flows* — The summary of how a company generates and uses its cash during a period of time

*Depreciation* — The cost of using equipment allocated over its useful life

*The Eight Basic Ratios for Financial Statement Analysis* —
A method of analyzing statements and comparing them to
industry standards

*Price and Volume Variances* — A method of explaining operational
results by isolating the effects of price and volume differences
from budgeted amounts

*Activity-Based Costing (ABC)* — The method of allocating overhead
expenses based on actual usage, not on arbitrary measure

# Day 4

## ORGANIZATIONAL BEHAVIOR

### Organizational Behavior Topics

Problem-Solving Model

Psychology Lesson

Motivation

Leadership

Creativity

On-the-Job Office Procedure

Crucial Conversations

Power

The Organizational Model and Structures

Systems Theory

Organizational Evolution and Revolution

Resistance to Change

Gig Economy and Working Remotely

NEW MBA GRADUATE: I have the answer! My Excel spreadsheet says that we should reorganize the company by geographic region rather than by product. We could save at least ten million dollars a year by cutting unnecessary staff and travel. We hypothetically implemented a similar plan at the Brandon Lee Company in a class discussion. It worked real well.

BOSS: Sounds great. You've been with the company seven months and you want to do a radical reorganization. I assume you already assembled a roster of redundant employees?

NEW MBA GRADUATE: Well, I've not thought it through *that* far yet.

Organizational Behavior (OB) classes attempt to teach MBAs how to deal with the human challenges in the workplace. Quantitative skills may provide the magic theoretical pill in the classroom, but OB tries to instill in young MBA Turks the human sensitivity to apply their MBA skills in the real world.

Many organizational theories are not unlike what you can find in books about self-awareness and sensitivity training at Barnes & Noble or Amazon. The reason for the similarity is that many of those books are written by the same professors who propound the academic theories that appear in MBA curricula. The difference is that faddish books about the "new" corporate rejuvenation theory or the "one-second manager" make more money than articles that appear in obscure academic journals.

Organizational behavior, the "touchy-feely" subject, is often where MBAs show their true colors. Sexism, prejudice, and greed rear their ugly heads in classes when seemingly open-minded students attempt to cope with the cases at hand. Regardless, the classes are a welcome relief to overworked MBAs. There is no need for intricate quantitative analysis or extensive reading. As with other MBA subjects, knowing the vocabulary and using it at the right moments goes a long way in establishing credibility on the job.

What is taught in the OB classes, if internalized, are the lessons that well may be the most influential in the careers of MBAs. Without people skills, MBAs are equipped with the power tools but are without the electric cord to use them.

# THE OB PROBLEM-SOLVING MODEL

Just as marketing offers seven steps to marketing strategy development, OB provides a three-step technique to solve organizational problems.

> Problem Definition
> Analysis
> Action Planning

## *PROBLEM DEFINITION*

The first step to solving an organizational problem is to know the source of the difficulty. Real problems are often masked by symptoms. It is easy to be misled into solving the symptoms instead of their cause. Unless the cause is dealt with, fresh headaches will undoubtedly arise. MBAs are taught several analytical techniques to aid in flushing out the sources of trouble.

*Want Got Gaps.* There is a problem when a gap or "deviation" exists between what a manager thinks "ought" to be occurring and what is "actually" occurring. Defining the problem entails viewing situations from the perspectives of all the participants and outlining their *Want Got Gaps.*

In the wake of a failure to introduce a critical new computer technology, a large service organization hired a new vice president, Hank Helpful, to lead the computer department out of its trouble. In his judgment the problem was caused by interdepartmental rivalries. He felt that the computer department was isolated and always at odds with the rest of the company. Hank saw the gap as follows:

I Want → Gap ← I Got

Interdepartmental → Gap ← Isolated Departmental
    Cooperation                       Islands

The VP felt that other gaps existed as well. The computer department believed it lacked the respect of the operational arm of the company. The people in the department felt that they were being treated as second-class citizens. Both perceptions were true. But the other sales and operating departments had their own gaps. They wanted timely computer services at an affordable cost.

In many instances, organizational problems are less easily diagnosed. Often managers do not know exactly what the gap is. Is there a gap at all? A manager's perceptions can cloud what is "actually" happening. That is often the cause of trouble in the first place.

*The Level of Problems.* When you know what gaps exist, it is then important to understand the ways in which they affect the organization. Problems can affect a company in three ways:

- Within or between certain people
- Within or between groups
- Within the whole organization

In the case of the computer department described above, the problem existed at all three of these levels. Each level had to be addressed to successfully "solve" it. The hard feelings between individuals occurred at a *personal* level. The interdepartmental squabbling was an *intergroup* problem. The company's failure to adopt competitive new technologies occurred at the *organizational* level.

*Source Problems and Causal Chains.* The goal of an effective MBA is to find the most important problems and solve those first. Those are called the *source problems.* Eliminate the source, eliminate the *symptoms.* Source problems, such as the lack of respect for the computer department, caused a multitude of other problems.

A graphical method used to get at source problems is to draw a *causal chain.* Using a causal chain, the company's interdepartmental problem would look like this:

Contributing Problems → Source Problem → Business Problem

Lack of Interaction →        Lack of Respect → Project Failures
Personality Differences     for Techies

## *ANALYSIS*

After defining the gaps and using causal chains, the MBA is taught to link the problems to their causes. In addition to drawing causal chains, during this analytical step you try to *understand* the causes. Why do they exist? What environmental factors play a role? By asking these types of questions you can begin to confront which causes can be corrected through management action. If one problem is insurmountable, different solutions have to be tried. In the example above, firing uncooperative people was an option for the vice president. Sensitivity training and interdepartmental discussions were other possibilities. As in a marketing plan, there are many possible avenues for action available to achieve a successful resolution to a problem.

## *ACTION PLANNING*

MBAs are taught to be decisive and *proactive*—a frequently used MBA adjective. After a thorough analysis, MBAs should be able to formulate a plan. The *action plan* has six important steps.

1. Set specific goals.
2. Define activities, resources needed, responsibilities.
3. Set a timetable for action.
4. Forecast outcomes, develop contingencies.
5. Formulate a detailed plan of action *in time sequence.*
6. Implement, supervise execution, and evaluate based on goals in step one.

As you can imagine, solving problems MBA-style is not simple. It requires time and effort. To add to your MBA vocabulary, you should refer to your menu of possible actions as *action levers*. This sounds forceful and progressive. An action lever may be a reward, a control, or a planning system.

The idea behind OB is to train MBAs to avoid tactical errors because they failed to take into consideration the people involved. With a framework to tackle challenges, the MBA curriculum inculcates in its students the theories and methods of the day so that they can use them.

## INDIVIDUAL AND ORGANIZATIONAL LEVEL OB TOPICS

The previous discussion covered the frameworks used to analyze a problem and implement a solution. The next sections deal with the topics that provide the background for that process. The MBA curriculum logically starts with the theories and topics that deal with the individual, then builds to larger organizational issues that become progressively complex with the addition of more people. Along the way, students are asked to apply their newly acquired skills to analyze and plan solutions to increasingly complex and challenging case situations.

### THE MBA PSYCHOLOGY LESSON: THE APCFB MODEL

In the effort to gain an insight into why people act the way they do at work, the MBA curriculum includes some form of the *APCFB model* pictured here. This model attempts to explain the cognitive process of linking external events to employee behavior. *Assumptions* affect the *perceptions* people have. Those perceptions affect the *conclusions*. And those conclusions prompt *feelings*. Ultimately those feelings drive *behaviors* that managers observe. By trying to understand this process, MBAs may have a chance to influence positive behaviors in themselves as well as in their coworkers. The model looks like that on page 129.

THE APCFB PSYCHOLOGY MODEL

"Why People Behave the Way They Do," Case UVA-OB-183, Figure 5. Copyright © by the Darden Graduate Business School Foundation, Charlottesville, Virginia.

Given an analytical tool, MBAs are made to believe that they can understand anything. However, confounding forces within people prevent perfect communication and understanding. We all see through *filters* that often prevent us from perceiving events accurately. Filters also prevent us from acting out our true desires. We all have internal *defense mechanisms* that act as additional filters to protect us from psychological damage. They also prevent an accurate psychological reading of other people. For example, if an insecure supervisor has a poor aptitude for numbers, then by way of defense, he may find fault with an analyst's technical presentation. That would help him avoid confronting his own ineptitude with numbers.

MBAs have a chance to affect *assumptions,* the beliefs we hold about the way the world or other people or ourselves *should* or *ought to* be. These assumptions make up our value system. Listed in order of ease of accessibility, assumptions include:

Expectations

Beliefs

Values

*Expectations* and to some extent *beliefs* can be changed through clear management intent and action. *Values* are deeply held assumptions that may be altered, if at all, only in time.

When a manager is able to tap into the values of subordinates, then real productivity may result. Personally, I place a high value on creativity and freedom. When my manager taps into that well inside me, she elicits my best work. For example, when my boss seeks an insightful marketing analysis, she presents me with an opportunity to express my creativity. Our goals are said to be *congruent* or equivalent because we are both aiming at the same thing. The desired behavior is produced. *Goal congruence* among the individuals of an organization makes the group productive. *Goal congruence* is a popular MBA phrase—it sounds great, and it is in fact meaningful.

Let's take the example of a strategic planning manager. She wanted to tap her team's creativity in developing plans to compete in an evolving marketplace. In the past, she had done all the creative work herself. Her staff members were simply used to crunch numbers. To elicit a change in their behavior, she had to learn to tolerate the trial and error that are part of the creative process. Because staff failures in the past had been met with firings and ridicule, the team would understandably be slow to comply with her wishes. The staff's assumptions stood in the way. To effect the desired change, she needed to build trust by rewarding creative behavior consistently.

The bottom line is that understanding a bit of psychology is useful if you wish to motivate people.

## *EXPECTANCY THEORY OF MOTIVATION*

Motivation is an elusive animal that all organizations want to capture. *Expectancy* theory outlines the factors that produce motivation with individuals. Managers, staff, and even you can use expectancy theory to attempt to understand employees' behavior.

> Motivation = Expectation of Work will lead to Performance
> × Expectation Performance will lead to
> Reward × Value of Reward

This equation may be helpful in isolating the source of a problem. Each of the equation's components can explain some aspect of motivation. If a marketing manager of a declining make of automobile has been losing market share to a better-manufactured and better-promoted competitor, he might feel that no matter what he does he will fail. That would naturally decrease his motivation. If the company never rewarded superior performance, that would also lead to discontent. And finally, if the reward were simply a set of keys to the executive washrooms, then a manager might think of working elsewhere.

Three academic heavyweights, Hertzberg, Maslow, and McClelland, believe that behavior is motivated by the urge to satisfy needs. Fred Hertzberg posits that motivation will be enhanced by maximizing the motivators or *satisfiers* on the job and minimizing the *dissatisfiers* or maintenance factors. A promotion or an award can be a satisfier. Maintenance factors don't necessarily bring happiness, but they are expected. A safe place to work and a living wage are typical maintenance factors. Abraham Maslow sees employee motivation as a function of meeting an employee's *hierarchy of needs.* The hierarchy is frequently depicted as a pyramid. The need for food and water is at the bottom of the pyramid, followed by the *need for safety,* the *need to belong,* and the *need for status,* while *self-actualization needs* are seen as the highest order of needs. These needs are met when a person experiences a sense of personal growth and self-fulfillment by accomplishing a challenging goal.

Finally, David McClelland proposes that people have three basic needs, the *need for achievement,* the *need for power,* and the *need for affiliation.* Whatever the theory, managers must recognize the needs of employees.

## *JOB DESIGN*

Another way to understand and affect employee motivation is to investigate the way a job is designed. Each job has certain *core job dimensions* that describe the duties performed. These duties lead to *critical psychological states* within employees that result in a variety of *outcomes.* Outcomes are the visible manifestations of work performance, while psychological states are hidden in the hearts and minds of people. If the human element is ignored, then quality and efficiency will suffer.

JOB DESIGN MODEL

| Core Job Dimensions | Critical Psychological States | Personal and Work Outcomes |
|---|---|---|
| Skill Variety<br>Task Identity<br>Task Significance | Experienced Meaningfulness of Work | High Internal Work Motivation |
| Autonomy | Experienced Responsibility for Outcomes of the Work | High Quality Work Performance<br>High Satisfaction With the Work |
| Feedback | Knowledge of the Actual Results of the Work Activities | Low Absenteeism and Turnover |

Adapted from "Introduction to Job Design," by Professor William Zierden, Case UVA-OB-91R, Figure 1. Copyright © by the Darden Graduate Business School Foundation, Charlottesville, Virginia.

If the MBA is confronted with a personnel problem, it may be the result of job design. A close study of the core job dimensions can often yield great benefits without significant costs. For example, at a Lockheed parts factory in Los Angeles, unskilled workers were hired and trained to assemble parts for jumbo jets fabricated at another factory. The employees were unmotivated and the quality of their output was poor. In talking with the workers, the managers realized that the work had no meaning to them. They did not understand what they were producing. To fix that, the workers were taken to the aircraft assembly plant to see where their parts were installed. They also met those who were inconvenienced when they received a defective product. Realizing the relevance of their work, the employees became more productive and part defects decreased. Their previously pointless assembly task acquired significance, and they responded by performing better. The result was a happier workforce that took pride in a job well done. The MBA term for such employee happiness is *quality of work life* (QWL). When employees are given the chance to be all that they can be, the word MBAs use to describe this is *empowerment*. You can hardly pick up a business book today without tripping over that word.

## MBA PERSONALITY TRAITS

Business schools teach young women and men business skills, but they also try to motivate their students to maximize their own potential. In that vein, MBAs are taught to be innovative leaders.

*Leadership.* The top MBA schools claim to be incubators for the business leaders of tomorrow. In this pursuit, organizational behavior classes probe the subject of leadership and its responsibilities. Some schools even send their students to the woods for Outward Bound experiences to unleash the leaders inside them and develop team skills. Leaders shape goals. Leaders develop new ideas. Leaders reach people on an emotional level. Managers, on the other hand, react to events. Managers solve problems, while leaders take on challenges. Of course, at the top business schools, everyone fancies himself or herself as a future captain of industry. At the end of the book in chapter 10, there is a Ten-Minute Leadership Coach to help you to succeed.

*The Leadership VCM Model.* The VCM leadership model proposes that the following three characteristics are part of a leader's personal profile:

- Vision
- Commitment
- Management Skills

Leaders exhibit these qualities in differing proportions. No particular mix works best. It all depends on the individual and the job situation. Steve Jobs could be viewed as being high on vision when he saw the potential for user-friendly personal computing in the 1980s. In the accounting profession, vision is not as critical, whereas *management skills* and *commitment* to long hours are the keys to success.

*Leadership Patterns.* There are as many ways to lead the troops as there are people. Leadership styles lie on a spectrum from *boss-centered* to *subordinate-centered.* In the 1960s, executives raced to be tested to see where they fell on the spectrum. Based on a *managerial grid,* they could be classified a "dictator" or a "wimp." Some bosses use their authority directly to press their people into action. They do the thinking, and the staff does the legwork. Others give their people the freedom to use their own wits to organize and accomplish tasks. The boss's function is to give general direction. Which leadership style a leader chooses is regulated by three basic forces:

- The forces within the manager
- The forces within the subordinates
- The forces of the situation

If the leaders do not have confidence in their subordinates, they cannot delegate tasks. If a staff doesn't have the ability to work un-

LEADERSHIP STYLES: VISION, COMMITMENT, AND MANAGEMENT

**Balanced**          **Visionary**          **Managerial**

Adapted from "Survey of Managerial Style," by Professor James Claw-son, Case UVA-OB-358, p. 14. Copyright © by the Darden Graduate Business School Foundation, Charlottesville, Virginia.

supervised, full delegation of authority is inappropriate. When the staff has a clear understanding of the business situation and how to address it, it's best to delegate authority.

It is important for a leader to understand his or her own personality traits. As you might imagine, a leader's insecurities may lead to an authoritarian style, regardless of what the situation may dictate. That is why self-awareness is important; it will enable you to avoid inappropriate management styles.

> My faults and my virtues are the same . . . Nothing is ever enough.
> I must check everything. It causes me problems—people think I
> don't trust anyone. But I must know what's going on.
> —Giorgio Armani, *Forbes*

*Creativity.* Not only are MBAs schooled to understand leadership, they are taught to become leaders by tapping their own creativity. Because *vision* is an element in the VCM pie, MBAs ought to nurture their own creativity. Everyone has *idea-friendly times* when they are most creative. For some it may be while in the shower, for others on the porcelain throne or in the car. Creative thought is often fleeting; you must be able to capture it in its tender, nascent stage. *What a Great Idea* by Chick Thompson suggests that we should always keep a pen, your iPhone, or a grease pencil (for the shower) handy in each of our *friendly* places.

The *mind-mapping* technique is also available. Take a blank piece of paper and start thinking about a creative challenge, then write down the subject and circle it. Proceed, in a completely uninhibited style, to scribble and circle all your related thoughts around that subject's key words and connect them like the spokes on a wheel. Each of the spokes should have spokes around it, and so on. No thought is too stupid! After it's all done, something may emerge from the jumble of free association. I've used the technique to think up titles, promotional copy, and project solutions for this book. Try it—you have nothing to lose.

An abbreviated mind-mapping session to develop the name for this book looked like the diagram at right.

*Entrepreneurship.* Touching on the traits of leadership and creativity is one of the hottest MBA topics, entrepreneurship. It is debatable whether entrepreneurship can be taught, yet all the top schools are researching this area and giving it a try. Studies of entrepreneurs reveal that they possess some combination of the following characteristics:

- Comfortable with ambiguity and uncertainty
- Belief that they control their own destinies
- Tenacity in completing tasks
- Low fear of failure
- Ability to identify opportunities

Entrepreneurial MBA incubators include classes on how to start a new venture and business plan contests. Visits from successful alumni provide inspiration and can be a source of contacts for the students.

If an MBA student skips the start-up and instead acquires a small business, it is called *entrepreneurship through acquisition* (ETA). It became quite the thing to do beginning in 2022.

*Type A and B Behaviors.* OB professors have introduced the concept of behavior typing into the curriculum as an added tool for personal understanding. Since most MBAs attending the Top Ten schools were admitted because their type A personalities helped them to the top of their college classes, it seems appropriate that they should understand that aspect of themselves. *Type A behavior* was originally identified in 1959 by two cardiologists, Meyer Friedman and Ray Roseman. They noticed that patients with severe coronary heart disease were often characterized by these traits:

- A Competitive Need for Achievement
- A Sense of Time Urgency
- Aggressiveness
- Hostility to Others and the World

MIND MAPPING FOR A BOOK TITLE

Additional manifestations of type A behavior include explosive, accelerated speech, interruption of others, a fast-paced approach to life, and impatience. Type A's always try to do more than one activity at once. That's where Outlook calendars are helpful. Type A's are often dissatisfied with life, showing a free-floating hostility. They evaluate their self-worth based on external achievements. One sure symptom is competition with others in noncompetitive situations. A classmate reported such a case: "During the interview season I was struck by a pizza company executive who boasted that his performance on the treadmill, during the company's annual physical, was superior to that of his coworkers." That executive was a type A.

On the opposite side of the spectrum, there are the type B's, who enjoy life and are more relaxed. Some type B's also sneak into business schools. Most individuals fall in the continuum between the two poles. Hopefully, by recognizing the type A signs, MBA hard chargers may be able to head off a heart attack by exercising some control over their behavior. If not, behavior typing can make good bar conversation for MBAs heading for coronary oblivion.

## *MBA OFFICE PROCEDURES*

The OB faculty, besides making students aware of their potentials and shortcomings, tried to teach us some practical interpersonal skills that would help us to succeed on the job.

*Active Listening.* One of the most valuable skills is to be able to *really* listen. *Active listening* helps you to gain a clear *perception* of situations so that you can effectively deal with them. It differs from conversation in three ways:

- You Respond to Information and Don't Lead.
- You Respond to Personal Information and Don't Give Advice.
- You Identify the Interviewee's Feelings as Well as the Content.

An active listener cedes control of the conversation to the other party. Given enough leeway, true motivations, feelings, and beliefs can come forth. After the active listening session runs its course, you can start to talk and act like an MBA know-it-all again.

*Performance Appraisals.* One of the most mismanaged tools for organizational improvement is the performance appraisal. Rating forms are sometimes used effectively for timely feedback and personal development. However, most of the time it is a task that is delayed until the appraisal has really lost all usefulness. *Effective* appraisals ought to have three types of goals:

Organizational
Feedback and Evaluation
Coaching and Development

*Organizational* goals aim to ensure proper conduct and levels of performance, placement, promotion, and pay. The *feedback and evaluation* aspects provide both employees and employers with a formal process and documentation of performance. *Coaching and development* should ultimately be the primary goals of an appraisal. How can we improve, rather than punish, unsatisfactory performance? Working together, the boss and the subordinate should agree on specific targets and timetables for improvement. These plans for the future lay the groundwork for a follow-up.

The problem is that managers tend to avoid this evaluation process. Subordinates are defensive. The appraisal must be timely; both participants must be prepared. The boss should foster an open climate of real communication (both ways) and make the purpose of the appraisal clear. As simple as the appraisal can be, it is seldom done right.

In addition to the potential for improvement, appraisals provide employers the documentation to legally fire an employee. Without documentation a disgruntled worker could sue the company for lack of just cause.

*Reprimands.* Sometimes an MBA will be called on to lower the boom. In line with my class discussions, the MBA should reprimand a subordinate using the following four steps.

1. **Check out the facts first.** Ask yourself if you caused the problem.
2. **Give warning that you need to talk about the problem.**
3. **Pause and express your displeasure.** Tell it exactly as you see it. Yelling is counterproductive.
4. **Display a caring attitude.** "I did not approve of your behavior, but you are still okay." "Let's learn from this and put it behind us." The idea is to do it firmly, clearly, and move on to new business.

"A good manager can balance his reprimands with praise."

*Managing Your Boss.* MBAs are not always bosses. Most start out as lowly analysts, planners, and associates. Ironically, these are the positions that operations classes characterize as corporate fat, ripe for trimming. Even if MBAs find themselves in more senior managerial jobs, it's a safe bet that they will have a boss to deal with. Even presidents have to deal with board members!

Management of the relationship *upward* is as important as managing your relationship below. That's why I've included it in this book. To give the MBA an edge, the curriculum includes a session on how to *manage your boss.* "Managing Your Boss" appeared in the *Harvard Business Review.* It was written by John Gabarro and John Kotter, and it captures the subject well.

"The first step to success on the job is to understand bosses and their context, including:

· Their stated and unstated goals and objectives
· The pressures on them
· Their strengths, weaknesses, blind spots
· Their preferred work styles

"The second step is to be introspective and assess yourself and your needs, including:

· Your own strengths and weaknesses
· Your personal style
· Your predisposition toward dependence on or resistance to authority figures

"The third step is to incorporate the first two steps and develop and maintain a relationship that:

· Fits both your needs and styles
· Is characterized by mutual expectations

· Keeps your boss informed — bosses hate surprises!
· Is based on dependability and honesty
· Selectively uses your boss's time and resources" *

Simply by asking a few questions at the start of the relationship, you can avoid making major political blunders in the future. Some bosses like a formal relationship, memos, and meetings with agenda. Others prefer e-mails, informal notes, and frequent unstructured meetings. Smart MBAs take the initiative to ask their bosses how they would prefer to communicate rather than guess. Careers often hang in the balance. I still keep Gabarro and Kotter's article at my desk as a reminder to manage my boss.

*Crucial Conversations.* Just as the author of *Managing your Boss* said, successful interactions with colleagues, and just about anyone else in your life, are the result of open "free flow of meaning" and "skilled" communications. Another book, *Crucial Conversations,* has been included in Top Ten MBA curriculums. Its relevance is the reason that 5 million copies have sold since 2002. The book is a step-by-step guide through tough conversations that must be had at "crucial moments." Failure to address issues can disproportionally affect organizations, relationships, careers, and lives. The big problem is the "lag time" between the identification of an issue and the most effective way to confront, discuss, and resolve it. It took a team of researchers, many years of careful observation, refinement, and coaching successes to develop these techniques.

Here are two key principles from *Crucial Conversations* for recognizing, building, and maintaining dialogue.

---

* Reprinted by permission of *Harvard Business Review,* "Managing Your Boss" by John J. Gabarro and John P. Kotter (January/February 1980). Copyright © 1979 by the President and Fellows of Harvard College; all rights reserved

1. *Learn to Look.* Are you actually having a true dialogue with people, or are they falling into "silence or violence"? Violence is acting out in destructive ways.
2. *Make it Safe.* Demonstrate *real* evidence that you care about their interests and that you respect them. You must have mutual purpose and respect to make progress.

The book also provides specific methods in each of the following areas:

*Choose Your Topic.* What is the right topic? Will it open the way to move forward? Will it help you attain what you really want to accomplish? Unbundle, choose, and simplify the topic.

*Start with the Heart.* Focus on what you really want and clarify what is most important to you. Avoid getting derailed by emotional side issues from the past, which can prevent the understanding of what is important now.

*Master Your Stories.* Separate the facts from the story. Realize *your* roll in the story. Am I seeing myself as the victim, villain, or helpless one in the stories? Ask, "Why would a reasonable, rational, and decent person do this?"

*STATE Your Path.* Share your facts. Tell your story. Ask others about their paths with genuine interest. Talk tentatively. Encourage testing the facts and stories.

*Explore Others' Views.* Actively explore other people's views; avoid unnecessary disagreements; mirror them; paraphrase them. Consider priming the pump with a question about your own possible shortcoming: "Am I being unfair?"

*Retake Your Pen.* Write your own story and affirm your own self-worth in the face of all detractors. Take criticism into account and make selective self-improvements on your own terms. (Most Important!)

*Move to Action.* Decide together how you'll decide to move forward. Document your decisions, follow up on them, and then hold everyone accountable.

This is only a summary of the *Crucial Conversation* process. This book is one of the best investments you can make (other than *The Ten-Day MBA*, of course).*

*Understanding Power on the Job.* If MBAs want power, then they ought to know more about what they seek. It's key to successful office politics. There are actually five types of power:

Coercive
Reward
Referent
Legitimate
Expert

*Coercive power* is based on fear. Failure to comply with a request could result in some form of punishment. A person with coercive power can influence or directly fire, demote, or transfer an employee. At a firehouse, the chief has the power to assign shifts. If you get on the chief's bad side, it could mean you work holidays.

*Reward power* is based upon the expectation of receiving praise, recognition, or income. It's the opposite of coercive power.

*Referent power* is derived from being a person whom other people admire regardless of formal job status. These people are said to have charisma to inspire and to attract followers. Star salespeople have this role in sales organizations.

*Legitimate power* is due to the formal status held in the organizational hierarchy. Those with this type of power can use it to reward, to ax, and to influence the lives of others in the organization. A shift foreman has the power to assign duties on an assembly line.

*Expert power* comes from one's own skill, knowledge, or experience. People with expert power have the ability to manipulate others. This is without regard to their position in the company. Often it is a

* Adapted from *Crucial Conversations: Tools for Talking When Stakes Are High*, 2002, Third Edition, McGraw Hill, by Grenny, Patterson, McMillian, Switzler and Gregory.

computer technician who may have the power to bring a senior executive to the IT department to fix a laptop. The boss must crawl for assistance. Crafty technicians fix programs so that they alone have the ability to tap into a critical database. This preserves their expert power. It's a manager's job to cross-train people to prevent the birth of such little generals in their organizations.

In the political gamesmanship of corporations, it is important for MBAs to recognize all the people in the organization with the power to influence their lives.

*MBO and MBWA.* MBO and MBWA are frequently used abbreviations in MBA babble. MBO means *management by objective.* It is a management style popularized by management guru Peter Drucker in the 1950s. Bosses delegate tasks by "negotiating a contract of goals" with their subordinates without dictating a detailed road map for implementation. MBO managers focus on the result, not the activity. At Frito-Lay, for example, a vice president might set a sales target for her regional sales managers. The managers decide what tactics and strategy are needed to meet the objective.

The MBO style is appropriate when your staff is competent. Chief executives of multinational corporations (MNCs) use MBO for their country managers abroad. Their bosses in the United States often have little knowledge of what is required for success in those international markets. MBO is appropriate in situations where you wish to build employees' management skills and tap their creativity and initiative. The drawback to MBO is the time needed to adequately negotiate and document the process. Therefore, MBO should be used in appropriate situations.

MBWA, *management by walking around,* was a theory expounded at Hewlett-Packard, the computer giant. HP executives were encouraged to be out of their offices working on building relationships, motivating, and keeping in direct touch with the activities of the company. MBWA is a simple concept, but it has become part of an MBA's portfolio of management theories.

## ORGANIZATIONAL LEVEL TOPICS

With a psychology lesson and a set of MBA office procedures to work with, the OB courses take a "bigger picture" look at organizations. With a larger scope also come grander theories and the vocabulary to accompany them.

### *THE BASIC ORGANIZATIONAL MODEL*

To understand an organization, you have to consider all of its components. Organizations are networks of related parts. Each element works together to support efficient operations. The MBA buzzword for it all is *organizational architecture.*

A noteworthy feature of the diagram is that the individual is at the center. The reason for this is that organizations are made not of brick and mortar but of people. Organizations affect those individuals. The theories in the previous sections focused on the individual. In the following sections the macro-view of the organizations is explored in MBA terms.

As shown in the diagram, six elements define organizations. Some are self-explanatory, but others have special MBA significance that you should be aware of.

*Strategy.* Strategy describes an explicit or implicit plan for success in the marketplace. When an airline decides to lure customers with either lower prices or better service, that is a corporate strategy. (Later in the book, I devote an entire chapter to this truly MBA topic.)

*Policies and Procedures. Policies* are formal rules that, in all but small companies, are captured in a handbook, while *procedures* are the observable ways in which a company conducts business. Vacation and benefits are policies that are codified. Routine tasks such as how waste paper should be separated for recycling may not be committed to paper. It's a procedure that is understood.

THE BASIC ORGANIZATIONAL MODEL

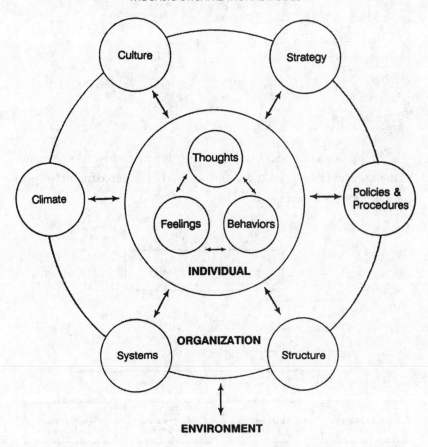

*Organizational Structures.* Structure vocabulary is a lexicon that no MBA can be without. It is a frequent subject of discussion in corporate meetings and is also an important tool for managing organizational behavior. Structures describe the hierarchy of authority and accountability in an organization. These "formal" relationships are frequently diagrammed in *organization charts*. Most companies use some mix of structures to accomplish their goals. People who are directly involved in producing or marketing the firm's products or services are called *line* employees. The others who advise, serve, and support the line are called *staff* employees. Line and staff employees can be organized along the following lines:

Functional
Product
Customer
Geographic
Divisional
Matrix
Amorphous

*Functional.* The functional form divides work by tasks, e.g., advertising, accounting, finance, and sales. These departments report to the senior executives.

FUNCTIONAL STRUCTURE

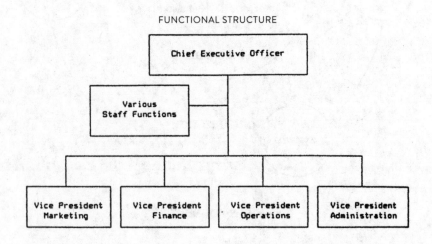

"Organizational Structure," written by Professor James Clawson, Case UVA-OB-361, Figures 1–8. Copyright © by the Darden Graduate Business School Foundation, Charlottesville, Virginia.

*Product.* The product structure groups all functions necessary to deliver a specific product. Product managers manage individual products as smaller businesses within a company. Black & Decker, for example, is divided into separate units responsible for power tools, small appliances, and accessories (see top chart, page 149).

*Customer.* The customer structure focuses on—you guessed it—the customer. Activities, such as production and marketing, are grouped

PRODUCT STRUCTURE

CUSTOMER STRUCTURE

with other functions to satisfy specific customer needs. The customer structure is common in service industries. Banks often divide responsibility by customer type. For instance, some loan officers are trained to serve business clients, others to serve individuals. Each has "expert" knowledge to deal with his or her customers' specific needs (see bottom chart, page 149).

*Geographic.* In this arrangement work is divided by location. Geographic structures cut across customers and products. Regional offices are established to manage the business. This is especially true of international businesses, where each country's office would adopt its own structure (see top chart, page 151).

*Divisional.* Divisions are independent businesses operating under the umbrella of a parent corporation. Unlike the previous four structures, divisions run somewhat autonomously. They do it all themselves, from marketing to buying raw materials. However, most divisions use the parent company for financing. For example, Amazon has ecommerce, cloud computing, and digital streaming divisions. These businesses are centrally owned but separately operated. Within each of the divisions there may be other organizational substructures (see bottom chart, page 151).

*Matrix.* The matrix structure departs from the principle of *unity of command:* only one boss for each employee. Here there are two or more lines of authority. The matrix is common in businesses involved in large, complex projects that require highly specialized skills. In this structure, both the product and the functional structures coexist. Employees report to both a project manager in charge of their assigned product and a functional manager who controls specific activities such as manufacturing, finance, and marketing. As you might expect, this organizational form can be confusing. It requires a staff that is flexible and professional. The defense and computer industries often opt for the matrix structure to handle large development projects (see chart, page 152).

GEOGRAPHIC STRUCTURE

DIVISIONAL STRUCTURE

MATRIX STRUCTURE

*Amorphous.* This is my personal favorite. The amorphous structure is no formal structure at all. It's the free bird. In these companies highly motivated and productive managers create and dissolve reporting relationships as the task at hand requires. In these companies, the structure incrementally grows as events dictate. Meta's Facebook started this way.

*Hybrid.* These entities are composed of a mix of operational structures. Most companies fall into this category. Amazon as described has a divisional structure. But within each division, there are geographic manufacturing organizations, matrix research staffs, and customer-sales-grouped organizations. On page 153 a single busi-

HYBRID STRUCTURE

ness is organized in a functional/product hybrid. The brand managers control their products and marketing, but they do not have complete control over the financing or operations of the business.

The choice of structure dramatically affects the operations of a company. There needs to be a *fit* between the business activities required and the corporate apparatus set up to produce and deliver the service.

Managers should select a structure that reflects their goals and strategy. The structure that is set up enables individuals to interact in ways that will best achieve goals. Informal reporting relationships form spontaneously, and these fail to be represented in the organizational charts kept by the personnel department. Recognizing both the formal and informal structures is crucial in executing a successful *action plan*.

An important issue related to reporting relationships is the *span of control*. The span describes the number of people who report to a

"YOU'RE FIRED, NEVINS, BUT WE'VE ENJOYED YOUR BEING HERE AND HAVE SOME
LOVELY PARTING GIFTS FOR YOU."

manager. During restructuring, downsizing, and recessions this topic becomes popular. Using an increased span of control, large corporations often fire middle-manager MBAs. The remaining managers have more staff. If a sales organization changes from a policy of one regional manager for every three regions to one for every four, that displaces 25 percent of the regional managers. MBAs call these layoffs a *reduction in force* (RIF), *demassing,* or *restructuring.* It's a nice, antiseptic way for managers to describe the firing of many people. Span-of-control policies are powerful organizational tools.

*Systems.* Each organization develops *systems* for allocating, controlling, and monitoring money, things, and people. Systems also perform informational activities by gathering information and channeling it to interested users. Systems fall into one of six categories:

*Money Allocation, Control, and Monitoring* —Accounting, investment, and budgeting systems

*Object Allocation, Control, and Monitoring* – Inventory and
   production systems
*People Allocation, Control, and Monitoring* – Human resource
   planning, employee data and appraisals
*Future Anticipation* – Strategic planning, marketing-sales planning,
   business development functions
*People Reward and Incentives* – Compensation schemes, bonus plans,
   profit-sharing plans
*Integrative* – Mixes of the first five. In well-managed companies,
   integrated systems forecast sales, which in turn dictates
   production schedules required to meet that need.

It is crucial to understand the systems of an organization, because they are the tools for change. Systems provide both a means and, at times, a barrier to corporate change.

*Climate.* This is a nebulous term that refers to the emotional state of an organization's members. Many companies hire expensive consultants to perform satisfaction studies to determine the "climate" of their organization so that improvements can be made. In service industries where people are the most valuable assets, such as law firms, investment banking houses, and consulting practices, the climate of the firm plays an important role in determining service quality.

*Culture.* This is another hazy term. Culture is the mix of behaviors, thoughts, beliefs, symbols, and artifacts that are conveyed to people throughout an organization over time. It may extend to such silly things as an unwritten rule that all men must wear white pinpoint oxford shirts or corporate lapel pins. Culture may include a belief about desired employee conduct. "Senior executives must always work past six o'clock." "It's important to look busy at all times." A main criterion for recruiting is often the perceived "fit" of interviewees with the organization. If a person does not appear to "fit" into the corporate culture, then he or she in many recruiters' eyes will probably not be an effective employee. Culture can also be toxic. When it includes racial and gender discrimination as well as tolerance of sexual harassment, it's illegal.

The six elements of an organization (strategy, policies, structure, systems, climate, and culture) dynamically affect one another. Each element interacts with the environment as a business strives toward its goals. The *problem definition/action planning* process requires that a manager look at all six elements of the organization model to determine which *action levers* will exist to implement positive change. If the environment changes, the organizational elements must adapt. MBAs like to refer to companies that can change as *learning organizations*.

Organizations that are stuck in the same old pattern of thinking and acting are said to be trapped by their *paradigms* or mind-set. High-priced consultants often counsel stagnant companies on how to break their old paradigms so that they can change and succeed. Use the word *paradigm* several times in a conversation tomorrow, and you're one step closer to becoming a Ten-Day MBA.

## THE HUMAN TALENT FLOW PYRAMID

The structure of a firm dictates not only how employees are grouped but also how they can advance in a firm. At each progressive stage the individual assumes more authority. People either leave, get fired, or are promoted. A handy MBA tool to track this flow of human capital is a pyramid diagram.

THE HUMAN TALENT FLOW PYRAMID

By tracking the flows of people in and out of an organization, we can clearly identify turnover problems, skill deficiencies, and entrenched management. The diagram helps to point out graphically the "leakages" and "blockages" of people flows within the organization. Employees enter all levels of the organization as depicted at the left and move up within the pyramid. If there is little movement from one level to another, this blockage may cause many people to become frustrated and leave to the right of the pyramid, a leakage. Discrimination issues such as "glass ceilings" for women and minority promotions can be analyzed using this pictorial technique.

## SYSTEMS THEORY AND ORGANIZATIONAL ANALYSIS

*Systems theory* is a concept that likens organizations to living organisms. Just as animals have their endocrine, digestive, and nervous systems, academics propose that organizational bodies have similar *subsystems* that enable them to live. When diagrammed, an organization looks like a paramecium.

The *management subsystem* is the organ that sets the goals, plans, and controls, similar to the brain. This is the role of executives.

The *adaptive subsystem* acts as a firm's eyes to monitor the environment. The system also makes sure that the firm's products and services are appropriate in a changing environment to ensure survival. Information gathered from market researchers, customer service representatives, and salespeople makes a company adaptive.

The *boundary spanning in subsystem* is the mouth. It controls the intake of the organization's food. In a company, this subsystem includes recruiting people, buying raw materials, and raising money.

The bowels of the company are the *production subsystem*. It converts the inputs into goods and services. In a manufacturing company, these are the factories.

The bowels lead to the *boundary spanning out subsystem*. The marketing crew helps the company produce its products and services. The personnel department deals with the outplacement of

SYSTEMS THEORY

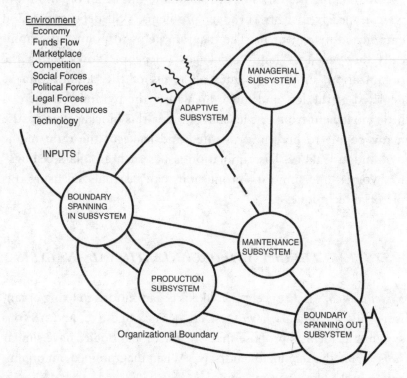

"Systems Theory and Organizational Analysis," by Professor James Clawson, Case UVA-OB-214, Figure 1. Copyright © by the Darden Graduate Business School Foundation, Charlottesville, Virginia.

employees who have not met company standards. And finally, the public relations department tries to put a good face on the company's actions.

Once the animal is breathing and functioning properly, the *maintenance subsystem* tries to keep the other subsystems working efficiently together. This cerebellum maintains a balance in the organization by coordinating all the movements of the body. Examples of the maintenance subsystems include employee incentives and company newsletters.

Systems theory provides yet another way of analyzing an organization to gauge its health or to make a change in its lifestyle.

## *EVOLUTION AND REVOLUTION*
## *AS ORGANIZATIONS GROW*

Larry E. Greiner of the Harvard Business School wrote a classic article with this title in the *Harvard Business Review* in July 1972, describing the growing pains that organizations go through.

Greiner proposed that organizations exhibit five predictable stages of growth called *evolutions* and five periods of crises called *revolutions*. His theory is readily applicable to many organizations. The growth pattern consists of tightening and loosening of management reins in response to changes within the organization and the environment.

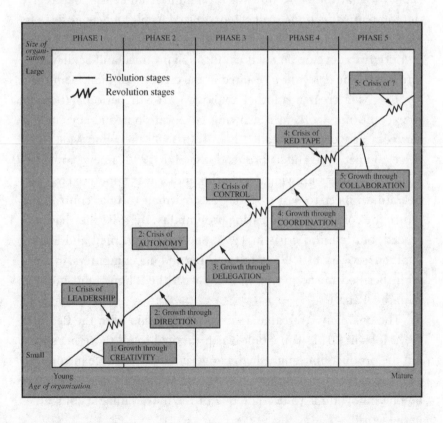

Reprinted by permission of *Harvard Business Review*. An exhibit from "Evolution and Revolution as Organizations Grow" by Larry E. Greiner, Volume 50, Number 4 (July/August 1972). Copyright © 1972 by the President and Fellows of Harvard College; all rights reserved.

The evolution/revolution pattern, as shown by Apple Computer, is an excellent way to put a company's history into MBA perspective. Apple Computer sprang forth from the *creativity* of Steven Jobs and Stephen Wozniak. Beginning in 1976, these two entrepreneurs were on a freight train of rapid growth until the company became so unwieldy that it almost jumped the tracks in 1983. Apple was faced with the *leadership crisis* of a growth company that didn't have anyone who could efficiently run its day-to-day operations. Jobs was a lofty visionary making speeches, while Wozniak was the magic technician.

The company started to run out of gas as its creative fuel ran low. Apple II sales slumped and the new Lisa computer failed. John Sculley (Wharton MBA '63) was brought in from Pepsi-Cola to give the company *direction*. Sculley reorganized Apple and cut costs in its bloated headquarters. Steve Jobs and his followers demanded more *autonomy* to develop a new breakthrough product, and Sculley gave it to them. The *delegation* resulted in the creation of the Macintosh.

The Mac created another explosive growth period. However, Jobs could not work in a growing corporate bureaucracy, and he started a new company called NeXT. In 1989 the aging Mac faced fierce competition, and as profits declined in 1990, a new Apple crisis of *control* was brewing. Michael Spindler was appointed as chief operating officer to assist Sculley as chairman to take control and return the company to increasing profitability. By 1992 they had succeeded, but fell into crisis in 1995. Steve Jobs returned and led yet another recovery in 1998 with the iMac and G3 computers, in 2002 with the iPod music player, in 2007 with the iPhone, and in 2010 with the iPad.

The company overcame a crisis of leadership with the death of Steve Jobs in 2011. Tim Cook was promoted to fill those big shoes, but the product line languished. However, in 2015 Apple introduced the Apple Watch, subscription services, Apple Pay, and significant iPhone innovations to become one of the most valuable companies in the world.

## *CHANGE MANAGEMENT STRATEGIES*

In addition to all the theory about the mind and corporate body, MBAs receive practical guidance for taking action in difficult situations. Even if an action plan is "perfect," there is always resistance to change. Even those well-thought-out plans such as the one the new MBA proposed to his boss at the beginning of this chapter may run up against a wall. Fortunately, John P. Kotter and Leonard A. Schlesinger formulated a tidy model to assist MBAs in their article "Choosing Strategies for Change" in the *Harvard Business Review* of March 1979. The appropriate course of action all depends on the situation.

**Situation → Action Needed for Change**

Company Lacks Information → Education and Communication Tactics

In a stodgily run manufacturing company in Salt Lake City, the employees were kept in the dark about corporate profitability. Judging by the expensive cars of the owner, they assumed that all was well. Unfortunately, the company was losing money and layoffs would be inevitable unless productivity rose. In this situation, the employees would need to be informed about the true condition of the company before they gave their full cooperation to work more efficiently.

You Need Information and You Have Little Leverage → Participation and Involvement Tactics

A metal fabrication plant in Kansas City hired a consultant to cure absenteeism. The consultant did not know the people, the personalities, or the town. Because she was an outsider, she had no power to demand cooperation for her investigation. She first had to gain the trust of the workers and begin to talk with them about the problems that prompted so many sick days. She needed their cooperation and involvement to define and solve a problem for the workers as well as for management.

A Japanese term *gemba*, meaning "the real place," describes just such a tactic called the *Gemba Walk*. Managers personally review the operation's flow to understand real problems and opportunities to reduce waste.

Adjustment Problems → Support and Facilitation Tactics

Instead of hiring new help, companies need to retrain their staffs. Companies must hire computer support staff to help learn new technology systems.

Your Desired Changes Will Cause Losses and Opponents Have Power to Block You → Negotiation and Agreement Tactics

In the 1980s robotics were introduced in the American auto industry. Japanese imports were taking jobs overseas. GM, Ford, and Chrysler chose to negotiate new agreements with the powerful United Auto Workers union to allow work-rule changes required by the new technology. If the corporations had decided to play hardball and impose their will upon the UAW, the union could have struck, and both parties would have ended up losing. By cooperating both had a chance of surviving and thriving.

You Have No Alternatives and No Money for Facilitation → Manipulation (Give No Choices)

In distressed companies there are often no alternatives to layoffs and wage cuts. A manufacturer of electronic switches in Trenton, New Jersey, gave its employees the choice of lower wages or no jobs at all. They took the pay cut, but the company failed anyway.

Speed Is Needed and You Have the Power → Explicit Orders and Coercion Tactics

This situation is most common in the consulting, law, and public accounting professions. The familiar scene begins with a client requesting a project due "yesterday." The partner calls in a lowly associate and demands that the assignment be completed "the day before yesterday." The partner says jump and the associate jumps. The partners hold the power. The rub is that employees burn out and leave. Fortunately for the firms, there are legions of eager college graduates to replace their ranks. If you choose coercion tactics, you have to be sure you have the power and are willing to deal with the consequences.

## THE GIG ECONOMY AND WORKING REMOTELY AND INDEPENDENTLY

Even before Covid, the gig economy was up and running with many people doing independent contract work for employers. Think Uber, DoorDash, Airbnb, Etsy, and freelance writers, artists, programmers, and designers working their gigs and side hustles.

Technology has played a key role with gig apps that connect workers and customers to companies. Within companies, remote collaboration is possible with the aid of Zoom, Slack, Google Meet, Microsoft Teams, Mural for *ideation* (brainstorming), and Trello for project management. Jobs and location have been decoupled, which expands the job pool and accesses those with diverse expertise. Project teams can be flexible to scale as needed.

From the workers' perspective, the control of the assignment is their choice, their own work/life balance choice, their flexible hours, their own location within the parameters of the temporary assignment. If things don't work out, they move on. If the employer isn't satisfied, there are no strings, no benefits, just an IRS 1099 income form to be submitted at year end.

In traditional employment situations, workers who desire autonomy and better work/life balance, and do not get it, may stay on by "quiet quitting." They will proactively adjust their schedules to meet their personal goals.

### Worker Challenges

1. No benefits
2. Work scheduling

3. Variable income
4. Work culture and relationship development and management
5. Personal career development

*Employer Challenges*

1. Recruiting
2. Training
3. Corporate culture development
4. Project management
5. Corporate liability for independent contractors. The managerial challenge depends on the extent of the command and control accepted by the organization.

In any case it is an economic and management challenge that is still a work in progress.

## AN OVERVIEW OF ORGANIZATIONAL BEHAVIOR

Above all, MBAs should think before they act. When MBAs need to take action, they should thoroughly analyze the situation, first from the perspective of the individual and then from an organizational vantage point, to create a coordinated and effective action plan. MBAs are not trained to be "organizational experts" by any means, but with a few theories and frameworks, they should have a better chance of acting effectively.

## KEY OB TAKEAWAYS

*Want Got Gaps* — Organizational problems
*Causal Chains* — The relationship of problems to one another

*Action Planning* — A specific series of activities to solve an
  organizational problem

*APCFB Model* — A human psychology model

*Goal Congruence* — People with similar goals work better together.

*Expectancy Theory* — Motivation is a function of how an employee's
  actions translate into a reward.

*VCM Leadership Model* — The vision, commitment, and management
  aspects of leadership

*Active Listening* — Listening to gain insight

*The Five Forms of Power* — Power is derived from more than a title.

*The Basic Organizational Model* — Strategy, policies, structure,
  systems, climate, and culture

*Structure* — The way a company organizes itself

*Span of Control* — The number of people a manager directly controls

*Paradigm* — A corporate mind-set or pattern of doing things

*Systems Theory* — An organization functions much like a body.

*The Evolution and Revolution Pattern* — Organizations go through a
  series of growth and crisis periods during their lifetimes.

**Crucial Conversations** — Important, emotionally charged
  conversations with high stakes.

# Day 5

## QUANTITATIVE ANALYSIS

### Quantitative Analysis Topics

Decision Tree Analysis

Cash Flow Analysis

Net Present Value

Probability Theory

Regression Analysis and Forecasting

Quantitative analysis (QA) is probably the most challenging and most important course in the MBA curriculum. It provides the basic tools principally used in finance, accounting, marketing, and operations. Therefore, these pages are not to be skipped over simply because you are not accustomed to dealing with numbers and statistics. Give it a chance!

Quantitative techniques provide MBAs with a way to distinguish themselves from their non-MBA peers. MBAs can make a splash with their bosses by creating sophisticated charts and graphs and by using impressive language. Hopefully, the conclusions they have to deliver are a welcomed story.

Using QA theories to solve business problems is the MBA's main job. Quantitative analysis helps MBAs remain objective when solving complicated problems. The theories behind the techniques are

"IT'S MY FERVENT HOPE, FERNBAUGH, THAT THESE ARE MEANINGLESS STATISTICS."

inconsequential. Their application to solve real business problems is what is important. Yet it should be noted that no matter how mathematically precise the tools of quantitative may appear, they are no substitute for an MBA's own best judgment.

## DECISION THEORY

Decision theory teaches how to break complex problems into manageable parts. Without a framework to attack difficult situations, such cases quickly become unmanageable. For example, QA can be used to help a wildcatter decide whether to drill for oil. The inherent risks of oil exploration, however, cannot be eliminated. A *decision tree diagram* can organize the problem's alternatives, risks, and uncertainty.

Decision tree analysis consists of the following five steps:

1. Determine all the possible *alternatives and risks* associated with the situation.

2. Calculate the *monetary consequences* of each of the alternatives.

3. Determine the *uncertainty* associated with each alternative.

4. Combine the first three steps into a tree diagram.

5. Determine the *best alternative* and consider the nonmonetary aspects of the problem.

Decision tree diagrams include *activity forks* and *event forks* at the junctures where alternatives are possible. For example, the decision whether to drill for oil represents an activity fork in the tree for an oil wildcatter. It is symbolized on a decision tree by a *square*. If the different alternatives are *subject to uncertainty,* that is an *event* fork. The uncertain outcome of a well producing oil would be considered an *event*. It is symbolized on a decision tree by a *circle*.

ACTIVITY FORKS                                    EVENT FORKS

Drill for Oil                                     Oil

Stay Home                                         Dry Hole

### *DECISION TREE EXAMPLE*

As an illustration of a situation where the decision tree could be helpful, consider Mr. Sam Houston of Texas. Mr. Houston is about to exercise his option to drill for oil on a promising parcel. Should he drill? If he hits a gusher, there is an estimated $1,000,000 to be gained. When he investigated all of the alternatives, Mr. Houston made the following list:

1. Sam paid $20,000 for the drilling option.

2. Sam could lower his risks if he hired a geologist to perform seis-

mic testing ($50,000). That would give him a better indication of success and lower his risk of wasting drilling costs.

3. Should he roll the dice and incur $200,000 in drilling costs without a seismic evaluation to guide him?

4. Sam consulted with oil experts. They believe Sam's parcel has a 60 percent chance of having oil without the benefit of any tests.

5. It has also been the experts' experience that if seismic tests are positive for the oil, there is a 90 percent chance there is "some" oil. And conversely, there is a 10 percent chance of failure.

6. If the seismic tests are negative, Sam could still drill but with a 10 percent chance of success and a 90 percent chance of failure.

7. Sam could decide not to drill at all.

Each piece of information above is incorporated into a tree diagram. A tree diagram graphically organizes Mr. Houston's alternatives.

Before you get too enthusiastic over the drawing of trees, you must determine what information is irrelevant. In this case, the $20,000 Sam paid for his drilling option is extraneous; it is a *sunk cost*. The money is out the door, sunk down a well. It isn't coming back no matter what Sam decides. Sunk costs are therefore excluded from decision trees.

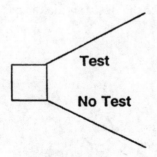

## *DRAWING A DECISION TREE*

The first step to drawing the tree is to determine the first decision (or *fork of the tree*) that needs to be made. Should Sam choose to test first? If seismic testing is chosen, it would precede all of the other activities that follow. It is reflected in the tree as a *square* at the first fork.

If Sam tests, it could result in a positive *event* (60 percent chance) or negative event (40 percent). If there are no tests, he can still choose to drill or not (square). Regardless of the results of the seismic report, Sam can still "choose" to drill or not. But once the oil rig is drilling, the existence of oil is an *uncontrollable* event. Either there will be a lucrative oil event or not.

The next step is to add the monetary consequences—they are like the "leaves to a tree." If there is oil, there would be a $1,000,000 payday. Drilling costs are $200,000 per well. Testing costs are $50,000 per well.

To know the potential financial outcomes of each decision, multiply the possible dollar outcomes by their probabilities at forks where there is an "event circle." ([$1,000,000 payday × .90 probability] + [$0 payday × .10 probability] = $900,000.) This gives you the *expected monetary value* (EMV) of the event, although the actual individual outcomes can be a range of values. At any circle, the probabilities must add up to 100 percent (.90 + .10 = 1.00) to denote that all possibilities are accounted for. Each fork is *mutually exclusive* of other alternatives, and within that alternative the probability is 100 percent or *collectively exhaustive*.

At *activity squares* the decision maker has the ability to choose

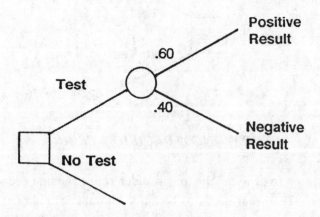

THE DECISION TREE OIL DRILLING

the best outcome. To determine the best alternative, subtract the applicable cost from the payoff of the alternative. You calculate the monetary consequences by beginning at the far right and working your way to the left. This process is said to be "folding back" or "pruning" the tree to arrive at your best action plan decision. At square forks you should choose the highest dollar alternative. At the circle multiply the possible payoffs by their probabilities.

The decision dictated by the tree is to throw caution to the wind and forgo the seismic tests. The expected monetary value of going ahead with testing is $370,000 (420–50), while the EMV of going ahead without tests is $400,000. You choose the highest *expected monetary value* (EMV). This relatively simple conceptual framework can be applied to new product development, real estate development, and store inventory level decisions. Whatever the decision to be considered, a decision tree structure forces the decision maker to take a comprehensive view of all the alternatives, to make an evaluation of the uncertainty (you often have to make your best guess about probabilities), and to explicitly calculate the dollar outcomes possible. The tree forces decision makers to state their assumptions explicitly. In this case, you may consider that the probability of oil when there is a test result to be misstated. In that case, using a different assumption, you may get the opposite final answer. Others looking at the same situation could see it otherwise. By comparing trees, analysts can debate specific assumptions in an organized way.

"Draw a tree and get a B" was the saying on exams involving decision trees. The complexity of seemingly simple problems can be seen using decision trees. Therefore, just creating an accurate tree framework was a challenge during a four-hour exam; it takes a lot of practice to become proficient. There is a tool in Excel called TreePlan that automates the drawing, but not the thinking.

THE DECISION TREE OIL DRILLING

(in thousands of dollars)

## CASH FLOW ANALYSIS

The term *cash flow* is often used in connection with leveraged buy-outs (LBOs), and it is the basis of financial analysis. Wall Street technicians may ponder briefly the qualitative aspects of their investment decisions, but ultimately, only the cash consequences have any real relevance for them. Cash flow analysis is based on the same information used by the accountant's Statement of Cash Flows. Cash flow analysis answers the simple question:

What does the investment cost and how much cash will it generate each year?

The cash generated by a company can be used to pay off debt, pay dividends, invest in research, purchase new equipment, or invest in a real estate development. The goal is to determine when and how much cash flows in a given case scenario.

In making an investment there may be several objectives in mind, but cash flow analysis concerns itself only with the dollars. A company's advertising may create goodwill with the public, for example, but if the benefits cannot be measured in dollars, cash flow analysis is not appropriate.

Cash flow analysis is as relevant to the purchase of a piece of machinery as it is to the acquisition of a corporation. So let us restate the first question asked:

What is the current investment and what are the future benefits? The steps to answer the question are:

1. Define the value of the investment
2. Calculate the magnitude of the benefits
3. Determine the timing of the benefits
4. Quantify the uncertainty of the benefits
5. Do the benefits justify the wait?

One important issue to consider is that cash flow analysis indicates cash flows, not profits. For example, a successful technology start-up company in Silicon Valley may be making an "accounting" profit of $3 million. But if the company requires a $20 million investment in research and a $30 million outlay to build a factory, the company is actually a net user of cash. In this case the company's profitability lies in the future.

Accounting profits, as reported in the income statement, are a short-term measurement of an investment in a time frame shorter than the life of the investment, whereas cash flow analysis is a technique used to evaluate individual projects over the life of the project.

The following specific information would be required to quantify the initial cash flows of a project:

*Cash Uses*
- Construction Costs
- Initial Inventory Stock
- Equipment Purchases
- Increases in Accounts Receivable (allowing customers to borrow from you for goods sold to them)

*Cash Sources*
- Sales of Equipment (if disposed of)
- Increases in Accounts Payable (borrowing from suppliers on materials purchased)

To determine the cash uses during the life of the project:

*Cash Sources*
- Revenues or Sales
- Royalties

*Cash Uses*
- Costs of Goods Sold
- Selling Costs

- General and Administrative Costs
- Taxes

*Depreciation,* which appears in income statements, is not relevant in cash flow analysis. Depreciation is an accounting allowance that says that if a piece of equipment has a useful life of five years, then one fifth of the cost in each year of use can be deducted from income. In a cash flow analysis, hard cash is used to buy the machine today, therefore it is shown as a use of cash at the time of purchase. Depreciation is only applicable inasmuch as it is used to reduce "accounting income," thereby reducing the "cash" out the door for taxes. In the Bob's Market example in the accounting chapter, the store expensed its cash registers and shopping carts over ten years even though they were paid for at the store's opening.

A second important point is that financing costs are not included in cash flow analysis. The investment decision is separate from the financing decision. At Intel there are thousands of projects and many classes of financing—debt (bonds, bank debt) and stock. To match debt with individual projects would be impossible. In reality, the finance department borrows to meet all of its current corporate needs, and it is the capital budgeting department that decides which projects to adopt. If the two decisions were linked, all projects that were financed by debt would look much better than those for which cash is paid up front, even though in substance they are the same.

## A CASH FLOW EXAMPLE

Quaker Oats is considering a $100,000 investment in a cereal filling machine for its plant in Kansas City. The benefits of fiber have spurred the demand for oatmeal to the point of exhausting plant capacity. If the machine is purchased, additional cereal sales of $80,000 could be made each year. The cost of goods sold is only $20,000 and the profits derived would be taxed at 30 percent. The increased sales will also require holding $10,000 in inventory. Quaker will partially offset that use of cash by increasing its payables by $8,000 to farmers for the oats and Smurfit WestRock Container for the boxes to net a $2,000 additional cash investment.

At the end of three years the machine will be worn-out, but the equipment will still be useful to a milling company in Mexico. Quaker plans to sell it to Molino Grande at a price of $10,000.

In this example the timing of cash flows is critical to determining the project's value, as shown in the statement of the details. A commonly used representation of the timing of cash flows is a bar graph. Each period, cumulative cash flow is reflected either below the line for

## THE TIMING OF CASH FLOWS
## QUAKER OATS FILLING MACHINE PROJECT
### (in thousands of dollars)

|  | YEAR 0 | YEAR 1 | YEAR 2 | YEAR 3 |
|---|---|---|---|---|
| Investment | − $100 | | | |
| Revenue | | + $80 | + $80 | + $80 |
| Cost of Goods Sold | | − $20 | − $20 | $20 |
| Taxes* | | − $ 9 | − $ 9 | − $ 9 |
| Increase in Inventory | − $ 10 | | | |
| Increase in Payables | + $ 8 | | | |
| Sale of Equipment | | | | + $10 |
| Total Cash Flow | − $102 | + $51 | + $51 | + $61 |

* Tax Calculation

| | | |
|---|---|---|
| Revenue | $ 80 | |
| Cost | − 20 | |
| Margin | $ 60 | |
| Depreciation | − 30 | (100 − 10)/3 |
| Earnings Pre-Tax | $ 30 | |
| Tax Rate | × .30 | |
| Tax | $ 9 | |

cash investments or above the line for returns. Our Quaker example is shown in the following bar graph:

Suppose that the cash flows are the same but the timing of the cash is advanced as follows (Scenario A):

or prolonged as follows (Scenario B):

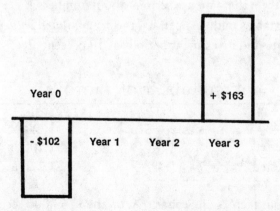

These diagrams raise the critical issue of the "value" of timing.

## *ACCUMULATED VALUE*

When the milling project produces cash, Quaker *reinvests* it rather than let it remain idle. Therefore if Quaker receives $51,000, $51,000, and $61,000 as described earlier, the company earns income with the cash for two more years in Scenario A than in Scenario B.

If the company has investment opportunities that yield 10 percent, then Scenario A will produce $34,230 more than Scenario B. I will show you the calculation in a moment.

The flows have an *accumulated value* at the end of three years of $163,000 plus earned interest of $34,230 that equals $197,230. Scenario A is clearly the better scenario.

A simpler calculation is to use the formula for the accumulated value or *future value* of a dollar:

Future Value of a $ in $x$ periods = ($ today) ×
$(1 + \text{Reinvestment Rate})^{\text{Number of Periods}}$

At 10% the factor for 1 year = $\$1 \times (1 + .10)^1 = 1.10$.

You don't have to memorize the factors or calculate them each time—you can use the tables provided in the appendix, or any basic business calculator. (The best calculator in my opinion is the Hewlett-Packard. Owning an HP, an MBA icon, also sends a strong signal to others that you are serious about numbers.)

Per the tables in the Appendix, the *accumulated value* factors for varying rates and investment periods at 10 percent are:

### ACCUMULATION FACTORS

| | | |
|---|---|---|
| $1 today | = | $1 today |
| $1 invested | = | $1.100 in 1 year |
| $1 invested | = | $1.210 in 2 years |

Using our factors on Scenario A, on the $163,000 received at the end of Year 1 and invested for two years till the end of Year 3, the accumulated value is:

Year 1's $163,000 × 1.2100 = $197,230 in 2 years or
$197,230 − $163,000 = $34,230 of reinvestment income

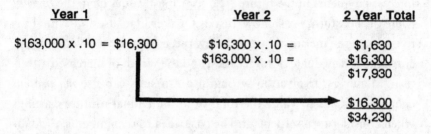

ACCUMULATED VALUE CALCULATION

| Year 1 | Year 2 | 2 Year Total |
|---|---|---|
| $163,000 x .10 = $16,300 | $16,300 x .10 = | $1,630 |
| | $163,000 x .10 = | $16,300 |
| | | $17,930 |
| | | $16,300 |
| | | $34,230 |

When evaluating projects or investments that extend into the future, it is not only the magnitude of the cash flows that is important, but also the timing and the subsequent use to which those flows can be reinvested.

## NET PRESENT VALUE (NPV)

Accumulated value analysis is a good tool to determine how much a retiree needs to invest today to have an adequate pension in thirty years, but it doesn't solve the problem of evaluating investments and projects today. Investments need to be evaluated in today's dollars. How much is Quaker's milling project worth today? How does it compare to a similar piece of equipment that costs $150,000 but lasts four years?

*Cash flow analysis determines the flows and the NPV technique values them in today's dollars. In that way different projects can be compared regardless of timing.*

If Apple Computer, for example, knows that a new Tangerine computer will be a surefire $5 billion hit, but that it will take ten years to develop, it may not make sense to invest in this project. Not only will that $5 billion be worth less due to inflation, but Apple could also use the money to invest in robotics, which will save Apple production costs *today*. Even if an NPV analysis justifies the

Tangerine, there may be strategic reasons that overshadow it. That's where the MBA must use management judgment.

Securities analysts see stocks and bonds as an equipment purchase. The stocks provide earnings and dividend payments, and bonds provide interest payments in the future. The securities' values lie in the *present value* of their future cash flow. Just as Quaker Oats uses NPV analysis to evaluate the merits of buying a new piece of production equipment, corporations evaluate new factories, and the worth of increased advertising. Lawyers involved in wrongful death suits can use *net present value* techniques to value the total of an individual's future earnings when considering a settlement. The basic idea to remember is: *A dollar today is worth more than a dollar received in the future.*

The Quaker Oats project yielded $163,000 over three years (51 + 51 + 61). As previously calculated, the $163,000 in cash flows would yield an additional $34,230 if the cash produced was reinvested at a rate of 10 percent in other company projects or an interest-bearing investment. Would you pay $163,000 for $163,000 to be received over three years? Of course not! You would be giving up the *time value of money,* or $34,230.

Using this simple logic, NPV analysis takes future cash flows and *discounts* them to their present-day value. This is the inverse of *accumulated value*. The formula is as follows:

$$\text{NPV} = (\$ \text{ in Future}) \times (1 + \text{Discount Rate})^{-\text{Number of periods}}$$

One dollar received one year from now, with a discount rate of 10 percent, would be worth:

$$\$1 \times (1 + .10)^{-1} = .90909$$

Using this formula, tables of *discount factors* tell the NPV of $1 at varying rates and for varying periods. Considering the 10 percent reinvestment opportunities available and the project's riskiness, $1 in the future is worth the following amounts today per the formula and tables:

## DISCOUNT FACTORS

| | | |
|---|---|---|
| $1 today | = | $1 today |
| $1 in 1 year | = | $.90909 today |
| $1 in 2 years | = | $.82645 today |
| $1 in 3 years | = | $.75131 today |

The cash flows of the Quaker project would be valued in the following way:

## FUTURE CASH × DISCOUNT FACTOR = NPV

| | | | | | |
|---|---|---|---|---|---|
| Start Year 0 | −$102,000 | × 1 | = | −$102,000 today | |
| in year 1 | $51,000 | × .90909 | = | $46,363.59 today | |
| in year 2 | $51,000 | × .82645 | = | $42,148.95 today | |
| in year 3 | $61,000 | × .75131 | = | $45,829.91 today | |
| The Quaker project NPV | | | = | $32,342.45 today | |

The evaluation of any project depends on the *magnitude* of the cash flows, the *timing,* and the *discount rate,* 10 percent in our case.

The discount rate is highly subjective. The higher the rate or *hurdle rate,* the less a dollar in the future would be worth today (see the appendix). It is called a hurdle rate because a project with a higher discount rate must generate more cash in the future to be worth the same value of today. The project thus has a higher hurdle to jump to stay even. In cases where the outcome of an investment is risky, as in our oil well example, a higher discount rate is appropriate. If the outcome of an investment is certain, as in the investment in a labor-saving device or in a U.S. Treasury bond, a lower rate is warranted. Companies not guided by an MBA's expertise will use only one hurdle rate for all investment decisions and thereby ignore the relative riskiness of projects. They end up rejecting sure things, and chasing high-risk projects. Under no circumstances should the interest rate of a company's bank debt be the rate that is used, unless it is just coincidence. *The risk of the project should determine the discount rate.* Stable companies can borrow at low interest rates, but they can invest in risky projects.

## INTERNAL RATE OF RETURN (IRR)

IRR is a derivative of NPV. Simply stated: The internal rate of return of an investment is the rate at which the discounted cash flows in the future equal the value of the investment today.

To find the IRR one must try different discount rates until the NPV equals zero. (Of course the HP calculator yields the IRR at a push of a button!) For the Quaker project the IRR is 26.709 percent. To confirm that number we can calculate the following:

### USING "26.709% DISCOUNT FACTORS"

| today | 1.00 | × | −102,000 | = | −$102,000 |
|---|---|---|---|---|---|
| 1 year | .78920 | × | $51,000 | = | $40,250 |
| 2 years | .62285 | × | $51,000 | = | $31,765 |
| 3 years | .49155 | × | $61,000 | = | $29,985 |
| | | | NPV | = | −0− |

Using IRR to rank projects is useful, but it does not consider the magnitude of the values. A small investment with proportionately large returns would be ranked higher than large investments with adequate returns. If Intel has a billion dollars allocated to research, it needs to deploy large sums of money to large projects that may have lower IRRs.

Ranking by IRR also neglects the hurdle rates or discount factors used in NPV analysis. Those hurdle rates, as I said, adjust for risk. All things being equal, the investment in equipment by Quaker may have a lower IRR than highly speculative research into a Swedish cancer cure by Merck, but the Quaker project could have a higher NPV. The equipment project's smaller cash flows would be discounted at a lower rate because of the lower risk involved. This could result in higher NPV. The cancer research would be assessed using a high discount rate of 50 percent. *Remember, the higher the discount rate, the less the cash is worth today and the more risk is implied.*

# PROBABILITY THEORY

*Probability theory* is a nice term for statistics, the subject that creates fear in the hearts of even the brightest CPAs in business schools. Actually, probability theory is a more accurate term because it describes how statistics are used to solve problems. Given the *probabilities* of striking oil, what should Sam Houston do? Out of eight hundred married MBA students in the Top Ten programs, how many spouses are likely to be ignored during the first year of the MBA program? It's all probability theory. Because most businesspeople shy away from statistics, here is an *opportunity* for MBAs to excel. I took a statistics course as an undergraduate and learned virtually nothing because I was taught theory, not problem solving. MBA programs concentrate on the practical aspects of statistics and tend to leave theory for mathematicians to sort out. If you are not familiar with statistics, *do not* skip this section. I cannot make you statistically proficient in a few pages, but if you give it a chance with some patient reading, I promise you that you will have enough working knowledge of the discipline to ask for help whenever appropriate. Preparing students by giving them a working knowledge of different subjects is the main thrust of an MBA education. In only two years, professors do not expect their students to become technical experts, but they expect them to recognize where they should seek the help of an expert to solve a particular problem.

## *PROBABILITY DISTRIBUTIONS*

In situations where multiple outcomes are possible, the result is a *distribution* of outcomes. Each possibility is assigned a probability. Through careful analysis, intuition, and judgment, all the possible outcomes of any *event* add up to 100 percent, like the event fork of a decision tree. The graph that shows a distribution of outcomes is called a *probability mass* or *density function*. If there are many possible outcomes, the curve is smooth and is called a *probability density function*. If there are only a few, an uneven curve is drawn, called a *probability mass function*.

*A Rainfall Example.* Rainfall in Seattle is an event resulting in a probability distribution. Seattle's rainfall, using hypothetical data, looked as follows in a table and in probability distribution charts on this and the next pages.

### SEATTLE DAILY RAIN MEASUREMENTS
### MARCH 2024

| DAILY INCHES OF RAIN | DAYS WITH × INCHES OF RAIN | DAYS AS % OF MONTH |
|---|---|---|
| 0 | 5 | 16% |
| 2 | 6 | 19 |
| 4 | 8 | 26 |
| 6 | 6 | 19 |
| 8 | 3 | 10 |
| 10 | 3 | 10 |
| | 31 | 100% |

### *THE BINOMIAL DISTRIBUTION*

Flipping a coin results in two possibilities, heads or tails. Therefore the *distribution* of outcomes of two coin flippings could have several possible outcomes if you consider "heads" a success.

2 successes, Heads/Heads
1 success/1 failure, Heads/Tails, Tails/Heads
2 failures, Tails/Tails

PROBABILITY MASS FUNCTION OF RAIN MEASURES
Daily Rainfall in Seattle
March 2024 (31 days)

Coin flipping gives rise to the most basic of distributions, called a *binomial distribution*. There are two outcomes in a binomial distribution, success and failure, each with an equal likelihood of occurring.

Seemingly arcane binomial distribution theories can be applied to such practical pursuits as stock market analysis. Success in a stock analysis would be a positive return on a stock in a month, and failure would be a loss or break even. In a historical study of the old AT&T share prices from 1957 to 1977, each month was examined to determine the rate of positive returns. It was found that 56.7 percent of the time there was a success.

The months studied were grouped into periods of three months each (quarters). Researchers noted that the frequency of actual successes was as follows:

| # *SUCCESSES* | *FREQUENCY OCCURRED* |
|---------------|----------------------|
| 0 | .088 |
| 1 | .325 |
| 2 | .387 |
| 3 | .200 |
| | 1.000 |

A coin-flipping mathematician created tables of numbers to solve all binomial distribution problems. In the AT&T case, the information needed to use a binomial table is:

r = number of successes possible = 0 to 3
n = number of trials = 3 (3 months in a quarter)
p = probability of success = 56.7%

Using this information, a standard binomial table predicts that the *expected* outcomes should be:

| # *SUCCESSES* | *FREQUENCY EXPECTED* |
|---------------|----------------------|
| 0 | .082 |
| 1 | .318 |
| 2 | .416 |
| 3 | .184 |
| | 1.000 |

Surprisingly, the binomial distribution matches rather well the actual results of the AT&T case. Given a guess of *probability of success* (p), the probability of positive monthly returns in a given quarter could be read off the table. Binomial distribution therefore has practical applications for assessing probabilities for portfolio managers, sales directors, and research analysts.

## THE NORMAL DISTRIBUTION:
## THE MYSTERY OF THE BELL CURVE

The *normal distribution* is the most widely used distribution and is most commonly known as the *bell curve*. At Harvard the bell curve is used to determine grades. The curve dictates that 15 percent of the class receive "Low Passes" ("loops").

When a *probability mass function* is based on many trials, the curve tends to fill in and become bell-shaped. We call this a *probability density function*. Such was the case with the two graphs describing rainfall in Seattle. The hump in the middle is caused by the *Central Limit Theorem*. It states that "the distribution of *averages* of repeated independent samples will take the form of the bell-shaped normal distribution." Why? Simply because a large number of independent samples tend to a central average.

The concept of "averages of samples" is pretty vague. In case applications the definition expands to include any large group of data. Why? Because the normal distribution is so easy to use and closely approximates reality anyway. Stock prices are the result of many market fluctuations that culminate in a return (profit or loss). The

THE BELL-SHAPED GRADING CURVE

**Probability**

Low Pass | Satisfactory | High Pass

15% | 70% | 15%

**Scores**

PROBABILITY DENSITY FUNCTION OF RAIN MEASUREMENTS

Daily Rainfall in Seattle

1980–2020 (14,600 days)

return can be considered an "average" of those market fluctuations. Just about anything can be rationalized as an average, hence the usefulness of normal distributions.

*Measures of the Normal Curve.* The bell-shaped curve is described by two terms, the *mean* and its *standard deviation* (SD). The mean ($\mu$) is the center of the curve. The mean is commonly called the *average*. It is the result of adding up the data and dividing by the number of data points. The standard deviation ($\sigma$) is how wide the curve appears. The SD can also be described as a measure of the "variability from the mean." These two terms are central to most probability concepts.

Other less-used measures of averages for a set of data are the *median*, the item in the middle of the list if sorted by size, and the *mode*, the item occurring most frequently in a data set.

As with the binomial distribution, the sum of all the outcomes as represented by the region under the curve equals 100 percent.

PROBABILITY DENSITY FUNCTIONS WITH CURVES
OF DIFFERENT STANDARD DEVIATIONS

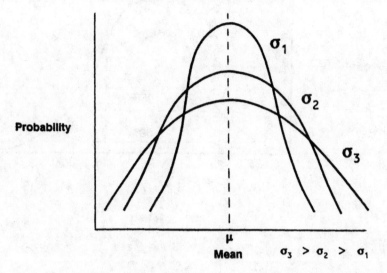

What makes the normal distribution's curve special is that for any given SD measure away from the mean or the center, the same probability exists for an event despite the normal distribution's shape.

*Normal Distribution Retailing Example.* Al Bundy, a shoe store owner, wants to make sure he has enough stock for all size requests. He purchased a study of ladies' shoe sizes from the Academy of Feet and received a stack of research data from survey responses.

He plotted the data on graph paper and it appeared as a normal distribution. He also entered the series of sizes in his calculator and hit the "Standard Deviation" key. The answer was 2. Al also took the average or mean of all the survey's respondents' sizes and found it to be 7. Looking at the graph he created, he saw that it looked like our trusty normal distribution.

Just by recognizing the shape, Al could apply the laws of the normal distribution curve. The laws governing the area under each side of the mean of all normal curves are the following:

NORMAL DISTRIBUTION OF SHOE SIZES

**Mean**

**Shoe Sizes**

1  SD = .3413
2  SD = .4772
3  SD = .49865
4  SD = .4999683

Using these rules, if Mr. Bundy stocks sizes 5 to 9 he has covered .6826 (2 × .3413) of the population. Increasing the sizes to 3 to 11, he has covered .9544 of the feet out there. If Al stocked sizes 1 to 13, .9973 of customers at his store would be satisfied with his selection. He can always special-order for those feet beyond sizes 1 to 13.

Of course normal distribution tables have been developed to determine the probability for any specific point on the curve (noninteger SDs away from the mean). To use the tables, a Z *value* must be calculated.

$$Z = \frac{[(\text{Point of Interest}) - \text{Mean}]}{\text{SD}}$$

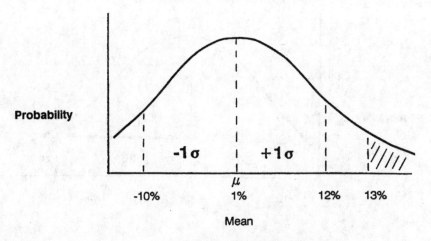

THE PROBABILITY DENSITY FUNCTION
Monthly Stock Returns of Pioneer Aviation

## A NORMAL CURVE FINANCE EXAMPLE

Let's apply these new pieces of probability theory to finance. The monthly stock returns of a volatile stock, Pioneer Aviation, are assumed normally distributed as shown by a plotted graph. A summary of historical returns shows a mean (center) of 1 percent and an SD (dispersion) of 11 percent. Gerald Rasmussen wanted to know what was the probability that next month's return would be less than 13 percent.

Using our new Z value tool we can figure it out:

$$Z = \frac{(13 - 1)}{11} = 1.09 \text{ SD away from the mean}$$

The normal distribution table I have provided in the appendix tells us that 1.09 SDs = .3621. The entire left side of the graph equals .5000, as any complete half of the distribution would. This holds true in all situations. There is a 50 percent chance of being above or below the center or mean in any normal distribution. Combining those pieces of information, I calculate there is an .8621 (.3621 + .50) probability that there will be a return of less than 13 percent,

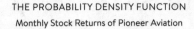

THE PROBABILITY DENSITY FUNCTION
Monthly Stock Returns of Pioneer Aviation

**Monthly Stock Returns**

and conversely a .1379 chance that it will be greater (1 − .8621). This is a real-world answer to a real-world business problem using statistics as our tools. Again, you may want to read this section several times; it's complicated. If it were easy everyone would get an "A" in stats class.

Statistics is not difficult if you do not dwell too long on theory. Other distributions exist, but are rarely used in business. The *Poisson distribution* (pronounced "pwasaun") is similar to the normal distribution but has a flaring tail on the right side of the graph. But most distributions are assumed to be normal to take advantage of the normal distribution's laws of standard deviations.

## CUMULATIVE DISTRIBUTION FUNCTIONS

A *cumulative distribution function* (CDF) is a cumulative view of a probability distribution. It takes a probability mass function, such as a bell curve, and asks, "What is the probability that the outcome is less than or equal to that value?" The normal curve tells you what the probability is for a given outcome, but the CDF tells you the probability for a given range of values. The CDF can also be used to marry our knowledge of uncertainty (probability theory) to our decision-making tool (decision trees). A CDF captures the range of possible outcomes of many-valued uncertain quantities.

To continue our oil well example, let's take the distribution of the possible values of oil that may be in the ground if oil is recovered:

| OIL VALUE | PROBABILITY MASS FUNCTION | CDF CUMULATIVE PROBABILITY "EQUAL TO OR <" |
|---|---|---|
| 50,000 | .005 | .005 |
| 75,000 | .01 | .015 (.005 + .01) |
| 150,000 | .03 | .045 (.03 + .01 + .005) |
| 200,000 | .08 | .125 |
| 300,000 | .12 | .245 |
| 750,000 | .15 | .395 |
| 1,100,000 | .21 | .605 |
| 1,200,000 | .15 | .755 |
| 1,400,000 | .12 | .875 |
| 1,700,000 | .08 | .955 |
| 2,000,000 | .03 | .985 |
| 2,500,000 | .01 | .995 |
| 6,000,000 | .005 | 1.000 |
| | 1.000 | |

In the tree constructed before, we used $1,000,000 as our payoff. That amount was the expected value (EMV) of the oil, because I conveniently chose it for the example. The distribution was actually a wide range of values. There was a .005 chance of a $6,000,000 payday and .005 chance of $50,000 as shown by the table of values. If you multiply each of the dollar values by their individual probabilities in the second column, the EMV equals $1,000,000, the EMV we used before.

Constructing a cumulative distribution function allows decision makers to arrive at the mean or EMV when they are not certain what it is to begin with. Drawing a CDF is a method of combining a series of your judgments about the probability of the upper, middle, and lower bounds of an unknown outcome to arrive at an EMV to use for decision making.

The CDF graph of ranges of outcomes resembles a big S. In the CDF, you see at a glance all the possible outcomes, not just static individual points. As shown by the following graph, Sam Houston believes that all his possible outcomes fall in the continuous "range" of $0 to $6,000,000.

CUMULATIVE DENSITY FUNCTION

Values of Possible Oil Drilling Outcomes

(in thousands of $s)

The range of probabilities from 0 to 1.0 in the CDF is divided into *fractiles,* or slices, using the *bracket median technique.* The CDF above is divided in that way. To divide the CDF probability ranges into five fractiles, for example, one would take the .1, .3, .5, .7, and .9 fractiles. Each of those fractiles would represent the average of the "ranges of values," 0 to .2, .2 to .4, .4 to .6, .6 to .8, and .8 to 1.0, respectively.

The .5 fractile is the same as the median, because half of the values are on either side of it. The median is not necessarily the same as the mean we used as the center of the normal distribution. The median is merely the center of the value range. The mean is the result of multiplying all the probabilities by the values, as was done to arrive at the $1,000,000 EMV for an oil discovery.

To marry this CDF concept to the decision tree to make important management decisions, imagine how you would represent all the values an oil well may produce. It would be a *range* of values that would be represented by a *fan* of possibilities. One could not possibly draw the infinite possibilities of branches on the tree, so we use a CDF to help out.

*Drawing a CDF.* To draw a CDF as shown on page 194, you use your own judgment and your research data. You need to ask yourself a series of questions:

> What value would occur where results are either higher or lower
>> 50 percent of the time (the median)?
> What value would be at the low end (.10 fractile)?
> What value would be at the high end (.90 fractile)?

With the answers to these questions, you can draw the CDF of what you believe the range of outcomes is. By picking five outcomes using the five fractiles from the CDF, you can draw the *event fan* of five possibilities and probabilities on a decision tree as five branches.

The expected monetary value is the same as in our first go-around, but that is only because I conveniently used the correct EMV to begin with.

A shortcut to using five fractiles is called the *Pearson Tukey Method*. Instead of five fractiles, the method uses only three—the .05, .5, and .95 fractiles. Their respective probabilities are .185, .63, .185.

For large problems the decision tree has been computerized by *Monte Carlo* simulation programs, the most popular being Oracle's Crystal Ball that also can be used with Excel spreadsheets. The tree and the parameters of the "event fan" CDFs are included in the computer model. The program runs many simulations to give you an idea of how things may really turn out. Some Fortune 500 companies use it. Financial planners use it to evaluate long-term returns on investment portfolios.

DECISION TREE OF OIL DRILLING USING THE
CUMULATIVE DISTRIBUTION FUNCTION

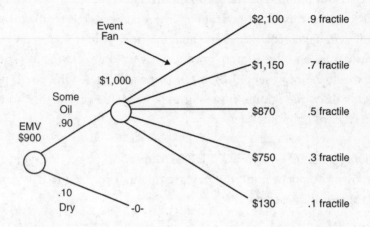

EMV = .9 [ (.2 X $130) + (.2 X $750) + (.2 X $870) + (.2 X $1150) + (.2 X $2100)] = $900

CDF and fractile analysis can be used for situations where the EMV of a branch of a decision tree is uncertain. However, the judgment of the analyst is most important. The tree is simply a tool that the MBA must use in tandem with his or her knowledge and intuition.

## REGRESSION ANALYSIS AND FORECASTING

*Linear regression* models are used in a variety of business situations to determine relationships between variables that analysts believe intuitively to be related. Once a relationship is established, it can be used to forecast the future. Commonly regression analysis is used to relate sales to price, promotions, and market factors; stock prices to earnings and interest rates; and production costs to production volumes. But of course one can use it as well to find answers to questions such as "What is the effect of temperature on the sales of ice cream cones?" The *independent variable* (X) in this scenario is the temperature. It is the variable that is believed to cause other things to happen. The *dependent variable* (Y) is sales. Temperature affects sales, not vice versa.

Regression analysis involves gathering sufficient data to determine the relationship between the variables. With many data points, such as year's worth of information on temperature and sales changes, a graph can be drawn with temperature along the X axis and sales along the Y axis. The goal of regression is to produce an equation of a line that "best" depicts this relationship. Regression tries to "fit" a line between the plotted data points so that the "squared differences between the points and the line are least." The *least squares method* requires a great deal of adding, subtracting, and multiplying. A business calculator or computer spreadsheet program will be necessary to do the heavy lifting.

## *AN ALGEBRA REFRESHER COURSE*

To set the stage for a *regression* example, let's review some basic algebra. You recall that a line is described by this algebraic formula:

$$Y = mX + b$$

Y = dependent variable (such as sales)
m = the slope of the line (the relationship between variables)
X = the independent variable (such as rain)
b = y axis intercept (where the line crosses the vertical axis)

The computer spreadsheet will calculate the linear equation ($Y = mX + b$) that defines the relationship between the independent and dependent variables. The program will determine whether the line that it has calculated as the best "fit" can be used as an accurate tool for forecasting.

## *AN ICE CREAM REGRESSION EXAMPLE*

The owner of a chain of twenty Ben & Jerry's ice cream shops noticed that as the temperature rose and fell, so did his sales. In an attempt to determine the precise mathematical relationship between sales and seasonal temperatures, he gathered the monthly sales data for the previous five years and the average temperatures for the months in question from the National Weather Service. His data looked as follows:

| MONTH | AVERAGE DEGREES F | SALES |
|---|---|---|
| January | 33 | $200,000 |
| February | 37 | 250,000 |
| March | 72 | 400,000 |
| April | 65 | 500,000 |
| May | 78 | 900,000 |
| June | 85 | 1,100,000 |
| July | 88 | 1,500,000 |
| August | 91 | 1,300,000 |
| September | 82 | 800,000 |
| October | 73 | 600,000 |
| November | 45 | 300,000 |
| December | 36 | 500,000 |

Using the "Regression" function of the spreadsheet, the owner generated the following Excel output:

## SUMMARY OUTPUT

### REGRESSION STATISTICS

| | |
|---|---|
| R Square | 0.70427945 |
| Standard Error | 243334.911 |
| Observations | 12 |

| | COEFFICIENTS | STANDARD ERROR | T STAT |
|---|---|---|---|
| Intercept | -379066.613 | | |
| X Variable 1 | 16431.5915 | 3367.036871 | 4.880134 |

## *WHAT DOES THIS MEAN?*

Wondrously enough, that block of information contains the equation for the line that describes the relationship between temperature and sales at Ben & Jerry's. First let's interpret the data in the output to get the line equation.

"Coefficient of the Y Intercept" = b = −379,066
"Coefficient of the X Variable" = m = 16,431

Placing that information into a standard linear equation as described in the algebra refresher, $Y = 16,431X − 379,066$, plotting the data points, and drawing the regression line described by the equation, the graph looks like this:

SALES OF BEN & JERRY'S ICE CREAM REGRESSION EXAMPLE

As shown by the graph, the regression line runs through the middle of the data points. By plugging temperature, X, into the equation, the *predicted* ice cream sales can be calculated. In Ben & Jerry's case, a temperature of 60 degrees would result in predicted monthly sales of $606,794.

$$Y = (16,431 \times 60 \text{ degrees}) − 379,066 = \$606,794$$

But just how accurate is this equation in predicting the sales of ice cream? The answer to this question is given to us by another number in the "Regression Output."

## R SQUARE EXPLAINED

The *R Square* value tells us "what percent of the variation in the data is explained by the regression equation given." In our case 70.4 percent of the variation of sales is explained by the regression equation. This is considered very high. In broader economic analyses, an R Square of 30 percent would be considered very high, since there are thousands of variables that could affect economies. In the ice cream business, one could imagine that in addition to temperature, store advertising, couponing, and store hours could also explain sales fluctuations.

But be careful! Do not read too much into the regression data results! Regression only says that changes in sales occur with changes in temperature in much the same way as described. It *does not* say that "temperature actually caused sales to move." But if a selected independent variable is reasonable and it is a good predictor of the desired dependent variable under study, use it.

Regression analysis points not only to positive correlations, such as ice cream sales and temperature, but also to negative correlations, such as interest rates and housing sales. If interest rates are high, housing sales are low. In this case the X coefficient is a negative number. These negative relationships are just as useful predictors as positive/positive relationships.

## STANDARD ERROR EXPLAINED

The "Standard Error of the Y Estimate and the X Coefficient" shown in the spreadsheet output are synonyms for the *standard deviations* of the Y and X coefficients of the regression line. In the Ben & Jerry's example, the standard error of the Y estimate (sales) is plus or minus $243,334 68 percent of the time. (It is listed in the Excel output found on the bottom of page 198.) In the same way the output shows that the standard error of the X coefficient (temperature) is 3,367. (It is listed in the Excel output found on the bottom of page 198.) A variety of analyses about the ranges of possible data values can be performed using standard deviations to show the variability of those numbers and the reliability of the resulting regression equation.

## *THE T STATISTIC MEASURE OF RELIABILITY*

The *T statistic* can help determine if the regression equation calculated by the spreadsheet is a good one to use for forecasting. The T statistic reveals if an X variable has a statistically significant effect on Y, such as temperature's effect on sales. You calculate the measure by dividing the X coefficient by its "Standard Error." The rule of thumb says if a T statistic is above 2 or below –2, the X variable has a statistically significant effect on Y. In our case $16,431/3,367 = 4.88$, a very high T-stat. It is also listed in the Excel output on the bottom of page 198. Therefore, an analyst would conclude that temperature is a good predictor of sales.

When considering whether a model is a good forecaster, it is necessary to have both a high R Square and a high T statistic. It is possible to create a model with more than one X variable. This is called *multivariable regression*. As the number of variables increases, so does the R Square. However, adding more X variables with low T statistics creates an inaccurate model. It is necessary to play with the model, adding and dropping independent variables to achieve high R Squares *and* high T statistics.

## *DUMMY VARIABLE REGRESSION ANALYSIS*

A trick employed in regression analysis is the use of *dummy variables* to represent conditions that are not measured in a numerical series.

Ones and zeroes are used to represent these conditions. For example, at Walmart, having the "hot" toy of the season in stock, a nonnumerical condition, catapults sales. The in-stock condition could be indicated in a data set by a 1, and out-of-stock condition could be designated by a 0, using dummy variables.

Given a hypothetical set of data at a Walmart store, you can see how it works.

### "HOT" TOY STOCK STATUS

| DATE | (1 = IN, 0 = OUT) | SALES |
|------|-------------------|-------|
| 12/1/05 | 0 | $100,000 |
| 12/2/05 | 0 | 100,000 |
| 12/3/05 | 1 | 200,000 |
| 12/4/05 | 1 | 200,000 |
| 12/5/05 | 0 | 100,000 |
| 12/6/05 | 1 | 200,000 |
| 12/7/05 | 0 | 100,000 |

The following regression output of the relationship between "hot" toys and sales is the result.

### SUMMARY OUTPUT

**REGRESSION STATISTICS**

| | |
|---|---|
| R Square | 1 |
| Standard Error | 0 |
| Observations | 7 |

| | COEFFICIENTS | STANDARD ERROR | T STAT |
|---|---|---|---|
| Intercept | 100000 | | |
| X Variable 1 | 100000 | 0 | 65535 |

This is a perfect model because the variation explained by the model's R Square is 100 percent and the T statistic is excellent. The T statistic is very large. The sales are $100,000 without the desired toys, and an extra $100,000 when they're in stock. The regression equation, using the spreadsheet output, is

$$Sales = \$100,000X + \$100,000$$

If the coveted toys are in stock, X = 1 and sales jump to $200,000. If not, X = 0, and sales total $100,000. Dummy variables are useful and can be used to match nonscaled data, such as stock status or a holiday, with other regularly scaled data, such as temperature, interest rates, and product defects, to produce useful regression models.

## OTHER FORECASTING TECHNIQUES

*Time series techniques* forecast outcomes based on changes in a relationship over time. In our ice cream example, the data points of temperature and sales were charted on the graph without regard to when they occurred. The regression relationship did not consider time. Obviously seasons affect Ben & Jerry's sales. Time series analysis considers time by plotting data as it occurs. The technique then attempts to "decompose" the fluctuations within the data into three parts:

- *The Underlying Trend* — Up, down, flat (a long-term measure)
- *The Cycles* — Hourly, daily, weekly, monthly (a short-term pattern)
- *Unexplained Movements* — Unusual or irregular movements caused by unique events and quirks of nature

Regression and moving averages are used to determine the trend and cycles. As you can imagine, time series forecasting is tedious and does not lend itself to a short and simple example. However, it is helpful at least to know that time series techniques exist.

## SUMMARY

This chapter has described the quantitative tools that perform the following functions:

Sort out complex problems with decision trees
Determine the value of cash received in the future —
cash flow analysis and net present value analysis
Quantify uncertainty with probability theory
Determine relationships and forecast with regression analysis and
other forecasting techniques

These are practical tools that MBAs use to meet business challenges. They give MBAs the power to make informed decisions and to distinguish themselves on the job. If you are reading this, that means you made it through this chapter. Congratulations on your persistence and courage to tackle one of the toughest MBA subjects.

## KEY QA TAKEAWAYS

*Decision Trees* — A way to graphically show and quantify multiple outcomes of a business decision

*Sunk Cost* — Investments made in the past that have no bearing on future investment decisions

*Expected Monetary Value (EMV)* — The blended value of a decision based on the probabilities and values of all possible outcomes

*Accumulated Value* — The total future value of cash flows with all earnings reinvested

*Net Present Value (NPV)* — The total present value of all cash flows "discounted" to today's dollars

*Internal Rate of Return (IRR)* — The discount rate that makes the net present value of the cash flows equal zero in today's dollars

*Probability Distributions* — The graph of all possible outcomes with their respective probabilities of occurring

*Binomial Distributions* — Probability distribution with only two possible
   outcomes

*Normal Distributions* — The bell-shaped probability distribution of all
   possible outcomes

*Standard Deviation* ($\sigma$) — The measure of the dispersion (width) of
   the normal distribution

*Mean* ($\mu$) — The arithmetic average of all outcomes

*Z Value* — A tool to measure probabilities of specific situations on the
   normal distribution curve

*Cumulative Distribution Function (CDF)* — A form of the normal
   distribution that shows the probability of being less than or equal
   to all possible outcomes

*Regression* — A mathematical method of forecasting using line
   equations to explain the relationships between multiple variables

# Day 6

## FINANCE

### Finance Topics

Business Structures

Beta Risk

The Efficient Frontier

Capital Asset Pricing Model

The Efficient Market Hypothesis

Investment Valuations

Discounted Cash Flows

Dividend Growth Model

Capital Budgeting

Capital Structure

Dividend Policy

Mergers and Acquisitions

I want to be an investment banker. If you had 10,000 shares I sell them for you. I make a lot of money. I will like my job very, very much. I will help people. I will be a millionaire. I will have a big house. It will be fun for me.

> —Seven-year-old schoolboy, "What I Want to Be When I Grow Up,"
> (from Michael Lewis's *Liar's Poker*, 1989)

In the 1980s, finance was the place to be. Even kids dreamed of a life on Wall Street. Machiavellian young MBAs were beside themselves with glee as a Wall Street hired them by the droves, offering them a shot at big bucks trading and deal-making as investment bankers. Unfortunately, the bubble burst in 1987 with the stock market crash, and MBAs were forced to seek less glamorous jobs by joining the financial staffs at banks, corporations, and mutual funds.

But like the seasons, Wall Street made a comeback in the 1990s, after the Internet meltdown in 2000, after the financial meltdown in 2008, and again after the Covid crash in 2020. MBAs from the top schools are put on the fast track and are paid significantly more than their non-MBA peers. On Wall Street and at hedge funds, MBAs make thousands more per year than non-MBAs in the same job. Moreover, job advancement is often limited to the MBA elite.

Do not read this chapter in isolation. If finance turns you on, a single-minded focus on this discipline could be hazardous to your business health. Finance is very quantitative, using numbers from the accounting and QA chapters. Finance also plays as much of a role in marketing as marketing does in finance. Marketers are responsible for their financial results. Financiers work hard to market themselves to new clients and to sell new stocks to existing ones.

## THE NATURE OF THE FIRM

Why do businesses exist? In a financier's eyes, the sole purpose of a firm is to maximize the wealth of its owners. In their pursuit of riches, people can organize their businesses in several ways. There are three basic legal *business structures* that entities take on in the United States. Each is chosen depending on the complexity of the business, liability preference, and tax considerations of the owners.

### *PROPRIETORSHIPS*

A *proprietorship*, commonly called a *sole proprietorship*, is a business owned by an individual or husband and wife. The owner reaps all the profits and has unlimited liability for all losses. If things go poorly, the owner's personal assets can be seized. It's a simple structure. As with a child's lemonade stand, no special government registration is required. Earnings are added to the individual's other income, and taxes are paid on the total income. Because it is not a separate legal entity that can be divided and sold in pieces, it is more difficult for a proprietorship to raise money in the financial markets.

## PARTNERSHIPS

When several individuals form a business, they often enter into a *partnership*. As in a proprietorship, each owner's share of the earnings is included on his or her personal tax returns. Depending on the nature of the business, there are two types of partnerships. In a *general* partnership, active owners, called *general partners*, have unlimited liability for all business debts. When the accounting firm of Laventhol & Horwath went into bankruptcy in 1990 because of auditing malpractices, creditors went after the personal assets of the partners to pay off the partnership's debts.

In a *limited* partnership structure, *limited partners* are shielded to the extent of their investment. The "limited" form is often used in real estate and oil exploration ventures to protect the investing partners that do not participate in management. In the real estate busts of the late 1980s, the early 1990s, and 2008, the limited partners in vacant building projects were able to walk away from their investments with no further liability. On the other hand, the general partners of the same projects were personally on the hook. As in the proprietorship instance, the ability to raise money or to sell partial interests in partnership structures is rather difficult.

## CORPORATIONS

*Corporations*, registered with a state, are legal entities that are separate from the individuals who own them. In the eyes of the law, a corporation is treated as an individual who conducts his or her own business independently. The assets and liabilities of the entity are owned by the corporation, not by the owners of the corporation. As with limited partnerships, owners of corporations have limited liability for the obligations of the business. In the case of a bankruptcy, the owners' personal assets are shielded from creditors.

A corporation's ownership is split into *shares of stock* that investors can purchase and trade in the financial markets such as the New York Stock Exchange (NYSE). Shares can be traded among investors without disrupting the business. When management and the board of directors who represent the owners decide that more money is needed, additional shares can be issued. An investor, whether he takes an active role or chooses to remain passive, is personally shielded from the liabilities of the company.

A major drawback of ownership in a corporation is *double taxation*. The corporation, like an individual, must pay taxes. When the corporation pays its owners a dividend, that dividend is taxable again as income to the individual.

There are variations to the *corporate* form. The *C Corp.*, as it is called by accountants and lawyers, works as described above, but there is also a *Subchapter S Corp*. These corporations have thirty-five or fewer owners. They agree to include the corporation's earnings in their personal tax returns as in the case of a partnership. In that way, the double-taxation hammer does not fall on the owners, while at the same time the corporation's limited liability advantage is maintained.

If you are interested in finance, you can take two different yet interconnected routes. There is the investments area, which is more glamorous, the thing that fortunes, headlines, and stock quotes are made of; and there is financial management, which is the "in the trenches" work that helps companies finance their growth, pay the bills, and make acquisitions. The two areas are interconnected because the performance of a business, for which the finance department is to a large extent responsible, affects its investors' share of the firm's profits. Let's start with the glamour.

## INVESTMENTS

### *RISK AND RETURN*

How can I profit by owning a large or small share of a corporation or other business? This investment decision is really a two-pronged question: What is the potential income, and how risky is the venture? The basic concepts of discounted cash flows and probability explained earlier in the QA chapter can be used to answer these valuation questions. Refer to them as you would look up old class notes.

A basic tenet of finance dictates that the return should be commensurate with the risk. If you know that an investment is a sure thing, then you should expect a lower rate of return in compensation for the lower risk. Accordingly, certificates of deposit insured by the Federal Deposit Insurance Corporation (FDIC) pay low rates of return. Wildcatting for oil involves a great deal of risk, but it also promises a huge jackpot if a well turns out to be a gusher.

*Types of Risk.* If risk applies to a whole class of assets, such as the markets for stocks, bonds, and real estate, it is called *systematic risk.* For instance, when the public believes that the stock market is a good bet (a so-called *bull market*), the market as a whole will climb. When the public leaves, the market "lays an egg" or "melts down," as the headlines read in the crashes of 1929, 1987, 2000, 2008, and 2020. Movements in the economy, interest rates, inflation, and pandemics are systematic factors that affect the entire market. In making any investment, you are exposed to the systematic risk of the market.

If the risk applies to a particular asset or to a small group of assets, it is called *unique* or *unsystematic.* An individual investment performance may be volatile because of specific risks inherent to the investment. If you own shares in Disney, for instance, and Mickey catches a cold, the stock could tumble. That type of risk can largely be compensated for by owning a number of investments. This is called *diversification.* By holding a broad portfolio of investments, investors can offset losses on some investments with gains on others. Diversification moderates the overall fluctuations of a portfolio.

## BETA: RISK WITHIN A PORTFOLIO OF INVESTMENTS

The market prices of stocks, IBM for example, fluctuate daily on the stock exchanges of the world. That *volatility* is equated with risk. A distribution of historical outcomes would show the risk graphically, as was shown for Seattle's rainfall and for shoe sizes in the QA chapter. To refresh your memory of probability distributions, the mean long-term historical return on common stocks was 12.1 percent with a standard deviation of 21.2 percent. Within one standard deviation, 68 percent of the time the stock market will return between +33.3 percent and –9.1 percent per year.

In addition to showing on a graph an individual investment's absolute volatility, financial analysts measure the risk of individual stocks or small groups of stocks by comparing their price movements with the entire market's movement. That measurement, *beta,* quantifies the risk of holding that particular investment versus own-

A PROBABILITY DISTRIBUTION OF HISTORICAL STOCK RETURNS

ing a very large portfolio that represents "the market." An example of such "market" portfolios are the collection of 500 stocks called the *Standard & Poor's 500* (S & P 500) or the 5,000 stocks that are included in the *FT Wilshire 5000*. The *Nikkei* index of 225 stocks represents the Japanese market. The DAX represents the German market and the FTSE reflects the British market.

The famous *Dow Jones Industrial Average* is a diverse collection of thirty of the most stable industrial companies in America (e.g., IBM, 3M, P&G, Coca-Cola, Boeing, and Apple). The Dow's thirty "blue-chip" stocks are traded on the NYSE and are not representative of the broader market, even though the press might have you believe that they are.

If a stock or portfolio moves in tandem with the market, it is said to be perfectly correlated with a beta of 1. IBM is such a stable company that it moves with the market with a beta of 1. If a stock moves in perfect opposition to the market, it is said to be negatively correlated, or to have a beta of –1.

There are no such perfectly negatively correlated stocks, but there are some stocks with low betas. Consolidated Edison has a .22 beta. When the market fluctuates down wildly, people still turn

HOW INVESTMENTS WITH DIFFERENT BETAS ACT

M = Market Movement   I = Individual Stock or Portfolio Movement

on the lights. However, in a big market rally Consolidated Edison is less likely to rise dramatically. Theoretically, a beta of 0 would mean an absence of risk. In that case the investments' betas would perfectly cancel each other so that there would be no risk regardless of the movement of the market.

A risky stock, like Tesla, has a beta of 1.48. A 1 percent fluctuation in the market would be magnified in a 1.48 percent movement in Tesla's price. Moderately risky stocks such as Amazon and Apple have 1.2 betas.

The behavior of the market is so important because most large investment decisions are made in the context of a large *portfolio,* or collection of investments. Although the risks of individual investments may be high, the overall risk will be lowered by investing in the right mix of investments to lower the portfolio's beta. Large mutual funds that own hundreds of investments, such as funds from Vanguard, Fidelity, and BlackRock, provide this kind of *diversification.* *Hedge funds,* on the other hand, are private equity (PE) pools for institutions and wealthy individuals that are able to take on more risk by making big bets on targeted investments. Notable hedge funds include Bridgewater Associates, Citadel, and Renaissance Technologies.

Mutual funds that mimic indexes of stocks such as the S&P 500 are called "index funds." Mutual fund portfolios price and trade once a day. Exchange-traded funds (ETFs) are low-fee alternatives to mutual funds of an index, an industry sector, or a commodity, that price and trade throughout the day.

Of course the beta number does not appear from nowhere. Beta is a statistical calculation of a correlation coefficient, the covariance of a stock with the market divided by the variance of the market. Betas can be calculated, but financial analysts will admit that investment information services, such as the Value Line Survey or Reuters, provide the beta coefficients. Calculating beta is tedious, and in true MBA fashion, this book will skip it.

## THE EFFICIENT FRONTIER

Given all the possible portfolios of assets, theoretically there is a perfect mix of investments at each level of risk. The graphical representation of these theoretical "best" portfolios lies on a line called the *efficient frontier*. The area below the efficient frontier line encompasses the attainable or feasible portfolio combinations. Theoretically above the frontier are the unattainable returns.

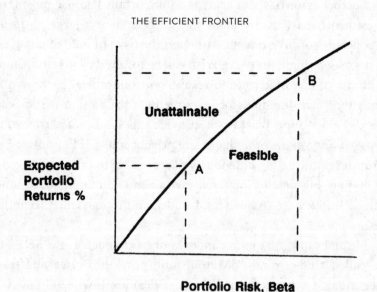

THE EFFICIENT FRONTIER

## *THE CAPITAL ASSET PRICING MODEL FOR STOCKS*

The *capital asset pricing model* (CAPM) determines the required rate of return of an investment by adding the unsystematic risk and the systematic risk of owning this asset. A simple formula, the CAPM says that the required rate of return is the risk-free rate plus a premium for unsystematic risk. That risk is the beta that you are already familiar with.

$$Ke = R_f + (K_m - R_f) \text{ Beta}$$

Required Return on an Equity Investment = Risk-Free Rate
+ (Avg. Market Return Rate − Risk-Free Rate) × Beta

Suppose you wanted to know in 2022 what IBM should return to be a worthwhile investment. The Value Line Survey told you that IBM had a conservative beta of exactly .84. The *Wall Street Journal* told you that the long-term risk-free U.S. Treasury bond pays a return of 4 percent. The final CAPM input requires some more homework. A study conducted since 1926 shows that the average return on the Standard & Poor 500 has exceeded the risk-free rate of investing in risk-free U.S. Treasury bonds by 7.4 percent. This is called the *market risk premium* (MRP). With those three CAPM inputs, an investment in IBM should return on average 10.2 percent.

$$4\% + (7.4\%) \,.84 = 10.2\%$$

Plugging many, many betas into the linear algebraic equation of the CAPM, you can generate a graph. That line is called the *security market line* (SML). In the IBM example, suppose that the return on IBM is actually 5 percent. That is less than the required rate of return determined by the CAPM. The theory suggests that a rational investor would sell IBM. If the return rate exceeded the required rate as determined by the CAPM, then the market is offering a bargain, and investors should buy the stock. It sounds great, but the CAPM tells

THE SECURITY MARKET LINE

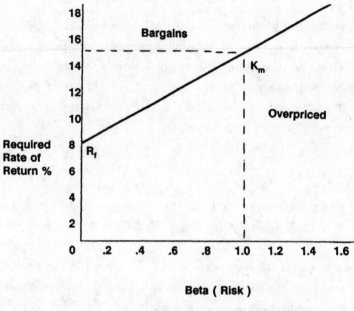

Beta ( Risk )

$R_f$ = Risk-free rate, $K_m$ = market rate

the required rate of return, not what an investment will actually return. For that you need tea leaves and a crystal ball.

The CAPM is the dominant model for estimating the cost of equity. Over 90 percent of Wall Street firms and all the financial advisers were employing this CAPM model in a 2013 survey.

## THE EFFICIENT MARKET HYPOTHESIS

The SML graph suggests that there are bargains in the market. But that begs the question "If the market is efficient, then how can there be bargains?" The *efficient market hypothesis* (EMH) alleges that to varying degrees the market reflects all current information. Therefore, no one can take advantage of market aberrations to "beat the market." Investors competing for profits are so numerous that quoted stock prices are exact indicators of value.

There are three degrees of belief in the efficiency of the market: *weak, semistrong,* and *strong.*

*Weak Form of Efficiency.* All information that caused past price movements is reflected in the current market price. Believing in the weak form means that no benefit is gained by charting stock price movements using *technical analysis* as a predictor of the future. However, by doing in-depth *fundamental analysis* about companies' operations and profitability, analysts can gain insights that will provide opportunities for big profits. Those gains are called *economic rents,* the excess returns over other investments with similar risk.

*Semistrong Form of Efficiency.* This camp believes that market prices reflect all *publicly* known information. Therefore, without insider information, no "abnormal" returns can be gained by poring over financial statements. The *Securities and Exchange Commission* (SEC) acts as a policeman to try to ensure that investors do not trade based on insider information. Believing in the semistrong form of efficiency means that fundamental analysis, conducted by reading financial statements and all public information, will not result in big gains. Insider trading is not gone. In 2022 an inside trader at Apple was caught trading their stock for five years with non-public financial information. The twist is that the person was an inside counsel responsible to enforce the ban on insider trading.

*Strong Form of Efficiency.* The true believers in market efficiency have faith that stock prices reflect all public and *private* information. That intense faith has been proven unfounded in many instances. The criminal trials of Ivan Boesky, Michael Milken, and Martha Stewart were well-publicized cases in which insider information was used to make profits that the public had no chance of making.

Research indicates that the *weak form* of market efficiency has held true over time. Naive beliefs in complete efficiency are not warranted. Stocks are generally fairly valued, yet some people deny even the weak form of the efficient market hypothesis. As mentioned, *chartists* or *technical* analysts graph price movements seeking patterns that will indicate price movement in the future. Meme stocks enthusiasts, for example GameStop, trade on message board information hoping that others will invest at higher prices regardless of financial fundamentals.

Investors that speculate that unforseen, hugely negative market events will happen are called *Black Swan* investors. When the market panics, they prosper.

## INVESTMENT TYPES AND VALUATION METHODS

In the QA chapter the concepts of discounted cash flows and net present value were covered in detail. A dollar held today is worth more than a dollar received in the future. That simple concept, applied to the cash thrown off by an investment, is in most cases the method used to value investments.

## THE BOND MARKET

A bond's value comes from the present value of its future cash flows. Bonds are issued by companies or governmental agencies to raise money at fixed rates of interest. Most pay interest, a *coupon,* semi-annually on the principal amount, called the *face* or *par value.* At the stated *maturity* date, the principal is repaid. Each 1 percent of interest rate is made of 100 basis points (BPS) and rate changes are quoted that way in the press.

In most cases the longer the maturity, the higher the interest rate that a company has to pay investors. Higher rates compensate investors for tying up their money for lengthy periods. Investors could miss out on higher returns if the market rates go higher; therefore, they must be compensated for that risk. The basic concept that higher rates accompany longer maturities is graphically depicted in what the investment world calls the *yield curve.* In 1992, it was up-

THE YIELD CURVE FOR U.S. TREASURY SECURITIES

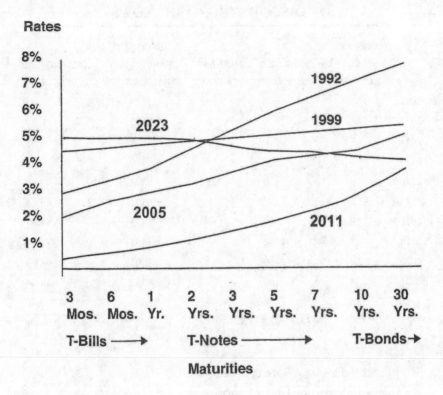

ward sloping with a 5 percent difference between short- and long-term interest rates. In 2005 the yield curve was sloping upward with a 2.5 percent difference, but at a much lower level of interest rates. In 2023 the yield curve was inverted: short-term rates were 1 percent *higher* than long-term rates, signaling an upcoming recession based on historical patterns.

*A Bond Valuation Example.* In 1991, Caterpillar Inc., the maker of heavy construction equipment, issued $200 million worth of 8 percent coupon bonds maturing in 2021. In June 2012, while the issue was still outstanding, the price for the bond was quoted in the *Wall Street Journal* as $100 for every $100 of face value. The value was determined not only by the rate of interest paid, but by three other factors:

## CATERPILLAR BOND VALUATION
## OF DISCOUNTED CASH FLOWS

| | INTEREST @ 8% COUPON | PRINCIPAL REPAYMENT | PAYMENT TOTAL × | DISCOUNT FACTORS @ 8% MARKET = | NET PRESENT VALUE |
|---|---|---|---|---|---|
| 2012 | $8 | $0 | $8 | .9259 | $7.41 |
| 2013 | 8 | 0 | 8 | .8573 | 6.86 |
| 2014 | 8 | 0 | 8 | .7939 | 6.35 |
| 2015 | 8 | 0 | 8 | .7350 | 5.88 |
| 2016 | 8 | 0 | 8 | .6806 | 5.44 |
| 2017 | 8 | 0 | 8 | .6302 | 5.04 |
| 2018 | 8 | 0 | 8 | .5835 | 4.67 |
| 2019 | 8 | 0 | 8 | .5403 | 4.32 |
| 2020 | 8 | 0 | 8 | .5002 | 4.00 |
| 2021 | 8 | 100 | 108 | .4632 | 50.03 |
| Total | $80 | $100 | $180 | | $100.00 |
| | | Face Value | | | Market Value |

The Stated Interest Rate (the *coupon* rate)
The Length of Time Until Maturity
The Risk of Default of the Issuer (investment researchers publish
    ratings)

The fact is that the market quote was $100. That indicated that the market valued the $100 payable in 2021, paying an 8 percent semiannual coupon, from a stable company at $100. The Moody's bond rating service confirmed a low default risk assessment by their A rating. Using the *net present value* concept, the cash thrown off by the bond, discounted at an 8 percent market discount rate in June 2012, equaled the bond's market value. Because the market rate equaled the coupon rate, investors paid neither a *premium* nor a *discount* on the face value of the Caterpillar bonds. The bonds had an 8 percent *yield to maturity* (YTM) on the $100 market value of the bonds.

Above is the calculation in detail; normally, however, you should use a calculator to do the math. Seeing it in this form helps you vi-

TIME AND DISCOUNT RATE EFFECTS ON PRESENT VALUE

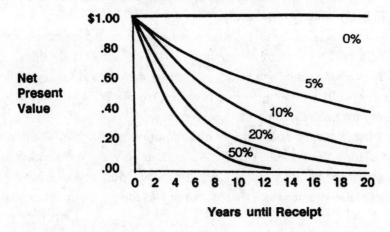

sualize the time value of money. If the market thought Caterpillar was on the verge of bankruptcy, or if the market interest rates on all investments skyrocketed in a period of high inflation, then investors might have required a 20 percent rate of return on their money. If that were the case, the $100 bond would have been worth only $49.69. The increased riskiness of the cash flows would reduce the bond's value. Conversely, a discount rate of 5 percent would have yielded a market price of $123.16. In that case an 8 percent coupon would be higher than the market rate and investors would pay a premium for the higher cash flows.

Graphically, cash discounted at higher rates is worth less. The further out the cash is received, the less it is worth to an investor today.

*Duration.* Another way of evaluating a bond is by calculating a bond's "average weighted maturity," called its *duration.* Duration is the time a bond takes to return half of its market price to the investor. It also measures the sensitivity of a bond to changes in market interest rates. The further in the future a bond is paid out, the more volatile its value. If a bond matures in one year, it would be considered a short-term bond; all the proceeds would be paid quickly and the bond's volatility would be low. Long-term bonds offer a fixed interest payout over many years. If market rates climb, an investor is locked into lower rates for a long time. As a consequence, the bond will be devalued dramatically.

In the case of the Caterpillar bond, it paid back 50 percent of the investors' $100 investment in nine years. That's the bond's duration. This is a long time for a bond; as a consequence, its value responded dramatically to swings in interest rates, from $49.65 with a 20 percent rate to $123.16 with a 5 percent rate.

Don't worry about the math—computers will do the calculations for you. As a Ten-Day MBA, you can now ask your broker not only for the bond's yield, but also for its duration, and he or she will know that you are more than a retiree looking for a safe investment.

*Other Types of Bonds.* There are five more types of bonds of note: zero coupon bonds, consuls, convertible bonds, callable bonds, and junk bonds.

A *zero coupon bond* bears no interest, but pays a lump sum at maturity. Investors value the bond the same way as one that pays interest, but there are no interest payments to discount.

A *consul* or *perpetuity* is a bond that never pays back the principal, but continues to pay interest forever. These bonds are unusual but they still are issued in the United Kingdom. The valuation technique is simple. The cash flow or interest payment is divided by the discount rate. A hypothetical example: London Telephone agreed to issue a $100 consul that pays $8 each year forever. If investors require a 10 percent rate of return, the value would be $80 ($8/.10)

$$\text{Value of a Perpetuity} = \frac{\text{Payment to be Received Forever}}{\text{Required Rate of Return}}$$

Sometimes a company adds an even more exciting provision called a *conversion feature* to bonds. *Convertible bonds* are convertible to common stock at a predetermined *conversion ratio*. For example, let's assume that Caterpillar's $1,000 face value of bonds was convertible into ten shares of stock or $100 per share. If Caterpillar's stock price rose above $100 per share, bondholders might consider converting their bonds into common shares of stock. Convertible bonds usually pay a lower interest rate than nonconvertible bonds, because they provide investors with an additional option.

The fourth type of bond is a *callable bond.* In some instances issuers want the option to buy back their bonds from the public if interest rates fall significantly after the issue date. In 1981, large corporations sold bonds paying 15 to 20 percent interest per year, the prevailing market rates. As interest rates fell later, in the 1980s and 1990s, the corporations that had included a *call provision* bought back their bonds at predetermined prices and issued new ones in the early 1990s paying 7 to 8 percent. This happened again in 2020 with sharply lower interest rates during the pandemic. Because call provisions limit unusually high rates of return, corporations have to pay a higher interest rate for the privilege of calling back the bonds.

The last classification, a high-yield bond, or so-called *junk bond,* is a bond that has a higher risk of default. Often their risk lies in that they may be *subordinated* to the claims of other bonds issued by a company. Junk bonds pay higher rates to investors, and most still pay their interest and principal on time. If the company does not have enough money to make payments on its borrowing, the subordinated debt holders get paid last.

Junk bonds have been around as long as there have been bonds. During the Civil War the Confederacy issued risky bonds that could be termed junk bonds. Billions of junk bonds were issued for takeovers in the late 1980s, by such well-known firms as RJR Nabisco, MCI, Macy's, and Metromedia. Junk bonds are not "junk"; they simply have a higher risk of default because they are issued by companies without stellar credit ratings.

## BOND VALUATION SUMMARY

Higher Risk of Default or Higher Market Rates → Higher Disc. Rate → Lower Bond Value

Lower Risk of Default or Lower Market Rates → Lower Disc. Rate → Higher Bond Value

Higher Coupon Rate or Shorter Maturity → Shorter Duration → Value Less Volatile to Mkt. Rate Chgs.

Lower Coupon Rate or Longer Maturity → Longer Duration → Value More Volatile to Mkt. Rate Chgs.

## THE STOCK MARKET

Stocks have no contractual terms of payment and no maturity. If earnings are adequate, most companies regularly pay dividends to stockholders. But there are no guarantees. Building on the teachings of accounting, equity ownership of a company entitles the owner to the *residual* claim on earnings and assets after all the other obligations, such as bonds, have been met. If there are no future earnings, there's little value to the stock. With adequate profits, bonds are paid on time and hopefully there is a portion left for stockholders.

Stocks are called by many names, depending on the company's characteristics.

### CLASSES OF STOCKS

| CLASS | DESCRIPTION | EXAMPLES |
|---|---|---|
| Growth Stocks | Rapidly Growing Companies | Alphabet, Tesla |
| Blue-Chip Stocks | Very Large Companies | Coca-Cola, Microsoft |
| Cyclical Stocks | Fluctuate Greatly with Economy | Ford, United Airlines |
| Penny Stocks | Risky, Small Companies with Low Share Prices | Jet Electro |
| Meme stocks | Low-priced stocks driven by social media frenzy | GameStop, AMC |

*The Dividend Growth Model.* One way that investment analysts try to value stocks is by valuing the dividend cash flow. This value model heavily weights dividend growth in its formula. However, it does not always yield a reasonable answer.

$$\text{Value per Share} = \frac{D}{(K - g)}$$

D = Annual Dividends per Share
K = Discount Rate or Required Rate of Return
g = Annual Dividend Growth Rate

The stock of Caterpillar Inc. is a good example. In 2022 the company paid a $4.80 yearly dividend per share. Using the CAPM equation, the required rate for Caterpillar's beta of .93 was 10.9 percent, the same as IBM's at the time [4% + 7.4% (.93) = 10.9%]. Caterpillar's board of directors had raised their dividend an average 5 percent for the last few years. With those inputs in the dividend growth model, the stock should have been worth $81.

$$\frac{\$4.80}{(.109 - .05)} = \$81.36 \text{ per share value}$$

But Caterpillar actually traded at $190 in June 2022. Either there must have been more than just dividends to the company, or the market had gone nuts. But probably not. Investors must also have valued the company's assets and future earnings as well.

How do analysts value technology companies that pay no dividends and some that make no money? There are no easy formulas, but the following are a few additional methods used by securities analysts to calculate value.

*Price-Earnings Ratio.* Analysts compare the ratio of the current stock price to the current or projected earnings per share (EPS). This *price-earnings ratio* (PE ratio) is probably the most widely used valuation method. It is simple. Everyone can divide price by earnings per share. Best yet, the EPS of most companies are widely published. If that ratio is in line with the industry of the business and with the market, then it may indicate the propriety of its current stock price. To illustrate the wide use of the PE ratio, the following was a stock picker's recommendation:

> Corestates Financial at $44, the old Philadelphia National Bank, has a low price-earnings multiple relative to other banks, and its dividend yield is higher than other banks mentioned. Strong buying interest exists.

The *PEG* ratio is a twist on the price-earnings ratio that factors in earnings growth. The PEG ration is calculated by dividing a company's PE by its projected long-term earnings growth rate. That growth projection is subject to a great deal of uncertainty. PEGs near or below 1.0 are considered possible bargains. In January 2005, Sina, an Internet software and service provider, traded at $30 and had an attractive PEG ratio of 0.6. By July 2011, the market had recognized the value, and Sina traded at $110 and had a PEG ratio of 5.

*Multiple of Book Value per Share.* This calculation using balance-sheet information divides the share price by the book value of assets per share. In 1992, ImClone Systems, a biopharmaceuticals company, sold at 331 times its book value. *Forbes* highlighted it as possibly overvalued, but the ratios of small, new companies are often unusual. Investors often value the potential success of start-up companies, not their current size. In this case, there was potential, as they developed a successful drug, Erbitux. Eli Lilly bought ImClone in 2008 for $70 a share, or eight times book value. Microsoft, an established growth company, for example, was priced at eleven times its book value in 2023.

*Price-to-Sales Ratio.* Stock price divided by sales is the formula. In 1999, eBay, Inc., the auction site, had a price-to-sales ratio of 1,681. With few sales, the multiple was large. Investors were buying the future of the Internet. As an established company in 2022, eBay had a sales-to-price ratio of three.

*Asset Value per Share.* When a company's assets value divided by the outstanding shares is more valuable than the price of the stock indicates, then analysts might overlook other ratios. The 1980s buy-out binge in oil stocks was due to their share prices being below the value of their oil and gas reserves. As a result, Getty, Gulf, Mesa, and Phillips engaged in a bidding war that made their shares soar.

*Multiple of Cash Flow per Share.* Some analysts value companies because of their ability to generate cash as measured by the company's cash flow statement. In Caterpillar's case, it produced $12.07 for each share outstanding in 2022. At $190 per share, the stock was priced at sixteen times cash flow. Looking forward, analysts projected cash flow $13.47 in 2023, and $15.23 in 2024 in later years, or twelve times the projected cash flow. That is where some bullish investors saw the value of Caterpillar. If a group of analysts valued the $15.23 cash flow per year in perpetuity at a 10.9 percent discount rate, the stock would have a net value of $140 (15.23/.109). To them, at $190 Caterpillar was a bit pricey.

In a stock market there are always buyers and sellers. Imbalances cause price movements. Many yardsticks of value exist, but the only one that truly matters is the current quote, no matter how crazy it may appear. If the market is willing to buy Caterpillar at $250, then *that* is its value. Of course, if there is more supply than demand, prices fall. But that's for our economics chapter.

*Preferred Stock.* This is the privileged cousin of common stock. Preferred shares, a hybrid of a bond and a common stock, are issued by many utilities and banks. Preferreds have the characteristics of a bond inasmuch as they pay a fixed dividend rate and have no voting rights. As in the case of common stocks, their dividends can only be paid if debt payments are made first, and there is no maturity. However, most issuers make provisions to purchase and retire their preferred stock over time. A preferred stock's claims on the assets of the firm are superior to common stock but are subordinated to debt.

Companies issue preferred stock when they want to borrow money but don't want to be contractually obligated to pay interest on time. Most preferred issues are *cumulative,* meaning that the total of all unpaid dividends must be paid before dividends on common stocks can be paid. Investors who like a more secure dividend, but like to have the benefits of partial equity ownership, choose preferred stocks.

## THE OPTIONS MARKET

Options are contractual rights to buy or sell any asset at a fixed price on or before a stated date. Options can be traded on real estate, bonds, gold, oil, currencies, mortgages, or even cryptocurrencies. An option is a way to gain control of a great deal of assets with little money. The opportunity for profits is high, and, accordingly, so are the risks.

Because these option rights are not the asset itself, they are called *derivatives.* Any security that is created that is valued based on the value of another is a derivative. Stock options, stock warrants, index options, commodity options, and commodity futures are examples.

Imagine G. R. Quick, a house buyer, who believes that prices are about to skyrocket. However, he needs six months to raise the down payment and get financing. A willing owner agrees to sell him his bungalow at $1,000,000, but wants $5,000 for the *option* to hold it off the market for six months. For six months Mr. Quick, the option holder, has the right, *but not the obligation,* to purchase the house for $1,000,000. If the real estate market falls, Mr. Quick can let his $5,000 option expire at a 100 percent loss.

But options can also be *very* profitable. If the bungalow increases in value to say $1,050,000, the return on the $5,000 option would be 1,000 percent. If he buys the house outright for $1,000,000, his return would be only 5 percent. The essence of options is to control the destiny of an asset with an investment of a fraction of that asset's value. The payoff is a leveraged payoff or a possible total loss if the underlying asset's value fluctuates.

Stock options work in the same way as in the real estate deal discussed. An *option* is "the right" to buy or sell a stock:

at a stated price — the *strike price*
by a certain date — the *expiration date*
at a cost for the privilege — the *option premium*

Options to purchase stocks are called *calls*. ("Call" in the stock
to buy.) Rights to sell a stock to somebody else are called *puts*. ("Put"
it to somebody else for sale.) The values of call and put options move
in opposite directions. If a stock price rises, then the value of a call
option to buy it, at a fixed price, increases. If a stock's price falls, its
call value decreases. Conversely, the value of a put option increases
when the underlying stock price falls and decreases when the stock
price increases.

On the Chicago Board Options Exchange (CBOE), the oldest
and largest exchange, traders buy and sell options on blocks of one
hundred shares of stocks in the same way as Mr. Quick bought an
option on real estate. Buyers of stock options buy the right to the
appreciation (calls) or depreciation (puts) of a stock for a period of
time. Sellers, called option *writers,* of *covered* options sell to buyers
the rights on the stocks that they own. If an option writer sells an
option on a stock not owned, the options are called *naked* options.
They are not covered.

There are two types of option valuations, *theoretical* and *market
value*. The theoretical value is the difference between the underlying stock's market price and the option's strike price. For example,
a call option to buy Nike at $95 when the market price of the stock

THE WAY OPTION VALUES FLUCTUATE

**Underlying Stock Price Movement**

|          | UP    | DOWN  |
|----------|-------|-------|
| **CALL** | Gain  | Loss  |
| **PUT**  | Loss  | Gain  |

is $100 would have a theoretical price of $5. However, options are written for extended periods of time. Therefore, the market value is the sum of the theoretical value plus a premium for the chance of profitable price movements until the expiration date. As the date of expiration approaches, there is less time for profits, so the premium erodes. On the expiration date, the option is settled for cash based on the optioned security's market value. The market value equals the theoretical value because there is no longer a premium for future gains.

*Option Valuations.* In 1973, Fisher Black and Myron Scholes published a model that became the industry standard for option valuations throughout the world. In the *Black-Scholes Option Pricing Model,* an option's calculated value is determined by five factors:

*Time until expiration* — The longer the optioned time, the more chance of a desired price movement. That's the time premium.

*The difference between the current stock price and the strike price* — The closer the strike price is to the current price the more probable it is that current price movements can meet or exceed it by the expiration date.

*The price volatility of the stock* — The more volatile the price movement of a stock, the more likely that a price movement could jump near the strike price.

*The market rate of interest on short-term government securities* — If the cost of financing the transaction is high, then the option price has to be higher to cover the handling costs of the transaction.

*Dividend payments on the stock* — Option owners do not collect the dividends on the underlying stock, but the stock price that influences the option price is affected.

One can calculate the approximate prices of calls and puts by placing these five inputs into a simple computer spreadsheet. Because everybody uses some form of the Black-Scholes model, the prices produced by these models are close to the market price. That is in sharp contrast to common stock valuations, in which investment analysts use thousands of methods to determine their own "correct" value.

*A Call Option Example.* Optimistic stock options traders buy calls to purchase stock if they believe the underlying stock will increase in the near term. For example, let's call our options trader Billy Peligro. On June 15, 2022, Billy saw Pfizer's common stock quoted at $54 per share in the *Wall Street Journal.* The call right to purchase one share of Pfizer by September at $55 traded at $2.69. Billy bet that Pfizer would trade significantly above $55 by September (SEP), and he paid $2.69 for the chance. If the option expired on the day of purchase in June, the option purchase price of $55 would have been "out of the money," by one dollar, and the option would be worthless. The value of a $55 call option of Pfizer graphically looks like a hockey stick. It varies with the stock price.

THE VALUE OF A PFIZER SEP $55 CALL OPTION

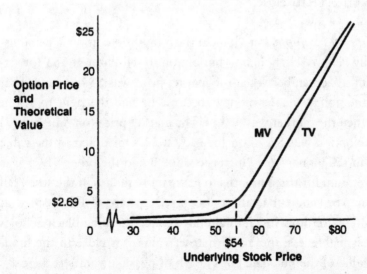

MV = option market value    TV = option theoretical value

THE VALUE OF A PFIZER SEP $55 PUT OPTION

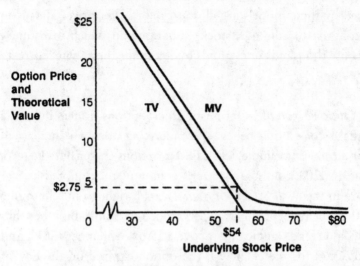

MV = option market value   TV = option theoretical value

But is $2.69 the correct price? Plugging the five factors of Pfizer's common stock and the particulars about the option into the Black-Scholes black-box spreadsheet, the outcome for your author was a $2.66 price. Pretty close!

*Put Option Example.* Let's look at the opposite situation, a pessimistic Billy Peligro. He bought a put option to sell Pfizer at $55 for settlement in September when the market price was $54 in June. That was one dollar "in the money" because he had the right to sell at $55 when the market was at $54. The market price (or "fair value") for the option was $2.75 on June 15, 2022. One dollar of the value was "in the money" (or "intrinsic value") and the other $1.75 was the premium for three months to make more money. If the stock fell further, Mr. Peligro had the right to sell a share of Pfizer stock at $55, no matter how low it might have gone. Checking Black-Scholes for reasonableness, the $2.75 market value was close to the modeled value of the put. The put's graph of possible values is the call's hockey stick in reverse.

*Options Strategies and Hedging.* Options are highly risky investments, but their risk can be reduced by *hedging*. Hedging is buying
an option to offset a possible decline in value in an owned investment. Like other options, it can be taken on many types of assets.
Suppose that a risk-adverse investor, Mr. Scared E. Cat, owned the
same share of Pfizer stock trading at $54, but because of the down-
side risk, he wanted to protect himself from a steep decline. The investor could have bought a three-month put option at a $50 strike
price for $1 in June 2011. The put would have ensured that he could
have sold his Pfizer share for at least $50 in the next three months.
The person who wrote the option believed that there was little risk
of that happening and was happy to take the $1 premium, hoping it
would have no value to Mr. Cat.

If Pfizer fell to $40, the put option that cost only one dollar
would be worth $10 at expiration. The put writer would be obli-
gated to pay up. For Mr. Cat, the option's $10 gain would partially
offset the $14 loss in the value of the stock from $54 to $40. That
is why many people view the options market as a way to shift risk
from one investor to another.

Option traders and portfolio managers use many options strategies in addition to simple hedges. Sophisticated investors combine
options and stocks in many ways, using *spreads, butterflies, condors,
straddles,* and *boxes.*

In addition to put options, an investor can *short* a stock if he or
she would like to bet that a stock's value will decline. In this transaction, you borrow the stock to sell it, with the hope of repurchasing it
later at a lower price. And just as with options, short selling can be
part of a hedging strategy. However, the short-selling speculators of
GameStop in 2020 were crushed in a *short squeeze* as meme stock
speculators bid up the stock to astronomical heights. Meme speculators forced the short-sellers to pay dearly to repurchase and close
their short positions.

## MORE ON DERIVATIVES

Derivatives are financial instruments that base their value on the value of other assets or variables. In addition to options already discussed, the most common derivatives are called *futures* and *swaps*. The underlying assets on which the derivatives are valued include stocks, commodities, currencies, and interest rates. They can also include other non-tradable items such as creditworthiness or even weather. When the underlying asset's value changes, the derivative's value changes in lockstep. As with the options described on Pfizer stock, investors can either hedge a risk or speculate on changes in asset values.

Derivatives called *futures* are contracts to buy commodities (such as gold, oil, or grain) or financial assets (such as the S&P 500 stock index) on a settlement date in the future. The contract can be settled on that date with either cash or the delivery of the commodity, depending on the contract. As the value of the underlying asset changes, the value of the future changes. Futures can be very risky because they are highly leveraged. Depending on the futures contract, investors can control 20 times the value of the asset with a *margin account* that is marked-to-market on a daily basis. If the asset's value moves down, the investor must supply more margin cash that day.

Using a derivative called a *swap*, a financial institution insures or "swaps" the risk of value changes of an asset with an investor or institution for a negotiated fee. Interest rate increases and bond payment defaults are the most common risks insured by swaps. Swap purchasers do not necessarily need to own the underlying asset involved; they may just be speculating that negative events will occur.

The financial crash in 2008 was caused by the collapse of real estate prices, but the derivatives made the crisis a meltdown. Large institutions, including insurance giant AIG, sold *credit default swaps* (CDS) to investors that insured bundles of residential mortgage debt, called *collateralized mortgage obligations* (CMO), against the risk of default. When the likelihood of higher-than-expected defaults increased, swap values increased to cover the losses, and AIG owed swap purchasers hundreds of billions of dollars. AIG thought the probability of high mortgage default was remote when it sold the CDSs, so it charged very little for the swap insurance contracts. Investors who believed the opposite eagerly bought the inexpensive CDSs. Ultimately the government had to take over AIG in 2008. Now everyone knows the term "toxic mortgage." See *The Big Short* movie quote in "*The Ten-Day MBA* Movie Guide" in Day 10: MBA Minicourses.

## FINANCIAL MANAGEMENT

How a company funds itself and maximizes the return on money raised from its shareholders or debt holders is the essence of *financial management*. MBAs who choose to go into financial management perform two major functions:

*Business Investment Decisions* — What assets should the firm own? In what projects should the business invest?

*Financing Decisions* — How should those investments be paid for?

### BUSINESS INVESTMENT DECISIONS

There are many investments that a company can make. It is a financial manager's job to help the management team evaluate investments, rank them, and suggest choices. The MBA term for such activity is *capital budgeting*.

In the quantitative analysis chapter, the Quaker Oats example described the techniques used to decide whether to invest in new cereal filling equipment. Quaker managers used discounted cash flows to calculate the net present value (NPV) of the project. In the marketing chapter, the decision to launch a new coffee brand was evaluated by a simpler measure, the payback period. Some investments, however, defy financial analysis. Charitable donations, for example, provide intangible benefits that financial managers alone cannot evaluate.

Investment decisions fall into one of three basic decision categories:

*Accept or Reject a Single Investment Proposal*
*Choose One Competing Investment over Another*
*Capital Rationing*—With a limited investment pool, capital rationing tells which projects among many should be chosen.

Each corporation uses its own criteria to ration its limited resources. The major tools that MBAs use are:

Payback Period
Net Present Value

*Payback Period Method.* Many companies believe that the best way to judge investments is to calculate the amount of time it takes to recover their investments:

Payback = Number of Years to Recover Initial Investment

Analysts can easily calculate paybacks and make simple accept-or-reject decisions based on a required payback period. Those projects that come close to the mark are accepted, and those falling short are rejected. For example, the managers of a small company may believe that all energy- and laborsaving devices should have a maximum three-year payback, and that all new equipment should "pay back" in eight years, whereas research projects should pay back in ten years. Those requirements are based on management's judgment, experience, and level of risk aversion.

By accepting projects with longer paybacks, management accepts more risk. The further out an investment's payback, the more uncertain and risky it is. The concept is similar to the measure bond investors use, *duration.* The longer it takes an investor to recover half of his or her bond investment, the riskier it is.

Payback period criteria are desirable because they are easy to calculate, use, and understand. However, they ignore the timing of cash flows, and accordingly, the time value of money. Projects with vastly different cash flows can have the same payback period. For example, a research project that repays a $100,000 investment evenly in $33,333 installments over three years has the same three-year payback as the single $100,000 return received at the end of three years.

Another shortcoming of using payback is that it ignores the cash flows received after the payback. What if the $100,000 research project with a three-year payback continued to churn out a stream of royalties forever as a result of a new invention? Clearly it would be worth much more than a project that had a onetime payout of $100,000 in the third year of the invention's life.

*Net Present Value Methods.* The same method used for valuing the cash flows of bonds and stocks is also used to value projects. It is the most accurate and most theoretically correct method.

The further in the future a dollar is received, the greater the uncertainty that it will be received (risk) and the greater the loss of opportunity to use those funds (opportunity costs). Accordingly, cash flows received in the future will be discounted more steeply depending on the riskiness of the project.

$$\text{NPV} = \text{Cash to Be Received} \times (1 + \text{Discount Rate})^{-\text{Number of Periods}}$$
(as calculated in tables in the appendix or by using business calculators and computers)

The ways in which a corporation wishes to fund itself are "financing" decisions independent of "investment" decisions. A *glaring* non-MBA mistake in evaluating projects is to use a discount factor equal to the cost of borrowing or cost of capital for the corporation as a whole. The individual projects that businesses may want to invest in are not as stable. Accordingly, financial managers *must* use a discount rate commensurate with the risk of the particular project. "Value" for the corporation as a whole is created by using the correct rate, but also choosing projects with returns above the corporation's cost of capital.

In the Quaker Oats factory example from the QA chapter, the cash flows looked as follows:

### 10% DISCOUNT

|         | CASH FLOW   | FACTOR  | NPV         |
|---------|-------------|---------|-------------|
| Today   | −$102,000   | 1.00000 | −$102,000   |
| Year 1  | $51,000     | .90909  | $46,364     |
| Year 2  | $51,000     | .82645  | $42,149     |
| Year 3  | $61,000     | .75131  | $45,830     |
| Total   | $61,000     |         | $32,343     |

The NPV method says that the project returned $32,343 in excess of the required rate of return for a project with that level of risk. Projects that have NPVs of $0 are also acceptable because they return the required rate. Those below zero are flatly rejected.

NPV has many advantages. It is flexible in making calculations that are useful in comparing different projects.

*Riskiness of Projects.* In calculating the NPV an analyst can use different discount rates. For example, if he or she considered the profits from Quaker Oats' new oatmeal filling equipment more risky, a 15 percent or 20 percent discount rate would value the project at $21,019 or $11,217 respectively.

*Unequal Lives of Projects.* An analyst does have the ability to value cash over many years by using different discount factors based on the risk-adjusted discount rate. The Quaker project could be compared with many other projects with cash flows of one year, ten years, or unlimited. The discount factor can be used to discount all cash flows to their present value for comparison.

*Scale Differences in the Size of Projects' Cash Flows.* The ability of the NPV method to discount cash at different amounts yields a "net" present value that is comparable among different-sized projects. The discount factor also values the cash flow at any time in the future.

Since capital needs to be rationed, what is an MBA to do if he or she needs to choose? NPV tells you the best projects, but not the best *group* of projects. The *profitability index* (PI) can be of help. The PI divides the NPV of the *future* cash flows by the initial investment. For example, the Quaker project has an index of 1.317.

$$\frac{\text{NPV of Future Cash Flows}}{\text{Initial Investment}}$$

$$\frac{\$46,364 + \$42,149 + \$45,830}{\$102,000} = 1.317$$

In situations where money is unlimited, all PIs above 1.00 would be accepted. All projects with a return over the risk-adjusted rate are attractive. With constrained resources, only the investment opportunities with the highest PI are chosen so that the group of investments may yield the highest NPV for the shareholders.

In those cases, it is up to the MBA analyst to try different combinations of the best projects using NPVs and PIs as guides to get the highest possible NPV for the entire group.

## BUSINESS FINANCING DECISIONS

A large number of MBAs devote their lives to finding the financing for the capital needs of businesses. The goal of corporate finance is to raise sufficient capital at the least cost for the level of risk that management is willing to live with. The risk is that a business will not be able to service its debt and will be forced into bankruptcy.

There are five basic ways of financing a company's needs:

Receive Credit from Suppliers
Obtain Lease Financing
Obtain Bank Loans
Issue Bonds
Issue Stock

*Supplier Credit.* Supplier credit is the easiest way that companies obtain financing. Companies buy goods and services and have anywhere from seven days to a year to pay their bills. When companies need more credit from suppliers, financial managers negotiate longer credit terms or larger credit lines. Cash managers can also *stretch their payables* to vendors by paying them late. In the case of Borders Books in 2011, vendors refused to extend them additional credit. The combination of creditors and debt holders forced the company into bankruptcy.

*Lease Financing.* Instead of buying equipment, many companies choose to lease equipment. This is a form of financing. Automobiles, computers, and heavy machinery can be financed for short periods or for longer periods. If the lease is for a shorter period, it is called an *operating lease.* At the end of the lease the property is still useful and is returned to the finance company. This is the case with two-year car leases.

Long-term leases are, in substance, ways of financing a purchase, rather than buying the temporary services of a piece of equipment. Such long-term leases are called *capital leases.* The *useful life* of the leased equipment is used up by the lessee, and at the end of the lease the equipment usually stays with the lessee for a *bargain purchase* price like $1. The accountants have specific rules that deal with the different kinds of leasing arrangements. For capital leases, the leased assets and the financing liability are recorded on the leasing company's books as though the company had bought the equipment outright.

*Bank Financing.* The next level of financing involves banks. Banks can loan money for long or short periods of time. If a company has a credit line or *revolver* with a bank, it draws down and pays back up to set limits of credit as cash is needed and generated by the business. The credit is often secured by the assets of the firm. If a business runs into trouble, it may not be able to pay the bank and go into bankruptcy.

When banks or investment analysts extend credit in the form of a loan or bond, they consider the *5C's of credit.*

- **Cash flow**—Are the cash flows enough to cover debt payments?
- **Collateral**—Is there enough collateral to repay the loan?

- **Conditions**—Are general economic conditions favorable for repayment?
- **Course**—Is the borrower headed on a good strategic course?
- **Character**—Is management qualified and morally inclined to honor repayment?

*Bond Issuance.* Bonds have fixed-interest-rate contractual payments and a principal maturity. The risk to the firm's owners comes if they cannot be serviced. In 1990 the Southland Corporation (7-Eleven stores) defaulted on its bond payment, and Ito-Yokado Corporation, the majority bondholder, exchanged its bonds for the ownership of the company and ousted the Thompson family from the company they had founded.

*The After-Tax Cost of Borrowing.* Interest payments for borrowing from vendors, bankers, or bondholders are tax-deductible, while dividends to shareholders are not. The after-tax cost of borrowing is the interest cost less the tax benefit.

After-Tax Cost of Borrowing = Borrowing Rate × (1 − Tax Rate)

The Caterpillar bond used in the earlier example continued to pay 8 percent interest on the issue maturing in 2021. In 2021 Caterpillar's corporate tax rate was projected at 29 percent. By deducting the interest expense on the tax returns, the company received, in effect, a 29 percent discount on its borrowing. The after-tax rate was 5.68 percent: 8% × (1 − .29).

As you learned in the accounting chapter, dividends are not tax-deductible, but interest payments are. That difference is an incentive for businesses to borrow rather than issue stock and pay dividends. This phenomenon is called a *tax shield* for borrowing. In the leveraged buyout binge of the 1980s, the tax shield was a spur to borrow huge amounts, such as the $26.4 billion Kohlberg Kravis Roberts borrowed to buy RJR Nabisco in 1989. That year the government subsidized this venture to the tune of approximately $800 million (26.4 × 10% × 30%). Not surprisingly, many taxpayers favor eliminating or restricting the tax subsidy for interest expenses to make acquisitions.

*Stock Issues.* Stock issues have noncontractual, non-tax-deductible dividend payments. Stock represents an ownership interest in the business and in all of its assets. If additional shares of stock are issued to raise cash, this is done at the expense of the current shareholders' ownership interest. New shareholders share their ownership interest equally on a per-share basis with the current shareholders. That is why analysts say that the new shares *dilute* the interest of existing shareholders.

Several markets are available to sell new stock issues: the New York Stock Exchange (NYSE) and the National Association of Securities Dealers Automated Quotations System (NASDAQ). When a stock is not listed on an exchange, but is *publicly* traded, it is traded *over the counter* (OTC). If a company's shares are not publicly traded, the company is said to be *privately* held.

Financial advisers called *investment bankers* assist in the sale of new shares in companies. Noted investment bankers such as Goldman Sachs Group and Morgan Stanley, employing many MBAs, work on these *initial public offerings* (IPOs) for large fees. These *I-bankers* assist in the preparation of the selling documents, called the *prospectus*. The prospectus outlines the issuer's history and business plans. The Securities Act of 1933 governs the disclosures required in this document.

*Special Purpose Acquisition Companies* (SPAC). In an effort to sidestep the SEC regulations concerning initial public offerings (IPO), financial engineers in 2015 created the Special Purpose Acquisition Company (SPAC). The SPAC's sponsors raised money from investors for an unspecified high-growth acquisition in the next two years. The SPAC shell company then became a publicly traded stock trading on the anticipation of a great deal. The acquired companies, such as Virgin Galactic and DraftKings, were merged into a SPAC; had access to the funds raised; and retained the majority of their ownership in the renamed publicly traded SPAC shares—a boom that started in

2015, peaked in 2020, and ended in a bust in 2022 when there was a lack of deals or when the new companies' values plunged.

*Repurchase and Reverse Repurchase Agreements.* A widely used form of very short-term, overnight debt financing and investments are called *repurchase agreements* (Repos) and *reverse repurchase agreements* (Reverse Repos). In a REPO transaction a borrower, usually a securities dealer, agrees to sell a government security overnight to an investor and then buy it back the next day with a night's interest added. In reverse REPOs the investing party, usually a corporation, buys the dealer's security overnight with cash, and sells it back and earns interest income on the overnight cash balances. This obscure market's trillion-dollar dance happens nightly.

*The Financing Mix's Risk and Reward.* The financing decisions in a corporation revolve around what is the best mix of debt and equity. That mix is called a company's *capital structure* policy. When managers make large changes in the debt-to-equity mix, they call it *restructuring*.

Theoretically, there is an optimal mix of debt and stock; however, there are no magic MBA formulas to establish that perfect ratio. MBAs can look to what worked in the past and to the mix of successful competitors. If the industry is cyclical, lighter debt loads are preferable in order to survive downturns. Good financial managers don't decide on a financing plan and forget it. Capital structures are *dynamic*. Decisions to shift the balance from equity to debt and back again should be continually reviewed to make sure the capital structure is appropriate at any given time.

Although there are no handy MBA formulas to solve once and for all the debt-versus-equity conundrum, there is a useful MBA acronym, FRICTO, whose initials stand for a useful checklist in sorting out capital structure issues.

*Flexibility.* How much financial flexibility does management need to meet *unforeseen* events, such as new competitors or lawsuits? For example, Johnson & Johnson never planned for the talc-based body powder litigation that cost the company dearly.

*Risk.* How much risk can management live with to meet *foreseen* events, such as downturns in the business cycle, strikes, and material shortages? Toy companies are known to produce hot toys that turn cold. Savvy managers should plan for the eventual sales drop-off by providing enough financial flexibility to survive the downturn. Accordingly, most toy companies have low debt-to-equity ratios.

*Income.* What level of interest or dividend payments can earnings support? Financial managers are required to forecast the results of operations to determine cash flows. Using those forecasts, and the degree of confidence a manager has in his or her projections, he or she can determine what level of payments the company can make.

*Control.* How much stock ownership does management want to share with outside investors? Many family business owners are leery of letting an outsider even know their income, let alone have a vote.

*Timing.* Does the debt market offer attractive rates? Has the market overvalued the firm's shares in the opinion of management? If so, then it makes sense to sell shares to the public. Conversely, if the stock is too cheap, then it is better to buy back shares from the public. After the crashes of 1987, 2008, and 2020, many firms took the opportunity to buy back their own shares. By reducing the number of shares outstanding, their share of debt financing grew as a portion of their capital structures.

In 1991 investors could not buy enough biotechnology stock. They paid high prices for even questionable start-ups. Smart managers tapped that market and sold shares to the eager public at high prices. In 1992, the days of easy money ended when biotech fell out of favor with investors. The same story repeated itself for Internet companies in 1995 until the meltdown in 2000. The real estate bubble peaked in 2006 and started to unravel in 2007. And again, more recently, the crypto-bubble peaked in 2020 and popped in 2022. A company's capital structure should be dynamic to take advantage of market conditions.

*Other.* Many other factors affect the paths managers take. At times, a company just can't find a bank to lend money, forcing an equity choice. In other circumstances interest rates are just unaffordable, forcing an equity choice. The reasons for capital structure decisions are many.

Key to financial structure is the discussion of ratios. In the accounting chapter, I explained the concept of *financial leverage.* Companies that maintain high levels of debt and little equity *leverage* their earnings for shareholders if there are profits. There are simply fewer shares to divide income by, yielding higher earnings per share. Conversely, highly leveraged firms wipe out the entire value of their equity when earnings falter and interest payments eat up all the profits.

Managers of highly leveraged firms must decide whether it is worthwhile to risk bankruptcy if their cash flow projections don't pan out in order to offer high returns to their shareholders. The Thompson family guessed wrong with 7-Eleven. Maybe if the Thompsons had used FRICTO, they might have avoided their losses?

The market value of shares already issued is also related to the risk of a firm's capital structure. If investors believe that debt levels are excessive, then they will pay less for the company's shares, since the debt payments could put earnings in jeopardy. Investors will also discount the market value of a company's debt for risk. That was the case with highly leveraged companies such as AMC, Norwegian Cruise Line, and American Airlines in the pandemic stock panic in early 2020. Many investors felt uncomfortable with the riskiness of their capital structures and avoided both the debt and equity of these highly leveraged companies.

*Modigliani and Miller,* a famous duo from MBA academia, created a series of "propositions" that discussed how debt affects the values of firms. In 1958, Franco Modigliani and Merton Miller did their pioneering work on the effect of debt financing with and without a tax advantage. In a perfect world, the more debt the better. The value of the firm increases with higher debt levels. However, in the real world, as seen in the previous paragraph, investors do consider the risk of insolvency in their valuations of both debt and equity.

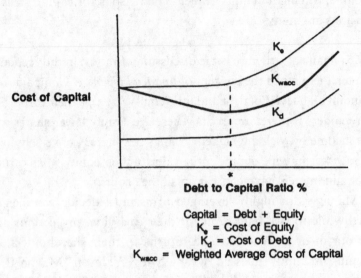

OPTIMAL CAPITAL STRUCTURE

The Cost of Capital

Capital = Debt + Equity
$K_e$ = Cost of Equity
$K_d$ = Cost of Debt
$K_{wacc}$ = Weighted Average Cost of Capital

OPTIMAL CAPITAL STRUCTURE

The Value of the Firm and the Weighted Average Cost of Capital

Capital = Debt + Equity

To summarize, the higher the percentage of debt to total capital, the higher a company's value, to a point. At the point where the risk of bankruptcy becomes significant, values fall. The cost of financing decreases as a company adds lower-cost tax-shielded debt to displace the higher returns required by equity investors. But like stockholders, debt holders become nervous at a certain point and require higher rates of return to compensate them for their risk. Study the two graphs on page 246 that illustrate the workings of capital structure.

*A Detailed Capital Structure Decision Example.* Although choosing the optimal capital structure is difficult, financial managers try to put together some numbers to make choices. If you are curious about the details and want to graduate from the *Ten-Day MBA* "cum laude," read on. If not, just skip to the next section, about "Dividend Policy." Making capital structure decisions involves a two-step process:

1. Calculate the WACC (weighted average cost of capital).
2. Value the *free cash flows* of the company, the value of the firm.

The first step is to calculate the *weighted average cost of capital* (WACC) of the entire firm by using the following formula and calculating a number of variables. The cost of equity ($K_e$) is the most difficult.

$$WACC = K_d (1 - t) \left( \frac{\text{(Market Value of Debt)}}{\text{Total Debt and Equity}} \right)$$

$$+ K_e \left( \frac{\text{(Market Value of Equity)}}{\text{Total Debt and Equity}} \right)$$

$$t = \text{tax rate}$$
$$K_d = \text{cost of debt}$$
$$K_e = \text{cost of equity}$$

Review the formula. Notice that the WACC uses the market values of debt and equity. The market is the true measure of how current bondholders and shareholders value their investments. The cost of debt can be obtained from the company's treasury department or can be found in the footnotes of the financial statements. It takes large boosts in debt financing to change the cost of debt. However, the cost of equity is a bit more complex to figure out.

The cost of equity heavily depends on the leverage of the firm. Because leverage means risk, we can use beta from the *capital asset pricing model* (CAPM). The CAPM helps calculate the required return on equity under different leverage scenarios.

$$K_e = R_f + (K_m - R_f) \times \text{Beta}$$

$$(K_m - R_f) = \text{Risk Premium}$$

The risk measure, beta, changes according to the risk of leverage. Financial MBAs take the current levered beta and unlever it to a no-debt, *unlevered* state (Step A), then lever it back up to any hypothetical capital structure (Step B).

Step A

$$\text{Beta}_u = \frac{\text{Beta}_l}{(1 + (1 - \text{tax rate}) \times \frac{\text{Debt}}{\text{Equity}})}$$

Step B

$$\text{Beta}_l = \text{Beta}_u \times (1 + (1 - \text{tax rate}) \times \frac{\text{Debt}}{\text{Equity}})$$

l = levered structure with debt
u = unlevered structure without debt

To illustrate: The treasurer of Leverco, Inc., wants to decide whether to choose a 0 percent, 25 percent, or 50 percent debt capital structure. To do so, he has laid out the facts and calculations in the following columns of numbers. The conclusion is the Leverco should have a 50 percent debt / 50 percent equity capital structure. That's the structure that maximizes the value of the firm while minimizing the WACC.

The same calculations demonstrated in Leverco's case were used to derive the two theoretical graphs of the "Optimal Capital Structure" on page 246. The first is the calculation of the weighted

# CAPITAL STRUCTURE DECISION CALCULATION
## LEVERCO, INC.
### SCENARIOS

| | 0% Debt | 25% Debt | 50% Debt |
|---|---|---|---|
| Book Value of Debt Ratio | | | |
| Book Value of Debt | $0 | $2,500 | $5,000 |
| Book Value of Equity | 10,000 | 7,500 | 5,000 |
| Market Value of Debt | $0 | $2,500 | $5,000 |
| Market Value of Equity | 10,000 | 8,350 | 6,700 |
| Market Value Debt Ratio* | 0% | 23% | 43% |
| Pretax Cost of Debt | .07 | .07 | .07 |
| Tax Rate | .34 | .34 | .34 |
| After-Tax Cost of Debt* Pretax Cost × (1 − t) | .0462 | .0462 | .0462 |
| Unlevered Beta | .8 | .8 | .8 |
| Levered Beta* Using the Step B formula | .8 | .958 | 1.194 riskiest |
| Cost of Equity* Using the CAPM formula: $K_e = R_f +$ Levered Beta × (Risk Premium) $K_e = .06 +$ Levered Beta × (.074) | .12 | .13 | .15 riskiest |
| WACC* Using WACC formula given | .12 | .11 | .105 least cost |
| Annual Cash Flow Before Interest and Taxes *"Free Cash Flow"* | $2,000 | $2,000 | $2,000 |
| Value of Company* (Value Cash Flow as a perpetuity) Free Cash Flow / WACC | $16,667 | $18,181 | $19,047 highest value |

*Denotes a calculation using a formula provided and historical values.

Adapted from "An Introduction to Debt Policy and Value," Case UVA-F-811. Copyright © by the Darden Graduate Business School Foundation, Charlottesville, Virginia.

average cost of capital. The second graph, using the lowest WACC shown, describes the maximum value of the firm. If you wish, you can try to recompute the calculations that are noted with an asterisk (*). These are the same computations that MBAs throughout the world use for capital structure decisions.

*Dividend Policy.* Financial managers must decide how much of a firm's profits should be paid out as dividends and must determine the size of dividends per share. This is called *dividend policy.*

To guide them in their policies, financial managers use at least two measures—*dividend yields* and *dividend payout ratios.* The market plays a big role in determining the *dividend yield* since it is derived by dividing the annual dividend payment by the current share price. Dividends may also be paid out as a certain percentage of earnings, called the *dividend payout ratio.*

$$\text{Dividend Yield} = \frac{\text{Annual Dividend}}{\text{Market Price per Share}}$$

$$\text{Dividend Payout Ratio} = \frac{\text{Annual Dividend}}{\text{Net Income per Share}}$$

Dividends are extremely important because they show clearly the cash-generating ability of the firm. Many analysts value companies based on the dividend cash flows. You saw that valuation method with the Dividend Growth Model earlier in this chapter.

Investors love stable, steadily growing dividends and hate any cuts. Therefore, managers try to avoid swings in dividend payouts at all costs. If an MBA miscalculates the ability of the company to maintain a dividend his or her job will be in real jeopardy.

There are five questions that astute MBAs ought to mull over as they formulate a policy that may directly affect their careers.

*Can the company do a better job by investing its earnings back into the firm than investors could by investing elsewhere?* If a company is growing and has many exciting investment opportunities, dividends should be small and earnings should be used internally.

*Who is your stockholder?* Do widows and orphans depend on your dividends for their incomes? This is the case with utility stocks, but not with start-up companies.

*What will stockholders' reaction be to any changes in dividend payments?* Changes in dividend payments are a powerful signal to investors. Investors react violently to any cuts in dividends, since they signal that the company is in trouble. Increases are not such a big deal. More often than not, dividend increases are expected and greeted with little fanfare. Increases in dividends show management's confidence that the business's earnings are strong enough over the long term to sustain an increased payout.

*What is the degree of financial leverage of the company?* To ensure that dividends will not be interrupted, companies should see to it that they can comfortably pay the dividends investors expect and demand.

*What is the growth strategy of the company?* Growth companies usually pay little to no dividends. They need cash to finance their own growth. Biotechnology companies, for example, retain all their cash to support long-term research needs.

If a company is strapped for cash and yet still wants to make investors happy, it can pay a *stock dividend*. This is a dividend that the company pays in shares of the company, not cash. Such dividends usually range from 2 to 5 percent of shares owned. For example, if you owned one hundred shares, you would receive two to five new shares. Investors end up with a greater number of shares, but since all shareholders receive the same percentage share dividend, their percentage ownership of the firm remains the same.

If a stock price is high, the company can also have a *stock split,* giving two or three shares for every share owned. It makes the stock more affordable and makes investors happy, but the percentage ownership remains the same. For very high-priced tech stocks, 2020 was a banner year for stock splits; both Google and Amazon split twenty for one and Tesla three for one.

# MERGERS AND ACQUISITIONS

Mergers and acquisitions (M&A) is one of the most exciting areas of finance. The same investment bankers who help companies raise money also help companies spend it. Many highly paid MBAs work in this field. "Strategic" reasons and methods for M&A are covered in the strategy chapter. This chapter will cover the legitimate financial reasons for mergers and acquisitions.

### Diversify the Company

Many companies attempt to lower risk by owning other businesses. Philip Morris renamed itself Altria and bought Kraft, General Foods, and Miller Brewing because it wanted to diversify. Tobacco usage was declining, lawsuits loomed, and new regulation limiting advertising was pending. Altria has since spun off those companies and bought UST to concentrate solely on tobacco, more business for dealmakers.

### Improve Sales and Earnings

AB InBev, the leader in brew, owned 630 beer brands in 150 countries. It decided to greatly expand sales and earnings by buying Anheuser-Busch in 2008 and SABMiller in 2016. Their brand-management expertise served them well in enhancing the values of these acquisitions.

### Purchase an Undervalued Company

Based on market conditions, corporations can sometimes buy companies at a bargain. Companies may also be a bargain if investors do not recognize the potential of valuable assets on the books valued at cost. Ted Turner bought MGM/United Artists in 1986 because MGM had an extensive movie library of classics that Turner felt was undervalued and not fully exploited. Real estate, timber, patents, copyrights, and other value could be overlooked or misjudged by the market.

### Lower Operating Costs

When companies merge, many cost savings are possible. With the absorption of a company, some of the acquired company's corporate overhead expenses can be cut. In manufacturing mergers, factories can produce larger quantities more efficiently.

Many companies are formed to consolidate fragmented industries by "rolling up" many mom-and-pop outfits, in hopes of achieving efficiencies. Office supply businesses, veterinary practices, funeral homes, Amazon sellers, and car dealerships have been rolled up.

## TYPES OF ACQUISITIONS

If two companies decide to join forces to become one company, this is called a *merger*. When Sperry and Burroughs merged in 1986, the merged entity was named Unisys.

If one company buys another company, it is called an *acquisition*. If both parties agree to the purchase, it is called a *friendly acquisition;* if not, it is called a *hostile takeover.*

Smaller companies that are attractive takeover candidates often agree to be purchased in friendly takeovers. Facebook (Meta) bought Instagram in 2012.

In other cases, the purchase can be nasty. In 1984, T. Boone Pickens notoriously tried to buy Phillips Petroleum in an unsuccessful hostile takeover. The management of Phillips was so opposed to the idea that in 1985 it borrowed $4.5 billion to buy back 47 percent of its common stock. This thwarted Pickens's efforts because it borrowed against the same assets that he was planning to mortgage.

The fourth type of acquisition that I have mentioned several times already in this chapter is the *leveraged buyout* (LBO). Many lenders are willing to loan money to takeover artists, such as leverage buyout and private equity funds. In the same way that a mortgage company makes a loan to a home buyer for a down payment of only 5 percent, banks, insurance companies, and bond investors lent money to these financiers to buy companies. The company that emerges from a leveraged buyout carries a high level of debt on which it must pay interest and principal.

## THE VALUATION PROCESS

To engage in M&A, you must assess the value of the targets. Cash flow is the main consideration. A business's cash flows are the result of operations, investing, and financing activities (the same activities that the accountant's statement of cash flows describes). In the accounting chapter, I used the example of tiny Bob's Market. By adding a few zeros to the numbers, it could be Safeway or Kroger. Because you are already familiar with Bob's Market, this section will continue with that example.

The total value of a company is called its *enterprise value* (EV). It is the present value of its projected cash flows. A company's EV is equal to its equity value (total outstanding shares × current market price) owned by shareholders, plus interest-bearing debt held by debt holders, less its surplus cash and marketable investments held beyond the firm's operating needs. Conversely, the equity would be equal to the company's EV less its debt plus its surplus cash and marketable investments.

Think of the enterprise value as the theoretical total takeover price. In the event of a buyout, an acquirer would have to pay shareholders for their equity and take on the company's debt. The market value of the equity may be different from an analyst's calculation of value based on cash flows projections, but that is how investors find opportunities.

Five steps are involved in calculating and evaluating a business's cash flows:

1. Analyze operating activities.
   Forecast the income statement; sales, cost of goods sold, selling, general, and administration expenses.
2. Analyze the investments necessary to replace and to buy new property, plant, and equipment.

3. Analyze the capital requirements of the firm.
   Determine the corporate working capital requirements.
4. Project the annual operating cash flows and terminal value of the firm.
5. Calculate the NPV of those cash flows to calculate the firm's value.

MBAs use many techniques or approaches to value firms. With all the flair a marketer displays in putting together a marketing strategy, finance jocks show their stuff in M&A valuations. The table below is one popular simplified method used by many in the financial community.

*1. Analyze operating activities and the firm's capital spending requirements.*
The first thing is to forecast sales and calculate the gross margins on sales and other operating expenses. But financial analysts must do more than just look at numbers. They must also review the industry, the competition, the markets for raw materials, and management's

### BOB'S MARKET, INCOME STATEMENT
### FOR THE YEAR ENDING DECEMBER 31, 2024
### (IN THOUSANDS)

|  |  | % OF SALES |
|---|---|---|
| Sales | $5,200 | 100% |
| Cost of Goods Sold (COGs) | 3,900 | 75 |
| Gross Margin | $1,300 | 25% |
| Selling, General, and Administrative (SG&A) | 1,256 | 24% |
| Earnings Before Interest and Taxes (EBIT) | $44 | |
| Taxes | 13 | |
| Net Operating Profit After Tax (NOPAT) | 31 | |
| Add Back: Depreciation (not a cash use) | 3 | |
| Less: Equipment Purchases | 3 | |
| Free Cash Flow | $31 | |

plans to run and grow the business. All these factors will affect the cash flow of business.

Discussions with Bob, his accountant, and his assistant manager revealed that the business is healthy and they expect sales to grow by 10 percent a year over a four-year period and then stabilize. They are confident that they will maintain a gross margin of 25 percent or a variable 75 percent cost of sales. They also believe that their SG&A expenses will remain a steady variable 24 percent of sales. The depreciation for equipment, which does not cost cash, can be added back, but Bob believes that he will be upgrading the store each year by reinvesting the $3,000 in new store fixtures. With that information, the cash flow forecast would look as shown below.

*2. Analyze the investments necessary to replace and to buy new property, plant, and equipment.*

Don't be shy. Consult with the engineers, purchasing department, and the accountants to get a good estimate of costs and useful lives.

## CASH FLOW PROJECTIONS (IN THOUSANDS)

|  | PRIOR YEAR | YEAR 1 | YEAR 2 | YEAR 3 | YEAR 4 |
|---|---|---|---|---|---|
| Sales | $5,200 | $5,720 | $6,292 | $6,921 | $7,613 |
| COGS @ 75% | 3,900 | 4,290 | 4,719 | 5,190 | 5,709 |
| Gross Margin @ 25% | $1,300 | $1,430 | $1,573 | $1,731 | $1,904 |
| SG&A @ 24% | 1,256 | 1,373 | 1,510 | 1,661 | 1,827 |
| EBIT | $44 | $57 | $63 | $70 | $77 |
| Taxes @ 30% | 13 | 17 | 19 | 21 | 23 |
| NOPAT | 31 | $40 | $44 | $49 | $54 |
| Add Back Depreciation | 3 | 3 | 3 | 3 | 3 |
| Less Equipment Purchases | 3 | 3 | 3 | 3 | 3 |
| Free Cash Flow | $31 | $40 | $44 | $49 | $54 |

*3. Determine the working capital needs of the business.*

Businesses need cash to operate. The level of working capital is most often a function of the volume of sales. The more sales that are generated, the greater the cash needs for making change at the cash registers and purchasing inventory. This need is balanced somewhat by the credit that vendors increasingly extend as the market's purchases from them grow in volume. This is an important part of the process; failing to consider the working capital needs could result in a cash squeeze.

When we look back at the balance sheet of Bob's Market, we see that Bob had $115,000 in current assets and $87,000 in current liabilities. That is a net working capital position of $28,000 (115 – 87).

Bob says that every week he needs 28 cents for every dollar of sales ($28,000/[$5,200,000 annual sales/52 weeks per year]). That covers his cash needs for inventory and register money offset by the additional financing extended by his grocery vendors. Added to the valuation calculation, the cash flow projection would look as follows:

## CASH FLOW PROJECTION (IN THOUSANDS)

|  | YEAR 1 | YEAR 2 | YEAR 3 | YEAR 4 |
|---|---|---|---|---|
| Free Cash Flow | $40 | $44 | $49 | $54 |
| Less Additional Working Capital Needs * | 3 | 3 | 4 | 4 |
| Net *Free Cash Flow* | $37 | $41 | $45 | $50 |

* (Sales / 52) × 28% – Prior Year's Working Capital Level

*4. Determine the terminal value of the firm.*

A business is presumed to be a *going concern* that will continue to operate indefinitely into the future. By valuing the cash flow to a certain point in time, you are ignoring ongoing value. That is why at the end of the financial projection, a *terminal value* must be calculated and added to the cash flow valuation. Trust me, it's complicated.

At Bob's Market the fourth year's cash flow was $50,000. If that cash is forecasted to be the same year after year, you could use the same valuation method that is used to value a perpetuity.

$$\text{Terminal Value} = \frac{\text{Terminal Cash Flow}}{(\text{Discount Factor} - \text{Growth})}$$

The proper discount factor to use in this case is the weighted average cost of capital (WACC). We use WACC because the *free cash flow* of the company is available to pay interest on debt *and* to pay dividends to equity holders. Therefore the proper discount factor takes into account the firm's entire capital structure, its debt *and* equity.

Bob's Market's capital structure is conservative. Its balance sheet lists only $10,000 of debt and $45,000 of equity. Its debt carries an interest rate of 10 percent. The cost of equity can be calculated using the Capital Asset Pricing Model. Using a historical long-term risk-free Treasury rate of 6 percent, the risk premium of 7.4 percent, and a .85 beta representing the lower risk of a low-debt grocery store, the cost of equity is 12.3 percent.

$$K_e = R_f + (K_m - R_f) \text{ Beta}$$

$$12.3\% = 6\% + (7.4\%)\ .85$$

Plugging the cost of equity into the WACC equation, the firm's weighted average cost of capital is 13 percent.

$$\text{WACC} = K_d(1 - t) \left( \frac{\text{Market Value of Debt}}{\text{Total Debt and Equity}} \right)$$

$$+ K_e \left( \frac{\text{Market Value of Equity}}{\text{Total Debt and Equity}} \right)$$

$$11.3\% = 10\% \ (1 - .30) \left( \frac{\$10,000}{\$55,000} \right) + 12.3\% \left( \frac{\$45,000}{\$55,000} \right)$$

Putting it all together in a valuation, the terminal value cash flow calculation would be:

$$\text{Terminal Value} = \frac{\text{Year 4 Free Cash Flow}}{\text{WACC} - \text{growth}}$$

$$\$442,477 = \frac{\$50,000}{11.3\% - 0\%}$$

*5. Calculate the NPV of those cash flows to calculate the firm's value.*

Add the terminal value to the present value of the first three years' projected cash flows, and the entire value of the firm can be calculated as follows:

### NET PRESENT VALUATION OF FREE CASH FLOWS
### (IN THOUSANDS)

|  | YEAR 1 | YEAR 2 | YEAR 3 | YEAR 4 |
|---|---|---|---|---|
| Free Cash Flow | $37 | $41 | $45 | $442 |
| Discount Factor @ 11.3% | .9010 | .8118 | .7315 | .6592 |
| Net Present Value | 33 | 33 | 33 | 291 |
| Total NPV | $390 | | | |

That's it! The grocery store's enterprise value is $390,000. The $5,000 in cash held by the store is not surplus cash; Bob needs it in the registers and to operate. (Cash is an asset on Bob's balance sheet shown in the accounting chapter.) To find Bob's equity value, take the enterprise value of $390,000 less the outstanding bank debt of $10,000 (also on his balance sheet), and that equals $380,000. That is what a takeover artist would expect to pay Bob for his store and assume its debt. That is how MBAs value companies large and small. Yes, it's a bit tedious, but mathematically not difficult to calculate. By keeping M&A a mysterious process, MBAs can charge more for their M&A services. Now you have the inside story.

## ADDITIONAL THINGS MBAS INCLUDE
## IN THEIR VALUATIONS

The valuation of Bob's Market assumes that the grocery store will be operated as Bob said it would. MBAs sometimes have different ideas. Companies being analyzed for potential acquisition are just like meat in a butcher shop—cut, sliced, and ground up as necessary. Analysts investigate the company from all angles. MBAs look at any opportunity to improve operations, lower expenses, and increase cash flow. They consider the sale of assets. The process is colored by the type of acquisition it is: merger, friendly, hostile, or leveraged. If the company is being taken over by a new management, then many changes are possible and likely. If the purchase is made with a great deal of debt, the new owners will want to increase cash flow and sell assets as soon as possible to pay off the debt incurred in purchasing the company. A sampling of things new owners will look for in these situations are:

"GOOD NEWS!
IT'S NOT A TAKEOVER, MERELY SOMEONE TAKING THE COMPANY FOR A JOYRIDE."

- Wage Concessions, Break Labor Unions
- Layoffs
- Lower Production Costs
- Reduce Working Capital Needs
    Lower Inventory
    Lower Receivables
    Increase Payables
- Gain Access to Employees' Pension Money
- Sell Real Estate
- Sell Patents and Rights
- Sell Divisions, Subsidiaries, Product Lines
- Sell Unnecessary Luxuries for Executives (jets, company apartments)

*The MBA Touch: Asking "What If?"* All the steps outlined can be investigated and plugged into mathematical formulas and spreadsheets. Analysts have to make many informed guesses. The real contribution an MBA can make to the process is not only an accurate evaluation of specific company information, but an experienced evaluation of the external factors that may affect the cash flows forecasted. How would a change in product costs affect the forecasted cash flows? How could the competitive environment in the industry affect sales? What if?

A proper MBA forecast of cash flows includes variations or "sensitivities" of key assumptions, so that decision makers can assess the risk inherent in the cash flows they are forecasting. The use of an Excel spreadsheet is imperative and its "Data-Table" function is the MBA tool to perform variation analysis. If you're not familiar with it, consider yourself computer illiterate.

In the airline industry, for instance, fuel prices, fares, and passenger load factors can produce swings in cash flows. Variations in key assumptions such as these three items dramatically change valuations and cash flows. In a leveraged buyout, owners are counting on projected cash flows to pay interest on the debt they carry. If they are caught short of cash, companies go into bankruptcy.

## *MAKING A BID*

MBA calculations and forecasts are fine and dandy, but they are often ignored. Sometimes the thrill of the hunt overcomes buyers, and they act like bidders in the heat of an art auction Also called the *winners curse*, the winner is often the one who overpays. Instead of a net-present-value cash-flow valuation, bidders use simpler rule-of-thumb methods, a multiple of earnings, multiple of EBITDA, multiple of NOPAT, or multiple of sales. In leveraged buyouts, the bid often simply represents the maximum amount of financing the acquisitor can obtain, or the maximum debt the targeted company's cash flow can carry. People differ, and accordingly, they have different motivations and methods in their M&A quests.

## FINANCIAL OVERVIEW

Simply stated, there are two main functions in the financial world: buying and selling. Businesses require funding; therefore, they either sell equity shares in their companies (stocks), or fixed-interest-payments securities (bonds). The investment community values these securities and buys and sells them.

The theoretical basis for financial analysis is the risk/reward equation, in which higher risks are associated with higher returns. Returns are calculated by determining the amount and the timing of cash flows.

The guiding principle of financial management is to maximize the firm's value by financing cash needs at the least cost possible, at a level of risk that management can live with.

## KEY FINANCE TAKEAWAYS

*Present Value* — The value of a dollar received in the future is less than a dollar on hand today. There is a time value of money.

*Beta*—A measure of risk inherent in a security or a portfolio of securities as it reacts to general market movements

*The Efficient Frontier*—The graph depicting the highest portfolio returns for a given risk level

*The Capital Asset Pricing Model*—$K_e = R_f + (K_m - R_f)$ Beta

*Duration*—The time it takes for a bond to pay back half of an investor's investment

*Bond Value Fluctuations*—If market interest rates go up, bond values go down, and vice versa.

*The Dividend Growth Model*—Value = $D/(K - g)$

*Call Option*—The right to purchase an asset at a fixed price for a limited amount of time

*Put Option*—The right to sell an asset at a fixed price for a limited amount of time

*The After-Tax Cost of Borrowing*—After-Tax Rate = Borrowing Rate × $(1 - \text{tax rate})$

*Capital Structure*—The mix of debt and equity of a company

*FRICTO*—Flexibility, Risk, Income, Control, Timing, and Other matters, the checklist to be considered in making capital structure decisions

*The Optimal Capital Structure*—One that minimizes the weighted average cost of capital and maximizes the value of the firm

*Enterprise Value (EV)*—The total value of a company

# Day 7

# OPERATIONS

*Operations Topics*

The History of Operations Research

The Problem Solving Framework

Flow Diagrams

Linear Programming

Gantt Charts

Critical Path Method

Queuing Theory

Inventories

Economic Order Quantities

Material Requirements Planning

Supply Chain

Quality

Information Technology

Operations is the only MBA subject that concerns itself with actually making products and providing services—the ultimate purpose of business. That is the line Production and Operations Management (POM) professors deliver each year to incoming MBAs. It must fall on deaf ears, since most MBAs go into finance, marketing, and consulting. It may be that recruiters feel MBAs are not sufficiently trained to be worth the high salaries paid in their plants and factories. From my interviews with recruiters and students, lack of interest on both sides is responsible for the lack of operational-bound MBAs.

Operational subjects are not all engineering and numbers. POM classes also have a humanistic side. The technical or quantitative approach presents students with a variety of mathematical tools with which to attack operational problems in a clinical fashion. The humanistic approach teaches students to look at operational problems from a worker's perspective as well. Clearly many business solutions lie in employee motivation.

## THE OPERATIONS HISTORY LESSON

Studies on methods to improve the production of goods and services have been conducted since the beginning of the twentieth century. Academics believed that if they only researched closely enough how businesses worked, they would stumble on that magic formula that would result in total efficiency. Much of that pioneering research was done on the factory floor. Because their names and theories are frequently mentioned in articles and MBA conversation, you had better add them to your business vocabulary.

### *FREDERICK TAYLOR*

Frederick W. Taylor, considered the "father of scientific management," developed his scientific management theories in the late 1890s and the early 1900s. He studied, measured, and documented the behavior of steelworkers. He showed that by breaking down a complex task into smaller component tasks, through a process that he called *job fractionalization,* each smaller task could be studied to find the most efficient way of accomplishing it. By successfully combining the most efficient elements, the best production methods could be adopted. Taylor performed countless *time and motion studies* using a stopwatch to find the "one right way" of doing things. In Taylor's opinion, it was in a worker's nature to "soldier," meaning to slack off. Therefore, it was management's responsibility to control the workplace and to force lazy workers to be efficient in spite of themselves.

## FRANK AND LILLIAN GILBRETH

The Gilbreths also studied ways to achieve peak factory efficiency. Their investigations led them to the development of a spectrum of seventeen types of body movements that covered the range of a factory worker's motion. Each motion was called a *therblig*. Like Taylor, the Gilbreths broke a complex task into its component parts. By understanding each element, one could simplify a job through the elimination of wasteful motion. Streamlining the task to its essential therbligs was key. Lillian's children wrote about her attempts to streamline the chores of parenting a family of twelve children in a humorous book entitled *Cheaper by the Dozen*. In 1984 the U.S. Postal Service commemorated her contribution to business and literature with a forty-cent stamp.

## ELTON MAYO

Elton Mayo is considered the father of the *human relations* movement of production management. In his search for efficiency, Mayo believed that the emotional state of workers is just as important as finding the right combination of movements.

Mayo's claim to fame came as a result of a series of experiments he conducted in 1927 at the Hawthorne Works of the Western Electric Company. In those studies, he varied the intensity of light on the shop floor in an effort to discover the degree of lighting that would result in the greatest productivity. He found that regardless of changes in lighting, worker productivity increased. Knowing that they were the subject of a study made the workers act differently. That phenomenon came to be known as the *Hawthorne effect*. Puzzled by the results, Mayo interviewed the workers and found that they had performed better because during the experiment they were being treated better by their supervisors. The assembly line workers were further motivated because their menial tasks acquired greater meaning as part of an experiment.

## *WORLD WAR II AND THE MANAGEMENT SCIENCE APPROACH*

As the technology and the scale of industrialization became more complex, operational problems became more difficult to solve. During World War II, production bottlenecks forced the government to turn to scientists and engineers to help achieve maximum military production. In seeking solutions, these pioneers created mathematical models to apply to production problems. Today this branch of operational study is called *operational research* (OR). Some of those models are presented later in this chapter.

## *THEORY X, THEORY Y, AND THEORY Z*

In 1960, Douglas McGregor of MIT renamed Taylor's scientific approach to management *Theory X* and dubbed Mayo's behavioral approach *Theory Y*. By repackaging these theories, he made a place for himself in the operational history books.

Theory X adherents, like Taylor, take a more "pessimistic" view of human behavior. They believe that people are inherently lazy and need to be pushed to produce with rewards and punishments. Workers lack creativity and ambition and have little to offer management other than their labor.

Theory Y adherents, like Mayo, believe that workers are self-motivated given a supportive work environment. Workers are inventive and should be consulted for ideas to improve productivity. They are also capable of assuming more responsibility for their work.

In the 1980s Theory Y was taken a step further. William Ouchi called the benevolent Theory Y used by Japanese management

*Theory Z.* In the mid-1980s some "experts" thought Theory Z was the secret of the Japanese competitive advantage. Using Z, the Japanese bring together management and workers in cohesive work groups. Everyone is part of a consensual decision-making process. To improve quality, workers and management work together in *quality circles.* Every employee is involved in *kaizen*—the continuous struggle necessary to improve all aspects of the self and of the company. MBAs refer to this as *continuous quality improvement* (CQI). When workers feel like partners in the business, they become more productive and committed to their jobs. For a manager, the Japanese word *gemba* describes their obligation to observe actual workflow, engage workers, and identify opportunities for continuing improvement.

## *THE CONTINGENCY APPROACH*

Because neither the scientific methods nor human relations approaches can be used successfully at all times, the proponents of the *contingency approach* believe that managers should alter and combine the two theories to fit the situation. If the classical methods of Taylor can be combined with a bit of Japanese Theory Z, so much the better if the result is good.

## THE PROBLEM SOLVING FRAMEWORK FOR OPERATIONS

Now that you have acquired a little historical perspective, you are ready to experience the core MBA operations education. Five issues arise when trying to produce a product or service:

*Capacity*—How much can I produce?
*Scheduling*—How am I going to do it?
*Inventory*—How much inventory is there and how can I reduce it?

*Standards* — What do I consider efficient production and quality
   output?
*Control* — Is the production process working?

An MBA's operations education is rudimentary. The object is to turn out not engineers, but managers who understand the manufacturing and service-rendering process. Each of the five issues raised above can and should be studied in great detail to achieve the most efficient production methods; however, in the spirit of this book, I will present only the highlights of some popular theories to offer you the basics.

## THE SIX M'S OF CAPACITY

To answer the question of how much you can produce, MBAs use six M's to guide them in manufacturing analysis. The M's focus on the areas that determine the limits of any production facility. Some schools teach only four M's, while others stretch the six into seven. In any case, M's are taught at all the Top Ten schools.

*Methods* — Have you chosen the best method of accomplishing the
   operational task? Are the machines placed in the most efficient
   factory-floor configuration?
*Materials* — Are the materials you need available and of good quality?
   Do you have the capability to purchase efficiently, store,
   and distribute the materials when needed by the production
   process?
*Manpower* — Do you have well-trained and productive workers
   and managers to accomplish your production goals? Are your
   workers sufficiently trained to operate any new technology that
   you may acquire?
*Machinery* — Do you have the right tools for the job? Do your
   machines meet your needs: capabilities, speed, reliability,
   technology?
*Money* — Is the cash to fund production available as needed? Is the

investment in factories, equipment, and inventories justified in light of the entire organization's priorities, capabilities, and other opportunities? Does the projected cash flow justify the investment? (A finance question.)

*Messages* — Do you have a system for sharing accurate and timely information among all members of the production team — people and machines? A machine needs to electronically share information about output and quality on an assembly line with its operator, as well as with other machines.

*Production methods* are of three basic types:

Continuous Process
Assembly Line
Job Shop

The more *standardized* the product, the more likely that a repetitive, high-volume production method is best. Oil refineries, for instance, use a *continuous* production process. Refining equipment works twenty-four hours a day. The operational focus at the refinery is to keep the equipment functioning smoothly. The downside of this kind of operation is that it is not flexible. Changes in the system usually require costly shutdowns and are slow to bring back online. The pandemic shutdown in 2020 wreaked havoc on the oil industry; oil flowed without buyers, driving prices to near $0 with no place to store it.

The old Henry Ford *assembly line* is a somewhat less continuous process. Auto production is broken down into separate tasks; each is performed repetitively in a series of workstations. The challenge is to coordinate the outputs of each task to maximize efficiency, and to minimize the need to hold a great deal of costly inventory. The assembly line method allows for some flexibility. Minor changes can be made to the process without a shutdown. Auto assembly lines can accommodate different combinations of optional equipment without interrupting the process.

The assembly line system can also be used to perform services. An enterprising surgeon in Russia who specialized in the removal of cataracts broke the operation into its component tasks and created a surgical assembly line.

To produce customized products, the *job shop* system is often best. In a job shop, the factory is set up to do many different tasks. Machinery is organized in work centers to tackle unique production jobs. Metal machine shops, print shops, hospital operating rooms, and furniture makers are commonly organized in this way. Each order is somewhat different, but the same basic equipment or instruments may be used for each job.

*Diagnosing Capacity Problems with Flow Diagrams.* Most MBAs are sent to factories as consultants rather than as plant managers. Instead of a wrench, they usually carry iPads with *flow diagram* template programs. These templates use rectangles, triangles, and diamonds. They are used to represent the manufacturing process. By mapping out the process, MBAs hope to find bottlenecks, inefficiency, and information-sharing problems. A clear sign that you are in the presence of an MBA is when he or she refers to production flows as *throughputs*.

In my experience, changing my car's oil at the gas station takes approximately twenty minutes; at Jiffy Lube, it takes only ten minutes. A simple process-flow-diagram analysis (page 272) tells why.

Jiffy Lube specializes in oil changes using an assembly line technique. The facility, the tools, and the workers are set up for only this task. Teams are used to complete the job as quickly as possible. Armed with your own template, you can act like a consultant too by diagramming any production process.

*Linear Programming: Dealing with Capacity Constraints.* Production is always faced with constraints. Materials may be scarce. Machines have production limits. Skilled labor is tough to find. The goal is to choose the best course of action within the prevailing constraints. What is considered best is the decision that will yield the largest output, the most revenue, and greatest profits at the least cost. Because often there are dozens of production constraints, to try to find an optimal solution by trial and error can be nearly impossible.

Corner Gas Station — I must leave my car, appointment necessary

Jiffy Lube — I wait for my car, no appointment necessary

Mercifully, a computer technique exists to do the work. It's called *linear programming* (LP). Linear programs use the *simplex method* to calculate their solutions.

Consider the Tangerine Computer factory, which produces two types of computers: a Deluxe and a Standard. The Deluxe model requires a special motherboard and two hard drives, whereas the Standard model requires one standard motherboard and one hard drive. However, the parts supply is limited to 30 Deluxe motherboards, 60 Standard motherboards, and 120 hard drives. If the profit on the Deluxe model is $500 and the profit on the Standard model is $300, how many of each unit should the factory produce? How do you sort it out?

The first step is to define the linear equation that will either maximize or minimize the desired results. In this case, Tangerine wants to maximize profits.

(X Deluxe Models × $500) + (Y Standard Models × $300) = Total Profits

The constraints on production are the parts supplies:

Deluxe Motherboard Use: (X units × 1) + (Y units × 0) < 30 units

Standard Motherboard Use: (X units × 0) + (Y units × 1) < 60 units

Hard Drive Use: (X units × 2) + (Y units × 1) < 120 units

The computer program tries many combinations until it has determined the production level that maximizes profits. In this case the solution is:

(30 Deluxe Models × $500) + (60 Standard Models × $300)
= $33,000 Max. Profit

In most production settings there are many models that a company can choose to produce. There are also many production constraints. LP can determine the best plan. There is a tool in Excel called Solver that can help solve linear programming problems like these.

Linear programming techniques can also be used to solve transportation and distribution problems. For example, McDonald's vendors have many warehouses, many franchisees, and a limited truck fleet. The goal is to find the cheapest way to ship the merchandise from a thousand or more possible warehouse/restaurant route combinations. Linear programming can do the job.

## SCHEDULING

*Henry Gantt and Gantt Chart Scheduling.* In the early 1900s Henry Gantt postulated that standards should be set not only for the performance of tasks, but also for their scheduling sequence. "Mr. Scheduling" felt that optimal timing should be determined so that the sequence of production tasks could be efficiently planned, coordinated, and performed. If scheduling ran amok, bottlenecks would occur and inefficiency would poison the system.

The *Gantt chart*, Henry Gantt's contribution to efficiency, is a grid in which tasks required in a production cycle are listed along one axis and their time sequence along the other. With a Gantt chart the entire production process can be scheduled, and critical tasks or bottlenecks can readily be identified. Gantt charts can be used in a variety of settings; they are not restricted to a factory. A project such as buying a house can be depicted in a Gantt chart (below).

*Critical Path Method of Scheduling (CPM).* The 1950s brought us a more sophisticated way of determining optimal scheduling: the *critical path method* (CPM). CPM is used for complicated production projects that require the coordination of many tasks. An even more complex form of CPM exists called *PERT,* Program Evaluation and Review Technique. However, today most businesspeople use PERT and CPM interchangeably.

Using CPM, production managers arrange each task or *activity* in sequential order and estimate the time needed to complete each one. Each time a task begins or is completed it is called an *event.* The CPM chart displays graphically all the events of a project. This enables a production engineer to estimate and manage the time to complete the job. Because all tasks are shown, the *critical* activities can be identified. The tasks that could potentially hold up a project are considered critical. The chart organizes and highlights the critical tasks, and it forecasts the time necessary to complete the entire project.

GANTT CHART FOR BUYING A HOUSE

| Week | 1 | 2 | 3 | 4 | 5 | 6 | 7 | 8 | 9 | 10 |
|---|---|---|---|---|---|---|---|---|---|---|
| Select Realtor | X | | | | | | | | | |
| Qualify for Mortgage | | X | | | | | | | | |
| House Hunt | X | X | X | X | | | | | | |
| Win Bid | | | | | X | X | | | | |
| Obtain Appraisal & Inspections | | | | | X | X | X | | | |
| Obtain Mortgage | | | | | X | X | X | X | | |
| Close on House | | | | | | | | | X | |
| Move In | | | | | | | | | | X |

To illustrate, Rosie Revere, production engineer at General Dynamics, would like to produce a new switch for a fighter plane. Rosie determined the five main activities involved in the project:

A: Design production machinery and prepare manufacturing drawings = 2 weeks
B: Prepare production facilities to receive new machines and parts = 4 weeks
C: Buy tooling and parts for production = 3 weeks
D: Stock parts and install production machinery = 1 week
E: Test new production line = 1 week

The CPM chart would look like this:

EJECTION SEAT SWITCH PROJECT CRITICAL PATH CHART

| Week 1 | Week 2 | Week 3 | Week 4 | Week 5 | Week 6 | Week 7 |

A = 2 wks.
2
C = 3 wks.
1
B = 4 wks.
1 wk.
Slack Time
3
D = 1 wk.
4
E = 1 wk.
5

= Critical Path = Shortest Path

Each task at General Dynamics is represented by an arrow for the activity and a circle for each event. As shown in the diagram, the shortest path to set up the production line for the switch is seven weeks. These activities along the longest path, called the *critical path*, determine and control the length of the project. When critical tasks can be accomplished faster, this is called *crashing the project*, because the project can be finished sooner. If designing the tooling could be sped up, that would crash the switch project. If any of the critical activities, such as designing the production tooling, is delayed, the project is delayed. Noncritical activities, such as preparing the facility, do not hold up the project. They have built-in *slack time*.

With large engineering, construction, and manufacturing projects, there are myriad tasks to keep track of. For these projects, computer software is available to help create the chart and do the timing calculations. The drawback to this wonder tool is the time needed to set up and manage the tedious CPM charts. "We all did them [CPM charts in the 1950s]," recalls Donald N. Frey, chief executive of Bell & Howell Co., "but it took so much effort to get the charts done, you might as well have spent the time getting the job done." Today they are created using a computer, and although still difficult and time consuming, CPM charts are doable as indispensable for large, complex projects.

*Queuing Theory to Schedule.* Ever been stuck in line at a bank? Trapped on hold while trying to order something by phone? Then queuing theory is a topic that you might find interesting. A *queue* is any line that either people or products wait in before they are serviced. Each person servicing a person in a queue is called a *channel*. MBAs use queuing theory to schedule workers and to design waiting lines to save money and improve service. The question of efficiency lies in the optimal number of channels needed per queue. For instance, a bank manager would like to have few tellers and short lines.

To answer queuing questions, you must determine several things:

A = Average number of random arrivals per unit of time
S = Average number of services provided per channel per unit of time
M = Number of available channels

With those items of information and a series of tables, you can make several calculations:

Utilization factor of the system = A/MS
Average Number Waiting = Total Number in Line − (A/S)

$$\text{Expected Waiting Time in Line} = \frac{\text{Average \# Waiting}}{A}$$

Let's continue the banking example: Consider a Citibank in lower Manhattan with one express teller who can process deposits at a rate of 50 per hour with an average customer arrival rate of 45 people per hour.

One Teller:
S = 50-customer-per-hour capacity per teller
A = 45 customers arriving per hour
$$A/MS = \frac{45}{1 \times 50}$$
= 90% utilization of one teller expected (very busy)

With that information and the abbreviated table below, the average number of people waiting in line should be 8.1.

| A/MS | M = 1 | M = 2 |
|------|-------|-------|
| .45 | .37 | .23 |
| .50 | .50 | .33 |
| .60 | .90 | .67 |
| .70 | 1.60 | 1.30 |
| .80 | 3.20 | 2.90 |
| .90 | 8.10 | 7.70 |

It would seem logical that by adding a second express teller, the average line would be cut from 8 to 4, wouldn't it?

Two Tellers:
$$A/MS = \frac{45}{2 \times 50} = .45$$
Expected Average Waiting Line
= .23 customers (from the table above)
No wait!

The waiting line would be reduced by over 97 percent by adding an extra teller. When the line is very busy, the second teller makes a *big* difference. Only queuing theory could tell you that. This teller problem is the simplest of examples. A whole "science" has been born around queuing. Academics have created books of tables and charts to answer many queuing dilemmas. Although you may not be an expert, you now know of the existence of queuing theory. That's how most MBA courses work. They teach you the fundamentals, but they expect that as an MBA, you'll seek out an expert to implement the program.

## INVENTORY

*The Balancing Act.* The optimal inventory level is a delicate balancing act. Inventory decisions are tough because different departments of the same company have different goals. When it comes to automobiles, marketers prefer to have too much rather than too little inventory. Salespeople want product for their customers. They hate to lose a sale because they are out of the hot SUV or EV (electric vehicle). Finance people want to carry the least amount of inventory possible. A smaller inventory investment leaves them with more cash on hand for other investments or to pay higher dividends. Production departments like to run as efficiently as possible. Long runs reduce the waste of multiple starts and stops, but can, of course, also be responsible for significant inventory buildups. MBAs call the process for getting all this right *supply chain management.*

*Inventory Vocabulary.* Inventory exists in one of three forms, be it in a factory or in a bakery:

*Raw Materials* — Flour, sugar, shortening, ready-made icing, etc.
*Work in Process* — Dough, pastry in the oven, pastry on cooling trays
*Finished Goods* — Cakes, cookies, and doughnuts ready for sale

Inventory includes not only the investment in materials, but also the investment in labor. As long as inventory remains in a company's possession, money is being tied up. A simple and illustrative way

INVENTORY FLOW DIAGRAM

of analyzing inventory levels is the *inventory flow diagram* above. It shows the type and value of a factory's inventory. As a product is made, raw materials are combined with labor to create finished goods of higher value.

*Reasons for Holding Inventory.* There are five major and legitimate justifications for holding inventory:

*Pipeline* — Inventory on hand to minimize production delays and maximize efficiency

*Cycle* — Suppliers have minimum order amounts that are greater than immediate need.

*Safety* — Stocks held to avoid a shortage because of uncertain production demands. Stockouts cost money when production is halted.

*Anticipatory* — Inventory held in anticipation of known demand

*Speculative* — Items purchased to beat supplier price increases

In efficient companies, materials arrive just in time for production. This is called *just-in-time* inventory (JIT). The Japanese are famous for this. Factory line workers request parts as needed with inventory order cards called *kanban*. However, JIT does not necessarily mean that parts suppliers produce at the exact rate of the automaker's assembly line needs. In reality the parts inventory sits in the warehouse of less powerful suppliers until it is called in by the auto manufacturers. True JIT has all manufacturing participants working in concert to meet production demands.

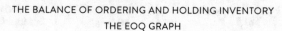

THE BALANCE OF ORDERING AND HOLDING INVENTORY
THE EOQ GRAPH

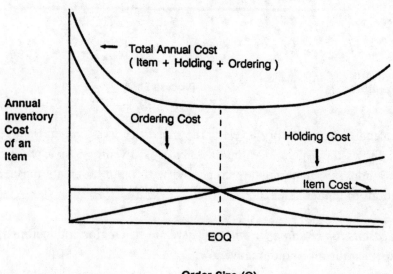

*Economic Order Quantity (EOQ).* Special EOQ formulas help MBAs find just the right quantity of inventory to order to keep parts, raw materials, or shelf items to a minimum.

The Economic Order Quantity formula is based on the trade-off of two costs associated with inventory.

*Carrying Costs* — The costs associated with storage, insurance, and financing of inventory. The opportunity cost of using the company's funds elsewhere should be considered.

*Ordering Costs* — The costs of ordering that include all the accounting and clerical labor and materials associated with placing an order

There are two extremes. A factory manager may choose to order huge quantities of parts infrequently, which reduces order costs, but maximizes carrying costs. Or he or she may order frequently to reduce carrying costs, maximizing ordering costs. The graph on page 280 shows that the least total cost is the inventory level when both ordering and carrying costs are minimized.

The EOQ formula tries to find that optimal point at which the total cost of both ordering and carrying is minimized.

The EOQ formula is:

$$\text{Economic Order Quantity } (Q^*) = \sqrt{\frac{(2 \times R \times O)}{C}}$$

Where:
Q* = Optimal inventory order quantity
R  = Annual unit requirements (Demand)
O  = Cost of placing an order
C  = Cost of carrying a unit of inventory per period

Consider an auto parts distributor that supplies a Kansas City assembly plant with replacement lamp bulbs for car dome lights. Its sales history indicates that a level demand of 2,000 bulbs throughout the year is most likely. Each time the distributor orders a shipment it costs $14 to process the order. A detailed study of costs reveals that it costs $.50 to carry each bulb in inventory for a year.

Economic Order Quantity

$$= \sqrt{\frac{(2 \times 2,000 \times \$14)}{\$.50}} = 335 \text{ units}$$

The formula calculates the most economic inventory order as 335 bulbs. Since the demand is 2,000 bulbs, this means that there will be about six orders per year (2000/335). Sounds simple. But it is not. The simple EOQ formula only works if the demand is *level*. When demand fluctuates wildly throughout the year, as in the case of a grocery store's demand for bagged ice, eggnog, or beer, the EOQ model has little value. Sophisticated computer programs perform a modified EOQ calculation more frequently to adjust the EOQ for fluctuating demand projections. In those situations the computer calculates varying optimal order sizes many times throughout the year. Even though the EOQ formula's application is limited, an MBA can talk intelligently with inventory experts if a problem arises. Because when inventory piles up unexpectedly, it is serious business.

"WE'RE STUCK WITH 700,000 BUSHELS OF CORN AND SOMEONE IS GOING TO HAVE TO EAT IT."

*Material Requirements Planning (MRP): Inventory and Capacity Management.* The knowledge of production scheduling and inventory control makes state-of-the-art manufacturing possible. MRP is a method for planning and controlling inventories required in a factory. Some say that MRP means "manufacturing resource planning," but under any name, MRP is a sophisticated system to improve manufacturing efficiency. MRP schedules production and calculates the optimal amount of inventory needed for efficient production. With products that have many parts, such as automobiles, appliances, and electronics, such a calculation can only be arrived at by using a computer.

To set up the system, the computer programmer must be familiar with the production process and material requirements. Then the computer can translate customer product demand into detailed orders to guide factory production and material requisitions from vendors.

The MRP process begins when production engineers determine the most efficient production method. For autos like a Honda Civic, for example, the assembly line is the most efficient production method. The process investigation must include every step of assembly, from sanding the raw steel body to driving the Honda out of the factory. Time and motion studies, such as those Taylor conducted nearly a century ago, might be necessary. The capabilities of both machine and worker must be known to determine the capacity of the factory. For instance, production engineers know exactly how many front quarter panels can be stamped out per hour and how many man-hours are required to operate the press.

Process engineers also have to detail *all* the part and material requirements of a product. The requirements list is called a Bill of Materials (BOM). It is recorded in the computer so that production demands can be "exploded" into exact material needs. For each Honda Civic, the MRP system would know that it needed two headlamps, forty-six two-inch screws, 4.2 quarts of paint, and hundreds

MATERIAL REQUIREMENT PLANNING SYSTEM

Customer Demand
↓
Production Planning
↓
Master Production Schedule
↓
Bill of Materials File ⟶ Material Requirements Program ⟵ Inventory Status File
↓
Production Plan
↓
Factory Floor Schedules        Inventory Requisitions        Orders to Vendors
(machine and labor needs)
↓
A Coordinated and Efficient Manufacturing Process

of other parts. The inventories of the materials are also tracked by MRP. In that way MRP can direct the factory manager to keep adequate part inventories to feed the production line needs. At the same time, MRP minimizes inventory levels by telling inventory clerks to order economic order quantities.

A "complete" MRP system, also called *enterprise resource planning* (ERP) software, coordinates the manufacturing process from forecasting customer demand, shipment of the finished product, managing the inventory in transit, and stocking the store shelf. The Master Production Schedule (MPS) within the computer sorts and stores all the information about demand, production, and materials and sends out orders to direct and coordinate manufacturing.

*Supply Chain Reality Check*. Knowing how inventory levels should be handled with EOQs, CPM and MRP, or the MBA way is not enough. Things do not work out well when the assumptions turn topsy-turvy, which happened during the pandemic in 2020.

Professor Willy Shih of Harvard outlined the "7 Principles of Supply Chains" to his classes in a *Wall Street Journal* article in 2022. "These 7 principles offer a way to look at how the supply chain does—and more recently, doesn't—work."

1. Supply Chains have many moving parts and layers.

   Companies can manage their own suppliers, but what about the sources that the suppliers rely on? "McKinsey estimated that the average auto maker has 250 tier-one suppliers and 18,000 suppliers across all layers"

   Like a "bullwhip," increased demand drives demand down the chain. When demand slows, the inventory buildup in the responding slowdown causes chaos at all levels, which happened post-pandemic in 2022. Forecasters like even, seasonally predictable demand; that's when everything works smoothly.

   On the distribution side, the path from the manufacturer to ship, port, truck, or rail to warehouse and to retailer was not a smooth process in the pandemic and post-pandemic period. Each step had its manpower and space allocation challenges. "Logistics" and "Supply Chain" became the buzzwords in every businessperson's vocabulary.

2. Sudden spikes can be easily misread or misinterpreted as longer-term demand shifts.

3. Because demand is hard to predict, many companies turned to just-in-time production. However, very lean inventories increase the risk of disruptions, delays, and outages. Not a good thing during a war or pandemic.

4. Ordering more than you need makes things worse. Over-ordering that which may only be transitory can cause over-ordering throughout the supply chain.

5. The longer the distribution chain, the more susceptible it is to disruption. The farther away from the consumer or the manufacturer, the more risks there are for sourcing and distribution problems. Clustered manufacturing that is closer to part manufacturers is less risky than overseas sourcing.

6. Congestion removes capacity from the system. By taxing an overburdened system, the velocity of the throughput is reduced. It's like a crowded highway in rush hour, which includes the ports, railways, trucking, and warehouses.

7. Bottleneck locations are hard to identify because very few people can see the whole picture. By just looking at what is immediately upstream or downstream, it is easy to lose perspective of the entire supply chain.

MBA inventory management tools are useful, but should be used judiciously.

## STANDARDS AND CONTROL

All the information about the production process necessary to create an MRP system or to use the other MBA efficiency tools provides the basis for the standards that managers use to measure and control performance. An MBA buzzword for using standards is the term *benchmarking*. This is where accountants jump in to help the operational side of the business. The *managerial accounting* section of the accounting chapter explained how accountants track and report production efficiency through the use of variances. The factory can vary by paying more than planned for materials (price variances) or using more materials or labor per unit produced (material and labor usage variance). By setting standards and seeing if they are met, production managers control the process.

## QUALITY

Operations classes take the concept of standards a bit further and deal with the issue of "quality," which is vital to competitiveness. What is quality, anyway? Quality only means that the product or service "meets the standards" set by either the manufacturer or the consumer. Quality does not necessarily mean a flawless product or service. Nor does it mean the most expensive product in its class like a Rolls-Royce. Quality products perform "as expected." Mundane things such as paper clips could be considered of high quality if they are not rusted and hold paper together well.

There are three important American "quality gurus" whose prescriptions were touted as the cure for troubled manufacturing: Joseph Juran, W. Edwards Deming, and Philip Crosby. Each has made a fortune writing, lecturing, and consulting about quality.

*Juran and Fitness for Use.* Joseph Juran uses the phrase "fitness for use" when speaking about quality. "Consumers should be able to count on the product for what they need or want to do with it." Manufacturers should produce quality products while "achieving high yields and minimal downtime."

*Fitness for use* has five "dimensions"; quality of design, conformance to manufacturing standards, lack of breakdowns, satisfactory performance, and the ease of maintenance of product after purchase.

*Deming, TQM, and Statistical Process Control.* W. Edwards Deming is famous for having taught the Japanese about quality in the 1950s, when American industry showed little interest in the subject. Deming quite simply proposed that quality could be achieved by identifying the causes of production problems throughout the process and by carefully monitoring production to stop errors before too many products were produced. Every step of the process is an opportunity for increased efficiency; hence the term *Total Quality Management* (TQM).

He divided problems into two categories, "common causes" and "special causes." Common causes are systemic problems, shared by many workers, machines, or product types. Special causes are those problems that relate to individual workers, machines, or material shipments.

Deming, with the help of Juran and W.A. Shewhart, developed a tool for identifying problems called *statistical process control* (SPC). "It is unlikely that two parts, even when produced by the same operator on the same machine, would ever be identical. The issue, therefore, was distinguishing acceptable variations from variations that could indicate problems." Statistical probability provides a method of making that distinction.

Production engineers make that distinction by studying the expected tolerance of each production task. For example, the filling machine at a Coca-Cola bottling plant does not pour exactly two liters into the two-liter jugs. The range of error is a few milliliters above or below two liters. Production engineers need to perform detailed studies to determine the usual amount of liquid squirted into each bottle. This exercise will result in a determination of the bell curve or statistical frequency distribution of filling quantities. If you remember the *normal* or *bell curve* discussion in the QA chapter, the range of variation that occurs 68 percent of the time was called *one standard deviation* or *one sigma* from the expected quantity. Any production measure outside a one-sigma-tolerance quality standard would signal a production problem. If a production manager desires, he or she can choose two- or three-sigma tolerances. *Six sigma* also refers to a program coined by Motorola that refers to a goal of a six-sigma standard or 3.4 defects per million. Many companies have six-sigma programs in place to reduce defects and increase profits.

In my Coca-Cola example, the production engineer selected a one-sigma tolerance and found that 68 percent of the time, the bottles measured in his or her sampling were filled within a range of ten milliliters above or below the desired two-liter level.

Using Deming's SPC, a filling-machine operator could take hourly batches of ten two-liter jugs off the assembly line. Using one-sigma tolerance, samples above two liters and ten milliliters would be above the *upper control limit* (UCL). For those measuring below two liters, 1,990 milliliters would be below the *lower control limit* (LCL). Measurements outside the limits would signal a "special problem," meaning a feeding line is crimped or clogged. The process would be considered "out of control," and the operator would be instructed to take corrective action. If after the correction the next samples are within the ten-milliliter tolerance, the process is "in control" and the machines are allowed to operate. (My Coca-Cola example of selecting the UCL and LCL was greatly simplified merely to expose you to the subject. The frequency and number taken in each sample by the operator greatly affects the statistical calculation of limits.) See chart below.

Using SPC, the filling-machine operator records his sample Coca-

BELL CURVE OF COLA FILL QUANTITIES

Frequency

68%

-1σ   +1σ

-10 ML        2 liters        +10 ML

Volume Dispensed

Cola measurements on SPC charts. On *X Bar Control Charts* the operator records the average (X Bar) of the sample measurement he or she takes every hour. The X Bar chart shows any tendency of the machine to drift or jump over time. If the chart is approaching a limit, the operator can investigate before the filling machine gets out of statistical control.

The *R (Range) Control Chart* reveals any tendency of the process to behave more or less randomly over time. It measures the range between the largest and smallest measurement in the same sampling used to create the X Bar charts. Within each group sample, the average of the sample measurements might mask unacceptable deviations. For example, a sample of a one-liter measurement and a three-liter measurement would average to two liters and appear acceptable on an X Bar chart. However, it is safe to expect that customers would be upset with half-filled bottles as well as bottles sticky from being grossly overfilled. In the case of being outside of an R chart's limit, the operator must also take corrective action.

The hypothetical SPC X Bar and R charts of a twelve-hour bottling shift on page 290 highlight problems.

The sudden change in X suggests that there is a mechanical problem or a new employee unfamiliar with the specifications.

The rise in R may signal that a machine is deteriorating, a machine control is vibrating and slipping out of specification, or a worker is getting tired.

*Crosby and "Quality Is Free."* Philip Crosby's claim to fame is the proclamation that "quality is free." He believed that if manufacturers improved quality, "conforming to requirements," total production costs would fall. Crosby proposed that the ultimate goal of a quality program is zero defects. Management must make a concerted effort to alter both the design and the production method to improve quality. In his opinion, any costs incurred in improving quality would be paid for by the saving of materials and labor that were once expended in correcting defects.

STATISTICAL PROCESS CONTROL CHARTS
COCA-COLA BOTTLING PLANT
X BAR AND R CHARTS

The sudden change in X suggests that there is a mechanical problem or a new employee unfamiliar with the specifications.

The rise in R may signal that a machine may be deteriorating, a machine control may be vibrating and slipping out of specification, or a worker could be getting tired.

*Genichi Taguchi and Poor Quality Is a Crime.* In addition to the Americans, Japanese quality expert Genichi Taguchi was a key quality proponent in postwar Japan. He taught from a spiritual perspective that "making poor products is worse than a thief." Society does not lose anything from a thief as it is a redistribution of wealth, but everyone loses when poor-quality products are made.

*Taiichi Ohno and the 8 Wastes of Production.* The seven wastes of production ("muda") were defined by Taiichi Ohno, father of the Toyota Production System. Some also include an eighth waste, underutilized talent.

*Transport*—An inefficient facility layout, poor production planning, poor scheduling can generate transport waste

*Inventory*—Any excess of inventory than necessary to produce goods or services in a just-in-time manner, poor forecasting

*Motion*—Any movement of people that doesn't contribute added value to the product like an inefficient plant layout

*Waiting*—Any idle time that occurs when production is not fully synchronized, such as production bottle necks

*Overproduction*—Producing more than is needed, faster than needed, or before it's needed

*Overprocessing*—Endless product or process refinements, excessive information, process bottlenecks, redundant reviews, and approvals

*Defects*—Loss of value when a product has to be scrapped because repairs deviated from specifications

*Underutilized Talent*—Employees performing unnecessary tasks when their talent could be utilized in ways that add greater value, or by not utilizing employees' critical-thinking abilities and feedback; allowing employees to work in silos, which prevents them from sharing their knowledge, is a waste

Eliminating the eight wastes from operations is the core of lean manufacturing. Manufacturers should focus on building processes that make waste obvious so that improvements can be made quickly.

## HOT TOPICS

With the basics of capacity, scheduling, standards, and control behind you, this chapter would not be complete without mentioning some of the trendy stuff that keeps popping up in the business press.

### *CYCLE TIME*

The time it takes for a company to convert a product idea into a new product or to improve an already existing product is called the *cycle time* of introduction. In Detroit the design and retooling for a new automobile may take two or more years. The turnaround for a new fashion item is often six months from design to store delivery. The faster a company can turn out a new product to meet consumer demand, the better the corporation will compete in the marketplace. Accordingly, rapid cycle times are a competitive advantage and a hot MBA topic. Some trendy MBAs call the battle to act faster *time-based competition.*

### *NEW TECHNOLOGY AND INTEGRATION*

New technology in and of itself is not necessarily a good thing unless it can be used effectively. General Motors spent billions of dollars in the 1980s for robotics to automate its assembly lines. With this lavish spending, GM hoped to achieve both higher quality and lower costs. However, GM lacked the technical expertise to integrate the new technology effectively into its operations.

Using traditional low-tech tooling and American workers, Japanese auto companies have met high productivity and quality standards in their U.S. assembly plants, to the chagrin of Detroit. In Honda's case, the use of flexible work rules, production work teams, and participative management has resulted in the productivity and quality gains that Detroit expected from its high-tech investments.

GM has since been a good learner from the Japanese and has closed that gap in its operations.

*Mass customization* was a new concept first promoted in 1992 by the Strategic Horizons group. Mass customization is based on the idea of tying computer-based information systems together with new modes of operation such as flexible manufacturing and just-in-time production. Using those linked systems, companies can provide each customer with the attractive, tailor-made benefits of the preindustrial craft era at the low cost of modern mass production. Products such as customized shoes, magazines, books, and computers can be provided in this manner. The development of 3D printing has permitted even more custom manufacturing on an even grander scale.

*Agile Methodologies* were created because the "manufacturing" process of software became such a complex task with questionable results. In 2001 a group of developers wrote the Agile Manifesto to tackle software development challenges of excessive planning and documentation that prevented the final product from pleasing its customers. Agile methodology is a way to manage a project by breaking it up into several phases, commonly known as *sprints*. Each day's meeting is called a daily *scrum*. It involves constant collaboration with stakeholders and continuous improvement at every stage of development. Once the work begins, the team "cycles" through the process of planning, executing, and evaluating the project to its best final product. Agile methodologies have also been applied to the development of new products and technologies.

## *INFORMATION TECHNOLOGY (IT)*

At many of the Top Ten schools, information technology has been added as a separate course. The topic has gained a life of its own in academic journals, the business press, and on the lecture circuit. As computers have become more powerful, and linked on the Internet via *cloud computing*, they have become a valuable tool in the gathering and integration of useful information for competitive advantages.

Those companies that know the most about their customers' preferences have an advantage over their competitors. Sales registers linked to large computers can yield daily information on consumer demand and preferences. Department stores, such as Macy's and Walmart, can track daily rack movement of their apparel to spot a hit dress or to cut back on orders for a fashion dud. The supermarket checkout scanners serve the same purpose. With limited shelf space, grocers can cull slow-moving items and replace them with more promising ones to maximize every foot of the aisle. Using the information in computer databases, advertising pitches can be targeted to the most likely prospects.

*Customer relationship management* (CRM) is the current hot topic in business automation. Complicated and expensive to implement, it is therefore fertile ground for MBA consultants. In theory it could automate every aspect of a company's relationship with its customers from customer data acquisition to customer retention. The contact with the customer can be in person, via e-mail, on the Web, or on the phone. Technological applications range from front-line customer data collection to providing customers and potential customers more accurate real-time data to answer their questions. Automated operators, called interactive voice response (IVR), can provide information or better route calls to the most competent service provider. Chatbots can also provide AI solutions on an even more sophisticated level. Within the corporation, a well-constructed database can identify opportunities for product development and additional markets for current products. The information that could potentially be part of a CRM system encompasses all parts of the organization, such as accounting, production, marketing, and finance. Technological barriers often keep these functions from interaction, making for an expensive and difficult implementation. Security of each function's data is critical.

As the scope of a CRM implementation can be so comprehensive, corporations must create a CRM strategy and then select the initial CRM application that delivers the greatest return on initial CRM investment.

The CRM cycle encompasses five functions:

**Product Development** — Research, concept development

**Sales** — Ordering, cross-selling, leads, forecasting, bidding and quoting

**Superior Customer Experience** — Personalization, service, queue management

**Retention and Win-Back Customers** — Loyalty programs, outbound efforts

**Targeting and Marketing** — Promotions, pricing, segmentation, behavior modeling, customer scoring, analytics

According to a Gartner Group survey, 55 percent of CRM projects do not produce results. With annual expenditures for CRM approaching $100 billion, it is important to avoid the common missteps: focusing solely on the technology, losing sight of the customer, lack of management support, inflexible business processes, underestimating change management, and undervaluing CRM's benefits.

MBA students are taught a lot of computer jargon so that they can be conversant in technospeak. MBAs hate to be outjargoned. Here's a small lexicon sampling.

*EDI* — Electronic Data Interchange, used to communicate orders between retailers and vendors

*API* — Application Programming Interface, used by companies to communicate with one another, especially order data

*POS* — Point of Sale systems, checkout registers

*AI* — Artificial Intelligence, computers that think like people through machine-learning on neural networks such as ChatGPT to answer questions and create wholly novel content

*RFID* — Radio Frequency Identification Inventory control tags

*HTTP* — Hypertext Transport Protocol, the way Internet browsers communicate with server computers

*HTML* — Hypertext Markup Language, the computer language of Internet Web pages

*Hypertext*—The system of interlinking Web pages

*Firewall*—Network protection from unauthorized access from outside computer users

*Moore's Law*—Intel founder Gordon Moore's idea that processing power doubles every eighteen months with proportionate decreases in cost

*Python*—Not a snake, a programming language like SQL, used to analyze databases

*Salesforce*—A leading CRM software provider

*SaaS*—Software as a Service, purchasing software on a subscription basis

*Cloud Computing*—using third-party computers to run vital operational functions such as Amazon Web Services (AWS), Microsoft Azure, Google Drive

Besides knowing the vocabulary, it is important that MBAs become knowledgeable technology buyers. The same equipment that can create a competitive advantage can also become a disadvantage if the equipment or the programming cannot be changed to suit the company's needs. Therefore computers and other technology purchases should be made after considering the company's long-range strategy.

## THE METAVERSE AND ARTIFICIAL INTELLIGENCE

*The Metaverse.* The metaverse or the 3D Internet must be included in *The Ten-Day MBA*. The PC age led to the Internet, which then led to mobile devices and cloud computing. The metaverse is a new ecosystem of connected interactive 3D technologies. Crypto technologies are separate but related technologies explained in the Economics chapter. Estimates predict that the GDP of the metaverse could eventually exceed that of the "physical world." Heady talk for sure. Current interactive virtual worlds are gaming ones like Roblox, Minecraft, and Fortnite Creative. Education, health care, and entertainment are virtually undeveloped.

Metaverse standards and protocols, like those developed for the Internet, have not yet been established. Virtual reality (VR) and augmented reality (AR) headsets and haptic bodywear are just being developed. It's real but not here yet. Facebook changed its name to Meta in 2021 and planned to invest $10 billion annually. Investors balked, so they cut the budget way back in 2022. Microsoft bought Activision Blizzard for $75 billion in 2022 to "provide the building blocks for the metaverse." Apple introduced their Vision Pro VR headset in 2023. But it is unclear how big the metaverse will be, and when it will actually arrive.

*Artificial Intelligence. Generative artificial intelligence* (AI) has emerged from closely held corporate secrets to mainstream tools in 2023. It has arrived. Instead of linear programming applications, AI's neural network computing applications can analyze data, learn, answer inquiries, and create wholly novel content. Chatbots integrate widely available Web data (sometimes inaccurately) to compose answers to user inquiries. AI can recognize patterns and relationships by mining *big data* sets that go beyond human capabilities, but AI can also drive cars and read medical imaging.

The OpenAI project widely released ChatGPT (Generative Pretrained Transformer) in February 2023. Microsoft integrated it into its Bing search engine. Google integrated its Bard chatbot into its search engine that month as well. The chatbots responded to inquiries coherently but not always accurately. But as their algorithms learn, the results will improve exponentially. This technology is not limited to text data creation. OpenAI's Dall-E bot, Midjourney, Stable Diffusion, and other bots do the same work with images, audio, and video to create their own unique content.

Questions about the ownership of AI's results and copyright infringement of their sources are yet to be sorted out. AI surveillance technologies and *deep learning* from big data pose privacy challenges. The issues facing the MBA are how to understand, to control, and to productively use this unpredictable and rapidly evolving technology. Something we missed with social media.

## OPERATIONS WRAP-UP

In all operational situations a five-issue framework applies: capacity, scheduling, inventory, standards, and controls. With that framework, a little history, some vocabulary, six M's, and a few formulas, the top MBA schools thrust their students into the business world. Imagine yourself as a consultant reviewing the operations of Onoff, Inc., a switch supplier to IBM. Onoff has been running short of cash. Product defects have plagued the factory, and costs have been rising. Based on the MBA knowledge culled from this chapter, you would start your investigation by asking a few questions:

> What is the management style used in the plant? Theory X, Y, or Z?
>
> Are the workers properly trained?
>
> Is the production equipment adequate? Efficient?
>
> Are there material supplier problems? Quality, Delivery problems?
>
> Is the production process efficiently configured? Consider a flow diagram.
>
> Can linear programming help develop a more profitable product mix?
>
> Could an MRP system be used to coordinate the entire production process, or a CRM system be used to manage the customer relationship?
>
> Are Economic Order Quantities used for inventory ordering to minimize inventories and to free up cash?
>
> Are there quality improvement programs in place? SPC, quality circles?
>
> Are adequate standards being set, monitored, and followed up timely?

Those are the types of questions that run through an MBA's head. With this chapter in mind, you too are able to ask the right questions.

# KEY OPERATIONS TAKEAWAYS

*Frederick Taylor* — Father of "scientific" production management
(Theory X)

*Elton Mayo* — Father of the "human relations movement" of
production management (Theory Y)

*Operational Problem Solving* — Capacity, scheduling, inventory,
standards, controls

*Six M's of Capacity* — Manpower, machinery, materials, money,
methods, messages

*Flow Diagramming* — Mapping out work flows to spot efficiency
opportunities

*Linear Programming* — Computer method of determining the optimal
solutions in situations with constrained capacity

*Gantt Chart* — A simple project-scheduling tool

*Critical Path Method (CPM)* — Sophisticated scheduling method for
projects

*Queuing Theory* — Mathematical tool to make waiting lines more
efficient

*Inventory Types by Stage of Production* — Raw materials, work in
process, finished goods

*Inventory Types by Reason for Holding* — Pipeline, cycle, safety,
anticipatory, speculative

*Economic Order Quantity (EOQ)* — Mathematical formula to minimize
inventory costs

*Material Requirements Planning (MRP)* — Sophisticated operational
inventory and capacity management tool

*Supply Chain* — The pathways to get vital manufacturing inputs

*Quality Gurus* — Joseph Juran, W. Edwards Deming, Philip Crosby,
Genichi Taguchi, and Taiichi Ohno

*Statistical Process Control (SPC)* — Statistical quality-control
technique

*Customer Relationship Management (CRM)* — A system of improving
and managing the entire relationship with the customer

# Day 8

# ECONOMICS

## Economics Topics

Supply and Demand

Microeconomics

Opportunity Costs

Marginal Utility

Elasticity

Market Structures

Macroeconomics

Keynesian and Monetarist Theory

Gross National Product Accounting

International Economics

We didn't have any models—I don't think anyone really had any models—to forecast the extent and severity of the home-price crash that spurred the 2008 financial crisis.

—Frank Nothaft, Freddie Mac Chief Economist,

from the *Wall Street Journal*

That may sound like a good excuse to play hooky on the day for economics, yet there is value in studying the subject. Economics cannot provide a clear picture, but it can supply some insights into

"I HAVE NO IDEA WHAT IT MEANS BUT I LOVE THE ACTION."

the "invisible forces" that underlie the movement of business around the world. As in the case of all other MBA subjects, some familiarity with this subject provides the chance to impress people at the office with how smart we are!

Schools like Chicago and MIT place a great deal of emphasis on learning classical textbook economics, but most others treat economics a bit more on an applied basis. Harvard and Darden have integrated economics into their international studies courses.

Economics can boast about only a few basic concepts. So how does one explain the endless volumes of complex academic literature that try to explain the booms and busts of business cycles? Like the Holy Grail, the perfect economic model is an elusive target that seduces many zealous professors and thousands of Ph.D.'s in private industry. In their wake over the past hundred years they have left thousands of magic formulas, graphs, and charts. An MBA should aim at understanding the fundamentals and the vocabulary of economics, then move on and leave the windmill theories for theoretical Don Quixotes to chase after. With that in mind, this chapter sticks

SUPPLY AND DEMAND FOR BEER

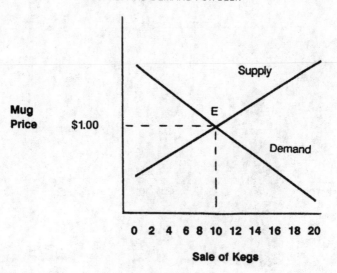

to the basics. It does not dwell on complicated formulas and difficult concepts that you would probably skip over, have no real use for, and forget in short order anyway.

Economics studies how society allocates the limited resources of the earth to the insatiable appetites of humans. Supply and demand are the forces at work. At what is referred to as *equilibrium* (E), the market price allows the quantity supplied to equal the quantity demanded. Suppliers are willing to sell, and consumers are willing to buy. Supply equals demand for a price. That, in a nutshell, is the basis of all economic theory.

For example, let's take a look at the local pub, Porth Tavern, which brews its own beer, Duff beer. Imagine you are a Heineken drinker and the bar is running a $1 special on mugs of Duff. The owner has ten kegs on hand, but feels if he were to charge the usual $6 per mug, he might only be able to sell one or two kegs. You like Heineken, but at a dollar, you decide to try the much cheaper brew. Here, in this bar, the "invisible hand" of economics is at work. At the "right" price, there is a demand for the ten kegs. The graph shows that as the price per mug increases, the brewery would be willing to produce more, but people would be less willing to buy.

SUPPLY AND DEMAND FOR AN ECONOMY

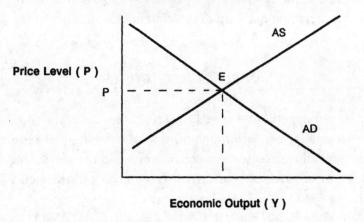

Generalizing from this simple relationship to an entire economy, aggregate supply (AS) equals aggregate demand (AD) at an equilibrium price and level of economic output. The graph is similar to the beer graph, the same relationship holds, but the elements measured constitute a much more serious MBA subject.

## LEVEL OF ECONOMICS: MICRO OR MACRO?

Students can study either *microeconomics* or *macroeconomics*. Microeconomics deals with the supply and demand equation of individuals, families, companies, or industries. The Heineken versus Duff competition was an example of a microeconomic battle. Macroeconomics, on the other hand, concerns itself with the economies of cities, countries, or the world as shown in the second graph. Simply put, "micro" economics deals with "small," specific situations; "macro" economics looks at the "big" picture of entire economics.

## MICROECONOMICS

Microeconomics is less glamorous than macroeconomics but is a little more practical. Since most of us are not likely to have a macro-effect on a whole economy, it is better if we concentrate on the few basic concepts that make up microeconomic knowledge.

## OPPORTUNITY COSTS

Because our appetites for goods and services are insatiable, decisions have to be made to determine how to allocate limited resources. Most often, the increase in production of a good or service requires that a cost or sacrifice be incurred. Economists call these costs *opportunity costs*.

For example, in the 1990s the demand for Harley-Davidson motorcycles had the company's factories operating at 100 percent of capacity. Harley controlled 60 percent of the big-ticket, big-bike market, and management was forced to decide how best to allocate limited production capacity to satisfy demand. They chose to produce several models for sale in the United States and abroad. As a result, Harley-Davidson incurred a significant opportunity cost because the company decided not to devote its entire capacity to its most expensive and profitable models for export to Japan. Had Harley tried to maximize short-term profits, it would have risked alienating the domestic market of devoted bikers—the very group that helped create the Harley mystique that the Japanese are buying. Opportunity cost, therefore, is the cost of choice, when output, time, and money are limited.

## MARGINAL REVENUE AND COST

A concept closely associated with opportunity cost is *marginal revenue and marginal cost*. Companies are motivated to maximize total profits by maximizing revenues and minimizing costs. If a business has the *opportunity* to sell even a single additional unit at a profit, it should produce it. The *marginal revenue* (MR) from the sale should exceed the *marginal cost* (MC) to produce.

Enterprises should continue to produce until their MR equals their MC. At that point of equilibrium the marginal profit on the next unit sold will equal zero. No profits are left on the table. Past that level, the marginal revenue of each additional unit sold decreases and the marginal cost increases. Experience tells us that the more units businesses try to push on the market, the less the market is willing to pay for these goods. The cost of producing one additional unit is minimal. But if there is no excess capacity and a company wants to produce more units, new workers will need to be hired, new equipment purchased, and a larger factory leased or built. Therefore, once a factory reaches capacity, the marginal cost of producing one additional unit increases beyond the cost of the last unit produced.

In the case of a cattle rancher, Bud Montana, the marginal cost of adding a steer to the herd is minimal. Fences still have to be mended and the pasture maintained. Since he is a *rational* decision maker, Bud will add cattle to the point that the marginal revenue from the sale of an additional steer will cover these marginal costs of raising this steer (MR = MC). If the cost of raising one additional unit becomes higher than the current market price, then Bud Montana will stop adding steers to his herd.

You might wonder why the demand curve is flat rather than

MARGINAL REVENUE AND COST EQUILIBRIUM

Competitive Environment

downward sloping, as in the case of other demand curves. It is because the price of beef is determined in a competitive auction. The few additional head of cattle that Bud might bring to the market will not affect the price that is determined by the output of thousands of ranchers and meat processors. If Bud had a corner on the beef market, or a monopoly, then presumably he would always produce and sell at the point where MR = MC. In that case, his marginal revenue curve would slope downward to the right as in the instance of the standard demand curve shown in the beer and macroeconomic illustrations.

The marginal cost and revenue concepts would also hold true for a cookie factory manager faced with a large special order. Imagine yourself in his or her apron. The customer wants to pay $1.00 per dozen for 100 dozens to be sold at a church fair. You have some excess capacity and so you go to your accountant and ask what your cost is to satisfy this order. She asserts that it would cost $1.45 per dozen. She gives you this breakdown as proof:

| | |
|---|---|
| Cookie Batter | $.80 |
| Labor | .25 |
| Factory Utilities | .20 |
| Factory Upkeep | .20 |
| Total Cost | $1.45 |

From that information you can see that the only *marginal* cost of running the automated cookie production line is the extra batter. The machine operator would be there anyway, and the large oven would be on anyhow. The factory would continue to require the usual maintenance.

The factory manager should welcome the order because he can make a marginal profit. The only reason to reject the order would be if word were to get out to regular customers that you sold the $2.00 cookies for $1.00. The rub is that if everyone paid the $1.00 special price per dozen, there would be no profits to pay for the fixed costs, such as the operator's salary and the cost of running the factory.

As shown in the example of steers and cookies, "marginal" costs and revenues are critical in making "marginal" pricing and production decisions. However, to evaluate profitability of an entire business, rather than one transaction, *total* revenue must exceed *total* costs to make a bottom-line company profit.

## MARGINAL UTILITY

*Utility* is a term used to describe the value of a product to a consumer. *Marginal utility* (MU) means the usefulness or utility of having an additional unit of a product. At some point a buyer is fully satisfied, and an additional unit is of no value. Going back to the beer example, suppose you are looking to forget whatever troubles you have and you order one beer at Porth Tavern. A second beer would be welcome and would in fact be of great marginal utility. Five hours later you've had twelve beers, played pool, danced, and forgotten your troubles. At this point, an extra beer would be of little value. The marginal utility of the thirteenth beer is negligible.

## PRICE ELASTICITY OF DEMAND

In the first illustration of supply and demand, Heineken drinkers were willing to buy Duff beer at a price. When the price was lowered, demand increased. Conversely, if the price had been higher, demand would have fallen. Buyers' responsiveness or *sensitivity* to changes in price is called *elasticity*.

Elasticity of demand is one of the few economic theories that my MBA alumni friends have reportedly used. Brand managers at Procter & Gamble, for example, want to know how a price change will affect demand for their brand of soap. Production foremen at Ford Motor Company want to know how price changes will affect their production requirements.

If consumers are sensitive to price changes, their demand is termed *elastic*. Consider the fast-food junkies' buying habits at Taco

Bell. Taco Bell lowered its prices by introducing "value meals." Consumers responded strongly by increasing their purchases. With tacos priced at a bargain, very little stood in the way of having a third or fourth helping. Competitors followed. Package deals at McDonald's gave permission to fence-sitters to order the large fries, large Coke, and apple pie with their Big Macs at a savings over ordering each item separately.

When consumers are not sensitive to prices, economists call their demand *inelastic*. Their purchasing behavior does not change with price changes. Necessities such as medical services or cigarettes fall into the inelastic category. When patients are in pain because of an appendicitis attack, they pay whatever the surgeon wants. Hard-core nicotine addicts accept cigarette price increases in the same way.

As you can see by now, the *price elasticity* of consumer demand for product is important to consider when pricing a product. To quantify elasticity, a descriptive *elasticity coefficient* is used:

$$\text{Elasticity of Quantity Demanded} = \frac{\% \text{ Change in Quantity Demanded}}{\% \text{ Change in Price}}$$

$$\text{OR}$$

$$\text{Elasticity of Total Revenue} = \frac{\% \text{ Change in Total Revenue}}{\% \text{ Change in Price}}$$

The higher the elasticity coefficient, the higher the price elasticity. A coefficient equal to or greater than 1 is considered elastic. For example, researchers have calculated elasticities for restaurant meals at 2 and medical services at .31. Usually a great deal of research is necessary to determine elasticity, but of course the process may be simplified at the expense of accuracy. Managers must analyze historical data and also try to sort out the nonprice influences that may have caused a demand change, such as weather and competition.

Another important aspect of elasticity is that it is not constant at all price levels. At different price levels elasticity may vary. This phe-

ELASTICITY OF DEMAND FOR HAMBURGER
(HYPOTHETICAL)

| Price per Pound | Total Pounds Demanded | Total Revenue | Elasticity of Quantity Demanded | Elasticity of Total Revenue |
|---|---|---|---|---|
| $5 | 1,000 | $5,000 | | |
| + 25% | −50% | −38% | 2.00 E | 1.5 E |
| $4 | 2,000 | $8,000 | | |
| + 33% | −50% | −33% | 1.50 E | 1.00 E |
| $3 | 4,000 | $12,000 | | |
| + 50% | −56% | −33% | 1.10 E | .67 I |
| $2 | 9,000 | $18,000 | | |
| +100% | −44% | +13% | .44 I | .13 I |
| $1 | 16,000 | $16,000 | | |

**E** = Elastic   **I** = Inelastic

nomenon is illustrated in a hypothetical table showing how people responded to price changes of hamburger meat sold by a particular butcher.

If you were a butcher, this information would confirm what you might expect. At lower price levels, affordable to most families, changes in prices do not prompt the cook of the house to switch to other meats. However, when prices are higher, in the $2 to $5 range per pound, hamburger loses its broad appeal. Shoppers demonstrate elastic demand by selecting hot dogs or even pasta instead of beef. Those with unlimited cash tend to be more price inelastic and buy regardless of the price. That is why the elasticity of "quantity demanded" differs from the elasticity of "total revenue." The die-hard beef eaters who are willing to buy at higher prices make up for the lost revenue of higher sales volumes.

The same concept of elasticity of demand can be applied to the supply side of the economy, but in the opposite direction. Higher prices encourage more production while simultaneously discouraging more consumption. Lower prices discourage production but encourage more consumption. At the point that the quantity supplied and the quantity demanded meet at a market price, the market reaches equilibrium.

## COMPETITIVE MARKET STRUCTURES

In addition to elasticity of demand, the competitive environment drives supply, demand, and prices. The greater the competition in a given market, the more sensitive the market price is to changes in supply and demand. In the gold market, there are many suppliers worldwide and the price fluctuates daily on commodity exchanges. The same holds true in the beef market in which Bud Montana operates. Now that you understand the principle involved, let's look at the four basic *market structures*.

*Pure Monopoly.* If there is only one seller with a unique product, then the seller is said to have a *pure monopoly.* The National Basketball Association controls professional basketball. Electric utilities are another monopoly. They are "price makers" because they can set the price of stadium tickets and of your utilities. And when a pharmaceutical company holds an exclusive patent, it can charge thousands of dollars for treatments that cost little to produce but cost a great deal to develop. Government regulation is usually the only restraint on greed. For a monopoly to exist there shouldn't be any close substitutes to which consumers can switch.

*Oligopoly.* When there are only a few suppliers for a product for which there are few substitutes, then what prevails is an *oligopoly.* With only a few competitors, prices can be maintained at high levels if the producers choose not to compete on price. If not, the market players can engage in price wars that can push prices down. Airlines are a good example of both of these conditions. Occasionally on busy routes price wars break out, but once it becomes clear that nobody can win, oligopolists return prices to higher levels.

*Monopolistic Competition.* In a market where there are many producers with products that can be differentiated, *monopolistic competition* can occur. Copy stores are known for this. The copies may be the same, but the service varies. FedEx Kinko's copy centers, for example, sell copies for fifteen cents each, while some economy shops charge only ten cents a copy. FedEx Kinko's justifies the higher price by being open twenty-four hours, and offering competent and friendly service in clean stores. The lower-priced shops provide bare-bones service. But the existence of discounters and at-home scanning place a lid on copy prices for the whole market. FedEx Kinko's would most likely experience a downturn if its prices were two or three times those of economy shops.

*Pure Competition.* In *pure competition* there are many competitors selling a similar, substitutable product. Marketing does not affect the price producers can get. Gold, silver, wheat, and corn are products that fit into this category. Many suppliers and buyers compete on commodity exchanges, and the prices are determined by the market forces of supply and demand. The producers are "price takers" from the market that arrives at prices by competitive bidding.

In summary, when you are thinking about the specific market conditions of an industry, a company, or the buying behavior of individuals, microeconomic theory governs. Industries produce the quantity that meets demand at an equilibrium price based on the competitive market structure. Companies produce the quantity at which the marginal revenue of the last unit produced equals the marginal cost. Individuals purchase based on their elasticity of demand.

## MACROECONOMICS

MBAs study macroeconomics to understand the forces that shape the larger economy in which their companies operate. Is a recession coming? Are interest rates heading up? Is inflation a threat? Those are legitimate questions that business owners need to ask and consider. Even though theories may not offer you the answers, knowing the fundamental principles of macroeconomics may provide the framework within which to make intelligent guesses about the future.

## THE BATTLE OVER HOW THE ECONOMY WORKS: KEYNES VERSUS FRIEDMAN

Economists rarely agree on what *drives* the economy. Just as there are Democrats and Republicans in politics, there are Keynesians and monetarists in economics. Keynesians hold that government intervention can significantly improve the operation of the economy. On the other hand, monetarists believe that markets work best if left alone with minimal government interference.

The fathers of these opposing economic camps were profoundly influenced by the times in which they lived. John Maynard Keynes of Cambridge wrote *The General Theory of Employment, Interest and Money* (1936), the cornerstone of modern Keynesian macroeconomics, in the midst of the chaos of the worldwide Great Depression of the 1930s. Keynes saw the hands-off policies of world leaders as a failure and felt that judicious and timely government intervention could have a stabilizing and beneficial effect on the economy.

In the boom years following World War II, Milton Friedman of the University of Chicago became a forceful advocate of the monetarist view of economics. He is the same person who asserts that a business's sole function is to make profits (see the ethics chapter). Having witnessed the prosperity of the Eisenhower and Kennedy years, he believed in the power of the market to heal itself. Friedman was convinced that government ought to keep its hands off the economy. In areas as varied as income tax policy, agricultural subsidies, public housing, and others, he thought governmental regulation had done more harm than good.

The macroeconomic debate of good-versus-evil government occupies an inordinate amount of time at MBA schools. Using the following chart as a guide, I feel confident you can argue both sides if you wish to, in true MBA form!

| KEYNESIAN THOUGHT | MONETARIST THOUGHT |
|---|---|
| Free enterprise without government intervention does not cause full employment. | Free market economics are best in the long run even at the cost of unemployment. |
| Unemployment is the big problem that needs a solution. | Inflation is the big evil; it is a tax on everyone. |
| With government spending and monetary policy, government should smooth out the business cycles. | Government tinkering makes the economy worse off in the long run. |
| Adequate information is available to take government action. | Available economic data are usually inaccurate and too late for useful government intervention. |
| Government spending can help spur efficient economic growth. | Government spending crowds out efficient private activity. |

This rather simplistic table covers the major theoretical macroeconomic arguments.

## GROSS NATIONAL PRODUCT, INFLATION, AND THE KEYNESIAN VIEW

The centerpiece of macroeconomics is understanding a nation's *gross national product* (GNP). GNP is the total market value of all *final* goods and services produced by an economy in a year. Changes in GNP are used as a measure of the health of an economy. The qualifier "final" is important. There is no double counting. An automobile, for example, is the sum of many components. Steel is counted in production only once, when the car is finished.

Because prices change from year to year, economists must adjust GNP for year-to-year comparisons. The cost of a pound of steel usually increases from year to year. If price levels rise, it is called *inflation*. GNP adjusted for inflation is called *real GNP*. If left unadjusted, the so-called *nominal GNP* could show dollar growth, even if the economy produced the same amount of goods and services.

To convert the unadjusted nominal GNP to real GNP, economists use a *GNP deflator* index. Using 2012 as a base year, the GNP deflator index then equaled 100. In 1960 it equaled 17. To translate, in 1960 the price of goods and services was 17 percent of what it was in 2012. During recessions and depressions real GNP falls, and during booms, it grows.

For example, imagine that in 2021 you produced in your kitchen one pound of saltwater taffy worth $1. Then the following year, you made an identical pound of candy, now worth $1.04 due to inflation. "Nominally," in "current" dollar terms in 2022, you produced 4 percent more value. But did you really? No. Your output was the same. Therefore, economists adjust nominal GNP numbers with a deflator to yield real GNP. With "real" figures analysts can measure and compare "real" growth in the economy.

In addition to a GNP deflator, economists use two more measures of inflation to gauge inflation's impact on the economy. The *consumer price index* (CPI) measures the price changes of a specifically defined basket of consumer goods and services that people buy most often. This shopping basket or collection of goods is kept constant from year to year. The *producer price index* (PPI) measures price changes of a collection of raw materials used most often by producers. The CPI index uses 1982–84 as its base years (1982–84 = 100). The PPI uses 2009 (2009 = 100). In 2022 the CPI was 292 and the PPI 139. That means that consumer prices in 2022 were 292 percent greater than they were in 1984 for identical goods.

There are also two additional variations of GNP measures called *net national product* (NNP) and *gross domestic product* (GDP). NNP considers the cost of using up machinery, factories, and equipment in production. In accounting, as I know you remember, they call that wasting of assets *depreciation*. NNP is GNP less the depreciation on the fixed assets used in the economy.

*Gross domestic product* is the part of GNP that is produced within a country's borders. It is an important statistic for economies heavily involved in trade. For example, Japan's GNP includes profits from Honda's assembly plants in the United States, but these profits would be excluded from its GDP. GDP is widely used.

*The GNP Equation.* The gross national product, in the Keynesian view, is composed of four types of spending that result in income for others. Each component can and should be influenced by the government's desire to maintain steady economic growth and low unemployment. When MBAs refer to the components of GNP, they call them the *drivers* of GNP.

$$GNP = C + I + G + X \text{ where:}$$
C is Personal Consumption
I is Private Investment
G is Government Purchases
X is Net of Exports over Imports

As illustrated by the equation, any increase in consumption, investment, or government spending will result in growth for the economy. Countries such as China, Japan, and Taiwan use exports as their engines for growth. The United States, by contrast, drags its economy with a yearly trade deficit.

As mentioned previously, the Keynesians' main goal is full employment. A lowering in GNP is distressing since it means fewer jobs. If the economy is operating at a level below full employment, then there is what is called a *GNP gap*. If the government intervenes in the equation by increasing spending, the economy will be buoyed up and there will be a rise in employment to close the gap.

Playing the devil's advocate, a monetarist would argue that the measures of the economy provided by government statistics are not accurate. Absent from GNP are the underground and unrecognized economies of crime, unreported earnings, and the output of caretakers working in the home. GNP also neglects to subtract the cost of environmental damage and add the value of leisure time produced.

*The Multiplier Effect and Fiscal Policy.* Keynesian theorists favor government spending to spur the economy because they believe in its positive impact. Spending by one person or by a government provides income to another individual or company. The way that such spending ripples through the economy in a repetitive cycle of spending and income is called the *multiplier effect.* How the Congress and the president decide to spend money is called the government's *fiscal policy.*

The Keynesians believe that a government's fiscal policy can "prime the pump" of a slow economy. In 2009 members of Congress raced to start public works projects to boost the economy during the deep recession. Road construction involves the purchase of rock, cement, steel, equipment, and labor, and the people involved in this work spend their wages and profits on food, housing, and clothes. The same was true in 2020 with the pandemic; massive amounts were spent for individual and business direct relief to avoid a depression. This *multiplies* throughout the community the effect of the original government spending.

Let's see the multiplier at work for $1,000,000 of those construction salaries. The workers' impact on the economy is dependent on their *marginal propensity to consume* (MPC) or spend the money they earn. If construction workers spent 80 percent of what they earned and saved 20 percent, they are said to have an MPC of .8. The higher the MPC, the greater the impact of their earnings on the economy. The effect on the economy would be calculated as follows:

$$\text{Spending Multiplier} = 1 / (1 - \text{MPC})$$

$$= 1 / (1 - .8)$$

$$= 5$$

The effect of $1 million of wages would result in $5 million ($1,000,000 × 5) of total spending in the economy. For members of

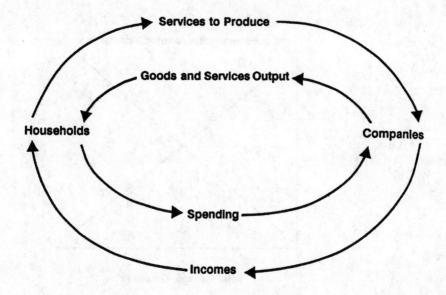

Congress who win public works projects and defense contracts for their districts, their vote-buying power is also multiplied by five.

*The IS/LM Curve of the Goods and Money Markets.* According to Keynes, interest rates are also powerful driving forces in the economy. Higher interest rates tend to retard the investments (I) that drive economic growth. It is unlikely that consumers will buy expensive items, such as cars and houses, if high interest rates make monthly payments unaffordable. The downward-sloping curve explaining this relationship is called the *investment and spending curve* (IS) (see charts on page 318).

Acknowledging the power of money, Keynes noted that the higher the interest rates, the higher the *liquidity preference* for money. On December 19, 1980, interest rates reached an all-time high of 21 percent, and people flocked to invest in money market funds. In 1992, when interest rates were hovering at 3 to 5 percent, investors rushed to shed their cash and ventured into the stock market. In 2003, with rates at 1 to 3 percent, and the stock market somewhat risky, investors rushed into real estate, which ended badly in 2007 and 2008. In the pandemic of 2020 rates hit rock bottom near zero, and both the real estate and stock markets took off. This relationship is illustrated by an

THE IS/LM CURVE

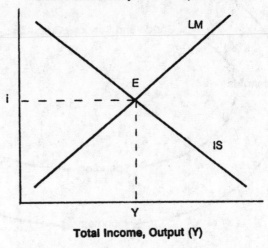

**Goods and Money Market Equilibrium**

Income = Output

THE IS/LM CURVE

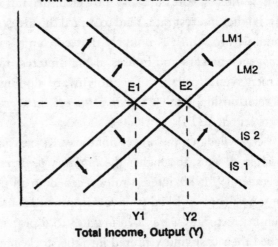

**With a Shift in the IS and LM Curves**

upward-sloping curve called the *liquidity and money curve* (LM). At some theoretical point there is an equilibrium point where the IS and LM curves meet at an equilibrium interest rate and a level of GNP.

The IS/LM curve is not fixed. It can change. If spending increases due to pump priming by the government during a recession, people will spend more in the aggregate. In this case, the entire IS curve will shift upward, resulting in higher interest rates and a higher GNP. If the money supply were also to be increased by the right proportion to accommodate the increase in spending, then interest rates could remain the same. That's in theory, of course.

There is not a single interest rate for the whole economy, nor can an accurate picture of how consumer spending responds to interest rates be drawn. That's why this is economics. The IS/LM curve is not precise; it does, however, illustrate a relationship that makes logical sense.

## ECONOMIC GROWTH AND THE MONETARIST VIEW

*What Is Money?* To begin a discussion on the monetarists, you need to know what they are talking about when they speak of what is dearest to their hearts—*money*. Money is the medium of exchange to buy and sell goods and services. Sounds simple, but is money just cash? No. When economists speak about measuring the money supply, they also include the "money equivalents" such as checking account balances and money market funds.

The money supply is referred to as *M1* and *M2*. M1, the most accessible money, includes only cash, checking account balances, and nonbank traveler's checks. M2 includes M1's components plus savings and money market accounts. In 2022, M1 and M2 equaled $20.6 trillion and $21.8 trillion respectively. The government closely monitors M1 and M2 money supply to gauge the economy's demand for money, and hence, its health.

*The Quantity Theory Equation of Money.* Whereas Keynes addresses the monetary dimension of the economy with the LM curve, monetarists consider money the main *driver* of GNP. The *Quantity Theory Equation* explains the monetarists' position. Changes in money supply cause direct changes in *nominal GNP*:

$$M \times V = P \times Q$$
Money × Velocity = Price Level × Real GNP
Money Supply = Nominal GNP

Monetary theories consider the money supply as the product of the amount of money and the *velocity* at which it travels through the economy. Velocity is the speed at which money changes hands. It is obvious that if a dollar remains under the mattress, it has little value to the economy. Its velocity is zero. If that same dollar were to change hands many times—be spent by some and be income to others—the rate of economic growth would be increased. Nonetheless, monetarists oddly believe that the velocity of money is constant.

The assumption of constant velocity is convenient if you look at the Quantity Theory Equation. Holding velocity constant makes the money supply the only determinant of growth in the economy. Keynesians find that proposition ludicrous. At different points in time, based on prevailing fear or euphoria, Keynesians believe there are changes in velocity. In a depression, for instance, people try to save whatever they can because they fear the next paycheck may be their last.

You might conclude from the equation that by setting the printing press on high speed, a government could send an economy into a high-growth gear. That may be true. The nominal GNP could be driven to new heights, but adjusted for inflation, the real GNP might remain the same or fall as a result.

Monetarists are most concerned about changes in price levels or inflation. If money is devalued by price increases, the real value of the economy's output is diminished. The trick is to have the wise Fed men in Washington increase the money supply just the right amount so that there may be economic growth with litle inflation.

Keynesians like a little inflation. That preference is supported by the research of A. W. Phillips of the London School of Economics, who claimed that higher inflation is accompanied by lower unemployment. The relationship between inflation and employment is shown by a graph called the *Phillips curve*. Monetarists don't buy it. They believe that an economy with lower inflation can also have low rates of unemployment. Historical data in the United States show that the Keynesian relationship was especially true in the period between 1950 and 1985, but it has not been consistently so over time, such as the period since 1985. In the period from 2012 to 2021, both inflation and unemployment were low, but that honeymoon ended when historic high inflation broke out in 2022.

*Monetary Policy Tools.* I mentioned that the supply of money can be manipulated. A group of seven people appointed by the president sit on the Federal Reserve Board of Governors in Washington. The *Fed*, as it is called, has three monetary tools at its disposal to regulate the economy.

*Change the discount rate.* Banks borrow money from the Federal Reserve at a *discount* rate and loan it at higher rates to customers. If the discount rate is lowered, the margin between the banks' loan rate and their cost from the Fed is higher. In turn, that encourages banks to make more loans to businesses and to consumers for homes, cars, and credit cards. Banks charge their best customers their lowest loan rate, called the *prime rate*. More loans increase the money supply in the economy and the multiplier effect starts. After September 11, 2001, the Fed lowered the rate to 1 percent to prevent a severe recession under extraordinary circumstances; that was lowered to zero after the 2008 financial meltdown, and again to zero during the Covid pandemic in 2020.

Like in the discussion of bonds, when describing interest rates, 100 basis points (BPS) is equal to 1 percent, so a Fed move of ½ percent is said to be 50 basis points.

You would think that setting interest rates, an impactful economic tool, is subject to a sophisticated set of rules, but it is not. It is a subjective process by the Federal Reserve shrouded in mystery. A transparent policy for rate changes based on explicitly targeted inflation and economic growth, by using the so-called Taylor Rule formulas developed in 1993, has yet to be adopted.

*Trade government securities.* The Fed actually trades in government securities in the financial markets. It buys and sells the government's own Treasury bonds. These trading transactions are called *open market operations.* When the Fed purchases government securities from the public it places more money in the hands of the public who sold them; the money supply increases. This is called *quantitative easing* (QE). In addition to the unprecedented lowering of rates to nearly zero, the Fed in 2008 through 2010 also bought over $2 trillion of governmental debt in an effort to bring the United States out of recession. During the pandemic shutdown in 2020, the Fed bought $8 trillion of Treasuries and mortgage-backed securities, flooding the economy with money to prevent a depression. When, in 2022, they began selling them, that is called *quantitative tightening* (QT), taking money out of the economy. When investors buy government securities sold by the Fed, money is drained from their pool of cash; the money supply decreases.

*Change the reserve requirement of financial institutions.* The Federal Reserve requires that financial institutions, such as banks and brokers, keep a prescribed percentage of the cash deposited by customers on hand. This cash is called a *reserve.* A *reserve requirement* is needed for banks to conduct daily transactions and accommodate depositors who wish to withdraw their funds. A reserve provides a measure of security. The rest of the depositors' money is loaned to customers. When regulators require a higher level of reserves, banks cannot loan as much money; this reduces the money supply in the economy.

If there is a crisis of confidence in a bank, a *bank run* on deposits can cause those reserves to be inadequate. Such was the case in the 2023 bankruptcies of both Silicon Valley Bank and Signature Bank. Federal regulators had to step in to backstop remaining depositors as tens of billions of deposits left their banks in a matter of a few days.

With these three tools, the Fed is able to change not only the money supply, but also the cost of money—interest rates. The Fed tries to gradually increase the supply of money as the economy grows. If this operation is performed correctly, inflation and interest rates can stay low and the economy can grow. If the money supply is kept too tight, a deep recession could occur, as it did in the early 1980s. If left to grow unrestrained, inflation can roar out of control, as has happened after the pandemic in 2022.

*Which Side to Choose?* If you are a conservative, you will gravitate to the Friedman camp. If you are politically liberal, Keynesian economics might be appealing since it calls for a more activist government. Regardless, the track record of both camps in keeping the economy on a steady course is not impressive. We still have recessions in the United States.

Both monetary and spending theories play significant roles in the workings of economic systems. It is a chicken-and-egg dilemma. Who starts the process? Monetary policy determines the supply of money, which in turn affects spending and GNP. Or does the Keynesian spending "tail" wag the monetarist "dog"? If you figure that one out, please write a book and set all the economists straight.

## *MORE ECONOMISTS YOU NEED TO KNOW ABOUT*

With Friedman and Keynes in your MBA grab bag, you need to know at least a little something about the following five economists. They are frequently mentioned as having shaped modern economics as we know it.

*Adam Smith and* The Wealth of Nations. Adam Smith is one of the world's earliest economists, but he is still much talked about. His book *The Wealth of Nations* (1776) described the "invisible hand" of competition as guiding an economic system based on self-interest. He saw the "wealth of nations" increase by the division of labor. Using the example of a pin factory, Smith described how productivity of a factory was enhanced when the different tasks were assigned to those workers with the appropriate skill. He observed cases in which ten people each performing a separate task turned out forty-eight thousand pins a day in an era when individuals were still turning out but a few pins.

*Joseph Schumpeter and "Creative Destruction."* This Harvard economist, long dead and forgotten, was resurrected in the 1980s. Schumpeter has been exhumed because he saw the *entrepreneur* as the crucial figure in economic life. If you have picked up any business periodical lately, you will not have failed to notice the word *entrepreneur* or some derivation thereof used with as much frequency as *a* and *the*.

Schumpeter considered capitalism "unruly and disconcerting, a system of flux rather than equilibrium." In *Capitalism, Socialism and Democracy* (1942) he wrote about capitalism as a process of "creative destruction." "Entrepreneurs create new industries that displace others in a painful and disquieting way." During the takeover and leveraged buyout craze of the 1980s, corporate raiders quoted Schumpeter to justify their actions and their profits as healthy activities that cleansed the capitalist system. For MBAs without the nerve to strike out on their own, theorists have created the term *intrapreneurs* as a consolation prize for those who are locked in corporations but still want to be agents of change.

*John Kenneth Galbraith and a Liberal View.* Galbraith, a Harvard economist, is known not for his grand theories or technical research, but for his broad policy statements. Although he is not considered a breakthrough thinker, his ability to give rousing lectures and market his books has given him a big name in economics. In 1951, Galbraith made a case for labor unions in *American Capitalism: The Concept of Countervailing Power.* In *The Affluent Society* (1958) he called for the economy to deemphasize production in favor of public services. In his 1967 *The New Industrial State,* Galbraith commented on the gradual move toward socialism in the United States.

*Arthur Okun and Okun's Law.* Arthur Okun studied economic growth and unemployment just as A. W. Phillips did. Okun, from Yale, was one of the most influential economists on the President's Council of Economic Advisers during the Kennedy and Johnson administrations. He found that higher levels of economic growth are accompanied by lower unemployment. His historical studies indicated that for every 2.2 percentage points of real GNP growth, unemployment falls 1 point. That rule of thumb was extensively used to justify the stimulative policies pursued by Washington in the 1960s.

*Arthur Laffer and the Supply-Side Economists of the 1980s.* Arthur Laffer is one of the best-known supply-side economists to emerge in the 1980s. Supply-siders believe in the incentive effects of reduced taxation. Tax incentives and federal spending reductions are critical in promoting growth by causing increases in savings and investment. When individuals and businesses keep more of their earnings, they can save and invest in projects, which in turn makes the economy more productive. This increase in productivity increases the level of "supply" and produces more wealth and economic growth.

While at the University of Southern California, Laffer developed what has come to be known as the *Laffer curve* to explain the incentive effects of tax rates. No, it's not a joke. The Laffer curve motivated the Reagan administration and the Congress to cut taxes in 1981. His theory suggests that tax revenues are correlated to the tax rate. His curve shows that total tax revenues increase as tax rates increase, but past a certain point, increases in rates decrease total tax revenues. Higher rates encourage tax cheating. Higher tax rates discourage people from working more. If rates are too high, reducing the tax rate will encourage people to work by making it more

THE LAFFER CURVE

Tax Revenue

E ?

0   20   40   60   80   100

Tax Rate %

profitable to do so. That in turn will increase gross tax receipts although the marginal tax on each dollar of income is smaller. The problem with the theory is that it is too abstract. There is, theoretically, an optimal tax rate, but nobody knows exactly what it is.

Other "radical" supply-side economists from the Reagan era who might creep into your economic conversations include George Gilder (*Wealth and Poverty*, 1981) and Jude Wanniski (*The Way the World Works*, 1978).

*Gary Becker and Behavioral Economics.* Gary Becker was one of the first economists to apply economic theory to topics belonging to sociology. He won the Nobel Prize in 1992. He argued that many types of behavior can be seen as rational and utility maximizing. Racial discrimination, crime, family organization, and drug addiction were topics of his most famous studies. Fellow University of Chicago professor Steven Levitt popularized the field in the book *Freakonomics*.

## INTERNATIONAL MACROECONOMICS

Taking an even broader view, macroeconomics in the international arena is a favorite of business schools. With the globalization of the world's economy, international economics has become a popular part of the MBA curriculum.

### THE COMPARATIVE ADVANTAGE OF NATIONS

In 1817, David Ricardo outlined the principles of *comparative advantage* in his work *Principles of Policy, Economy and Taxation*. A comparative advantage of a nation is its ability to produce a product at a lower cost than its trading partners. Nations theoretically should maximize the production of goods that they produce most efficiently because of availability of land, labor, or good weather. Even if a country is able to produce a product at an absolute lower cost relative to another nation, that nation should maximize the output of products that it produces more efficiently than other nations. Ricardo proposed that Portugal export wine to England and import wool from England even though both products are produced at absolutely lower costs in Portugal. The rationale is that Portugal is more efficient at producing wine than wool and it has a limited productive capacity. Therefore its capacity is best utilized for wine, and thus wool should be imported from England.

In the U.S.-Japanese trading relationship, the United States should maximize its ability to produce food at a lower cost. America has plenty of good farmland, machinery, fertilizer, technical expertise, and labor. U.S. farm productivity is three times Japan's. Japan, on the other hand, is good at producing electronics and automobiles. Theoretically, if these were the only two countries in the world, the United States should slash all electronics production and shift its emphasis to food production. The Japanese, conversely, should stop their inefficient food production. In reality, however, there are other national agenda and special interests at work that prompt nations to erect trade barriers. These prevent the efficiencies of comparative advantage from working. Trade barriers such as taxes on imports, import quotas, or other trading rules are governmental attempts to protect domestic industries and jobs. MBA schools consistently preach that tariffs and trade barriers are "bad," and free trade is preferred for long-term economic growth.

## BALANCE OF PAYMENTS

Just as companies keep track of their transactions with financial statements, entire nations keep track of their international transactions via *balance of payments* (BOP) accounting. The BOP registers the changes in a country's financial claims and obligations with all other countries. It is similar to an accountant's cash flow statement. Balance of payments accounting shows changes in *foreign exchange* for a period of time. Foreign exchange is the balance of liquid assets such as cash and gold reserves that can be used to make international payments.

| SOURCES OF FOREIGN EXCHANGE | USES OF FOREIGN EXCHANGE |
|---|---|
| Merchandise Exports | Merchandise Imports |
| Travel Expenses of Foreigners Here | Travel of Citizens Abroad |
| Transportation Receipts of Domestic Carriers from Foreigners | Transportation Expenses by Residents Paid to Foreigners |
| Fees and Royalties Received | Fees and Royalties Paid Abroad |
| Foreign Investment Income | Interest and Dividends Paid Abroad |
| Government Foreign Aid Received | Government Foreign Aid Given |
| Private Transfers of Money into the Country | Private Transfers of Money Abroad |
| Increases in Foreign Liabilities | Increases in Foreign Assets |

The sources and uses above show in broad terms the items that most frequently enter into a foreign exchange ledger. Excluded from the count are the international drug trade and other unreported activities. The press usually ignores the whole BOP picture and focuses only on the *merchandise trade deficit*. It is easier to say that the United States in 2021 ran a $1 trillion merchandise trade deficit. Journalists ignore that the U.S. ran a $230 billion surplus in trading services, such as consulting and engineering, and a net surplus of investment income of $39 billion. That leaves a net trade deficit of $821 billion in a $23 trillion economy.

Having enough foreign exchange is extremely important. The collapse of the currency in Zimbabwe in 2008 came as a result of insufficient foreign exchange in its central bank to make good on the purchases made by its government and citizens. When foreigners went to convert their claims into U.S. dollars, the central bank was emptied of its foreign exchange. Without convertibility, everyone dumped their nearly worthless Zimbabwe dollars. One U.S. dollar was worth a trillion Zimbabwe dollars, and the government abandoned its currency.

## *EXCHANGE RATE AND PURCHASE PRICE PARITY*

The *exchange rate* is the rate at which one country's currency is converted into another's. In July 2022, one U.S. dollar could buy 6.7 Chinese yuan, 135 Japanese yen, 84 percent of one British pound, and one European Union euro. The euro was at a twenty-year low after the Russian invasion of Ukraine. In the 2000s with a weaker U.S. dollar, traveling in Europe was expensive for American citizens. Post-Covid in 2022 the U.S. dollar was more valuable and things were cheaper. What makes one country's currency worth more than another's? It's the old supply-and-demand relationship. International currency traders have to keep the following four factors in mind when trying to predict the gyrations of world currencies:

- Trading Demands for Currency to Pay for Goods and Services

  When the United States needs to buy French wine, importers sell U.S. dollars and buy euros to make payment in EU currency.
- Demands for Currency for Attractive Investments

  Higher relative interest rates in the United States prompt purchases of bonds by foreigners.

  Higher U.S. relative rate of economic growth prompts purchases of stocks by foreigners.
- Demands for a Safe Haven in Times of Uncertainty

  In times of war or chaos, investors seek the currencies of stable governments.
- Lower Inflation Relative to Other Countries

  In 1987 the U.S. inflation rate was 3.6 percent, and the Lebanese inflation rate 723 percent, which reflected the chaos of their civil war.

Lebanese investors naturally wanted to hold their investments in U.S. dollars because their pound's value was eroding quickly. The theory of *purchasing-power parity* describes the way that currencies' values adjust versus each other because of inflation. If one country's inflation is higher than another's, then its currency will be adjusted downward to compensate for the annual loss of value. During the Lebanese civil war in 1986 and 1987, the country's exchange rate went from 38 to 496 pounds to the dollar, a loss of 86 percent to compensate for the loss of inflation.

Exchange rate movements are critical for companies involved in international trade. If exchange rates change between the time of signing a contract and its settlement, anticipated profits can be wiped out by currency fluctuations. Imagine if a farmer wanted to sell one U.S. dollar's worth of beef to Japan. At the 2022 exchange rate the farmer would charge 135 yen, expecting a 5 percent profit. But when paid, the farmer might need 150 yen to buy the same one dollar, because of a rate change. Although the yen payment would have remained constant at 135 yen, the currency fluctuation would have caused a 11 percent loss in U.S. dollar buying power. Companies and individuals use the futures and options markets to offset or *hedge* losses on this kind of currency transaction. This is not unlike the stock-option hedging described in the finance chapter.

## EXCHANGE RATE SYSTEMS

Exchange rates are governed by the host country's exchange rate system. With a *floating* exchange rate, the value of the country's currency can freely move based on the factors described above. With a *fixed* exchange rate system, the host government tries to change interest rates or buy and sell foreign currencies to maintain a fixed value against the U.S. dollar, the EU's euro, or a basket of currencies. This is called *pegging* the value of the currency to another. Between 1945 and 1971 under the Bretton Woods system, the U.S. dollar was pegged against a certain amount of gold, and all other currencies were pegged to the U.S. dollar. That system ended in 1971 when many countries decided to allow their currencies to float.

Counties cannot just do anything with their currencies. A concept called the *impossible trilogy* says a government can have only two of the following three options:

Independent monetary policy
Fixed exchange rates
Absence of capital controls

For example, if a country chooses a fixed exchange rate, it has to abandon an independent monetary policy or impose capital controls to maintain its fixed peg versus the other independent currency. If a country decides to maintain a peg in volatile times, it becomes expensive to keep a fixed rate of exchange. When a fixed system begins to fail, as it did in Mexico in 1994 and Southeast Asia in 1998, there is a currency "crisis" as the currencies fall to their true levels, causing trade and investment disruptions.

By pulling together the topics of domestic interest rates, international capital flows, and currency rates, Gregory Mankiw of the University of Chicago has created a *three-panel diagram* to represent the world's economics system, as presented on page 332.

Within each country, such as the United States, the supply and demand for loanable funds determine the level of domestic real interest rates. At that equilibrium interest rate, savers of dollars supply funds and investors' demand for dollars is satisfied.

The interest rate paid on dollar-denominated investments can be either attractive or not in the international marketplace. The country's riskiness, currency demands of international trade, and the interest rate itself determine the country's net capital outflow. These outflows supply the international currency market with dollars. Based on the international supply and demand for dollars, the dollar's exchange rate is established.

These three variables—domestic interest rates, capital flows, and exchange rates—interact simultaneously in the international macro-

THE WORLD ECONOMY AND THE 3-PANEL DIAGRAM
(From Wikipedia, the free encyclopedia)

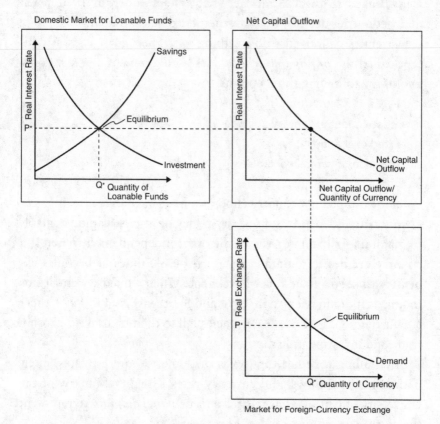

Market for Foreign-Currency Exchange

economic system at a constantly fluctuating point of equilibrium as depicted in a three-panel diagram. It's macroeconomics in a nutshell.

## CRYPTOCURRENCY 101

*Blockchain History.* Cryptocurrencies, including Bitcoin (BTC), Ether (ETH), Dogecoin, Tether, and others, are a medium of exchange, store of value, or a speculative investment, all depending on who you talk to.

The cryptocurrency idea started in October 2008 with a white paper named "Bitcoin: A Peer-to-Peer Electronic Cash System" posted under the pseudonym "Satoshi Nakamoto." Because financial intermediaries such as banks were charging too much to process electronic transactions, Bitcoin wanted to replace those intermediaries. The system launched in January 2009, with the imbedded code, "The Times 03/Jan/2009 Chancellor on the brink of a second bailout for banks." The code revealed an additional motive to create a monetary system independent of any governments' central banks that manage the money supply.

*Blockchain Explained.* The Bitcoin blockchain system is a network of decentralized computers. They maintain a public ledger of transactions and confirmations of transfer of assets called Bitcoin. The Bitcoin code is stored in digital wallets. The wallet's address must be the same for receiving and sending Bitcoin.

The Bitcoin blockchain is a database of the most recent ledger transactions, which also contains all prior transactions. It shows the ownership of all current Bitcoins in the blockchain. The point is that once a transaction is posted, it cannot be erased or modified. The Bitcoin software that runs the Bitcoin universe is called Bitcoin Core: a 450-gigabite database, stored at Github, a Microsoft-owned Web site. A group of five to six coders serve as maintainers, stewards of the updates and bug patches to the Bitcoin Core open-source software.

Full node computers process the updates that are "hashed" out by many miner node computers. The miners add the new transaction data—called a block—to the blockchain in a very intensive process using a lot of computing power and electricity. The miners are compensated for their work with newly minted Bitcoins. Miners are constantly working on updating the most recent blockchain with the most recent transaction blocks.

While U.S. dollars can be created without bounds, the maximum number of Bitcoin is limited by the technology to 21 million. *Bitcoin blockchain* describes the technology. *Bitcoin cryptocurrency* describes the currency itself.

Blockchain technology can be used to create a decentralized blockchain ledger of ownership of all kinds of assets and to verify authenticity and past history. Ethereum technology blockchains have created tokens to represent digital assets such as NFTs (nonfungible tokens) for art, music, videos, gaming, or intellectual property. The blockchain technology is currently being used for health-care records and supply chain data.

Cryptocurrency exchanges such as Coinbase and Binance are places to buy and trade cryptocurrency. Each currency resides on its own blockchain, but you trade them on the exchange. You can hold your cryptocurrency and NFTs in *hosted wallets* on an exchange, or on your own computer in a self-custody wallet with your private key or "seed phrase" for security.

Crypto has its negatives too. Crypto is unregulated against fraud, theft, and lost keys (passwords). Crypto technology does not safeguard against illegal activity, hacking, or money laundering. It is not easy to trade cryptocurrencies for goods and services; their value is extremely volatile. Fraudulent cryptocurrencies, such as Squid Games' SQUID token, just disappeared overnight in 2021. This is called a *rug pull.*

Crypto trading is facilitated by DeFi (decentralized finance). In that way people can trade or leverage trades for their speculative bets. Cryptocurrency lenders take in deposits; hold your cash and crypto; pay high interest rates on their deposits. Celsius Network bank failed in 2022 when its loans to traders soured, leaving depositors in the lurch. Later that year the major crypto exchange FTX swiftly collapsed when its loans of customers' assets to traders at the affiliated Alameda Research became worthless. Both FTX and Alameda went bankrupt and FTX's sponsored token FTT also became worthless. No regulators or deposit insurance came to the rescue of customers. James Mackintosh wrote in the *Wall Street Journal* in the fall of 2022 that all crypto coin is simply "a gambling token dressed up as an investment asset."

Stablecoins are cryptocurrencies that try to peg their value to the dollar. This makes them more a medium of exchange rather than just a speculation. Tether and USD coin are backed by traditional assets; however, some coins are kept to their pegs by an algorithm. Some flawed algorithm coins have had spectacular failures, such as TerraUSD and Luna in 2022. U.S. regulators had their sites trained on regulating the stablecoins as securities in 2023.

With that said, billions have been made and lost in crypto trading. Bitcoin and Ether were said to have peaked in 2021 at $68,781 and $4,379 per token. The total market cap of all cryptocurrencies was approximately $1 trillion U.S. dollars in March of 2023. The uses of blockchain technology had not been fully realized and the new decentralized Internet called Web3 had not yet been built out.

## COUNTRY ANALYSIS

B-schools teach students what to consider when trying to make predictions about a country's future. Since MBA schools aspire to turn out presidents of large multinational corporations, they must prepare these future captains of industry to evaluate investment opportunities abroad.

A *country analysis,* as developed at the Harvard Business School, is a four-step process that attempts to organize all available economic, social, political, and geographic data for strategy development.

1. Analyze Past Performance
   External Measures: balance of payments, exchange rates
   Internal Measures
       General: GNP, inflation, employment
       Supply Side: interest rates, investment, capacity
       Demand Side: consumption, income distribution
       Social Side: human migrations, population growth, education
2. Identify the Country's Strategy
   Goals: autonomy, productivity, equity
   Policies: fiscal, monetary, trade, social
3. Analyze a Country's Context
   Physical: size, population, geography
   Political: government type, stability, corruption, leaders
   Institutions: government agencies, business, labor, religion, agriculture
   Ideological: role of government, family, culture, individualism
   International: trade advantages, competitiveness
4. Make a Prediction Based on Steps 1, 2, and 3

Let's take a country that is deep in debt, experiencing high inflation, and mired in political gridlock—as an example, the United States of America in 2023. Assume that you are in 2023 and that you are Franz Danninger, a Swiss banker at the Bank of Zurich. You are considering whether you should invest your clients' money in the United States as part of your global portfolio. Gather the data outlined in the three steps of country analysis and make a prediction.

If Franz were to make several forecasts of the future, MBAs would call that *scenario analysis*. The same facts supporting a recessionary prediction could also support a scenario of an economic boom or bust in the United States. An astute manager should make contingency plans in the event that one of these alternative scenarios begins to develop.

Country analysis is a multipurpose tool that provides a way to sort out all the reams of economic data that are available on a nation. As a new MBA you now have the framework that global strategists use in the boardrooms of multinational corporations and that economic analysis departments of the world's most prestigious investment firms employ.

## ECONOMICS IN REVIEW

As this chapter has shown, microeconomics and macroeconomics are not that complicated if you wish to know only the MBA basics.

*Microeconomics.* Supply equals demand at an equilibrium price. Consumers try to minimize opportunity costs and maximize marginal profits and utility. If they respond to price changes, economists call their behavior elastic.

*Macroeconomics.* Keynesians like government and consumer spending. Friedman and his monetarist friends place their faith in the control of the money supply. It looks like both camps have valid points to make, but neither has a corner on explaining how economies work. In any case, supply equals demand at an equilibrium price. That much they agree on.

*Global Macroeconomics.* The economies of the world keep track of their activity using balance of payments accounting. If they are doing a good job, inflation stays low, economic growth remains steady, foreign reserves stay high, and the local currency maintains its value. If not, a country may end up in an economic quagmire. If you want to be a crystal ball reader and want to predict where your favorite nation is headed, use the country analysis framework to make a prediction.

## KEY ECONOMICS TAKEAWAYS

*Microeconomics* — The study of individual, family, company, and industry economic behavior

*Macroeconomics* — The study of the behavior of entire economies

*Equilibrium* — The point at which the quantity supplied equals the quantity demanded and a mutually agreeable price is determined

*Marginal Revenue and Cost* — The added revenue and cost of producing and selling one additional unit

*Elasticity* — The change in buyers' demand as a result of price changes

*Market Structures* — The competitive environment in an industry determined by the number of sellers and the product's characteristics

*Keynesian Theory* — Spending and consumption are the main drivers of an economy.

*Monetarist Theory* — The size and growth of the money supply determines the growth of the economy. Money makes the world go around.

*Gross National Product* — The total amount of final goods and services produced by an economy over a period of time

*The Spending Multiplier*—The economic ripple effect of money being circulated in an economy: spending for one person is income for another.

*Fiscal Policy*—A government's spending policy

*Monetary Policy*—A government's policy of controlling the supply of money and interest rates

*Adam Smith*—The economist who wrote about the "invisible hand" of capitalism in *The Wealth of Nations* in 1776

*Arthur Laffer*—1980s economist who developed the Laffer curve, which illustrated that lower tax rates would result in higher tax revenues

*Balance of Payments*—The accounting for the inflows and outflows of foreign exchange of a country

*Country Analysis*—A systematic framework to organize economic data and make predictions about the prospects of a nation

# Day 9

## STRATEGY

### Strategy Topics

The Seven S Model

Environmental Analysis

The Value Chain

Integration and Expansion Strategies

Industry Analysis

Competitive Strategies

Signaling

Portfolio Strategies

Competitive Life Cycle

Globalization

Synergy

Incrementalism

S trategy is the most exciting course in the MBA curriculum because it gives you the chance to put all your new skills to work. Most professors insist that strategy be taught after completing most of the core courses, because it requires a background in all the MBA disciplines. Strategy classes place students in the chairman of the board's chair, and MBAs love that feeling. As my strategy professor told us, exposure to strategy concepts alters the way you look at businesses. Strategic thinking involves a comprehensive analysis of a business in relation to its industry, its competitors, and the business environment in both the short and the long term. Ultimately, strategy is a company's plan to achieve its goals.

Corporate managements often do not know clearly what they want or how they'll get there. When this is the situation, a boardroom discussion could resemble a scene from Lewis Carroll's *Alice's Adventures in Wonderland:*

> ALICE: Would you tell me, please, which way ought I to go from here?
> CHESHIRE CAT: That depends a good deal on where you want to get to.
> ALICE: I don't much care where—.
> CHESHIRE CAT: Then it doesn't matter which way you go.

Corporations need well-thought-out strategic plans or inevitably they will become victims of the marketplace instead of being the victors who shape it.

## STRATEGY AS PART OF AN ORGANIZATION: THE SEVEN S MODEL

Strategic plans cannot be formed in a vacuum; they must *fit* organizations, just as marketing plans must be suited to products. Two separate stages characterize strategic planning: *formation* and *implementation*. Strategists should always devise their plans with an eye toward implementation. Thomas J. Peters, of *In Search of Excellence* fame, created the *Seven S model* showing that strategy ought to be interwoven within the fabric of an organization. Actually Peters created the model with Robert H. Waterman and Julien R. Phillips, but Peters, an exceptional speaker, is usually given most of the credit. Their model provides a structure with which to consider a company as a whole, so that the organization's problems may be diagnosed and a strategy may be developed and implemented. If a strategy requires radical reorganization, it's called *reengineering*. If not, it is described as *organizational tinkering*. The Seven S's are:

- Structure
- Systems
- Skills
- Style
- Staff
- Superordinate Goals/Shared Values
- Strategy

The diagram illustrates the "multiplicity" and "interconnectedness" of elements that influence an organization's ability to change. The other notable feature in the diagram is that there is "no starting point or implied hierarchy." In any one organization, different

THE SEVEN S MODEL

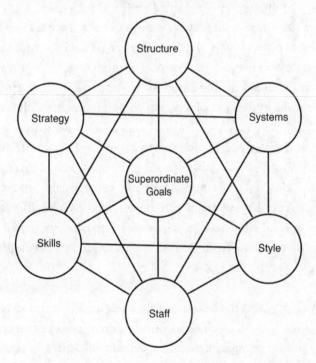

Reprinted from *Business Horizons,* June 1980. © 1980 by the Foundation for the School of Business at Indiana University. Used with permission.

factors may drive the business. In an "excellent" organization, each of the S's complements the others and consistently advances the company's goal. This is not any different from a marketing plan, which should be *internally consistent* and *mutually supportive,* as explained in the first chapter. The Seven S model is a helpful tool to organize one's thoughts in order to define and effectively attack complicated problems.

If you recall the *basic organizational model* outlined in the organizational behavior chapter, the Seven S's should look familiar. Strategy theorists borrow ideas and concepts from other MBA disciplines and integrate them. Here the same S's appear but with some additions and deletions.

*Structure.* A corporation's *structure* affects its strategic planning and its ability to change. As explained in the OB chapter, a company's structure may have a customer or a geographic focus. For instance, if a company decides to alter its strategy to become more responsive to its customers, it may need to adopt a *customer* structure, which will channel all the skills of a company to meet customers' specific needs. In the case of a power tool manufacturer, the competition may demand a change from a *functional form,* which separates manufacturing, sales, and finance, to an organization with two customer divisions. One division would serve household consumers and the other industrial customers. These market segments have different needs that could most effectively be serviced by two focused divisions. In special situations, a temporary structure such as a matrix could be overlaid to form project teams skilled in developing new products.

*Strategy.* This refers to the *actions* that a company plans in response to or in anticipation of changes in its external environment, its customers, and its competitors. The spectrum of strategies a company can use is the focus of this chapter.

*Style.* It sounds like a new addition to the *basic organizational model,* but this S is more closely related to *culture.* Culture or style is the aggregate of behaviors, thoughts, beliefs, and symbols that are conveyed to people throughout an organization over time. Since it is hard to change a company's ingrained culture, it is important to bear it in mind when developing a new strategy. If a consumer products company has a conservative bent, it will need to be convinced, beyond a shadow of a doubt, of the efficacy or viability of a new product. Historically, Procter & Gamble was in the slow-to-innovate category, but lately its behavior has been changing. P&G had test-marketed Bounce fabric softener for years before introducing it across the country. By contrast it rolls out new products in months now.

*Staff.* With no warm bodies, there's no company. By *staff* Peters means the human resource *systems,* which include appraisals, training, wages, and the intangibles, such as employee motivation, morale, and attitude. With a motivated workforce, companies are able to adapt and compete. Top management often ignores this S because they feel that it is not significant on one hand and too touchy-feely on the other. "Let the human resources department deal with it" is the common attitude. This soft factor is essential, however, because without employee cooperation a company will not have the ability to succeed.

*Skills.* Closely related to staff are the distinctive abilities and talents that a company possesses. *Skills* may range from the ability of a staff to speak Spanish, to an understanding of statistics, to computer literacy, for instance. Certain companies are strong in particular areas. Du Pont and 3M are known for their superb research and development capabilities. International companies need people with language skills and in-depth knowledge of other cultures and customs. American Express for one acquires these skills by hiring knowledgeable nationals in the markets in which it competes.

*Systems.* The procedures, both formal and informal, by which an organization operates and gathers information constitute the *systems* of a company. As I mentioned, Peters considers the systems relating to personnel part of *staff.* With this S, Peters is concerned with the systems that allocate and control money and materials as well as gather information.

When a company confronts a major challenge in the marketplace, management must have detailed data about its operations, customers, and competition to determine the gravity of the situation. Managerial accounting systems provide operational data about production and costs. Marketing research and sales tracking systems give information about the customers. Competitive intelligence systems provide insight as to what other companies are up to.

*Superordinate Goals.* This last S is at the core of an organization. According to Peters, "The word *superordinate* literally means *of higher order.*" *Superordinate goals* are the guiding concepts—values and aspirations, often unwritten—that go beyond the conventional statements of corporate objectives. "Superordinate goals are the fundamental ideas around which a business is built." For example, Peters wrote in 1980 that Hewlett-Packard's superordinate goal was to have "innovative people at all levels in the organization." 3M's superordinate goal was to produce "new products," while IBM's was "customer service."

*Mission and Vision Statements.* These are often mentioned when companies speak about their goals. A mission statement should be a short and concise statement of goals and priorities. Unfortunately they are often long, bland, and tedious documents. When senior executives return from expensive executive programs from one of the Top Ten schools, frequently they form a mission statement task force or hire a consultant for this purpose. This exercise has a large element of "keeping up with the Joneses." If a company incorporates a mission statement in its annual report, then all of its competitors go off to cook up theirs. Campbell Soup Company's annual reports boasted a well-written mission statement in 2022:

> To nourish people's lives by offering a wide variety of convenient,
> delicious, and affordable food choices that can help everyone enjoy
> a balanced, healthful diet.

Their goals were clear. The wording of the mission statement is often crafted to address the most important constituency at the time.

*Vision statements* take a more forward look to set corporate goals. Altria's vision in 2022 was "Our vision by 2023 to responsibly lead the transition of adult smokers to a smoke-free future." Some companies have both a mission and a vision statement.

Apart from the politics involved in their creation, a mission and vision statement can be a useful surrogate for a firm's superordinate goal, if it doesn't have one.


## A SEVEN S MODEL EXAMPLE

When all of a company's S's move in concert, it can be a formidable competitor. The early success of Apple Computer can be said to have been derived from the balance of its S's. It had an entrepreneurial *style* fostered by its founders that attracted the brightest and most creative *staff*. With their cutting-edge technological *skills,* the founders organized Apple in a loose corporate matrix *structure* that fit the personalities of the people and the task of creating new products. Apple developed reinforcing *systems* to reward innovation and to track operations. Their rewards supported Apple's shared values of teamwork and fun to achieve its *superordinate goal*—placing the best user-friendly computer in every household. Apple's *strategy* was to create a proprietary, user-friendly system for the home, school, and graphics markets. All the S's fit together well and were mutually supportive of its goals.

Do your own MBA analysis of your favorite organization. List the Seven S's on a sheet of paper and dig in. A strategic consultant with an MBA would do exactly the same thing you can now do with the Seven S model. But a consulting firm would accompany the study with fancy computer graphics, put it in a binder, and charge your company a small fortune.

## ENVIRONMENTAL ANALYSIS

*Environmental Analysis* is a big-picture strategic tool that looks at the macro factors and trends that influence competition within industries. It's an important place to start organizing your thoughts about the larger context in order to make strategic decisions.

*Demographic Trends*—Current and emerging population trends of growth, age, income, gender, migrations. An aging population is a favorable trend for health-care products.

*Sociocultural influences*—Emerging values, lifestyle, fashion, beliefs, and societal attitudes that influence consumer demand and labor issues. A heightened value for life-work balance, how remote work impacts recruiting, and retention of talent are sociocultural influences.

*Technological Developments*—New technologies that influence consumer habits, needs and demand, product substitutes, obsolescence, material usage, and production efficiencies. New battery technologies can lower costs, increase outputs and longevity, reduce product sizes, and alter the use of key materials.

*Macroeconomic Impacts*—Inflationary trends, exchange rates, wages, interest rates, business cycle, and monetary policies. Key cost and wage inflation affects manufacturing, pricing, and consumer demand.

*Political and Legal Pressures*—Analysis of relevant laws, regulations, policies, and international conflicts. Transfer laws pertaining to key intellectual property could affect sourcing and exports. The war in Ukraine in 2022 created a wide range of impacts and influences.

*Global Trade Issues*—Impacts of globalization, international trade organizations, treaties and tariffs, and regime changes. Increases in trade barriers and tariffs influence product sourcing and export markets.*

* Adapted from *The Strategist's Toolkit*, by Harris and Lenox, Darden Business Publishing, 2013, pp. 21–22.

# THE VALUE CHAIN AND INTEGRATION

When an MBA begins the strategic analysis of any company, one of the first questions should be "What business is it in?" The value chain and integration concepts help to answer that question.

## VALUE CHAIN

After the basic question has been answered, the next step for a strategic analyst is to assess the *value* a company adds to its products. The apparel industry's value chain looks like this:

Wool → Fiber → Yarn → Cloth → Clothing → Distribution → Retailing → Consumer

At each link in the chain, a *channel participant* adds value to the product as it makes its way to the consumer. First, the raw materials must be produced, harvested, or mined. These factors of production—wool, cotton, and chemicals—are combined to manufacture clothing. Once it is produced, marketers must promote, distributors transport, and retailers sell the clothing to the consumer.

## INTEGRATION

*Forward and Backward Integration.* A company can perform at any link in the value chain. When a company operates in areas further down the value chain, it is said to be *forwardly integrated* toward the consumer. For example, if an orchard owner grew and sold his fruit to the public, he would be considered forwardly integrated toward the buyer. The grower could decide to sell at a lower price than the grocery store or to sell at the grocery's price and make the additional profit.

If a business operates in areas closer to the raw materials, then the company is said to be *backwardly integrated*. International Paper, which owns its own forests and paper-manufacturing facilities, would be classified as being backwardly integrated.

You can see a company as either forwardly or backwardly integrated depending on the point in the value chain at which you view that company. If you consider the orchard owner primarily as a grower, then you might view his business as forwardly integrated toward the retailing end of the chain. If you believed that his main business was retailing fruit to the public, then you could say that his business is backwardly integrated because he grows what he sells. International Paper is backwardly integrated to its timberland operations and forwardly integrated to its consumer paper-product manufacturing and distribution activities.

Forestry ← *Backward Integration* ← **International Paper** → *Forward Integration* → Consumer Paper

*Vertical and Horizontal Integration.* Industries can also be viewed *vertically* and *horizontally*. *Vertically integrated* is a term used for companies that participate at many levels of the value chain in an industry. International Paper is vertically integrated because it owns both the trees and the paper mills. The term can describe both *forwardly* and *backwardly integrated* companies. The key is that several value-adding functions are being performed by one firm.

When Exxon purchased Mobil to become ExxonMobil, it acquired a competitor at the same level in the value chain. This is called *horizontal integration*. Exxon chose not to move to another value-adding activity. Instead Exxon moved sideways or horizontally. If the new ExxonMobil had bought Apache Oil Exploration, it would be vertically integrated. In this hypothetical case, a new value function would have been added to ExxonMobil's manufacturing operations in the automobile industry.

Strategic analysts review industries' value chains to identify current and future sources of competition. When chemical companies sought higher profits, they forwardly integrated into higher "value added" products such as fibers for cloth and carpet. With the likes of Du Pont, the fiber link of the chain became more competitive.

Integration strategies may result in obvious benefits such as secured inputs and lower costs, but the disadvantages include a higher exposure to the downturns in a single industry. All of the corporation's eggs are in one basket. In lean times, an ExxonMobil refinery can't squeeze concessions from its oil suppliers if the supplier is ExxonMobil. In the same way, General Motors can't dump excess engine inventories on its customers if the only user is the company itself.

## LEVELS OF STRATEGY

*Strategy* is a broad term. It commonly describes any thinking that looks at the "big picture." In fact, it is more complex. There are three levels of strategy to be considered:

*Functional Strategy* — The value activities engaged in
*Business Strategy* — How to fight the competition, tactics
*Corporate Strategy* — What businesses should I be in?

When putting on the strategy hat, you must ask yourself, "At what level do I wish to think? Functional, business, or corporate?"

## FUNCTIONAL STRATEGY

*Functional* strategies are those operational methods and "value-adding" activities that management chooses for its business. The functional strategy of Altria Group's Philip Morris USA, for example, has been to lower costs by utilizing the most advanced processing technologies. If Philip Morris USA felt vulnerable to a single supplier of tobacco, a good functional strategy would dictate that it use multiple suppliers.

## BUSINESS STRATEGY

Business strategies are those battle plans used to fight the competition in the industry that a company *currently* participates in. They are on a higher level than functional strategies, but there is obviously an overlap between how a company operates and how it competes. Philip Morris USA's *business* strategy has been to beat its competition by crowding store shelves with many different brands and by spending heavily on advertising to promote its brands.

## CORPORATE STRATEGY

Corporate strategy looks at the whole gamut of business opportunities. The original parent company Philip Morris's corporate name change to Altria made it clear. Altria's *corporate* strategy led the company to diversify away from tobacco products and toward consumer goods. Altria's executives reviewed the tobacco industry's growth potential, the legal environment, and the increased health awareness among consumers and concluded that it was wise to be in more "healthful" businesses. Its purchases of General Foods, Kraft,

Nabisco, and Miller Brewing were made with that corporate strategy in mind. By 2009 Altria sold all those businesses to maximize shareholder value as the market found Philip Morris USA to be toxic when the legal environment for tobacco turned negative. The food companies were more valuable as separate companies. The remaining company doubled down on tobacco and nicotine by first acquiring Juul e-cigarettes in 2018 for $13 billion. However, a regulator crackdown in 2022 on marketing and selling to kids practically shut down Juul. Undaunted Altria acquired NJOY e-cigarettes in 2023 for $2.75 billion. Corporate strategy is dynamic.

## EXPANSION STRATEGIES

Academics love to create diagrams to show off their theories and to make them easier to use. One of the simplest of the strategic diagrams is the *Ansoff matrix*. H. I. Ansoff created it in 1957 as a clear way to classify routes for business expansion. What determines the strategy classification is the newness of the product to the company and the firm's experience with the intended market. The "newness" of the product or market is determined by how "new" it is to the company contemplating the strategy, not by the age of the product or market itself.

The power of the matrix lies in that it can be used for any industry. Ansoff created a vocabulary to communicate a strategic direction in a few words. If Hershey Foods Corporation wanted to sell more chocolate bars in the United States, that would be a *penetration* strategy (existing product, existing market). If they intended to sell chocolate in Eastern Europe, that's an *expansion* strategy (existing product, new market). Using a *related diversification* strategy, Hershey could develop a new bubble gum and sell it in the United States (new product, existing market). If it wanted to sell automobiles in Nepal (new product, new market), that would be *unrelated diversification*. A company always has a menu of expansion options. The catch is that there has to be enough money and management time to expand effectively. If Hershey's management were to decide

THE ANSOFF MATRIX

**PRODUCT**

|  | **OLD** | **NEW** |
|---|---|---|
| **OLD** | Market Penetration | Related Diversification (Product Development) |
| **NEW** | Expansion (Market Development) | Unrelated Diversification |

**MARKET** (label at left, between OLD and NEW rows)

Adapted with the permission of *Harvard Business Review*. An exhibit from "Strategies for Diversification" by H. Igor Ansoff, Volume 35, No. 5 (September/October 1957). Copyright © 1957 by the President and Fellows of Harvard College; all rights reserved.

to expand in all four of the directions described above, they could end up with many businesses that are inadequately managed. There are only so many hours in an executive day. Even if managers could run the new ventures, the company might lack the cash to fund them adequately.

## INDUSTRY ANALYSIS

Along with the language to discuss expansion (integration and diversification), you also need tools to help develop a strategy to survive. Michael Porter of Harvard has developed the *Five Forces Theory of Industry Structure* to help companies survive in a competitive environment. His books, *Competitive Strategy* and *Competitive Advantage,* are truly cornerstones of strategic thinking. If you must buy business books (other than *this* one), they are the ones to purchase. Porter's theories can be used to formulate survival strategies for your current business, as well as to evaluate the "attractiveness" of other industries for expansion. Porter offers tools for investigating the five forces that determine the level of competition and, consequently, the level of profit in an industry.

The five forces that drive industry competition are:

- Threat of Substitutes
- Threat of New Entrants
- Bargaining Power of Suppliers
- Bargaining Power of Buyers
- Intensity of Rivalry Among Competitors

## A FIVE-FORCES EXAMPLE

Let's apply the model to the tin can industry, which would be viewed by Porter as extremely competitive because of the array of forces at play within the industry. The *suppliers* of steel have many other industries to sell their steel to. Therefore, the canning industry does not have much leverage in the market. Porter focuses on power, the ability of one participant in the value chain to force its will on others in the chain.

The *users* of cans are primarily the small group of large food processors. Users can wield their power to force the can industry to reduce prices by playing one competitor against another.

Processors the size of Del Monte can also threaten to *substitute* plastic packaging for cans. Many food processors have moved to plastic packaging. Consequently, competition intensifies as the demand for cans shrinks.

Making matters worse is that can-making machines can easily be purchased by *new entrants*. Efficient can production is accomplished at low cost and at relatively low volumes. This opens the industry up to new competitors if profit margins are at an attractive level. Del Monte, if it wished, could buy packaging equipment and produce for itself. Because the manufacturing technology is widely available and reasonably priced, the *barriers to entry* are low. Ease of entry increases the level of potential competition.

PORTER'S FIVE FORCES THEORY OF INDUSTRY STRUCTURE

Reprinted with the permission of The Free Press, a division of Macmillan, Inc., from *Competitive Advantage: Creating and Sustaining Superior Performance* by Michael E. Porter. Copyright © 1985 by Michael E. Porter.

Because these four forces make the industry highly competitive, the fifth force, *rivalry among existing firms,* is equally intense. Salespeople know their competition well because they compete for orders from a shrinking group of customers. This competitive force includes the possibility of bitter price wars. Under certain circumstances, competitors will adopt artificially low prices regardless of the impact on profit because they want to win the account at all cost. The industry's competitive intensity results from all five forces exerting their pressures on the industry as seen in Porter's model.

What's a company to do in this sort of competitive environment? Crown Holdings of Philadelphia has pursued a strategy of adding *value* to its product. It offers expert consulting services to solve clients' packaging problems, quick delivery to lower clients' inventory costs, and customized and innovative packaging to enhance brands and engage customers. On the cost side, Crown Hold-

## PORTER'S FIVE FORCES THEORY OF INDUSTRY STRUCTURE

**Entry Barriers**

Economies of scale
Proprietary product differences
Brand identity
Switching costs
Capital requirements
Access to distribution
Absolute cost advantages
  Proprietary learning curve
  Access to necessary inputs
  Proprietary low-cost product design
Government policy
Expected retaliation

**Rivalry Determinants**

Industry growth
Fixed (or storage) costs/value added
Intermittent overcapacity
Product differences
Brand identity
Switching costs
Concentration and balance
Informational complexity
Diversity of competitors
Corporate stakes
Exit barriers

Threat of New Entrants

Bargaining Power of Suppliers

New Entrants

Industry Competitors

Intensity of Rivalry

Bargaining Power of Buyers

Suppliers

Buyers

Threat of Substitute

Substitutes

**Determinants of Supplier Power**

Differentiation of inputs
Switching costs of suppliers and firms in the industry
Presence of substitute inputs
Supplier concentration
Importance of volume to supplier
Cost relative to total purchases in the industry
Impact of inputs on cost or differentiation
Threat of forward integration relative to threat of backward integration by firms in the industry

**Determinants of Substitution Threat**

Relative price performance of substitutes
Switching costs
Buyer propensity to substitute

**Determinants of Buyer Power**

Bargaining Leverage
Buyer concentration versus firm concentration
Buyer volume
Buyer switching costs relative to firm switching costs
Buyer information
Ability to backward integrate
Substitute products
Pull-through

Price Sensitivity
Price/total purchases
Product differences
Brand identity
Impact on quality/performance
Buyer profits
Decision makers' incentives

Reprinted with the permission of The Free Press, a division of Macmillan, Inc., from *Competitive Advantage: Creating and Sustaining Superior Performance* by Michael E. Porter. Copyright © 1985 by Michael E. Porter.

ings has focused on low-cost production, which allows it to price its products competitively. Not only has the company survived, it has prospered.

As a prospective entrant into the tin can industry, one should ask:

Is this an attractive industry for me to be in?
Can I duplicate the Crown Holdings strategy?
Can I win in a price battle if I choose to enter?
What is the profit potential for me if I choose to enter?
Could my money be better invested elsewhere?

Regardless of the industry, the same questions must be asked when a manager wishes to expand into a new field. Even if expansion is not contemplated, the Porter model offers insight on how to compete more effectively within one's own industry. Please review the *determinants* of the Five Forces in the detailed Porter model *very* carefully. Those are the questions that MBAs ponder to gain competitive advantage.

The forces at play in an industry are dynamic. The essence of strategy is to understand the current forces and to use them to your advantage. In waste disposal, Waste Management Inc. lobbies hard for enactment of stringent environmental regulations. Why? Because only a few companies are able to comply with them. In that way, regulation simultaneously assists Waste Management and hinders its competitors. Stringent regulation creates *barriers to entry* for *new entrants* and, most important, increases the profits of the remaining waste disposal players. Pharmaceutical companies press for the regulation of the vitamin and nutritional-supplement industry for the same reason. Who will survive the streaming entertainment wars? Apple TV+, Disney +, Netflix, Paramount +, Hulu, YouTube, Amazon Prime?

## GENERIC STRATEGIES

There are many ways for a company to analyze its competitive challenges. One such way is the Five Forces framework outlined by Porter that we have just discussed. But most options for action fall into what are called *generic strategies*. A generic strategy is one that can be used across many industries, from dish towels to computers. Porter has aptly captured the three major strategies in a matrix of functional and business strategic possibilities:

Cost Leadership
Differentiation
Focus

THREE GENERIC STRATEGIES

**STRATEGIC ADVANTAGE**

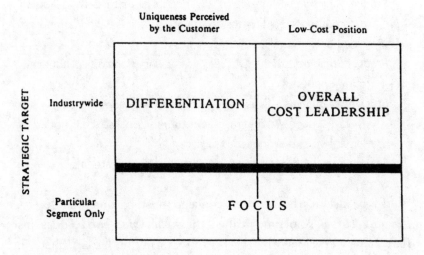

Reprinted with the permission of The Free Press, a division of Macmillian, Inc., from *Competitive Strategy: Techniques for Analyzing Industries and Competitors* by Michael E. Porter. Copyright © 1980 by The Free Press.

## *COST LEADERSHIP AND THE LEARNING CURVE*

The simplest strategy is *cost leadership.* By achieving the lowest cost of production in an industry, a company can either reduce its prices or keep the increased profits to invest in research to develop new and better products. *Low-cost producers* (LCPs) can also choose to use their profits to advertise and market their products more vigorously.

An operations concept related to cost leadership is *economies of scale.* This means that as one produces more, costs per unit fall. As factories produce more, they learn and become more efficient in several ways.

These "learning" efficiencies can come from six sources:

*Labor Efficiency* — Learning through repetition or automation. Tremendous progress has been made in factory automation by using robots and computer-aided manufacturing (CAM).

*New Processes and Improved Methods* — Less costly ways to do the same task

*Product Redesign* — Redesign to lower costs of materials and labor. If a computer is used to design the product, it is called computer-aided design (CAD).

*Product Standardization* — Decreasing the variations of a product's components

*Efficiencies of Scale* — Doubling factory capacity does not cost twice as much. Adding machines or additional space is not as expensive as starting from scratch.

*Substitution* — Using less expensive but adequate materials

To be useful, the learning concept must be quantifiable. The *learning curve,* sometimes called the *experience curve,* does just that. It was developed by the Boston Consulting Group (BCG) in the 1960s to attach numbers to economies-of-scale benefits believed to exist. They found that each time the "cumulative" volume of production doubled, the cost of manufacturing fell by a constant and predictable percentage.

For example, a consultant's investigation of a manufacturing task could identify an "80 percent learning curve." This means that for every doubling of accumulated production, the next unit produced would cost 80 percent of the first unit, or 20 percent less. Computer spreadsheet models exist to perform the mathematics. The important point to remember is that "accumulated production" starts with unit one, not the first produced that month or year, but the very first one off the assembly line using that manufacturing method.

THE LEARNING CURVE EFFECT
COST OF PRODUCTION OF RAZOR BLADES

| Units Produced | Unit Cost | Math per Unit | Production Method |
|---|---|---|---|
| 1 | $10.00 | | By Hand |
| 2 | 8.00 | $10 \times .8$ | |
| 4 | 6.40 | $8 \times .8$ | Manual Assembly Line |
| 1,048,576 | .12 | $10 \times (.80)^{20}$ | |
| 2,097,152 | .09 | $10 \times (.80)^{21}$ | Fully Automated |

To demonstrate the math involved, I have hypothesized what the effects of an 80 percent learning curve would have been on the cost of producing disposable razors for Gillette.

The math demonstrates that after the razor production doubles twenty-one times, the cost per unit decreases 20 percent each time from a cost of $10.00 to $.09. A simple learning curve can also be seen graphically as shown:

RAZOR BLADE LEARNING CURVE

**80% Learning**

**Total Units Produced**

The strategic implications of the learning curve lie in *moving down the learning curve* before competitors do. A firm wishing to maintain cost leadership will strive to produce more units than its competition. That way its production costs will be decreased more quickly.

The concept of "dumping" products below cost is a tactic the Japanese had used in the electronics industry while pursuing a cost leadership strategy. These forward-thinking companies sold video recorders at low prices, expecting to realize profits as they increased production at a lower cost. Japanese manufacturers calculated their profits using a five-year rather than a one-year time horizon. Therefore, they planned losses for their first year, so that larger profits could be realized in years three and four. American competitors saw the industry as unattractive and plagued by irrational pricing, while the strategic-minded Japanese companies walked away with the market. As the older products matured, the Japanese used the profits from their sale to develop new products like DVDs. But DVDs died with the advent of video streaming. Drawing from the same playbook, China leapfrogged Japan in the production of large-screen TVs.

As a product matures in its *product life cycle* and becomes widely adopted, as described in the marketing chapter, the curve becomes less useful. To double accumulated production would require tremendous increases in volume that are simply not realistic. Profits are also likely to be low. In this situation, the remaining competitors have the chance to catch up, if they haven't given up.

Learning curves are not static. A new process or material may increase worker productivity and thus alter the curve. In the razor instance, a new curve may be at work at, say, "75 percent learning" because of a new assembling machine, instead of 80 percent as shown. That is called *jumping to a new curve*. In this situation, the running total of accumulated units produced is set to zero, and the new curve takes effect. When production doubles, the next unit produced will cost 75 percent of the first one using the new process, or 25 percent less. With products that are continuously innovated, the learning curve is of little use. New curves are formed all the time, and there is not much time to "move down" any of them.

## DIFFERENTIATION

As discussed earlier, *differentiation* is a prime marketing objective. It involves making your product or service appear different in the mind of the consumer. With products, this means offering better design, reliability, service, and delivery. With services, a point of differentiation can be employee courtesy, availability, expertise, and location. Products and services can be differentiated via advertising, even if they are virtually the same. A media campaign can convince the consumer that one is better. For instance, consumers could be persuaded that Nike shoes are better than Converse because of a celebrity endorsement.

## FOCUS

Using a *focus* strategy, a company concentrates on either a market area, a market segment, or a product. The strength of a focus strategy is derived from knowing the customer and the product category well. Companies establish a "franchise" in the marketplace. In the beer market, dominated by titans such as Anheuser-Busch, Coors, and Miller, little Hudepohl Beer ("Hudy") holds its own in Ohio. The giants can boast lower costs and slick marketing, but they do not enjoy the local "cult" following. Hudy pursued a loyal following over the years through local exposure and community involvement. Hudy *focuses* on Ohio.

## COMPETITIVE TACTICS: SIGNALING

Signaling is a key strategic tool. It involves letting your competitors know what's on your mind. Combatants signal what they plan to do or what steps they will take in response to a competitor's move. Of course, a company can also bluff. Signaling is used to prevent disastrous (and costly) price wars. Direct contact with the competition to set prices or allocate markets is illegal! Antitrust laws forbid this behavior. But by judiciously signaling, companies can achieve the desired outcome without time behind bars.

In the airline industry, signaling is commonplace. On reservation screens across the country, a daily cat-and-mouse game goes on. For example, Delta may briefly lower fares significantly on its prized routes from Atlanta to Los Angeles in response to United Airlines' price cuts along the same route. The Delta price move says, "United, if you want to play games on this route, it'll be bloody." If United responds by raising prices, in effect they are signaling, "Let's call a truce." If United keeps the low fare, it is signaling its intention to do battle. It's just like poker.

Six common types of *legal* signals are:

*Price Movements* — to signal intentions and to penalize unacceptable behavior

*Prior Announcements* — to threaten, to test competitors' resolve, and to avoid surprises. In the retailing industry announcements that a strong company will "meet or beat any competitor's price" sends a strong signal of a company's resolve. A smaller and weaker competitor should probably not compete only on price.

*Media Discussions* — to communicate your rationale for actions and to convey your thoughts to the competition. Because executives of competing companies are barred from communicating with each other directly, they do it indirectly via the media.

*Counterattack* — to hit your competitor's home market with a price cut or promotion in retaliation for their encroachment on your turf. Say New York was Maxwell House coffee's best market, and Folgers best was California. If the Maxwell House brand manager attacked Folgers turf with aggressive pricing and promotion, his counterpart at Folgers would be up in arms, to put it mildly. He would have two options: one, to defend California aggressively; or two, to take the offensive and attack Maxwell House's New York market. If he chose the second option, he would be signaling his anger and suggesting that a truce might benefit them both.

*Announce Results* — to communicate clearly to the competition the results of an action to avoid a costly misunderstanding. In test-market situations a manufacturer could clearly announce a failure in hopes of dissuading a competitor from counterattacking other established products. In pricing battles, a competitor could announce that the price cut is for only a limited time, in an effort to avoid signaling a long-term intention to keep prices low.

*Litigation* — to tie up a competitor in court. In a lawsuit, a company can express its displeasure on a number of issues, such as patents and trademark infringement.

THE PRISONER'S DILEMMA

|  | Silence | Confess |
|---|---|---|
| **Silence** | Freedom for Both | Light Sentence/ Tough Sentence |
| **Confess** | Tough Sentence/ Light Sentence | Moderate Sentence for Both |

(In the case where the two prisoners act differently, the confessing prisoner gets a lighter sentence.)

## *SIGNALING, THE PRISONER'S DILEMMA AND GAME THEORY*

A related signaling concept is the *prisoner's dilemma,* as it is frequently referred to in corporate battles. As the story goes, two people are arrested for a murder and separated so that they cannot communicate. The police do not have enough evidence to convict either man, but if they can convince either man to confess and testify against the other, they will then have a strong case against one of them. The police promise each a lighter sentence if he turns state's evidence against the other. If they both refuse to confess and implicate each other, they will go free for lack of evidence. But what each prisoner does not know is how the other will act. Can one trust the other to keep quiet?

In competitive situations such as prevail in the airline industry, this scenario is similar to two companies that maintain high prices, each trusting the other to do the same. It is always tempting to break this silent pact, because a price war could result in the elimination of the other carrier. If they decide to cooperate in this unstable arrangement, they are both caught in a prisoner's dilemma.

All forms of signaling will be doomed if a competitor acts "irrationally." In that case, any attempt to call a competitive truce would go unheeded because in an irrationally competitive mind, winning, rather than maximizing profits, is the goal.

*Game theory* is the formal study of competitive interactions. It analyzes possible outcomes in situations where people are trying to score points from each other, whether in bridge, politics, war, or business. You do this by trying to anticipate the reactions of your competitor to your next move and then factoring that reaction into your actual decision. Computers' powers of calculation have allowed game theory to become a practical business tool. In 1994 a Nobel Prize was awarded for the study of game theory.

That same year, game theory gained wider acceptance when it was used extensively by bidders in the federal government's auction of 120 megahertz of air frequency for PCS, personal communication services. The FCC set up such a complicated bidding system that sophisticated decision-making tools were a necessity. With multiple bidders and fifty-one markets to auction off, bidders used applied-game-theory programs to analyze their competitors and make their bids. After 112 rounds of bidding, the government raised $7.7 billion.

## PORTFOLIO STRATEGIES

If signaling sounds like fun, its enjoyment is eclipsed by the pleasure MBAs take in playing portfolio games. *Portfolio strategy* is considered the highbrow area of *corporate level* strategic planning. It is the dominion of MBAs and of the elite management consulting firms headquartered in Boston and New York. In the 1960s, many academics and executives believed that if a corporation could put together the right *portfolio* of unrelated and countercyclical businesses, it would be immune to economic downturns. Accordingly, the concept of diversification became the craze of the decade. A prime example is General Electric, a company that was involved in 160 businesses during the sixties.

But in the 1970s, when profits declined and Wall Street became dissatisfied with *unrelated diversification,* boards of directors ran to consultants for help. They wanted to know what businesses they should be in, which they should continue in, and which they should sell. Cash was scarce and a strategy had to be found that would help funnel their limited capital to the best prospects. After many divestitures in the decades since, GE totally split apart in 2021.

As you might expect, each consulting firm developed its own theory and matrix model to answer the portfolio management problem. Knowledgeable MBAs are familiar with the four major portfolio models, and you should be too.

## THE BOSTON CONSULTING GROUP'S
## GROWTH/SHARE MATRIX

The Boston Consulting Group's (BCG) model uses market growth rates and relative market share to classify companies into four categories. Their studies showed that high market share was highly correlated with higher ROI (return on investment) and lower costs because of *learning curve effects*. Therefore, the theory suggests that it is best to have a stable, high market share in some businesses to fund the cash needs of other businesses. There are four classifications that rest on that premise.

The *Star* is a high-market-share business in a high-growth industry. Stars grow and finance themselves. Alphabet, the owner of the

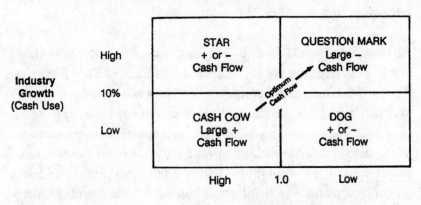

THE BCG BUSINESS PORTFOLIO CHART

Google search engine, is a good example of a self-financing growth company. Its profit margin of 30 percent on sales of $258 billion in 2021 was ample to meet its cash needs for new and existing projects. Characteristically, these types of companies exist in competitive markets and require vigilant managements to maintain their enviable positions on the BCG matrix.

*Cash cows* are high-market-share businesses in low-growth industries. These gems provide the cash to fund other businesses or dividends. Yesterday's stars, tobacco companies, are today's cows.

*Dogs* are small-market-share businesses in low-growth industries. These businesses are going nowhere and consume corporate cash and management's time in an attempt to stay competitive. In the steel industry many companies are dogs. Their plants and equipment need expensive modernization, but with softer demand and increased foreign competition, they do not warrant additional investment by their parent companies. As a consequence, boards of directors that agree with this assessment have let their steel plants rust.

*Question marks* are small-market-share businesses in high-growth industries. To grow they need cash. Some strategists call them "problem children." If they become successful, they will become stars, and later, cash cows. If they fail, they either die or become dogs as their industries mature. Start-up biotechnology, crypto, and AI firms fall into the question mark category. Expensive research has to be funded in the hope of producing a miracle drug, blockchain technology, or generative AI breakthrough.

All this animal talk is fun until it is *your* business that the consultants label a dog. Dogs are not necessarily bad businesses. They just aren't the type of businesses that large corporations want in their portfolio. Wall Street investors demand a level of sales growth and cash generation that dogs cannot provide. Many millionaires have been minted as the dogs' management and buyout artists have taken these companies off larger corporations' hands. My acquisitions course was taught by a number of visiting "professors" who had profited nicely from the housecleaning of large corporations' troublesome critters.

Portfolio strategies have their drawbacks. They assume that businesses in a portfolio have no significant *linkages*, which is often not the case. Many collections of businesses share technical, marketing, and support functions. Using shared resources is difficult when using portfolio concepts because they dictate a continual juggling act of companies to maximize growth and cash. Historically, with few exceptions, only investment bankers and advising consultants have profited from the juggling transactions of trading the BCG *animals*. The other beneficiaries of company juggling are the managements of these portfolio companies. If a business is not working out, there is no need to fix it. Just sell it to them!

## MCKINSEY & COMPANY'S MULTIFACTOR ANALYSIS

McKinsey & Co. takes a different approach to portfolio juggling. In response to dissatisfaction at General Electric in 1970 with the BCG's two-variable model, McKinsey developed its own. The guidance is the same from both models: sell, hold, or invest in a business in the portfolio. In McKinsey's vocabulary, you *harvest* a cash cow and *divest* a dog.

The model has two general variables that govern a business evaluation: *industry attractiveness* and *business strength*. McKinsey's model is not simple. Each variable is determined by a number of industry factors. In any given industry, some factors will be of greater importance than others.

The McKinsey model has nine quadrants versus BCG's four. The six generic courses of action dictated by the model are:

- Invest and Hold
- Invest to Grow
- Invest to Rebuild
- Selectively Invest in Promising Areas of the Business
- Harvest, Milk the Cow
- Divest, Sell the Dog

Although the McKinsey model is attractive because it takes into account many factors, nonetheless the evaluation is subjective. As shown by the matrix, the individual factors culminate in a "high," "medium," or "low" assessment. For example, Walmart's sales growth is accessible through its published annual report, but how can one objectively quantify Walmart's "image"? It is a component that McKinsey uses in evaluating a business's position in its matrix. It's all subjective.

THE MCKINSEY COMPANY POSITION / INDUSTRY
ATTRACTIVENESS SCREEN

| Business Position | | Low | Medium | High |
|---|---|---|---|---|
| | High | S | I | I |
| | Medium | H | S | I |
| | Low | H | H | S |

Industry Attractiveness

I = Invest / Grow    S = Selectivity / Earnings    H = Harvest / Divest

## ARTHUR D. LITTLE'S SBU SYSTEM

Arthur D. Little (ADL) is another bastion of MBA portfolio experts. ADL has cooked up a system that revolves around the SBU, the *strategic business unit* and lifestyle change. When similar businesses of a corporation are grouped into SBUs, portfolio strategies become less complicated because there are fewer units to worry about. Businesses in different SBUs have little association with one another other than the financial ties imposed on them by the parent corporation.

The ADL portfolio process has four steps:

1. Classify all the businesses of a corporation into SBUs.
2. Place the SBUs into a matrix.
3. Evaluate the conditions of the industries in which each SBU operates.
4. Decide.

ADL's matrix has twenty-four quadrants compared to McKinsey's nine. The two variables that are operative in ADL's model are *industry maturity level* and *competitive position*. Needless to say, these are similar to McKinsey's and BCG's. However, ADL vocabulary derives its inspiration from traffic signals rather than the animal world. SBUs either with high market share or in an attractive market are classified as *green*. Those caught in the middle are *yellow*. And the poor prospects with low market shares or in mature markets are branded *red*, as shown below.

Based on their traffic light classification, the consultants devise appropriate strategies for each SBU owned: *build, maintain,* or *liquidate.* For green SBUs there are many different strategies available. For the red ones, the options available are constrained by the poor "condi-

THE ADL STRATEGIC BUSINESS UNIT MODEL

|  |  | Embryonic | Growth | Maturity | Aging |
|---|---|---|---|---|---|
| **Competitive Position** | Leading | G | G | G | G |
|  | Strong | G | G | G | Y |
|  | Favorable | G | G | Y | R |
|  | Tenable | G | Y | R | R |
|  | Weak | Y | R | R | R |
|  | Nonviable | R | R | R | R |

**Industry Maturity**

G = Green   Y = Yellow   R = Red

tions" in which they find themselves. Once the SBU is classified, the consultants turn to their palette of generic strategies such as *focus, penetration,* or *diversification* to construct appropriate tactical plans.

## THE COMPETITIVE LIFE CYCLE—PRODUCT AND TECHNOLOGY PORTFOLIO ANALYSIS

From a marketing standpoint, the product life cycle (PLC) has a strategic twist called the *competitive life cycle* (CLC). The CLC has only three stages for new products and technologies—*emergent, growth,* and *mature.* By the time decline occurs, the industry has already moved on to another CLC. Even component parts go through CLCs like microprocessors and batteries.

The S-curve is the shape that depicts the cumulative revenues that new products generate, similar to the PLC on page 19.

As new products or technologies emerge, old S-curves cease to be relevant and a new S-curve of competition begins. That's called *jumping to a new S-curve.* It is strategically important for a company to plan for the CPC by creating a portfolio of products and technologies that will survive the inevitable decline of any given product in the portfolio.

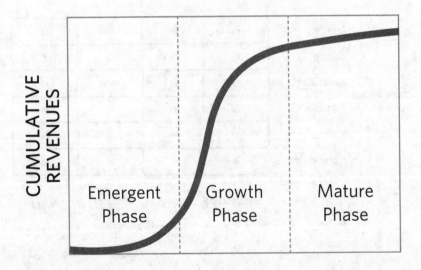

The emergent stage begins with a "disruption" of the old CLC with a new technology. Think iPhone for the cell-phone industry.

As the emergent phase progresses, there is an "annealing" process (a term for strengthening steel) where the new product or technology becomes more standardized with a dominant design. Think EVs (electric vehicles).

When sales accelerate during the growth phase, competitors scale up their production. As direct competition grows, that leads to the mature phase, where a "shakeout" occurs. Think Ikea value-priced furniture with few competitors, but then Wayfair comes to disrupt.

The cycle goes back to square one, where a new "disruption" occurs and the whole process repeats. The speed of the process is highly dependent on the industry: furniture slow; electronics fast.

The executive team is required to forecast the timing of the CLC stages and inflection points in order to strategically plan resources, and to focus and monitor competitors.

In 2023 EVs were annealing in the emergent phase, while laptops were in the mature phase waiting for a disruption. Dedicated GPS devices were disrupted by Waze and other apps. The same could be said for the taxi industry, which was disrupted by Uber and Lyft.\*

## OTHER STRATEGIC CONSULTING
## FADS TO KNOW ABOUT

In any strategic marketing analysis, as mentioned in the marketing chapter, you should evaluate your own company's *core competencies* in the context of evaluating your competition. Beginning in 1990, consulting firms made an entire assignment out of investigating what your company does well. For example, at Frito-Lay, the distribution system is key.

Another popular assignment was to focus on *customer retention*. Bain & Co., the theory's leading exponent, created an entire practice out of it. The goal of such an assignment is to figure out how to create loyal customers and retain them. To accomplish that, companies and consultants perform extensive consumer research to understand customer buying habits and satisfaction. Consultants examine the customer base to discover who the best customers are so that they can be singled out for special treatment. Often the "best" customers generating the most sales are not the same as those generating the most profits. In addition, systems are set up to gather and store customer data so that marketers can easily and effectively contact the customer. It is more effective to retain good customers than to constantly churn new ones. This took a sinister turn in 2009 when McKinsey used its expertise to advise Purdue Pharma how to "turbocharge" opioid sales.

In 1993, James Champy and Michael Hammer's book *Reengineering the Corporation* set a new consulting fad in motion. Their "reengineering" consultancy CSC-Index drafted on their book's success and provided expert advice on how to rethink everything your corporation may do. As reported in the *Boston Globe* in April 1995, "Managers should abandon hierarchal structures in favor of em-

\* Adapted from *The Strategist's Tool Kit*, by Harris and Lenox, Darden Business Publishing, 2013, pp. 33–42.

ployee teams, to develop systems that cut across traditional fiefdoms such as sales and marketing, and to use computer technology to eliminate a lot of paper-pushing and paper-pushers."

Stern Stewart & Co. innovated in the financial area by creating a method of restating a company's income so that management could concentrate on improving its stock performance. *Economic value added* (EVA) or *market value added* (MVA) was a new strategic consulting concept that gained importance in 1993. EVA is the difference between a company's net operating income after taxes and its cost of capital. Accountants have called the measure "residual income" for years, but Stern Stewart modified it and coined the EVA term.

> EVA = ANOPAT – Cost of Capital % × (Adjusted Total
>    Assets – Current Liabilities)
> ANOPAT means the Adjusted Net Operating Profit
>    After Taxes

The idea is that a company's financial performance should be judged by the return generated after deducting the cost of capital provided by shareholders. The GAAP accounting measure of "net income" used on financial statements does not do that. During a consulting assignment the client company would learn the new methodology, and its management would be guided toward strategies focusing on the factors that could possibly boost its stock price.

## GLOBALIZATION AND STRATEGY

The world is becoming increasingly economically interdependent. Thus strategic planning on a global scale has become a timely concern. The MBA buzzword is *globalization*. It is a rather nebulous term, but it is a "hot" topic and efforts are made to interject the word *global* into all MBA courses and writings.

The possibility of globalization depends on the classification of the industry in which a business operates. If an industry is *national* in nature, it can successfully operate without being threatened by large *multinational corporations* (MNCs) swooping in and either trying a hostile takeover or competing in some sense. Baking and trucking are two examples of national industries. Automobiles and computers, on the other hand, are examples of global industries. The necessity of heavy research spending and significant learning curve effects tend to favor large MNCs. Whatever the industry, forces are at work that either facilitate or impede globalization.

Forces encouraging globalization:

*Improved Communications and Transportation* — 5G cell-phone service, cable, satellite, supersonics

*Fewer Trade Restrictions* — Lower tariffs, duties, uniform regulations

*Convergence of Consumer Needs* — People everywhere are beginning to have the same tastes.

*Technological Complexity and Change* — Emerging high-tech industries require larger investments and worldwide efforts to keep pace with rapid change.

*MNC Rivalries* — MNCs fight for world domination of their particular industries.

Forces hindering globalization:

*Cost of Coordination* — More managers, communication costs

*Geographic Restraints* — Transportation constraints and logistical barriers of operating over wider areas

*National Differences* — Taste preferences, usage, media, language, distribution channel differences

*Protectionism* — Tariffs, government subsidies, regulatory approvals

The debate over which classification, global or national, an industry belongs to is not as important as investigating the forces that do or don't make it so. If a company finds itself in an emerging global industry, it must take action or it will be overtaken by others. Because the classification lies on a spectrum that ranges from national to global, the courses of action available are also in that range. A threatened automaker could lobby the government to close its market to foreigners to make an industry national. On the other hand, in the same situation the automaker may choose to pursue an aggressive expansion strategy, as Chinese manufacturers have done.

When speaking of globalization, MBAs often refer to Thomas Friedman's *The World Is Flat* (2005). He viewed the world as a level playing field in terms of commerce because of technological advances. Friedman outlines what he calls "flatteners" that "converged" to create an integrated, hypercompetitive, global marketplace.

## SYNERGY AND STRATEGY

*Synergy* is the benefit derived from combining two or more businesses so that the performance of the combination is higher than the sum of the individual businesses. When you are making portfolio acquisitions and divestitures, synergy becomes a key issue. Mistakes are often made when the synergistic effects of combining businesses are not explicitly defined and quantified. There may be possibilities for shared production, distribution, and markets, but these *linkages* or *interrelationships* must be scrutinized before including them in the price of an acquisition or merger target. Overpaying for synergy is called the *synergy trap*. The purchase price should always be greater than the opportunity costs of other uses. In a merger, the target company has to be valued so that the appropriate number of shares of the parent's stock is exchanged for the target's.

The four types of business linkages are:

*Market Linkages*
Customer Bases — same buyers
Distribution Channels — same path to the consumer
Brand Identifications — transference of a brand's name and equity to
    other products
*Technological Linkages*
Operations Technologies — factory processes
New Product Technologies — research
Information Technologies — data collection, databases

*Product Linkages*
Product Line Extension Possibilities
Excess Production Capacity — to be used for other products
Materials Procurement — buyer power with suppliers enhanced
Staff Functions — The same accountants and personnel staff can
  provide services across product categories.

*Intangible Linkages*
Shared Managerial Know-How: Experience with same type of buyer
Similar configuration of the value chain
Similar generic strategies used

In November 1994, Quaker Oats thought it had the perfect match for its Gatorade sports drink: Snapple fruit juices and iced teas. The acquisition cost $1.7 billion. Already a leader in noncarbonated beverages with the Gatorade brand, Quaker vaulted to the position of being the third-largest beverage company behind Coke and Pepsi. Quaker's analysts thought that its powerful distribution system, shared manufacturing, and economies of scale could vault this New Age beverage to new heights of sales and profitability. It had many linkages going for it. However, Coke and Pepsi both aggressively entered the market with lower-priced Lipton and Nestea tea drinks. Coke's Fruitopia brand attacked Snapple at the high end as well. In the end, New Age became "old hat" by 1997 and Snapple's sales collapsed. Taking a $1.4 billion loss, Quaker sold the company for $300 million to Triarc Companies, the maker of RC Cola and Mistic fruit juices. Despite the linkages, the trendy nature of the product itself overwhelmed any synergies that may have existed for the transaction. Triarc, on the other hand, found value by returning to the strategies that had built the brand and in 2000 sold Snapple for $1.5 billion to soda maker Cadbury Schweppes.

Even when synergy does exist, there are often significant costs associated with making two organizations work together. Decision making may be hampered by lengthier processes of approval. Increased organizational inflexibility may be the by-product of a larger organization. In rapidly changing markets, this inflexibility could be a strategic disadvantage.

## STRATEGIC SKEPTICISM

The preceding discussion may have given the impression that corporations are successful as a result of expert strategic planning. In the area that I call *strategic skepticism,* strategic planning is not quite the analytical process preached by academics.

According to James Brian Quinn of MIT's Sloan School, strategy is considered to be a process of *logical incrementalism.* In his view, strategy is the result of many smaller decisions taken over a long time. Other theorists also hold that strategy is not as formal a process as that presented in the preceding pages. Strategy can take five forms, all starting with *P*:

- Plan
- Ploy
- Pattern
- Process
- Perspective

In one company, strategy is the result of a formal *plan.* In another, strategy is the execution of a successful tactical *ploy.*

Strategy can also be just a *pattern,* a *process,* or *perspective* of conducting business and making decisions. In my own experience in a small jewelry business, we followed a simple philosophy. We treated our customers well, gave them the best prices, and were completely honest about the merchandise. This consciously chosen way of conducting business was a successful *strategy.*

Strategy can be the product of an entrepreneur's insight as a result of being hit with the boom of his or her sailboat, or it can be a series of ad hoc plans that develop over time. Either way, the formal planning processes sold by consultants are not always the answer.

History is often rewritten to suit the theories of strategic planners. One version of the success of Honda motorcycles described Sochiro Honda as a free spirit driven by will and a dream. He had no grand plan. The success of the company was the product of his burning desire to build a winning racing motorcycle and his slow, step-by-step introduction of his motorcycle into the U.S. market in 1958. Luckily for Sochiro, the United States placed few restrictions on his "inconsequential" Japanese import.

Consultants at BCG told a much different story about Honda to their British motorcycle industry clients. In their view, Honda had calculated to *go down the learning curve* to achieve lower costs and build world market share through low pricing. The company's dominant market share allowed for large investments in research and advanced manufacturing techniques. BCG reported that Honda's market leadership also allowed the company to advertise and promote Honda at lower costs per bike. Which version of history is true? Personally, I gravitate toward the more colorful story, but the cost leadership principle obviously played a large role in Honda's success, planned or not. In fact, if theory is used in conjunction with a manager's own good judgment and common sense, strategy can be a winning mix of art and science.

## STRATEGY AND CHINESE WARFARE

No lesson on strategy would be complete without mentioning Sun-tzu, a Chinese military strategist of the fourth century B.C. Somehow his maxims have entered into many an MBA conversation about strategy. I imagine the irascible Mr. Honda quoting him quite often. Sun-tzu's book, *The Art of War,* even sat on my former boss's desk. Quoting Sun-tzu is sure to make you either sound terribly smart or appear like the ruthless insider trader Gordon Gekko in the movie *Wall Street.* Here are a few choice quotes for your next business meeting, if you dare use them:

> All warfare is based on deception.
> Offer the enemy a bait to lure him; feign disorder and strike him.
> For to win one hundred victories in one hundred battles is not the acme of skill. To subdue the enemy without fighting is the acme of skill.

In war, numbers alone confer no advantage. Do not advance relying
on sheer military power.

Thus, what is of supreme importance in war is to attack the enemy's
strategy.

See *The Ten-Day MBA* Movie Guide in Day 10: Minicourses for
more!

## STRATEGIC IMPLEMENTATION

As I indicated at the beginning of this chapter, strategy development
without an eye toward implementation is a waste of time. Strategic
changes are an easy topic for MBAs to talk about, but are not easy
to accomplish. A clever quote won't cut it. I cannot possibly tell you
how to turn around a failing business in a chapter, but I can put strategic thinking into perspective. Contrary to what some academics
would lead you to believe, no one tactic or trick constitutes strategy;
rather, strategy is how the "totality" of a company works together to
achieve goals.

Executives do not think up or implement strategy in one day.

Leaders have to discern which factors are within their control
and which are not. MBAs call those factors within their control the
*action levers.* Strategists must also deal with the reality of human
resistance to change. They must set tangible goals, formulate their
action plan, and develop contingency plans if things do not go as
intended. This is the same action-planning sequence outlined in the
organizational behavior chapter.

Strategy is dynamic. Executives must review their strategy continuously to ensure that it reflects the changes in the business environment, the company, and its goals. *The source of competitive
advantage is the pursuit of an evolving strategy that cannot easily be
duplicated by competitors.*

## KEY STRATEGY TAKEAWAYS

*The Seven S model* — Strategy is how all of a company's S's work together.

*Environmental Analysis*—A look at the macro factors and trends that influence competition within industries

*The Value Chain* — The process of producing and delivering goods and services

*Integration* — Ways to expand a business: backward, forward, vertically, horizontally

*Ansoff Matrix* — Four strategies for business expansion

*Porter's Five Forces Theory* — Five forces that determine the competitive intensity of an industry

*The Learning Curve* — The more units produced, the lower the cost per unit falls due to production efficiencies.

*Signaling* — Indirectly communicating with competitors

*The Prisoner's Dilemma* — The captive nature of competitive relationships within an industry

*Portfolio Strategies* — The theories large multibusiness corporations use to decide which companies they should buy, sell, or hold

*Competitive Life Cycle*—The cycle through which new products and technologies emerge, grow, and mature

*Globalization* — The worldwide competition inherent in certain industries due to a variety of globalizing factors

*Synergy* — The incremental profits generated by the combination of two companies that share resources

*Incrementalism* — The concept that strategy is not a grand scheme but is developed over time, step-by-step

# *Day 10*

---

# MBA MINICOURSES

RESEARCH AND COMPETITIVE INTELLIGENCE GATHERING

PUBLIC SPEAKING

NEGOTIATING

INTERNATIONAL BUSINESS

MBA MOVIE GUIDE

BUSINESS LAW

BUSINESS WRITING

REAL ESTATE INVESTING

LEADERSHIP COACH

FINANCIAL PLANNER

## THE TEN-MINUTE MINICOURSE ON RESEARCH AND COMPETITIVE INTELLIGENCE GATHERING

It is said that information is power. That is why MBA schools teach students research skills. The key to efficient and productive research is to know where to seek information. By putting a little more effort into your job, you as a Ten-Day MBA may get that brilliant insight or fact that may elude your less industrious colleagues. Of all the sections in this book, this one may be the most valuable to you, so I finish with it. Suppose you need facts about a competitor, a person, or an industry; the following are some of the *right* places to look.

## THE INTERNET

When you log on to search sites, review the optimal syntax for searches so that you can keep searches with a thousand responses to a minimum. By limiting your search terms with the correct syntax, you will save a great deal of time.

*Optimal Google Searching.* When doing a Google search, use the optimal syntax to ask your research questions. It will save you a great deal of time, believe me. Use quotes around exact phrases to limit results to an exact phrase or topic ("Ten Day MBA"). Use a hyphen to exclude words you do not want in your search (MBA -Harvard). Use a colon to search an individual Web site ("Ten day MBA" site:Amazon.com). Use the asterisk as a wildcard to get at incomplete information (Ten * MBA). Use the word OR to search two items of related interest (Darden OR "University of Virginia").

*Factiva.* A great affordable service for researching business subjects is Factiva. The database includes thousands of sources from the Dow Jones and Reuters databases that are mostly not available for free.

*United States Patent and Trademark Office.* You can search existing trademarks and patents at www.uspto.gov. It is a great source of competitive information and can aid you in your product-naming and development activities.

*Google Trends.* Google Trends is a great and free way to search for trends in new products, consumer needs, emerging technologies, etc. With graphics you can see keyword search traffic that reveals trends over time. For example, if you have a product for "sciatic back pain," you can search that term and see if there is interest in the problem and how it is trending.

*Amazon Ecosystem Intelligence.* A Web site called Hellium10.com is a deep dive into the Amazon world. At Hellium10 you can look for new product opportunities and trends. It has a very powerful set of tools. Alibaba.com is a source of product information as well. In any case, if you are developing a new product, do not skip over extensive Amazon searches.

## BOOKS AND ONLINE DATABASES

*Standard & Poor's Industry Surveys* — This multivolume set provides excellent, timely, in-depth research of twenty major industries.

*Macrotrends.net* — An excellent source of corporate financial information, share prices, financial statements, charts, and ratios, both current and historical.

*Value Line Investment Surveys* — This source provides detailed, up-to-date company information for investors in seventy-six industries.

*Plunkett's Industry Almanacs* — This multivolume set describes industries and companies (www.plunketresearch.com).

*Gale Research* — Gale Research publishes a series of books that are the cornerstones of all good business libraries:

· *Market Share Reporter* — This book presents market share data that appear in public sources. It's a timesaver!

· *Business Rankings Annual* — This book gives business ranking data that appear in public sources. It is a good industry source.

· *Encyclopedia of Associations* — Most industries and products have associations, trade groups, and clubs. These organizations are happy to assist people to learn about them, their membership, or their interests. Many publish research studies, membership directories, and newsletters. Their people can also lead you to other sources of information. Do not overlook the *Encyclopedia of Associations*.

*Local Market Audiencet Analyst* — This annual study published by SRDS is one of the best sources of marketing information. It combines demographics, lifestyles, and media habits.

*Congressional Quarterly's Washington Information Directory* — This book puts all the resources of the Washington bureaucracy at your fingertips. The entries about the Commerce Department are helpful for international trade. If you pay your income taxes, you have paid for this service. Why not use it?

*Google Scholar* — A database of university research papers.

## *INTERNATIONAL BUSINESS*

*Doing Business in . . .* This series published by PwC is an excellent
   source of information for the international businessperson.
   It discusses the customs and a variety of the finer points of
   international business.

## *EXPENSIVE RESEARCH*

*The Lexis-Nexis Research Database* — This expensive online computer
   service is available at some libraries and businesses. It allows
   access to whole libraries of news, financial, and marketing data.
   Keyword searches must carefully be defined because so much
   data is available. Seek free sources of information first if you
   are cost-conscious. If not, this is one of the most powerful
   databases that exists. It will save you a lot of time.

*Find/SVP* — Provides off-the-shelf studies of most product
   categories. Their well-written reports range in price from a few
   hundred to several thousand dollars. Their studies contain much
   of the information that is available for free from other sources,
   as well as some proprietary research.

*Financial Databases* — Factset, Capital IQ, Bloomberg, Investex,
   Mergent Horizon, and SDC are expensive financial databases
   available at corporate and library institutions.

## *INTERVIEWS*

Information can always be gathered by talking to people. The biggest mistake is to finish an interview and neglect to ask for referrals to other sources. After networking with several company or industry insiders, you can name-drop your way to other people. By mentioning the name of someone they already know, you make interviewees feel more at ease, and they become more generous with their information.

## *TRADE SHOWS*

If you really want to know about an industry, attend its annual trade show. In one location you will get to see all the major players and new products. The show directory serves as an encyclopedia of industry contacts. There are several online sources for domestic and international trade shows. I have regularly attended the hardware, housewares, medical products, toy, gift, and automotive trade shows.

## *KEEPING CURRENT*

There are a few newspaper and magazine apps and Web sites that MBAs must make time for. MBAs must be informed, and these publications give them the information edge. How can they expect to talk and think intelligently if they do not know what is going on in the world? To succeed, you must read.

*The Wall Street Journal* — If you don't have time to read more, just read the front page. It gives you the business news that you need to know.

*Forbes* and *Barron's* — These are the best business magazines. For news, there is the *Journal*, but these magazines give you the trends and the types of stories and analyses that are written for the intelligent business reader.

*Advertising Age* — Most business magazines have a financial bent, but *Advertising Age* comes at business from a pure marketing perspective. It is the trade magazine of the advertising world. It gives a person a well-rounded business outlook. Since most products are advertised, it is a good source of competitive information.

Local Paper/Local Business Journals — If you don't know the business players in your community, they will probably never know you.

## THE TEN-SECOND MINICOURSE ON PUBLIC SPEAKING

1. Know your audience.
   Their interests, attention span
2. Know your own capabilities.
   Can you deliver a joke?
3. Keep it simple.
   Detailed information is best delivered in print.
   Speeches should deliver a concept and motivate.

   *KISS* — Keep It Short and Simple.

## THE ONE-MINUTE MINICOURSE ON NEGOTIATING

1. Know your opponent.
   Temperament, history, capabilities, resources
2. Know yourself.
   Temperament, history, capabilities, resources
   When the desires of two individuals clash, there is a tension that some people handle better than others. It's best not to fool yourself about your own temperament. Try to work either to improve your ability to handle conflict, or to learn to compensate for it.
3. Do your homework.
   Understand the impact of possible settlement scenarios.
4. Determine your strategy and limits ahead of time.
   Do not get caught up in the "need to win" at all costs.
5. Review each negotiation afterward to gain knowledge for the next negotiation.
   What can I improve on? What can I learn from my opponent?

## THE ONE-MINUTE MINICOURSE ON CONDUCTING INTERNATIONAL BUSINESS* (AND FOREIGN POLICY)

1. Understand the host's culture, values, customs, and beliefs. Don't assume that your values are shared.
2. When you are in a foreign country, you are a guest. They are the host and they have the power.
3. You are a foreigner and you will never *really* understand them.
4. Multinational corporations get their competitive advantage from their ability to transfer their experience across borders and avoid mistakes.
5. International investment is a long-term investment. The measure of its return should also be a long-term one.
6. You will have little success without true respect for the host country and its people. If you do not respect them, they'll know it.
7. In international business there is a lot of room for ethical decision making. Act as your own policeman.

## *THE TEN-DAY MBA* MOVIE GUIDE: TOP 15 QUOTABLE QUOTES

There may not be many real-life watercooler conversations anymore, but your colleagues are bound to talk about movies. These movie plots and references to the business world are what you need to know to be a well-rounded Ten-Day MBA. Here is a list of the top fifteen.

1. *Wall Street* (1987): hostile takeovers, leveraged buyouts, stock manipulation, insider trading; starring Michael Douglas as Gordon Gekko. He said:
   "Greed, for lack of a better word, is good. Greed is right. Greed works."
   "Money never sleeps, pal."

---

* These notes on international business were taken from a case discussion led by Professor Neil H. Borden Jr. at the Darden Graduate School of Business at the University of Virginia, used with permission.

2. *The Godfather* (1972): big business, leadership. This is a movie with many notable quotables by Don Vito Corleone, played by Marlon Brando:

> "The lawyer with the briefcase can steal more money than the man with the gun."
>
> "I'm gonna make him an offer he can't refuse."

3. *The Inventor: Out for Blood in Silicon Valley* (2019): the Theranos blood analyzer start-up story, deception, Silicon Valley culture, start-up funding, whistleblowing; starring Elizabeth Holmes and Tyler Shultz as themselves.

> Elizabeth Holmes: "Fake it till you make it."

4. *9 to 5* (1980): sex discrimination; starring Dolly Parton, Jane Fonda, Lily Tomlin.

> Franklin Hart, Jr. (Dabney Coleman): "I'm not such a bad guy!"
>
> Judy Bernly (Jane Fonda): "You're a sexist, egotistical, lying, hypocritical bigot."
>
> Franklin Hart, Jr.: "So I have a few faults; who doesn't?"

5. *Putney Swope* (1969): advertising industry, diversity, discrimination; starring Arnold Johnson.

> Putney Swope (Arnold Johnson): "Rockin' the boat's a drag. You gotta sink the boat."

6. *Moneyball* (2011): the Oakland A's story, use of statistics; starring Brad Pitt, Jonah Hill.

> Billy Beane (Brad Pitt): "When your enemy's making mistakes, don't interrupt him."

7. *The Big Short* (2015): 2007 financial meltdown, mortgage fraud, fundamental financial analysis, SWAPS; starring Steve Carell, Ryan Gosling, Christian Bale, Brad Pitt.

> "The truth is like poetry, and most people f***ing hate poetry." (overheard at a bar in the movie)

8. *Thank You for Smoking* (2005): the big tobacco story, lobbying, PR; starring Aaron Eckhart as Nick Naylor.

> Nick Naylor (Aaron Eckhart): "That's the beauty of argument: if you argue correctly, you're never wrong."

9. *Steve Jobs* (2015): the Apple story, start-ups, creativity, leader-

ship; starring Michael Fassbender as Steve Jobs, and was written by Aaron Sorkin and Walter Isaacson.

> Steve Jobs (Michael Fassbender): "People don't know what they want until you show it to them."

10. *Glengarry Glen Ross* (1992): salesmanship, real estate, leadership, motivation; starring Alec Baldwin, Jack Lemmon, Al Pacino.

> Blake (Alec Baldwin): "Always be closing!" (ABC).

11. *The Founder* (2016): the McDonald's story, start-ups, franchising; starring Michael Keaton as Ray Kroc.

> "Business is war. It's dog eat dog, rat eat rat. If my competitor were drowning, I'd walk over and I'd put a hose right in his mouth."

> "If you've got time to lean, then you've got time to clean."

12. *Boiler Room* (2000): stock fraud, salesmanship, motivation; starring Ben Affleck as Jim Young.

> "There is no such thing as a no-sale call. A sale is made on every call you make. Either you sell the client some stock or he sells you a reason he can't. . . . Either way a sale is made."

13. *Margin Call* (2011): 2007 financial meltdown, the Lehman Brothers story, financial leverage and trading; starring Jeremy Irons, Kevin Spacey.

> John Tuld (Jeremy Irons): "Maybe you could tell me what is going on. And please, speak as you might to a young child. Or a golden retriever. It wasn't brains that brought me here [to become chairman]; I assure you that."

14. *The Wolf of Wall Street* (2013): the Jordan Belfort story, stock fraud, leadership, motivation; starring Leonardo DiCaprio, Matthew McConaughey, Jonah Hill.

> Jordan Belfort. (Leonardo DiCaprio): "Sell me this pen." (By the way, that's a common interview question for sales jobs.)

> Mark Hanna (Matthew McConaughey): "Nobody knows if a stock's going up, down, or f***ing sideways, least of all stockbrokers. But we have to pretend we know."

> Agent Patrick Denham (Kyle Chandler): "Let me give you a little legal advice: Shut The F*** Up!"

15. *The Social Network* (2010): start-ups, leadership, IP ownership issues; starring Jesse Eisenberg, Justin Timberlake.

Mark Zuckerberg (Jesse Eisenberg), in response to accusations of stealing the Facebook concept: "A guy who makes a nice chair doesn't owe money to everyone who has ever built a chair."

# THE TWENTY-MINUTE MINICOURSE ON BUSINESS LAW (THE TWENTY-MINUTE LAWYER)

You could call it "The Twenty-Minute Lawyer," but this section is really a review of the most basic concepts of business law. No divorce law here. As the law is open to many interpretations, a strict interpretation of any of these concepts or related wording could fill a book and could be debated by legal scholars, but in the spirit of *The Ten-Day MBA,* they are outlined here in quick order. Discussions about business structures such as partnerships and corporations have already been discussed in the finance chapter.

## *COMMON LAW*

*Common law* is the basis of law in the United States. Often it is called *case law.* Common law is the framework of laws and guidelines that has been developed based on prior case decisions and opinions. A court's decision is called a *holding. Stare decisis* means that the court should follow the direction of prior court decisions, especially superior court rulings. When the court breaks that tradition, it is unsettling, as we saw the Supreme Court reversal of Roe v. Wade in 2022. The requisites of the American legal system are that it is predictable, flexible, understandable, and reasonable. Two types of law based on the platform of common law play key roles in the system.

## SUBSTANTIVE AND PROCEDURAL LAWS

*Substantive laws* are the actual rules and regulations that define legal behavior. These include the rights and obligations that people have in society. *Procedural laws* govern the way those rules and regulations are implemented or accessed within the system of justice, in an attempt to impose an order for using the system fairly and efficiently.

When lawyers actually apply the law, they refer to the state and federal codes called *statutes*. Statutory laws are the word-for-word substantive rules enacted by the state and federal legislatures or governmental agencies. These laws include criminal law, tax law, and governmental regulations. To investigate how those statutes were applied in actual case situations, a lawyer refers to the body of rulings or *opinions* called case law. By combining statutes and opinions, a lawyer can make a case for his or her client in court following procedural rules of the court.

For the MBA, business transactions are important, thus you hear a great deal about the *Uniform Commercial Code* (UCC). This is a special body of law that combines both the statutory and the case law for business purposes. It is a comprehensive statute adopted by each state that covers the major areas of business transactions, including sales contracts and commercial paper. Its "uniformity" provides a stable set of rules for interstate commerce. Without the UCC, doing business in each state would be like doing business in a foreign country.

## THE LEGAL PROCESS

A standard legal action has nine steps:

1. *Jurisdiction* — For a court to hear a case, it must have *jurisdiction* to hear the subject matter and the power to bind the parties.
2. *Pleadings* — *Pleadings* are the necessary paperwork to begin the trial process. The *plaintiff* files the initial paperwork, called a *complaint* or petition. The plaintiff asserts that the *defendant* has done

a wrong and requests a punishment or remedy. In law notes, *plaintiff* is written as the Greek letter pi (π) and *defendant* as the Greek letter delta (Δ).

3. *Discovery*—Lawyers gather the required information and witnesses before a trial during *discovery*. Each side is allowed to see the evidence held by the other side. Unlike what you may have seen in the movies, there should be no surprises.

4. *Pretrial Conference*—Often held for federal civil cases, at this meeting lawyers and the judge try to organize and narrow the issues of the case to the most important ones to make the trial more efficient. Often out-of-court settlements occur at this point.

5. *Trial*—The trial is proceedings before the court. If a jury is selected, the process of selection is called *voir dire*. The location of the trial is called the *venue*. The jury decides the factual disputes, and the judge interprets the law and instructs the jury. If the plaintiff's case has no merit, a *summary judgment* can be made by the judge, ending the case without further trial.

6. *Jury Instruction by the Judge and the Verdict*—The judge instructs the jury about the issues of law involved in its decision. The jury makes its determination about the facts and penalty within its authority.

7. *Posttrial Motions*—This step includes asking the court, for various reasons, for a retrial and indicating why a new trial is warranted. Errors of law and procedure, jury misconduct, or unusual damage awards can be the basis for an appeal. Rarely is new evidence the basis for a successful appeal.

8. *Appeal*—Generally each party of a lawsuit is entitled to one appeal at an *appellate* court. The paperwork outlining the basis for the appeal is called a *brief*. It is filled with the rather lengthy arguments and with citations of prior court decisions and applicable statutes to make the case for a new trial.

9. *Secure or Enforce the Judgment*—Send the person to jail or collect the money.

## SETTLING A BUSINESS DISPUTE WITHOUT THE COURTS

If they want to avoid the courts to settle a dispute, the parties can bring in a neutral peacemaker.

Mediation — A *mediator* has a nonbinding authority to direct the parties to a fair settlement. However, the parties can back out if they do not like the decision.

Arbitration — An *arbitrator* has the power to bind the parties of a dispute. The decision is final and there are no appeals. These arbitrators are registered, trained professionals.

## CRIMES AND TORTS

The law revolves around one person doing something wrong to another. A wrong can be classified either as a crime or a tort.

Crime — A *crime* is a wrong against society. It can be punished by jail, probation, and fines based on statutory law. Punishable crimes are committed with intent, called *mens rea*, or by negligence. Defenses include self-defense, necessity, and insanity.

Tort — A *tort* is a private wrong against a person or property. It includes acts such as strict product liability, fraud, assault, and theft, also called *conversion*. Torts result from intentional wrongful acts or negligent acts. Torts are punishable by monetary awards based on civil case law. To be found negligent, the offender must have breached a duty to the plaintiff or *standard of care* to act as a prudent person of ordinary skill. If a person is hired for a specialized skill, the standard would be that of the profession or trade. In addition, the accused person must have caused the act for which he or she is being charged, either directly or proximately. In the case of employers, they may be held responsible for the acts of their employees acting within the scope of their duties. This liability of employers is called *respondent superior*.

*Burden of Proof* — In criminal actions, guilt must be found "beyond a reasonable doubt." In civil verdicts, guilt is based on a "preponderance of the evidence."

Often cases have both a criminal and a civil component. For instance, in a criminal embezzlement case, the defendant can be sent to jail for stealing. In a civil proceeding, the plaintiff can try to recover the money and be awarded monetary damages by the court. Defenses to tort actions include the truth (refuting the allegation), consent ("done with my consent"), and insanity.

## CONTRACTS AND PROPERTY LAW

In most business relationships people enter into contracts with one another for a benefit. Although the word *contract* is frequently used in conversation, a contract has a specific legal definition. In legal notes a contract is written as a *K*.

*Contracts* — A *contract* is a legally enforceable agreement, either express or implied, between two or more parties. Four conditions must be met for a contract to be valid:

1. **Capacity of Parties** — The parties must have legal authority and mental capacity to enter into the agreement. Minors can disaffirm their contracts, but adults cannot disaffirm a contract with a minor. The only exception is for items called necessaries such as food and shelter.

2. **Mutual Agreement (Assent) or Meeting of the Minds** — There must be a valid *offer* and an *acceptance*. The offer must clearly indicate an intent to make a contract, be definite as to its terms, and be communicated to the other party. Generally advertisements are not valid offers; rather they are "invitations to deal." An

offer can be withdrawn anytime before acceptance. Silence does not constitute acceptance.

3. **Consideration Given** — There must be value given for the promise to be enforceable.
4. **Legality** — You cannot enforce a contract dealing with illegal goods or actions.

## *PROPERTY*

Business revolves around property, and gathering the most of it for yourself. Property is not only a thing, but also the collection of rights and responsibilities associated with the property. There are several classes of property:

*Real Property* — Land

*Personal Property* — Property not attached to land or building. Personal property is also called *chattel*.

*Fixture* — *Personal property* attached to *real* property

*Intellectual Properties (IP)* — Creative property that has no physical form

*Patents* — *Patents* are twenty-year rights to novel, useful, and not obvious inventions or processes. Before June 1995 patents lasted seventeen years.

*Copyrights* — A *copyright* is the right to written works for the life of the author plus seventy years. Before January 1978, a copyright could last up to seventy-five years.

*Trademarks* — These are renewable twenty-year rights for marks used in a trade of business.

## *UNIFORM COMMERCIAL CODE (UCC) ARTICLE 2: SALES CONTRACTS*

The UCC mentioned previously covers many aspects of property-related transactions and contracts. It is such an important part of the law that it is covered in greater depth here and in separate sections that follow. The property-related part of the act defines a "merchant" as a person who regularly deals in the goods included in the contract. Transactions between merchants are considered special and have different levels of documentation required for a contract to be enforceable.

**Bailment**—A *bailment* is a temporary transfer of possession, not ownership, of property from a *bailor* to a *bailee* for a limited time and a special purpose. Sending your laundry to the cleaner is a bailment.

When a person delivers personal property in a bailment, the *standard of care* required by the bailee depends on the mutual benefit of the relationship. If the bailment is for the sole benefit of the bailor, only "slight degree of care" is required. "Do me a favor: Please keep this at your house for me while I'm away" is one example. If the bailment is for the mutual benefit of the parties, such as a paid warehouse, a "reasonable degree of care" is necessary. If the only benefit is for the bailee, an "extreme degree of care" is required. ("Can I use your car this weekend?")

**Sale**—A *sale* is a permanent transfer of ownership in exchange for a *consideration* or payment. The seller can convey no more rights than he or she owns, with three exceptions:

1. A good title can pass to a "bona fide purchaser in good faith." As a purchaser you have no knowledge that a bad title exists.
2. If you buy from a retailer, who has already sold the same type of goods to others, you are a "buyer in ordinary course." The buyer can have good title even if the retailer may not.
3. If you buy from a dealer in a type of goods, even if the dealer has the goods on a bailment, you are a "buyer in ordinary course." The buyer can have clear title even though the dealer did not own the goods.

**Shipment Contracts**—Several terms you may see on shipping documents and invoices indicate when the risk of loss passes from the seller to the buyer: the most common in *FOB, free on board*. At the FOB point the risk of loss passes to the buyer. *CIF* may appear on invoices as well. A CIF price includes cost of goods, insurance, and freight.

*Product Liability*—Product liability concerns the warranties that manufacturers and sellers make about the goods they sell. *Express warranties* are written or spoken promises about the performance of a product. *Implied warranties* are the promises made with the sale of goods that do not need to be written or said. *Merchantability* is an implied warranty meaning that the goods are fit for the ordinary purpose for which they were made. A pen is made for writing, not for performing surgery. *A warranty of fitness* is another implied warranty more specific to the particular purpose for which the seller knowingly sells the product. If the seller knowingly sells an item for a purpose, it should perform that function. *Strict liability* is also implied and it covers the failure of products when used properly to perform safely or effectively as reasonable persons would expect.

*Statute of Frauds*—The *statute of frauds* provision requires that certain important contracts be in writing to prevent fraud. Contracts concerning the following six subjects must be in writing:

1. Sales of goods of value greater than or equal to $500
2. Sale of land
3. Contracts for services not to be performed within one year's time
4. Promise to pay the debt incurred by another person
5. Promises of an estate's executor to pay the expenses of the estate out of his or her own pocket
6. Promises of a dowry in a marriage arrangement

The agreement does not need to be in one written document. If the basic terms of the agreement can be pieced together with several documents that were signed by the party being sued, these can be construed as a valid contract.

*Parol Evidence Rule*—The *parol evidence rule* prohibits the parties from disputing the written contract by citing evidence external to the contract. There are many exceptions to this rule, however, that make the parol evidence rule more of a guideline than a strict rule. For example, evidence that a contract was entered into under duress or by fraud can be admissible evidence that a court will consider outside the contract.

*Privity Rule*—The *privity rule* allows only those parties named in a contract to bring a lawsuit relating to a contract. The scope can be expanded to include those who are assigned rights created by the contract or third-party beneficiaries who receive the results of the contract's performance.

*Force Majeure*—Acts of God, such as hurricanes or floods, can be valid excuses for nonperformance of a contract. *Force majeure* is often included as an express clause of a contract.

*Novation*—In a contract between two parties, one party may re-assign his or her duties to a third party and be excused from the contract. The new third party assumes those duties and responsibilities to perform the contract as written. Assuming someone else's home mortgage is an example.

*Elements of a Contractual Lawsuit*—Lawsuits must include the following elements:

1. Proof that a contract exists
2. *Breach* or nonperformance of the contract
3. Proof of damages

If a clause is included in the contract specifying the penalties for nonperformance, it is called *liquidated damages*.

## UNIFORM COMMERCIAL CODE (UCC) ARTICLES 3 AND 4: COMMERCIAL PAPER

*Commercial or negotiable paper* is a document that can be traded for value by its holder independent of the parties that created it. Checks are negotiable paper. To be negotiable, a paper must have the following characteristics:

1. It must be in written form.
2. It must be signed by the party promising to pay.
3. It must include an *unconditional promise* to pay.
4. It must specify payment of a *sum certain* in money.
5. It must be payable *on demand* or by a point or points certain in time.
6. It must be payable to order of a specific person or *to bearer*.

When a negotiable paper is traded, people will often obtain it improperly and sell it to innocent buyers. A *holder in due course* (HIDC) can obtain more rights than the seller has if the HIDC buys it without knowledge of seller's invalid ownership.

## *AGENCY AGREEMENTS*

*Agency* is the legal relationship between two parties in which one person acts for another. Although it is not part of the UCC agency, it is a key component of business law. The legal relationship of agency can occur four ways:

1. **Contract** — In a written, oral, or implied contract, the parties enter into an agency agreement, and the person is liable for the agent's acts on his behalf.
2. **Ratification** — The person accepts the results of the other person, who is acting for him or her as an agent. The person is responsible for the agent's activity.
3. **Estoppel** — The person allows another to act as his agent and allows others to believe that this relationship exists. Liability arises when another party performs some act for that agent based on the agency relationship.
4. **Necessity** — If a person in a special situation cannot act and someone in good faith helps another, an agency agreement exists.

## BANKRUPTCY LAW

There are no debtors' prisons anymore. The bankruptcy laws provide a mechanism for people and businesses to get a new start or to arrange payment on more favorable terms.

Chapter 7 — A trustee liquidates the remaining assets of a business to pay debts as best as possible. After bankruptcy, the debts, except for special debts such as alimony and child support, are *discharged*.

Chapter 11 — A court-appointed officer approves a *restructuring* plan to pay the debts over time. The person or business continues operating with the restructured debt load. The payments to creditors theoretically should not be less than they would have been under Chapter 7 bankruptcy.

Chapter 13 — This form of personal bankruptcy is available to individuals with regular income and less than $100,000 of unsecured debts and less than $350,000 of secured debts. The debtor submits a payment plan to the court that can last a maximum of five years.

## UNIFORM COMMERCIAL CODE (UCC) ARTICLE 9: SECURED TRANSACTIONS

A body of rules covers the acts of creditors to protect their interest in personal property and fixtures from other third-party claims. Those protected rights are called *security interests*.

A creditor can have a secured interest if a borrower *pledges* collateral to the creditor by giving it to him or her for safekeeping. Taking an item to a pawnshop is a good example of pledging collateral.

In the absence of actually holding the property, such as jewelry, the creditor *attaches* the property with a *perfected* security interest against third-party claims. The creditor can *perfect* his or her interest in two ways:

1. **Attachment**—In this process, the creditor obtains a signed written agreement describing the debt and the property. The debtor must have received value for the security interest and the debtor has legal rights to the property.
2. **Filing a Financial Statement**—A security interest can be secured by filing a financial statement signed by the debtor and creditor. The statement must be filed with the appropriate state, county, or local authority considered valid in the state where the property exists or where the debtor lives. Banks usually make a UCC filing to protect their interests in the collateral for loans outstanding. The filing is a public record that puts others on notice that the property is attached.

A special type of security interest is a *purchase money security interest (PMSI)*. In these transactions, the consumer goods sold (such as cars, furniture, or other household goods) are the collateral for the loans the seller makes to finance the purchase. In these cases, no filing is necessary.

*Default* occurs when a creditor does not pay or perform a contractual obligation. When property is seized by the courts to satisfy debts, a *priority of claims* governs who has rights to the property. The party that is first to *perfect* its interest in a property has priority over other creditors.

## SEVERAL ACTS BUSINESSPEOPLE NEED TO KNOW ABOUT

*Federal Trade Commission Act*—The Federal Trade Commission (FTC) works to prohibit unfair and deceptive business practices. The FTC is especially active in regulating advertising claims and product labeling.

*Sherman Antitrust Act*—This act governs those practices that "actually" restrain trade. Price fixing, setting production quotas in an industry to manipulate prices, dividing a territory to limit trade, deliberately excluding businesses from an industry, and tying arrangements among vendors are all prohibited. (A *tying relationship* is one in which a business is contractually obligated to buy products from a particular source to the exclusion of others.)

*Clayton Act*—This act prohibits monopolistic practices and mergers that "lead" to lessened competition. In this way some mergers are not allowed by the courts because they "may lead" to lessened competition. For example, having the same people on the board of directors of several related companies in a particular industry could lead to lessened competition and be prohibited by the Clayton Act.

*Robinson-Patman Act*—This act prohibits the discriminatory pricing of a product based on factors other than actual cost differences in making and delivering the product to the customer.

In a nutshell, we've covered the abbreviated body of notes from a typical business law course taught at business school. Do seek the advice of an attorney if you need it, but at least now you "can walk *their* walk and talk *their* talk."

## THE ONE-MINUTE MBA BUSINESS WRITING COURSE

1. Present your purpose explicitly and as close to the first sentence as possible. Don't waste readers' time. Have a clear purpose for writing any memo.

2. Keep your tone personal, accessible, and respectful. Write as if the receiver were sitting with you. Do not use too much technical jargon or try to impress others with your vocabulary. Do not write while you are either angry or upset: the memo, text, or e-mail will not go away if you have a change of heart. Do not blame someone or write anything negative about someone in your company unless absolutely necessary and you have all the facts.

3. Use the active voice, not the passive voice if at all possible.
   Active: Steve Silbiger wrote this book.
   Passive: This book was written by Steve Silbiger.

4. Eliminate extra words, facts, and long sentences. Use headings to break up different thoughts to eliminate transitional paragraphs. Try to keep your memo to one page. Additional information can be attached.

5. Use "spell and grammar" check twice before you send a memo. Read the final draft before you send it, preferably after a good night's rest.

## THE TEN-MINUTE REAL ESTATE INVESTOR

Since a great proportion of the wealth of the world's richest people was created investing in real estate, every MBA should know the basics of real estate. The object of real estate investing is to create wealth by leveraging your initial investment, taking advantage of government tax benefits, and selecting excellent undervalued properties.

Cash flow is the critical element in real estate investing. Cash flow allows you to pay the bills and pay yourself. Cash flow is calculated by subtracting the mortgage payment and other operating expenses from the rent you collect. With the cash flow you can maintain and increase your property portfolio and pay yourself. For a residential property the lease is a simple monthly payment contract. Commercial property leases come in two types. In a *gross lease* the tenant pays the rent and the owner pays all operating expenses other than utilities. In a *triple net lease,* the tenant pays the rent, taxes, insurance, utilities, and maintenance.

With the lease payments there are three types of operating expenses. Operating expenses have a fixed, a variable, and a planned portion. *Fixed* expenses include taxes and insurance, which are often paid in large payments annually or quarterly. *Variable* expenses include utility payments not assumed by the tenant, repairs, maintenance, and a provision for vacancies between tenants. In addition, *planned* expenses are those with a longer useful life, such as a new roof, furnace, or exterior siding or painting.

## PROPERTY ANALYSIS WORKSHEET

**Address:** _____

_____

**Basic Return**

1. Value of the Property      _____
2. Loans on Property      _____
3. Equity in Property      _____
4. Gross Income _____ Mo. × 12 =      _____
5. Expenses _____ Mo. × 12 =      _____
6. Loan Payments _____ Mo. × 12 =      _____
7. Interest (_____ Loan Amt. × ___ %) =      _____
8. Loan Payoff (Line 6 − Line 7) =      _____
9. Cash Flow (Line 4 − Line 5 − Line 6) =      _____
10. Depreciation Deduction*      _____
11. Tax Shelter (Line 10 − Line 9 − Line 8) =      _____
12. Tax Savings (Tax Bracket ___ % × Line 11) =      _____
13. Property Profit (Line 8 + Line 9 + Line 12) =      _____
14. Basic Return (Line 13 / Line 3) =      _____

**Return on Equity**

15. Cash Flow (Line 9)      _____
16. Loan Payoff (Line 8)      _____
17. Tax Savings (Line 12)      _____
18. Appreciation ___ % × Line 1 =      _____
19. Total Investment (Lines 15 + 16 + 17 + 18) =      _____
20. Return on Equity (Line 19 / Line 3) =      _____

* Depreciation equals the property value less land value divided by 27.5 years for residential or 39 years for commercial real estate.

A large part of your investment profit is from the reduction of mortgage principal paid for by the renters. As the balance of the loan is paid, your equity increases as time passes, even if the property's value remains the same.

As discussed in the finance chapter, leverage increases the return on your investment. This is one of the few transactions in which the average person can be engaged in very leveraged transactions. Mortgages with 5 percent down are leveraged at a twenty-to-one ratio. At 20 percent down, your gains are leveraged by a factor of five. That is why large returns are possible on a relatively small investment. As a property increases in value, you can borrow against the equity and invest in more properties or take cash. In an era of rising property values, fortunes are created. In declining markets, investments can be wiped out. However, real estate is far more durable than a biotechnology stock. Unless the property has an extreme environmental problem, one person's bust lays the groundwork for another investor's fortune.

Appreciation in property values come from inflation, supply and demand in the market, and the opportunities for other uses for the property. If a residential property has commercial possibilities, it can become more valuable. That is called the property's "highest and best use." Real estate investing is a local business. Prices differ greatly by city, neighborhood, and block. If you think that the value of the investment lies in fixing up the property, then get competent appraisals of the fixes required.

The deductibility of loan interest for tax purposes is a tax shelter provided to all property owners that subsidizes your purchase. As opposed to nondeductible credit-card interest, the government helps you by lowering your after-tax cost of borrowing. The U.S. government also has programs from the Department of Housing and Urban Development (HUD), Federal Housing Administration (FHA), and the Veterans Administration (VA) that can help you obtain the financing required to buy properties.

Tax depreciation is another way the government subsidizes your purchase with a tax deduction. Tax depreciation for U.S. properties is 27.5 years for residential properties and 39 years for nonresidential. The value of the land must be subtracted from the cost of the property being depreciated. Check your property tax bill for the assessed value of the structure and the total assessment. Use that ratio to multiply by your purchase price to estimate the depreciable portion of your investment.

Profits realized in real estate transactions can be rolled over into new property purchases without a tax on the profits. It's a unique asset in that way. In an IRS 1031 tax-deferred exchange, you are able to roll over your equity much the way you roll over the profits of an individual retirement account into another IRA account. In this case your real estate investing can create a considerable nest egg without a great deal of risk. In these exchanges you must roll the entire proceeds into "like-kind" property and not take any cash, debt relief, or other things of value out of the rollover transaction.

There are several ways to evaluate properties. The *capitalization rate method* is a simple way to value an investment property. The value of the property equals the net income from the property (rent less operating expenses) divided by a capitalization rate. The capitalization rate is what investors expect to make on their investment based on the prevailing interest rates, appreciation, and the riskiness of the rents. A capitalization (cap) rate of 6 to 8 percent in 2023 was a common goal based on the riskiness of the cash flows. In the case of property that has a net income of $20,000, it would be valued at $250,000 using this method ($20,000 / .08). Of course if improvements can be made to improve the net income, the property may be more valuable under the new owner's management.

Another valuation is a thumbnail method of using a *gross rent multiplier,* but it is fraught with inaccuracies. The most accurate valuation method is to complete a full NPV analysis of the cash flows and expected appreciation, discounted at a rate that compensates you for the risk of ownership as explained in the finance chapter. Also the analysis should include some variation analysis of key variables to test the robustness of the projections.

Financing the investment can take the form of a conventional bank loan, government loan, mortgage, or seller financing.

The plan for real estate success is summarized in a five-part plan:

1. Learn about real estate as an investment.
2. Research properties in your area.
3. Plan how to invest your money.

4. Invest according to your plan.

5. Manage your investment to meet your goals.

The worksheet on page 404 can help you calculate the return on a prospective real estate investment.

## THE TEN-MINUTE LEADERSHIP COACH

One of the newest areas for MBA education is leadership. Personal leadership coaches are the rage for corporate executives, and they cost hundreds of dollars an hour for their advice. I discussed the theories of leadership in chapter 4, "Organizational Behavior," but many MBA programs have created leadership courses so that their students can be leaders themselves and, down the road, become large donors to their school.

Being an effective leader involves having the self-confidence to make decisions, motivating others, and assuming responsibility for your actions. In a nutshell, to become an effective leader you have to overcome your fears and anxieties. It goes beyond a weekend of climbing ropes. Most of the fear and anxiety of business leaders is over losing control. Other fears that stem from this include the common fear of going insane, fear of embarrassing yourself in front of others, and fear of failure. You create fear within yourself, and only you can calm yourself to be effective. "If you knew that you could handle anything that came your way, what would you possibly have to fear?" Therefore "all you have to do to diminish your fear is develop the trust in your ability to handle whatever comes your way." This wisdom comes from Susan Jeffers, Ph.D., the author of *Feel the Fear and Do It Anyway.* "Whatever happens to me, given any situation, I can handle it." But what about really horrible things? You may experience uncontrollable events, but if you do your best, then you cannot ask for any more of yourself.

Many things create the fear within you. Lucinda Basset's *From Panic to Power* pinpoints your family and upbringing as the primary causes.

- You may have had a strict upbringing that controlled you through fear and guilt.
- Your family did not easily express emotions and did not easily give you praise or approval.
- Your parents may have had high expectations for you that you could not possibly meet.
- You may have overreacting family members who created a negative environment of nervousness in your house.
- You may have lost a family member or had one incapacitated by disease or addiction.

It sounds horrible, yes, but most families, mine included, have elements from the list that have formed our personalities, habits, and dispositions. They lead people to be perfectionist, guilty, obsessive, nervous, sensitive, overreacting, overly concerned about the opinions of others, and apparently in control all the time. Many of these same traits have driven you to be successful as a student and as a businessperson, but at a point, they hold you back from being a great leader.

The first step of improvement is to recognize that you have these fears and can conquer them. When you have this feeling of a loss of control, which is the basic core fear, you accept it. The anxiety is created by an external source in most professional situations. That creates an internal anxiety, such as nervousness or a sweaty brow. It is your choice how you react. Don't fight the anxiety, understand it.

When you deal with external events, your mind tends to create cognitive distortions of the real situation causing you needless anxiety. As explained by David Burns, M.D., in *Feeling Good,* the ten categories of these poisonous cognitive distortions to watch out for are:

1. *All-or-nothing thinking:* If it is not perfect, it is a failure.
2. *Overgeneralization:* A single negative event is a never-ending pattern of defeat.
3. *Mental filter:* Filter out the entire positive and concentrate on the negative.

4. *Disqualify the positive:* Reject positive as it does not count and maintain negative beliefs regardless.

5. *Jumping to conclusions:* Anticipating negative reactions from people and negative consequences.

6. *Magnification or minimization:* Exaggerate the importance of a negative event or minimize the importance of a positive one.

7. *Emotional reasoning:* Your negative emotions reflect the reality of the real world around you.

8. *Should statements:* You motivate yourself with *should*s and *shouldn't*s as if you need to be whipped and punished to do something. The consequence of these *must*s and *ought to*s is guilt.

9. *Labeling and mislabeling:* Negatively label yourself a loser or others as idiots.

10. *Personalization:* You are the cause of negative external events that you are not responsible for. This causes guilt.

When stressed, take a few breaths and use a "positive inner dialogue" to get over it. Positive thoughts create positive feelings. Negative thinking is a bad habit that you can break . . . with *practice.* Training the noise in your head, "the chatterbox" as Jeffers calls it, is your key. You can choose to have this voice constantly berating you, doubting your decisions with countless what if scenarios and regretful *I should have*s. Alternatively, you can choose to have a kind internal voice tell you, "You are a capable and talented person, and if things don't work out, you can handle it. You can't control the world, but you can control how you react to it and learn along the way to make better decisions in the future."

Jeffers suggests that when you make a decision, look at what you can gain, not what you can lose. Do your homework to make sure you have all your facts to make a realistic and informed decision, establish your priorities, and trust your intuition and lighten up.

After making a decision, do not wed yourself to what you thought "should be" the outcome: throw away that picture. If things do not work out perfectly, accept responsibility and correct the situation. Avoid wasting your time trying to "protect" the righteousness of the decision that you made. You cannot change the past: you can only affect the future. Feeling guilty is not a productive treadmill to run on. Forgive others and yourself and be solution-oriented.

If you are having negative thoughts, Basset suggests that you need to recognize the thoughts for what they are and raise the "stop sign" right there. Ask yourself if the thoughts are true, realistic, rational, and reasonable. Use your positive internal voice to put things into perspective and assure yourself that you can handle it, and make yourself feel positive. Positive self-talk is better than a bad habit of negative talk. In a positive and powerful mental state, you solve the problem by *doing,* not *worrying.* If you are busy *doing,* you are not busy *worrying.* "Change your mind and change your mood." The distraction of being active solving your problem, or perhaps taking some time out to exercise, listen to some music, or do something else positive, will provide time for the initial anxiety to pass. That enables you to become a more positive and productive leader for your next challenge.

Many other experts have similar advice. Spencer Johnson's *The Present* is a great book about an old man's sage advice about becoming happy as a result of focusing on action in "the present." "Be in the present, focus on what is right now. Use your purpose to respond to what is important to you. Learn from the past. Learn something valuable from it and do something different in the present. Plan for the future and see what a wonderful future would look like and make plans to help it happen. Put your plan into action in the present."

In Johnson's *Who Moved My Cheese?,* with examples of mice and little people caught in a maze, he focused on taking action in the face of a changing world. He advocated accepting change as part of life, proactively anticipating change, and dealing with it. Accepting change and dealing with it is more productive and better for your well-being than being paralyzed by fear and anxiety. People survive and thrive.

Leadership coaches touch on the practical as well as the big life-planning issues. Tools that leadership coaches suggest include keeping organized and prioritized by creating daily to-do lists. The lists enable you to check things off during the day and feel productive, even though you are not solving every issue at your company. Don't overschedule your day; it is a method of avoidance. To effectively network and keep connected, you must keep an updated contact list. If you include significant keywords with your entries, such as *Masters* with someone whom you met at the Augusta golf classic, you can more effectively find people when you don't remember their names.

On the big life issues, coaches will help you create a detailed set of goals for yourself: company, professional, personal, professional relationships, family relationships and community. Then you will review it periodically with the coach to make sure that you are on track and that your actions are in line with your goals. Stephen Covey's 7 *Habits of Highly Effective People* tells us to "take responsibility, make your mind up about what is important to you, and live by it. Seek first to understand, then to be understood." His eighth habit, added in 2004, was "find your voice, your calling, your soul's code, and inspire others to find theirs."

Leadership coaches, as you can imagine, see themselves as *life coaches* as well and recommend regular exercise, healthy diets, not smoking, cutting back on caffeine, meditation, and getting proper sleep. They recommend a *360-degree evaluation* to gain self-awareness from your superiors, your colleagues, and your direct reports. Coaches may offer other advice: Eat a piece a fruit each day and you are less likely to eat junk food. Smile more; your smile makes other people happy, which in turn makes you happy. Don't accept the TV news' picture of the world; it is a distorted, negative view. Give back; doing good for others is just as good for you. Many of these factors affect your general level of stress and anxiety and, therefore, affect your productivity as a business leader.

## THE TEN-MINUTE FINANCIAL PLANNER

Business schools want their students to be as successful as possible in meeting their personal financial goals. Several top schools offer courses on financial planning and financial management. No subject is more important to MBA students than their personal wealth creation. The keys to becoming a millionaire are straightforward. Since the average MBA is earning a salary that puts him in the top 10 percent of earners, all it takes is discipline and some planning.

**Rule 1: Pay Yourself First.** Automatically save a minimum of 10 percent of your earnings.

*Maximize your tax-deferred savings opportunities.* Take full advantage of all 401(k) or 403(b) plans available. Take full advantage of employer matches. Take advantage of all the tax benefits from Uncle Sam. If you are in the 25 percent tax bracket, you are in essence already getting a 25 percent return on your savings by avoiding the taxes versus trying to save it from your check after you get it. If you get an employer match, you doubled your money. What you earn in a mutual fund investment is icing on the cake. It would be tough to beat those returns. It is important that your investment is automatically taken from your check before taxes are taken from the money.

If your employer does not have a 401(k) plan available, you need to maximize your other tax-deferred savings options. Maximize available Traditional IRAs, Roth IRAs, and Simple IRAs. Automatically invest with systematic payments from your paycheck or from your own checking account if possible. If you have self-employment income, you are able to save much more money tax-deferred. Create an Individual Person 401(k) or SEP IRA.

If you follow this plan, you are assured to amass more than a million dollars over your working career even with a moderate income.

**Rule 2: Own Your Home.** Own your home; don't rent if you plan on staying for an extended period of time. Renting a place does not build up any wealth for you, but it does for your landlord. As with the tax-deferred accounts, the federal government is subsidizing your home. The subsidy is your tax deduction for your mortgage interest. If you have a 25 percent tax rate, the government is paying 25 percent of your interest. In the first years of the mortgage, when most of the payment is for interest, the government will be paying 25 percent of your entire mortgage payment. That deal is hard to turn down.

Thirty-year and fifteen-year mortgages are available if you plan to stay more than just a few years in a home. The fifteen-year mortgage has a lower interest payment, takes half as long to own your home, and forces you to save more with a higher monthly payment. The thirty-year has a little higher interest rate, but takes twice as long to pay off. On the positive side of thirty-year mortgage, you can afford a larger house, which in a market of rising values allows you more financial leverage. Few investments allow you to have the same amount of leverage as your home mortgage. In a 20 percent down-payment situation, you control five times the value of real estate with your real estate investment.

If you want to accelerate your ownership and your savings, set up biweekly payments, make extra payments to principal each month, or make an extra month's payment to principal each year. You could own your house totally in ten years if you wish. Make sure to shop to compare interest rates and fees. Use bankrate.com.

*Own rental property.* When you are further along with the payments on your house, you will have built up considerable equity. You can use the equity in your home to buy another home for yourself or to buy a rental property. In that case the renters will be saving for you, as they pay off your mortgage on that property. See "The Ten-Minute Real Estate Investor" for guidance on the economics of real estate.

**Rule 3: Create an Emergency Fund and an Investment Portfolio.** Everyone needs an emergency fund. Experts suggest three to six months expenses as appropriate, but longer is okay if that is what makes you sleep well at night. You need to pay yourself first to create this nest egg with a set amount each month until you reach your goal. This account will not have the benefit of a government subsidy because it comes out of your paycheck after taxes have been taken. The money should be inaccessible. Shop for the highest money-market rates and CD rates at bankrate.com to ensure you get the best deal.

Once your emergency fund is created, you need to invest the same amount or more in an investment account holding longer-term investments. This account can be earmarked for education, to start a business, and or retirement.

**Rule 4: Invest Wisely.** Investing your portfolio is not a place to express your creativity. Choose the long-term mutual fund winners as rated by Morningstar.com and *Forbes*. Diversify stock investments across asset classes such as large, mid-, and small-capitalization company mutual funds and across investment styles such as value, blend, and growth investing. Bonds should likewise be diversified, across short-, medium-, and long-term maturities. Holding a portfolio of individual bonds to maturity is a risk-reduction strategy against rate changes as you are locked in to the return calculated at the time of your purchases. In addition, choose funds with low expenses. Lower expenses have been highly correlated with higher returns. You must also monitor your entire portfolio, not just individual holdings. Track and analyze your entire portfolio with Morningstar.com's portfolio tracker. Shop for CD and money market rates at bankrate.com.

You may choose to take a portion of your savings to invest in risky opportunities, but be disciplined, keep it to a small portion of your nest egg.

**Rule 5: Be Selectively Extravagant but Pervasively Frugal.** The expense side of the ledger can be just as important as the saving and investment side. Of course you must enjoy life; life is not a dress rehearsal. But you need to be selective about how you spend your money. To feed your passion, whatever it may be, golf or even wine collecting, you may need to be selectively extravagant, but for things that are not important, you need to be prudently frugal.

As widely reported, over a lifetime a $5-a-day caffe-latte or cigarette habit can cost you more than a million dollars of lost retirement saving. Driving a moderately priced reliable car for one hundred thousand miles instead of trading frequently for a pricey luxury car permits you to avoid many car payments, the steep cost of depreciation, and interest charges. This plan also is worth a million dollars to you over your lifetime.

Another area for savings involves the use of credit cards. Some experts say that you should not use them because it psychologically divorces your spending from the actual use of cash. If you do choose to use your credit card, use one that provides a cash benefit such as cash-back from Discover or Capital One. Do not roll over a balance from month to month, as the interest charges are far more than you can earn from your other investments.

**You have done it! Congratulations! You have finished your nine core MBA courses and your tenth day of intensive MBA minicourses. Fill in your diploma and display it proudly!**

Ten-Day
MBA

By the authority of the author,
this diploma confers upon

_____

the degree of Ten-Day MBA
and herewith all the rights and privileges of
a Master of Business Administration
from the University of the Self-Taught

Steven Alan Silbiger

Author

# Appendix: Quantitative Analysis Tables

# Present Value of $1

## PRESENT VALUE FACTOR OF $1 = $(1 + r)^{-n}$

$r$ = discount rate    $n$ = number of periods until payment

| PERIODS = N | 1% | 2% | 3% | 4% | 5% | 6% | 7% | 8% | 9% | 10% | 12% | 14% | 15% | 16% | 18% | 20% | 25% |
|---|---|---|---|---|---|---|---|---|---|---|---|---|---|---|---|---|---|
| 1 | 0.9901 | 0.98039 | 0.97087 | 0.96154 | 0.95238 | 0.9434 | 0.93458 | 0.92593 | 0.91743 | 0.90909 | 0.89286 | 0.87719 | 0.86957 | 0.86207 | 0.84746 | 0.83333 | 0.8 |
| 2 | 0.9803 | 0.96117 | 0.9426 | 0.92456 | 0.90703 | 0.89 | 0.87344 | 0.85734 | 0.84168 | 0.82645 | 0.79719 | 0.76947 | 0.75614 | 0.74316 | 0.71818 | 0.69444 | 0.64 |
| 3 | 0.97059 | 0.94232 | 0.91514 | 0.889 | 0.86384 | 0.83962 | 0.8163 | 0.79383 | 0.77218 | 0.75131 | 0.71178 | 0.67497 | 0.65752 | 0.64066 | 0.60863 | 0.5787 | 0.512 |
| 4 | 0.96098 | 0.92385 | 0.88849 | 0.8548 | 0.8227 | 0.79209 | 0.7629 | 0.73503 | 0.70843 | 0.68301 | 0.63552 | 0.59208 | 0.57175 | 0.55229 | 0.51579 | 0.48225 | 0.4096 |
| 5 | 0.95147 | 0.90573 | 0.86261 | 0.82193 | 0.78353 | 0.74726 | 0.71299 | 0.68058 | 0.64993 | 0.62092 | 0.56743 | 0.51937 | 0.49718 | 0.47611 | 0.43711 | 0.40188 | 0.32768 |
| 6 | 0.94205 | 0.88797 | 0.83748 | 0.79031 | 0.74622 | 0.70496 | 0.66634 | 0.63017 | 0.59627 | 0.56447 | 0.50663 | 0.45559 | 0.43233 | 041044 | 037043 | 03349 | 0.26214 |
| 7 | 0.93272 | 0.87056 | 0.81309 | 0.75892 | 0.71068 | 0.66506 | 0.62275 | 0.58349 | 0.54703 | 0.51316 | 0.43235 | 0.39964 | 0.37594 | 0.35383 | 0.31393 | 0.27908 | 0.20972 |
| 8 | 0.92348 | 0.85349 | 0.78941 | 0.73069 | 0.67684 | 0.62741 | 0.58201 | 0.54027 | 0.50187 | 0.46651 | 0.40388 | 0.35056 | 0.3269 | 0.30503 | 0.26604 | 0.23257 | 0.16777 |
| 9 | 0.91434 | 0.83676 | 0.76642 | 0.70259 | 0.64461 | 0.5919 | 0.54393 | 0.50025 | 0.46043 | 0.4241 | 0.38061 | 0.30751 | 0.28426 | 0.26295 | 0.22546 | 0.19381 | 0.13422 |
| 10 | 0.90529 | 0.82035 | 0.74409 | 0.67556 | 0.61391 | 0.55839 | 0.50835 | 0.46319 | 0.42241 | 0.38554 | 0.32197 | 0.26974 | 0.24718 | 0.22668 | 0.19106 | 0.16151 | 0.10737 |
| 11 | 0.89632 | 0.80426 | 0.72242 | 0.64958 | 0.58468 | 0.52679 | 0.47509 | 0.42888 | 0.38753 | 0.35049 | 0.28748 | 0.23662 | 0.21494 | 0.19542 | 0.16192 | 0.13459 | 0.0859 |
| 12 | 0.88745 | 0.78849 | 0.70138 | 0.6246 | 0.55684 | 0.49697 | 0.44401 | 0.39711 | 0.35553 | 0.31863 | 0.25668 | 0.20756 | 0.18691 | 0.16846 | 0.13722 | 0.11216 | 0.06872 |
| 13 | 0.87866 | 0.77303 | 0.68095 | 0.60057 | 0.53032 | 0.46884 | 0.41496 | 0.3677 | 0.32618 | 0.28966 | 0.22917 | 0.18207 | 0.16253 | 0.14523 | 0.11629 | 0.09346 | 0.05498 |
| 14 | 0.86996 | 0.75788 | 0.66112 | 0.57748 | 0.50507 | 0.4423 | 0.38782 | 0.34046 | 0.29925 | 0.26333 | 0.20462 | 0.15971 | 0.14133 | 0.1252 | 0.09855 | 0.07789 | 0.04398 |
| 15 | 0.86135 | 0.74301 | 0.64186 | 0.55526 | 0.48102 | 0.41727 | 0.36245 | 0.31524 | 0.27454 | 0.23939 | 0.1827 | 0.1401 | 0.12289 | 0.10793 | 0.08352 | 0.06491 | 0.03518 |
| 16 | 0.85282 | 0.72845 | 0.62317 | 0.53391 | 0.45811 | 0.39365 | 0.33873 | 0.29189 | 0.25187 | 0.21763 | 0.16312 | 0.12289 | 0.10686 | 0.09304 | 0.07078 | 0.05409 | 0.02815 |
| 17 | 0.84438 | 0.71416 | 0.60502 | 0.51337 | 0.4363 | 0.37136 | 0.31657 | 0.27027 | 0.23107 | 0.19784 | 0.14564 | 0.0178 | 0.09293 | 0.08021 | 0.05998 | 0.04507 | 0.02252 |
| 18 | 0.83602 | 0.70016 | 0.58739 | 0.49363 | 0.41552 | 0.35034 | 0.29586 | 0.25025 | 0.21199 | 0.17986 | 0.13004 | 0.09456 | 0.08081 | 0.06914 | 0.05083 | 0.03756 | 0.01801 |
| 19 | 0.82774 | 0.68643 | 0.57029 | 0.47464 | 0.39573 | 0.33051 | 0.27651 | 0.23171 | 0.19449 | 0.16351 | 0.11611 | 0.08295 | 0.07027 | 0.06961 | 0.04308 | 0.0313 | 0.1441 |
| 20 | 0.81954 | 0.67297 | 0.55368 | 0.45639 | 0.37689 | 0.3118 | 0.25842 | 0.21455 | 0.17843 | 0.14864 | 0.10367 | 0.07276 | 0.0611 | 0.05139 | 0.03651 | 0.02608 | 0.01153 |
| 21 | 0.81143 | 0.65978 | 0.53755 | 0.43883 | 0.35894 | 0.29416 | 0.24151 | 0.19866 | 0.1637 | 0.13513 | 0.09256 | 0.06383 | 0.05313 | 0.0443 | 0.03094 | 0.02174 | 0.00922 |
| 22 | 0.8034 | 0.64684 | 0.52189 | 0.42196 | 0.34185 | 0.27751 | 0.22571 | 0.18394 | 0.15018 | 0.12285 | 0.08264 | 0.05599 | 0.0462 | 0.03819 | 0.02622 | 0.01811 | 0.00738 |
| 23 | 0.79544 | 0.63416 | 0.50669 | 0.40573 | 0.32557 | 0.2618 | 0.21095 | 0.17032 | 0.13778 | 0.11168 | 0.07379 | 0.04911 | 0.04017 | 0.03292 | 0.02222 | 0.01509 | 0.0059 |
| 24 | 0.78757 | 0.62172 | 0.49193 | 0.39012 | 0.31007 | 0.24698 | 0.19715 | 0.1577 | 0.1264 | 0.10153 | 0.06588 | 0.04308 | 0.03493 | 0.02838 | 0.01883 | 0.01258 | 0.00472 |
| 25 | 0.77977 | 0.60953 | 0.47761 | 0.37512 | 0.2953 | 0.233 | 0.18425 | 0.14602 | 0.11597 | 0.0923 | 0.05882 | 0.03779 | 0.03038 | 0.02447 | 0.01596 | 0.01048 | 0.00378 |
| 26 | 0.77205 | 0.59758 | 0.46369 | 0.36069 | 0.28124 | 0.21981 | 0.1722 | 0.1352 | 0.10639 | 0.08391 | 0.05252 | 0.03315 | 0.02642 | 0.02109 | 0.01352 | 0.00874 | 0.00302 |
| 27 | 0.7644 | 0.58586 | 0.45019 | 0.34682 | 0.26785 | 0.20737 | 0.16093 | 0.12519 | 0.09761 | 0.07628 | 0.04689 | 0.02908 | 0.02297 | 0.01818 | 0.01146 | 0.00728 | 0.00242 |
| 28 | 0.75684 | 0.57437 | 0.43708 | 0.33348 | 0.25509 | 0.19563 | 0.1504 | 0.11591 | 0.08955 | 0.06934 | 0.04187 | 0.02551 | 0.01997 | 0.01567 | 0.00971 | 0.00607 | 0.00193 |
| 29 | 0.74934 | 0.56311 | 0.42435 | 0.32065 | 0.24295 | 0.18456 | 0.14056 | 0.10733 | 0.08215 | 0.06304 | 0.03738 | 0.02237 | 0.01737 | 0.01351 | 0.00823 | 0.00506 | 0.00155 |
| 30 | 0.74192 | 0.55207 | 0.41199 | 0.30832 | 0.23138 | 0.17411 | 0.13137 | 0.09938 | 0.07537 | 0.05731 | 0.03338 | 0.01963 | 0.0151 | 0.01165 | 0.00697 | 0.00421 | 0.00124 |

# Future Value of $1

## FUTURE VALUE FACTOR OF $1 $= (1 + r)^n$

$r$ = discount rate $\quad$ $n$ = number of periods until payment

| PERIODS =N | 1% (1.01) | 2% (1.02) | 3% (1.03) | 4% (1.04) | 5% (1.05) | 6% (1.06) | 7% (1.07) | 8% (1.08) | 9% (1.09) | 10% (1.1) | 12% (1.12) | 14% (1.14) | 15% (1.15) | 16% (1.16) | 18% (1.18) | 20% (1.2) | 25% (1.25) |
|---|---|---|---|---|---|---|---|---|---|---|---|---|---|---|---|---|---|
| 1 | 1.01 | 1.02 | 1.03 | 1.04 | 1.05 | 1.06 | 1.07 | 1.08 | 1.09 | 1.1 | 1.12 | 1.14 | 1.15 | 1.16 | 1.18 | 1.2 | 1.25 |
| 2 | 1.0201 | 1.0404 | 1.0609 | 1.0816 | 1.1025 | 1.1236 | 1.1449 | 1.1664 | 1.1881 | 1.21 | 1.2544 | 1.2996 | 1.3225 | 1.3456 | 1.3924 | 1.44 | 1.5625 |
| 3 | 1.0303 | 1.06121 | 1.09273 | 1.12486 | 1.15763 | 1.19102 | 1.22504 | 1.25971 | 1.29503 | 1.331 | 1.40493 | 1.48154 | 1.52088 | 1.5609 | 1.64303 | 1.728 | 1.95313 |
| 4 | 1.0406 | 1.08243 | 1.12551 | 1.16986 | 1.21551 | 1.26248 | 1.3108 | 1.36049 | 1.41158 | 1.4641 | 1.57352 | 1.68896 | 1.74901 | 1.81064 | 1.93878 | 2.0736 | 2.44141 |
| 5 | 1.05101 | 1.10408 | 1.15927 | 1.21665 | 1.27628 | 1.33823 | 1.40255 | 1.46933 | 1.53862 | 1.61051 | 1.76234 | 1.92541 | 2.01136 | 2.10034 | 2.28776 | 2.48832 | 3.05176 |
| 6 | 1.06152 | 1.12616 | 1.19405 | 1.26532 | 1.3401 | 1.41852 | 1.50073 | 1.58687 | 1.6771 | 1.77156 | 1.97382 | 2.19497 | 2.31306 | 2.4364 | 2.69955 | 2.98598 | 3.8147 |
| 7 | 1.07214 | 1.14869 | 1.22987 | 1.31593 | 1.4071 | 1.50363 | 1.60578 | 1.71382 | 1.82904 | 1.94872 | 2.21068 | 2.50227 | 2.66002 | 2.82822 | 3.18547 | 3.58318 | 4.76837 |
| 8 | 1.08286 | 1.17166 | 1.26677 | 1.36857 | 1.47746 | 1.59385 | 1.71819 | 1.85093 | 1.99256 | 2.14359 | 2.47596 | 2.85259 | 3.05902 | 3.27841 | 3.75886 | 4.29982 | 5.96046 |
| 9 | 1.09369 | 1.19508 | 1.30477 | 1.42331 | 1.55133 | 1.68948 | 1.83846 | 1.85093 | 2.17288 | 2.35795 | 2.77308 | 3.25195 | 3.51788 | 3.80296 | 4.43545 | 5.15978 | 7.45058 |
| 10 | 1.10462 | 1.21899 | 1.34392 | 1.48024 | 1.62889 | 1.79085 | 1.96715 | 2.15892 | 2.36736 | 2.59374 | 3.10585 | 3.70722 | 4.04556 | 4.41144 | 5.23384 | 6.19174 | 9.31323 |
| 11 | 1.11567 | 1.24337 | 1.38423 | 1.53945 | 1.71034 | 1.8983 | 2.10485 | 2.33164 | 2.58043 | 2.85312 | 3.47855 | 4.22623 | 4.65239 | 5.11726 | 6.17593 | 7.43008 | 11.64153 |
| 12 | 1.12683 | 1.26824 | 1.42576 | 1.60103 | 1.79586 | 2.0122 | 2.25219 | 2.51817 | 2.81266 | 3.13843 | 3.89598 | 4.8179 | 5.35025 | 5.93603 | 7.28759 | 8.9161 | 14.55192 |
| 13 | 1.13809 | 1.29361 | 1.46853 | 1.66507 | 1.88565 | 2.13293 | 2.40985 | 2.71962 | 3.0658 | 3.45227 | 4.36348 | 5.49241 | 6.15279 | 6.88579 | 8.59936 | 10.69932 | 18.18989 |
| 14 | 1.14947 | 1.31948 | 1.15259 | 1.73168 | 1.97993 | 2.2609 | 2.57853 | 2.93719 | 3.34173 | 3.7975 | 4.88711 | 6.26135 | 7.07571 | 7.98752 | 10.14724 | 12.83918 | 22.73737 |
| 15 | 1.16097 | 1.34587 | 1.57797 | 1.80094 | 2.07893 | 2.39656 | 2.75903 | 3.17217 | 3.64248 | 4.17725 | 5.47357 | 7.13794 | 8.13706 | 9.26552 | 11.97375 | 15.40702 | 28.42171 |
| 16 | 1.17258 | 1.37279 | 1.60471 | 1.87298 | 2.18287 | 2.54035 | 2.95216 | 3.42594 | 3.97031 | 4.59497 | 6.13039 | 8.13725 | 9.35762 | 10.748 | 14.12902 | 18.48843 | 35.52714 |
| 17 | 1.1843 | 1.40024 | 1.65285 | 1.9479 | 2.29202 | 2.69277 | 3.15882 | 3.70002 | 4.32763 | 5.05447 | 6.86604 | 9.27646 | 10.76126 | 12.46768 | 16.67225 | 22.18611 | 44.40892 |
| 18 | 1.19615 | 1.42825 | 1.70243 | 2.02582 | 2.40662 | 2.85434 | 3.37993 | 3.99602 | 4.71712 | 5.55992 | 7.68997 | 10.57517 | 12.37545 | 14.46251 | 19.67325 | 26.62333 | 55.51115 |
| 19 | 1.20811 | 1.45681 | 1.75351 | 2.10685 | 2.52695 | 3.0256 | 3.61653 | 4.3157 | 5.14166 | 6.11591 | 8.61276 | 12.05569 | 14.23177 | 16.77652 | 23.21444 | 31.948 | 69.38894 |
| 20 | 1.22019 | 1.48595 | 1.80611 | 2.19112 | 2.6533 | 3.20714 | 3.86968 | 4.66096 | 5.60441 | 6.7275 | 9.64629 | 13.74349 | 16.36654 | 19.46076 | 27.39303 | 38.3376 | 86.73617 |
| 21 | 1.23239 | 1.51567 | 1.86029 | 2.27877 | 2.78596 | 3.39956 | 4.14056 | 5.03383 | 6.10881 | 7.40025 | 10.80385 | 15.66758 | 18.82152 | 22.57448 | 32.32378 | 46.00512 | 108.42022 |
| 22 | 1.24472 | 1.154598 | 1.9161 | 2.36992 | 2.92526 | 3.60354 | 4.4304 | 5.43654 | 6.6586 | 8.14027 | 12.10031 | 17.86104 | 21.64475 | 26.1864 | 38.14206 | 55.20614 | 135.52527 |
| 23 | 1.25716 | 1.5769 | 1.97359 | 2.46472 | 3.07152 | 3.81975 | 4.74053 | 5.87146 | 7.25787 | 8.9543 | 13.55235 | 20.36158 | 24.89146 | 30.37622 | 45.00763 | 66.24737 | 169.40659 |
| 24 | 1.26973 | 1.60844 | 2.03279 | 2.5633 | 3.2251 | 4.04893 | 5.07237 | 6.34118 | 7.91108 | 9.84973 | 15.17863 | 23.21221 | 28.82518 | 35.23642 | 53.10901 | 79.49685 | 211.75824 |
| 25 | 1.28243 | 1.64061 | 2.09378 | 2.66584 | 3.38635 | 4.29187 | 5.42743 | 6.84848 | 8.62308 | 10.83471 | 17.00006 | 26.46192 | 32.91895 | 40.87424 | 62.66863 | 95.39622 | 264.6978 |
| 26 | 1.29526 | 1.67342 | 2.15659 | 2.77247 | 3.55567 | 4.54938 | 5.80735 | 7.39635 | 9.39916 | 11.91818 | 19.04007 | 30.16658 | 37.8568 | 47.41412 | 73.94898 | 114.47546 | 330.87225 |
| 27 | 1.30821 | 1.70689 | 2.22129 | 2.88337 | 3.73346 | 4.82235 | 6.21387 | 7.98806 | 10.24508 | 13.10999 | 21.32488 | 34.38991 | 43.53531 | 55.00038 | 87.2598 | 137.37055 | 413.59031 |
| 28 | 1.32129 | 1.74102 | 2.28793 | 2.9987 | 3.92013 | 5.11169 | 6.64884 | 8.62711 | 11.16714 | 14.42099 | 23.88387 | 39.20449 | 50.06561 | 63.80044 | 102.96656 | 164.84466 | 516.98788 |
| 29 | 1.3345 | 1.77584 | 2.35657 | 3.11865 | 4.11614 | 5.41839 | 7.11426 | 9.31727 | 12.17218 | 15.86304 | 26.74993 | 44.69312 | 57.57545 | 74.00851 | 121.50045 | 197.81359 | 646.23485 |
| 30 | 1.34785 | 1.81136 | 2.42726 | 3.2434 | 4.32194 | 5.74349 | 7.61226 | 10.06266 | 13.26768 | 17.4494 | 29.95992 | 50.95016 | 66.21177 | 85.84988 | 143.37064 | 237.37631 | 807.79357 |

# Table of the Normal Distribution

Each number in the table is the area under the normal density curve which lies between the mean and "Z" standard deviation units from the mean.

$Z = (x - \text{mean}) / \text{Standard Deviation}$

| Z | 0.0 | 0.01 | 0.02 | 0.03 | 0.04 | 0.05 | 0.06 | 0.07 | 0.08 | 0.09 |
|---|---|---|---|---|---|---|---|---|---|---|
| 0.0 | 0.000 | 0.004 | 0.008 | 0.012 | 0.016 | 0.0199 | 0.0239 | 0.0279 | 0.0319 | 0.0359 |
| 0.1 | 0.0398 | 0.0438 | 0.0478 | 0.0517 | 0.0557 | 0.0596 | 0.0636 | 0.0675 | 0.0714 | 0.0753 |
| 0.2 | 0.0793 | 0.0832 | 0.0871 | 0.091 | 0.0948 | 0.0987 | 0.1026 | 0.1064 | 0.1103 | 0.1141 |
| 0.3 | 0.1179 | 0.1217 | 0.1255 | 0.1293 | 0.1334 | 0.1368 | 0.1406 | 0.1143 | 0.148 | 0.1517 |
| 0.4 | 0.1534 | 0.1591 | 0.1628 | 0.1664 | 0.17 | 0.1726 | 0.1772 | 0.1808 | 0.1844 | 0.1879 |
| 0.5 | 0.1915 | 0.195 | 0.1985 | 0.2019 | 0.2054 | 0.2088 | 0.2123 | 0.2157 | 0.219 | 0.224 |
| 0.6 | 0.2257 | 0.2291 | 0.2324 | 0.2357 | 0.2389 | 0.2422 | 0.2454 | 0.2486 | 0.2518 | 0.2579 |
| 0.7 | 0.258 | 0.2612 | 0.2642 | 0.2673 | 0.2704 | 0.2734 | 0.2764 | 0.2794 | 0.2823 | 0.2852 |
| 0.8 | 0.2881 | 0.291 | 0.2939 | 0.2967 | 0.2995 | 0.3023 | 0.3051 | 0.3078 | 0.3106 | 0.3133 |
| 0.9 | 0.3159 | 0.3186 | 0.3212 | 0.3238 | 0.3264 | 0.3289 | 0.3315 | 0.334 | 0.3365 | 0.3389 |
| 1.0 | 0.3413 | 0.3438 | 0.3461 | 0.3485 | 0.3508 | 0.531 | 0.3554 | 0.3577 | 0.3599 | 0.3621 |
| 1.1 | 0.3643 | 0.3665 | 0.368 | 0.3708 | 0.3729 | 0.3749 | 0.377 | 0.379 | 0.381 | 0.383 |
| 1.2 | 0.3849 | 0.3869 | 0.3888 | 0.3907 | 0.3925 | 0.3944 | 0.3962 | 0.398 | 0.3997 | 0.4015 |
| 1.3 | 0.4032 | 0.4049 | 0.4066 | 0.4082 | 0.4099 | 0.4115 | 0.4131 | 0.4147 | 0.4162 | 0.4177 |
| 1.4 | 0.4192 | 0.4207 | 0.4222 | 0.4236 | 0.4251 | 0.4265 | 0.4279 | 0.4292 | 0.4306 | 0.4319 |
| 1.5 | 0.4332 | 0.4345 | 0.4357 | 0.437 | 0.4382 | 0.4394 | 0.4406 | 0.4418 | 0.4429 | 0.4441 |
| 1.6 | 0.4452 | 0.4463 | 0.4474 | 0.4484 | 0.4495 | 0.4505 | 0.4515 | 0.4525 | 0.4535 | 0.4545 |
| 1.7 | 0.4554 | 0.4564 | 0.4573 | 0.4582 | 0.4591 | 0.4599 | 0.4608 | 0.4616 | 0.4625 | 0.4633 |
| 1.8 | 0.4641 | 0.4649 | 0.4656 | 0.4664 | 0.4671 | 0.4673 | 0.4686 | 0.4693 | 0.4699 | 0.4706 |
| 1.9 | 0.4713 | 0.4719 | 0.4726 | 0.4732 | 0.4738 | 0.4744 | 0.475 | 0.4756 | 0.4761 | 0.4767 |
| 2.0 | 0.4772 | 0.4778 | 0.4783 | 0.4788 | 0.4793 | 0.4798 | 0.4803 | 0.4808 | 0.4812 | 0.4817 |
| 2.1 | 0.4821 | 0.4826 | 0.483 | 0.4834 | 0.4838 | 0.4842 | 0.4846 | 0.485 | 0.4854 | 0.4857 |
| 2.2 | 0.4861 | 0.4864 | 0.4868 | 0.4871 | 0.4875 | 0.4878 | 0.4881 | 0.4884 | 0.4887 | 0.489 |
| 2.3 | 0.4893 | 0.4896 | 0.4898 | 0.4901 | 0.4904 | 0.4906 | 0.4909 | 0.4911 | 0.4913 | 0.4916 |
| 2.4 | 0.4918 | 0.492 | 0.4922 | 0.4925 | 0.4927 | 0.4929 | 0.4931 | 0.4932 | 0.4934 | 0.4936 |
| 2.5 | 0.4938 | 0.494 | 0.4941 | 0.4943 | 0.4945 | 0.4946 | 04948 | 0.4949 | 0.4951 | 0.4952 |
| 2.6 | 0.4953 | 0.4955 | 0.4956 | 0.4957 | 0.4959 | 0.496 | 0.4961 | 0.4962 | 0.4963 | 0.4964 |
| 2.7 | 0.4965 | 0.4966 | 0.4967 | 0.4968 | 0.4969 | 0.497 | 0.4971 | 0.4972 | 0.4973 | 0.4974 |
| 2.8 | 0.4974 | 0.4975 | 0.4976 | 0.4977 | 0.4977 | 0.4978 | 0.4979 | 0.4979 | 0.498 | 0.4981 |
| 2.9 | 0.4981 | 0.4982 | 0.4982 | 0.4983 | 0.4894 | 0.4984 | 0.4985 | 0.4985 | 0.4986 | 0.4986 |
| 3.0 | 0.49865 | 0.4987 | 0.4987 | 0.4988 | 0.4988 | 0.4989 | 0.4989 | 0.4989 | 0.499 | 0.499 |
| 3.1 | 0.49903 | 0.4991 | 0.4991 | 0.4991 | 0.4992 | 0.4992 | 0.4992 | 0.4992 | 0.4993 | 0.4993 |
| 3.2 | 0.4993129 | 0.4993 | 0.4994 | 0.4994 | 0.4994 | 0.4994 | 0.4994 | 0.4995 | 0.4995 | 0.4995 |
| 3.3 | 0.4995166 | 0.4995 | 0.4995 | 0.4996 | 0.4996 | 0.4996 | 0.4996 | 0.4996 | 0.4996 | 0.4997 |
| 3.4 | 0.4996631 | 0.4997 | 0.4997 | 0.4997 | 0.4997 | 0.4997 | 0.4997 | 0.4997 | 0.4998 | 0.4998 |
| 3.5 | 0.4997674 | 0.4998 | 0.4998 | 0.4998 | 0.4998 | 0.4998 | 0.4998 | 0.4998 | 0.4998 | 0.4998 |
| 3.6 | 0.4998409 | 0.4998 | 0.4999 | 0.4999 | 0.4999 | 0.4999 | 0.4999 | 0.4999 | 0.4999 | 0.4999 |
| 3.7 | 0.4998922 | 0.4999 | 0.4999 | 0.4999 | 0.4999 | 0.4999 | 0.4999 | 0.4999 | 0.4999 | 0.4999 |
| 3.8 | 0.4999277 | 0.4999 | 0.4999 | 0.4999 | 0.4999 | 0.4999 | 0.4999 | 0.5 | 0.5 | 0.5 |
| 3.9 | 0.4999519 | 0.5 | 0.5 | 0.5 | 0.5 | 0.5 | 0.5 | 0.5 | 0.5 | 0.5 |
| 4.0 | 0.4999683 | 0.5 | 0.5 | 0.5 | 0.5 | 0.5 | 0.5 | 0.5 | 0.5 | 0.5 |
| 4.5 | 0.4999966 | 0.5 | 0.5 | 0.5 | 0.5 | 0.5 | 0.5 | 0.5 | 0.5 | 0.5 |
| 5.0 | 0.4999997133 | 0.5 | 0.5 | 0.5 | 0.5 | 0.5 | 0.5 | 0.5 | 0.5 | 0.5 |

# MBA Abbreviation Lexicon

| Abbreviation | Translation | Subject | Page |
|---|---|---|---|
| ABC | activity-based costing | A | 118 |
| AIDA | attention/interest/desire/action | M | 6 |
| B2C, B2B | business to consumer/business | M | |
| BCG | Boston Consulting Group | S | 365 |
| CAPM | capital asset pricing model | F | 215 |
| CDF | cumulative distribution function | Q | 192 |
| CDS | credit default swap | F | 234 |
| CLC | competitive life cycle | S | 370 |
| COGS | cost of goods sold | A | 94 |
| CPA | cost per action | M | 48 |
| CPG | consumer packaged goods | M | 27 |
| CPM | critical path method of scheduling | OP | 274 |
| CPM | cost per thousand | M | 40 |
| CRM | customer relationship management | OP | 294 |
| DE&I | diversity, equity, and inclusion | ET | 73 |
| DTC (D2C) | direct to consumer | M | |
| EBIT | earnings before interest and taxes | A | 95 |
| EBITDA | earnings before interest, taxes, depreciation, and amortization | A | 95 |
| EMV | expected monetary value | Q | 171 |
| EOQ | economic order quantity | OP | 280 |
| ESG | Environmental, Social, Governance criteria | ET | 72 |
| EVA | economic value added | S | 373 |
| FASB | Financial Accounting Standards Board | A | 77 |
| FIFO | first in first out | A | 83 |
| FRICTO | flexibility, risk, income, control, timing, other | F | 243 |
| FSI | freestanding insert | M | 42 |
| GAAP | generally accepted accounting principles | A | 77 |
| GDP | gross domestic product | E | 314 |
| GNP | gross national product | E | 313 |
| GRP | gross rating points | M | 39 |
| IPO | initial public offering | F | 242 |
| IRR | internal rate of return | Q | 182 |

| | | | |
|---|---|---|---|
| IT | information technology | OP | 293 |
| JIT | just-in-time inventory | OP | 279 |
| LBO | leveraged buyout | F | 253 |
| LCP | low-cost producer | S | 357 |
| LIFO | last in first out | A | 83 |
| M&A | mergers and acquisitions | F | 252 |
| MBO | management by objective | OB | 145 |
| MBWA | management by walking around | OB | 145 |
| MNC | multinational corporation | S | 374 |
| MRP | material requirements planning | OP | 282 |
| NNP | net national product | E | 314 |
| NOPAT | net operating profit after tax | A, F | 95, 255 |
| NPV | net present value | Q | 179 |
| PE | price-earnings ratio | F | 225 |
| PE | Private equity | F | 213 |
| PLC | product life cycle | M | 17 |
| POP | point of purchase | M | 43 |
| QWL | quality of work life | OB | 133 |
| RIF | reduction in force (layoff) | OB | 154 |
| ROE | return on equity | A | 112 |
| SBU | strategic business unit | S | 368 |
| SEC | Securities and Exchange Commission | F | 217 |
| SEO | Search Engine Optimization | M | 46 |
| SKU | stock keeping unit | M | 30 |
| SMSA | Standard Metropolitan Statistical Area | M | 13 |
| SOX | Sarbanes-Oxley Act | ET | 70 |
| SPC | statistical process control | OP | 287 |
| SWOT | strengths, weaknesses, opportunities, threats | M | 21 |
| TRP | total rating points | M | 39 |
| TQM | total quality management | OP | 287 |
| WACC | weighted average cost of capital | F | 247 |
| YTM | yield to maturity | F | 220 |

SUBJECT KEY: A = Accounting; E = Economics; ET = Ethics; F = Finance; M = Marketing; OB = Organizational Behavior; OP = Operations; Q = Quantitative Analysis; S = Strategy

# *Permissions*

Grateful acknowledgment is made for permission to use material from the following:

## DAY 1: MARKETING

Assael, Henry. *Consumer Behavior & Marketing Action*, 4th ed. Boston: PWS-Kent Publishing Company, 1992, p. 100.

Cullum, Leo. Cartoon, "Down in Accounting Flexing My Muscles."

Cullum, Leo. Cartoon, "I Have Credibility."

Newton, Derek A. *Sales Force Management—Text and Cases*. Copyright © 1990 by Richard D. Irwin, Inc., pp. 7–9.

## DAY 2: ETHICS

Cullum, Leo. Cartoon, "Out of My Depth."

Freeman, R. Edward, and Daniel R. Gilbert. *Corporate Strategy and the Search for Ethics*. Copyright © 1988, pp. 24–41. Adapted by permission of Prentice Hall, Englewood Cliffs, N.J.

## DAY 3: ACCOUNTING

Cullum, Leo. Cartoon, "The Phoenicians Were the *First* Accountants."

Cullum, Leo. Cartoon, "News from Accounting." *The New Yorker*, March 18, 2002. Copyright © 2002 by The New Yorker Magazine, Inc.

## DAY 4: ORGANIZATIONAL BEHAVIOR

Clawson, James. "Organizational Structure," Darden School Case UVA-OB-361, Figure 1–8, pp. 11–18. Copyright © 1988 by the Darden Graduate Business School Foundation, Charlottesville, Virginia.

Clawson, James. "Survey of Managerial Style," Darden School Case UVA-OB-358, Figure, p. 14. Copyright © 1988 by the Darden Graduate Business School Foundation, Charlottesville, Virginia.

Clawson, James. "Systems Theory and Organizational Analysis," Darden School Case UVA-OB-214, Figure 1, p. 9. Copyright © 1983 by the Darden Graduate Business School Foundation, Charlottesville, Virginia.

Cullum, Leo. Cartoon, "Ice Water in Your Veins."

Cullum, Leo. Cartoon, "Lovely Parting Gifts for You."

Gabarro, John J., and John P. Kotter. "Managing Your Boss." *Harvard Business Review* (January/February 1980), Exhibit, "Managing the Relationship with Your Boss," p. 99. Copyright © 1979 by the President and Fellows of Harvard College; all rights reserved. Reprinted by permission.

Greiner, Larry E. "Evolution and Revolution as Organizations Grow." *Harvard Business Review* (July/August 1972), Exhibit II, "The Five Phases of Growth," p. 41. Copyright © 1972 by the President and Fellows of Harvard College; all rights reserved. Reprinted by permission.

"Why People Behave the Way They Do," Darden School Case UVA-OB-183, Figure 5, p. 16. Copyright © 1986 by the Darden Graduate Business School Foundation, Charlottesville, Virginia.

Zierden, William E. "A Framework for Understanding Organizations," Darden School Case UVA-OB-183, Figure 5, p. 16. Copyright © 1986 by the Darden Graduate Business School Foundation, Charlottesville, Virginia.

Zierden, William E. "Introduction to Job Design," Darden School Case UVA-OB-91R, Figure 1, p. 2. Copyright © 1975 by the Darden Graduate Business School Foundation, Charlottesville, Virginia.

## DAY 5: QUANTITATIVE ANALYSIS

Cullum, Leo. Cartoon, "Meaningless Statistics."

Oksman, Warren, and Sherwood C. Frey. "Introduction to Analytical Probability Distributions," Case UVA-Q-205, pp. 5, 6, 14. Copyright © 1980 by the Darden Graduate Business School Foundation, Charlottesville, Virginia.

## DAY 6: FINANCE

"An Introduction to Debt Policy and Value," Case UVA-F-811, p. 1. Copyright © 1989 by the Darden Graduate Business School Foundation, Charlottesville, Virginia.
Cullum, Leo. Cartoon, "It's Not a Takeover."
Cullum, Leo. Cartoon, "Limited Partners."

## DAY 7: OPERATIONS

Cullum, Leo. Cartoon, "We're Stuck with 700,000 Bushels."

## DAY 8: ECONOMICS

Cullum, Leo. Cartoon, "I Have No Idea What It Means."

## DAY 9: STRATEGY

Ansoff, H. Igor. "Strategies for Diversification." *Harvard Business Review* (September/October 1957), Exhibit I, "Product Market Strategies for Business Growth Alternatives," p. 114. Copyright © 1957 by the President and Fellows of Harvard College; all rights reserved. Reprinted by permission.
Harris, Jared D., and Michael J. Lenox. *The Strategist's Tool Kit, 7th edition.* Copyright © 2013 by Darden Business Publishing, pp. 21, 22, 33–42.
Porter, Michael E. *Competitive Strategy: Techniques for Analyzing Industries and Competitors,* Figure 2–1, p. 39. Reprinted with the permission of The Free Press, a Division of Simon & Schuster. Copyright © 1980, 1998 by The Free Press.
Porter, Michael E. *Competitive Advantage: Creating and Sustaining Superior Performance,* Figure 1–1, p. 5, Figure 1–2, p. 6. Reprinted with the permission of The Free Press, a Division of Simon & Schuster. Copyright © 1985, 1998 by Michael E. Porter.
Waterman, Robert H., Thomas J. Peters, and Julien R. Phillips. "Structure Is Not Organization." *Business Horizons,* June 1980, Figure, p. 18. Copyright © 1980 by the Foundation for the School of Business at Indiana University. Used with permission.

## DAY 10: MBA MINICOURSES

Borden, Neil H., Jr. "Class Notes on Conducting International Business," Darden Graduate School of Business, Charlottesville, Virginia, used with permission.

# Index

accounting, 75–122
  accounting methods, 83–84
  accounting profits, 104, 174
  allocations to accounting periods,
    79–80
  balance of payments and, 327
  cost and activity-based accounting,
    118–119, 122
  fundamental concepts of, 78–85
  fundamental equation of, 87–88,
    100–101, 121
  GAAP, 3, 77–78
  managerial accounting and variances,
    115–118
  misstatement of earnings and,
    119–120
  rules of, 77–78
  see also financial statements
Accounting Standards Codification
  (ASC), 77
accrual accounting, 79–80, 93, 95, 104,
  121
accumulated value, in cash flow analysis,
  178–179, 180, 204
achievement, McClelland and need for,
  132
action levers, 128, 156, 379, 405
action planning
  marketing and, 32
  organizational behavior and, 127–
    128, 153, 156, 161, 165, 379
  quantitative analysis and, 171
active listening, 139, 165
activity-based costing (ABC), 118–119,
  122
activity forks, in decision trees, 168
activity ratios, 109, 111–112

activity squares, in decision trees,
  170–171
advertising, 7, 11, 19, 38–40, 61
affiliation, McClelland and need for,
  132
Affluent Society, The (Galbraith), 324
after-tax costs, of business borrowing,
  263
agency agreements, 399
aggregate supply (AS)/aggregate demand
  (AD), 303
Agile methodology, operations and,
  293
AIDA (Attention/Interest/Desire/Action),
  6, 48
algebra refresher, 197
allocations to accounting periods, 95
amorphous organizational structures,
  152
amortization, 95
Annual Statement Studies, 114–115
Ansoff, H. I., 351–352
Ansoff matrix, 351–352, 380
APCFB model, organizational behavior
  and, 128–130, 165
arbitration, 393
Art of War, The (Sun-Tzu), 378–379
Arthur D. Little (ADL), 368–370
artificial intelligence (AI), 294, 297
assembly line production, 270–271
asset value per share, 227
assets
  on balance sheet, 86–93
  noncurrent asset (NCA), 91
Attention/Interest/Desire/Action (AIDA),
  6
awareness, marketing and, 7

balance of payments (BOP), 327, 338
balance sheet, 86–93, 121
    accounting process and, 88–90
    cash flow statement's link to, 100–101
    contents of, 86–87
    example of, 89–93, 97–98
    fundamental accounting equation and, 87–88, 108
    income statement's link to, 98–99
    liquidity and, 90–91
    owners' equity and, 92–93
    T accounts and, 88–89
    working capital and, 91
bank financing, as business decision, 240–241
bankruptcy law, 400
barriers to entry, 22–23, 353, 356
Basset, Lucinda, 407–408, 410
Becker, Gary, 326
behavioral economics, 326
behavioral market segmentation, 14
bell curve (normal distribution), in probability theory, 187–192, 205, 287–288
benchmarking, 285–286
Beta, 211–214, 263
binomial distribution, in probability theory, 184–186, 205
bitcoin (BTC), 332–335
Black, Fisher, 230
Black-Scholes Option Pricing Model, 230–231
Black Swan investors, 218
blockchains, 332–335
blocking strategy, competitive analysis and, 25
bonds, 218–223, 241–242, 263
book value per share, 226
bosses
    boss-centered leadership, 134
    managing of, 141–142
Boston Consulting Group (BCG), 358, 365–367, 369, 378
bracket median technique, cumulative distribution and, 194

brand equity, marketing and, 33–34
brand loyalty, 18, 42
break even point, economics of marketing plan and, 53–56, 61
budgets, in managerial accounting, 115–118
Burns, David, 408–409
business law, 390–402
    agency agreements, 399
    bankruptcy law, 400
    commercial paper, 398–399
    common law, 390
    contracts, 394–395
    crimes and torts, 393–394
    dispute settling without courts, 393
    federal legislation and, 401–402
    legal process, 391–392
    property law, 395
    sales contracts, 395–398
    secured transactions, 400–401
    substantive and procedural laws, 391
business strategy, 350
business structures, 207–210
    corporations, 208–210
    partnerships, 208
    proprietorships, 207–208
buyer's remorse, 8
buying process
    marketing and, 5, 6–12, 60
    personal selling and, 41
    promotional decisions and, 38

C corporations, 209–210
call to action (CTA), 48
callable bonds, 223
calls, in options market, 229, 231–232, 263
capacity
    linear programming and constraints of, 271–273
    marginal costs and, 205
    material requirements planning and, 282–284
    six Ms of, 269–273, 299

capital asset pricing model (CAPM),
    215–216, 225, 248, 263
capital budgeting, business decisions
    and, 235–239
capital leases, business financing and,
    240
capital structure, of business, 243,
    246–249, 263
*Capitalism, Socialism and Democracy*
    (Schumpeter), 324
capitalization ratios, 109, 110
captive sales force, 37
cash basis accounting, 79–80, 121
cash flow
    business investment decisions and,
        238–239
    importance of cash to business,
        99–100
    investing and, 403
    multiple per share, 227
    valuation for M&As and, 254–259
cash flow analysis, 172–183
    accumulated value, 178–179, 204
    example of, 175–183
    internal rate of return (IRR), 182–185,
        204
    net present value (NPV), 179–182,
        204
    uses of, 172–175
cash flow, statement of, 99–107, 121
    balance sheet's link to, 100–101
    example of, 102–107
    uses of, 102
causal chains, organizational behavior
    and, 126–127, 164
Central Limit Theorem, 187
Champy, James, 372
change management, organizational
    behavior and, 161–163
channel intermediaries, 27–28, 30
channel margins, 28–30, 37, 60
channel power, 30–31, 60
channels of distribution. *See* distribution
    channels
chart of accounts, 88

chatbots, 294, 297
"Choosing Strategies for Change"
    (Kotter and Schlesinger), 161
click-through rate (CTR), 48
coaching and development, office
    procedures and, 139–140
coercive power, organizational behavior
    and, 144
collateralized mortgage obligations
    (CMOs), 234–235
Committee of Sponsoring Organizations
    of the Treadway Commission
    (COSO), 71
common law (case law), 390
*Competitive Advantage* (Porter), 352
competitive analysis, 21–26, 58–59
    barriers to entry and, 22–23, 353,
        356
    competitive factors and market
        analysis and, 20
    market share leverage and, 23
    perceptual mapping and, 23–25, 34,
        60
    positioning and, 25–26
    product pricing and, 50–51
    SWOT and, 21–22
competitive life cycle (CLC), 370–372,
    380
*Competitive Strategy* (Porter), 352
conservatism, in accounting, 81–82
consistency, in accounting, 83–84
consul (perpetuity) bonds, 222
consultation process, personal selling
    and, 41
consumer analysis, marketing and, 4–15,
    58
    buying process, 5, 6–12
    need category, 5–6
    promotional decisions, 37–38
    segmentation, 4–5, 12–15
consumer price index (CPI), 314
consumer sales promotions, 41
contests, sales promotions and, 42–43
contingency approach, to operations,
    268

contingent liabilities, 81
continuous production, 270
continuous quality improvement (CQI), 268
contracts, law and, 394–395
convertible bonds, 222–223
cookies, web sites and, 47
cooperative advertising, 36
cooperative payments, 36
core competencies, strategy and, 372
corporation, as business structure, 208–210
cost accounting, 118–119
cost of goods sold (COGS), 80, 83–84, 94–95
cost per action (CPA), 48
cost-per-lead (CPL), 48
cost per thousand (CPM), in advertising, 40, 46
cost plus pricing, 49
country analysis, international business and, 335–336, 338
coupons, sales promotions and, 41–42
covered options, 229
Covey, Stephen, 411
"crashing the project," 275
creative/creatives, advertising and, 39
"creative destruction," 324
creativity, as personality trait, 135–136
credit default swaps (CDS), 234–235
credit, 5 Cs of, 240–241. See also debt
credits, in accounting, 88, 97
crimes and torts, 393
Critical Path Method (CPM) Scheduling, 274–276, 299
Crosby, Philip, 286, 289–290
crucial conversations
    office procedures and, 142–144
    organizational behavior and, 165
cryptocurrency, 332–335
cultural relativism, 65–66
culture
    as element of organizational behavior, 155
    in Seven S model, 342–343

cumulative distribution function (CDF), 192–196, 205
cumulative stock issues, 228
current assets, accounting for, 104–105
customer relationship management (CRM), 294–295, 299
customers
    organizational structures and focus on, 148–150
    strategy and retention of, 372
cycle time, operations and, 292

debits, in accounting, 88, 97
debt
    debt to equity ratio, 112
    as fixed obligation, 110
    as noncurrent liability, 91
decision tree analysis, 167–172, 193, 204
DeFi (decentralized finance), cryptocurrencies and, 334
demand side platform (DSP), 48
Deming, W. Edwards, 286–288
demographic segmentation, marketing and, 13
depreciation, 95, 104, 121, 175, 315
derivatives, 228–235
differentiation
    marketing and, 33–34
    strategy and, 356–357, 360–361
diffusion, product life cycle and, 17
direct sales, 45–46
discount factor
    business investment decisions and, 237–238
    in cash flow analysis, 180–183
    financial management and, 258–259
discount rate, government policies and, 321
distribution analysis, marketing and, 7–8, 18
distribution channels
    competitive analysis and, 26–31
    marketing mix and, 36–37, 60
distributions, in probability theory, 204

diversification
  of investments, 211, 213
  strategy and, 351–352, 364–365
dividends
  accounting and, 92–93, 96, 99, 106, 112
  business finance and payment of,
    250–251
  dividend growth model, 224–225,
    250, 263
  dividend payout ratios, 250
  dividend yield, 250
  paid on stocks, 224–228
  paying in stock shares, 251
divisional organizational structures, 150,
  151
Dodd-Frank Wall Street Reform and
  Consumer Protection Act, 71
dollar amount per order, 46
double entry accounting system, 88
double taxation, corporations and,
  209–210
Drucker, Peter, 145
Du Pont Chart, 113–114
dummy variables, 201–202
duration, bond market and, 221–222,
  236, 263

early adopters/early majority, marketing
  and, 18
earnings before interest and taxes
  (EBIT), 95
earnings before interest, taxes,
  depreciation, and amortization
  (EBITDA), 95
earnings, cautions about misstatement
  of, 119–120
economic order quality (EOQ),
  280–282, 299
economic value added (EVA), 373
economics, 300–338
  cryptocurrency and, 332–335
  economists of note, 323–326
  international economics, 326–337
  macroeconomics, 303, 311–326,
    336–337

marketing plans and, 51–57, 59
microeconomics, 303–311, 336, 337
supply and demand and, 302–303
economies of scale, 357–358
effective cost-per-X (eCPL, eCPA,
  eCPM), 48
efficiency studies, operations and,
  265–268
efficiency variances, in managerial
  accounting, 117
efficient frontier, business investments
  and, 214, 263
efficient market hypothesis (EMH),
  216–218
8 Wastes of Production, 291
elasticity coefficient, 308
elasticity of demand, 307–309, 337
employment, Keynesian theory and,
  312–321
empowerment, of employees, 133
end game strategy, marketing and, 20
enterprise resource planning (ERP)
  software, 284
enterprise value (EV), 254, 259, 263
entity, in accounting, 78
entrepreneurship, as personality trait,
  136
entrepreneurship through acquisition
  (ETA), 136
environmental analysis, as strategic tool,
  346, 380
environmental, social, and governance
  (ESG) investing, 72–73, 74
equilibrium (E), in economics, 302–303,
  305, 309, 319, 331–333, 337
equity leverage, 245
ethics, 62–74
  ESG and, 72–73, 74
  example issues and, 63
  relativism and, 64–67, 74
  Sarbanes-Oxley Act and, 69–72, 74
  social responsibility of businesses,
    63–64, 73
  stakeholder analysis and, 64, 67–68,
    74

event forks, in decision trees, 168, 184
evolution, organizational behavior and, 159–160, 165
exchange rate systems, 329–332
exchange-traded funds (ETFs), 213–214
exclusive distribution, 18, 35
expansion strategies, 351–352
expectancy theory of motivation, 131–132, 165
expected monetary value (EMV), 170–171, 193–196, 204
expenses, recorded as debts on balance sheet, 97
expert power, organizational behavior and, 144–145

Federal Reserve Board, monetary tools of, 321–323
feedback and evaluation, office procedures and, 139–140
*Feeling Good* (Burns), 408–409
FIFO (First In First Out) inventory, 83–84
finance, 206–263
    business financing decisions, 236–251
    business structures, 207–210
    financial management, 210, 235–251
    mergers and acquisitions, 252–262
    *see also* investments, business finance and
Financial Accounting Standards Board (FASB), 77, 78
financial leverage, 24, 110, 112–114, 245, 251, 413
financial management, 210, 235–251
    business financing decisions, 239–251
    business investment decisions, 235–239
financial planning, personal, 411–415
financial statements, 85–107
    balance sheet, 86–93
    cash flow statement, 99–107
    income statement, 93–99
    using ratios with, 108–115, 121

financing activities, in cash flow statement, 106
financing costs, cash flow analysis and, 175
fiscal policy. *See* government monetary policies
fiscal year, 97
Five Forces Theory of Industry Structure, 352–356, 380
5 Cs of credit, 240–241
fixed costs, 52–53, 403
flow diagrams
    capacity problems and, 271
    inventory and, 278–279
    operations and, 299
focus strategy, 356–357, 361
footnotes, in financial statements, 84, 247
foreign exchange, economics and, 327–329
Four Cs of Internet Marketing, 4, 31
Four Ps of marketing mix, 32–51, 59, 60
fractiles, cumulative distribution function and, 194–196
Freeman, R. Edward, 66–67
freestanding inserts (FSIs), 42
frequency, advertising and, 39
Frey, Donald N., 276
FRICTO, business financing decisions and, 243–245, 263
Friedman, Meyer, 137
Friedman, Milton, 64, 312, 366–367. *See also* monetarist economic theory
Friedman, Thomas, 375
fulfillment, promotional decisions, 48–49
functional organizational structures, 148
functional strategy, 350
future value
    in cash flow analysis, 178
    table of, 419
futures and swaps, 234–235

Gabarro, John, 141–142
Galbraith, John Kenneth, 324

game theory, 364

Gantt Chart Scheduling, 273–274, 299

Gantt, Henry, 273

*gemba,* 161–162, 268

general partners, 208

*General Theory of Employment, Interest and Money, The* (Keynes), 312

Generally Accepted Accounting Principles (GAAP), 3, 77–78

geographic organizational structures, 150, 151

geographic segmentation, marketing and, 13

gig economy, organizational behavior and, 163–164

Gilbreth, Frank and Lillian, 266

Gilder, George, 326

global macroeconomics, 326–336
    triple-panel diagram of, 331–332

globalization, strategy and, 373–375, 380

goal congruence, 130, 165

going concern concept, in accounting, 82–83

government monetary policies
    Federal Reserve Board and, 321–323
    impossible trilogy of, 331
    Keynes and full employment, 312–321

granular sales data, 23

Green, Scott, 71

Greiner, Larry E., 159

gross domestic product (GDP), 314–315

gross margin, 93–95, 121

gross national product (GNP), 325, 337
    Keynes and full employment, 313–319
    monetarists and, 315–316, 319–320

gross rating points (GRPs), 39

growth/share matrix, strategy and, 365–367


Hammer, Michael, 372

Hawthorne effect, 266–267

hedge funds, 213

hedging, as options strategy, 233

Hertzberg, Fred, 131

hierarchy of needs, 131

high-involvement products, 9–12

historical costs, in accounting, 82–83

holding, in business law, 390

human relations movement, operations and, 266–267

human talent flow model, 156–157

hurdle rate, in cash flow analysis, 181, 182

hybrid organizational structures, 152–153


impossible trilogy, of government economic policy, 331

in-store demonstrations, sales promotions and, 43–44

incentives, to dealers and employees, 43

income statement, 93–96, 121
    balance sheet's link to, 98–99
    contents of, 93, 95–96
    entries to, 96–98
    example of, 94–95

incrementalism, strategy and, 377, 380

industry analysis, strategy and, 352–356

inelastic demand, 308

inflation
    Federal Reserve and, 322–323
    GNP and, 314, 320–321
    international business and, 336–337
    Keynesian economics and, 320–321

influencers, 7, 47, 48, 66

information search, marketing and buying process, 7

information technology (IT)
    jargon of, 295–296
    operations and, 293–296

innovators, marketing and, 18

integration
    operations and, 292–293
    strategy and, 347–349, 380

interactive voice response (IVR), 294

internal control rules, Sarbanes-Oxley and business ethics and, 70, 71

internal rate of return (IRR), 182–183, 204

International Accounting Standards Board (IASB), 77–78
international business
  globalization and, 373–375, 380
  tips for conducting, 387
International Financial Reporting Standards (IFRS), 77–78
internet
  role in channels of distribution, 31
  search engines, web marketing, and vocabulary of, 46–48
inventory
  operations and, 268, 278–285
  reasons for holding, 279–280, 299
  stage of production and, 278–279, 299
investing activities, in cash flow statement, 105–106, 107
investment and spending curve (IS), 317–319
investment bankers, 242
investments, business finance and, 210–235
  bond market, 218–223
  capital asset pricing model for stocks, 215–216, 263
  efficient frontier and, 214, 263
  futures and swaps, 234–235
  investment decisions and, 235–239
  options market, 228–233
  risk and return and, 210–214
  stock market, 224–228
"invisible hand," in economics, 302, 323
IS/LM curve, 317–319

Jeffers, Susan, 407, 409
job design organizational model, 132–133
job fractionalization, 265
job shop production, 271
Johnson, Spencer, 410
journal entries
  to balance sheet, 88–89
  to income statement, 96–98
junk bonds, 223

Juran, Joseph, 286, 287
just-in-time inventory (JIT), 279–280

kaizen, 268
kanban, 280
key performance indicators (KPIs), 39
Keynes, John Maynard, 312
Keynesian economics, 312–321, 333–337
Kotler, Philip, 2
Kotter, John, 141–142, 161

Laffer, Arthur, 325–326, 338
late majority, marketing and, 18
leadership
  as personality trait, 133–135
  tips for, 407–411
learning curve (experience curve), 358–360, 365, 374, 378, 380
learning efficiencies, strategy and, 356–360
learning organizations, 156
lease financing, as business financing decision, 240
least squares regression method, 197
legal process, steps in, 391–393. See also business law
legitimate power, organizational behavior and, 144
leverage
  CAPM and, 248
  equity leverage, 245
  financial leverage, 24, 110, 112–114, 251, 413
  market share and competitive analysis, 23
leveraged buyout (LBO), 100, 173, 253
liabilities, 81, 86–93, 105
LIFO (Last In First Out) inventory, 83–84
limited partners, 208
line extension, marketing and, 32, 33–34
linear programming (LP), capacity constraints and, 271–273, 299

linear regression. *See* regression analysis and forecasting

linkages, synergy and, 375–376

liquidity
  on balance sheet, 90–91
  cash flow statement and, 104
  liquidity preference, 317
  liquidity ratio, 109
  money curve and, 317–319

losses, recognizing in accounting, 81–82

low-cost producers (LCPs), 357

low-involvement products, marketing and, 9–12

M1 and M2 (money supply), 319

Mackintosh, James, 334

macroeconomics, 303, 311–326, 336–337
  country analysis and, 335–336, 338
  economists of note, 323–326
  Friedman, monetarism, and economic growth, 312–313, 315–316, 319–323, 336–337
  Keynes, full employment, and government policies, 312–321, 333–337

management by objective (MBO), 145

management by walking around (MBWA), 145

managerial accounting, 115–118, 286, 344

*Manager's Guide to the Sarbanes-Oxley Act* (Green), 71

"Managing Your Boss" (Gabarro and Kotter), 141–142

Mankiw, Gregory, 331

margin accounts, for trading derivatives, 234

marginal propensity to consume (MPC), 316–317

marginal revenue (MR) and marginal costs (MC), 304–307, 337

marginal utility (MU), 307

margins and costs, 26–31, 37

market analysis, 16–20, 58
  competitive factors, 20
  product life cycle, 17–20
  relevant market, 16–17

market risk premium (MRP), 215

market share leverage, 23

market structures, 310–311, 337

market value added (MVA), 373

marketing, 1–61
  competitive analysis, 21–26, 58–59
  consumer analysis, 4–15, 58
  distribution analysis, 26–31
  economics of plan, 51–57, 59
  market analysis, 16–20, 58
  marketing mix development, 32–51, 59
  need for internal consistency and mutual support in, 3, 32, 36, 57, 342
  revision of plan, 57–58

marketing mix (4 Ps), 32–51, 59, 60
  place of sale decisions, 35–37
  pricing decisions, 49–51
  product decisions, 32–35
  promotional decisions, 37–49

markup on selling price, 28–30

Maslow, Abraham, 131

mass customization, 293

matching, in accounting, 79–80, 93, 95

material requirements planning (MRP), 282–284, 299

materiality, in accounting, 84–85

matrix organizational structures, 150, 152

Mayo, Elton, 266–267, 299

MBA degree programs, ranking of schools offering, xii–xvi

McClelland, David, 132

McGregor, Douglas, 267

McKinsey & Company, 65, 367–369, 372

mean ($\mu$), in quantitative analysis, 188–191, 193, 194–195, 205

media clutter, 40

mediation, 393

medium, 188
mergers and acquisitions (M&A), 252–262
    financial reasons for, 252–253
    making bid, 262
    types of, 253–254
    valuation process for, 254–261
metaverse, 296–297
microeconomics, 303–311, 336, 337
Miller, Merton, 245
mind-mapping, creativity and, 136, 137
mission statement, in Seven S model, 344–345
mode, in normal distribution, 188
Modigliani, Franco, 245
monetarist economic theory, 312–313, 315–316, 319–323, 336–337
money
    monetarism and money supply, 319–323, 333
    Quality Theory Equation of money, 319–321
    time value of, 180, 220–221, 237
monopolistic market structure, 310–311
Monte Carlo simulations, 195
motivation, expectancy theory of, 131–132
movies, references to and quotes about business in, 387–390
multifactor strategic analysis, 367–368
multinational corporations (MNCs), 145, 374
multiplier effect, fiscal policies and, 316, 321, 338
multivariable regression, 201
mutual funds, 213–214

naive relativism, 65
natural law, as ethics framework, 66
need categories, marketing and, 5–6, 60
negotiating tips, 386
net income, in accounting, 96–99
net national product (NNP), 314–315
net operating profit after tax (NOPAT), 95, 262

net present value (NPV)
    bond market and, 220
    business investment decisions and, 235, 237–239
    in cash flow analysis, 179–182, 204
    M&A and, 262
net working capital, 91, 104–105, 121
net worth. See owners' equity
New Industrial State, The (Galbraith), 324
new technology, operations and, 292–293
Newton, Derek A., 41
noncurrent asset (NCA), 91
noncurrent liability (NCL), 91
normal distribution (bell curve)
    in probability theory, 187–192, 205, 287–288
    table for, 420

objectivity, in accounting, 80–81, 82
Ohno, Taiichi, 291
Okun, Arthur, 324–325
oligopoly market structure, 310
online marketing, 46
open market operations, 322
operating activities, in cash flow statement, 104–105, 107
operating income, accounting for, 96
operating leases, business decisions and, 240
operating profit, in accounting, 95
operational research (OR), 267
operations, 264–299
    current topics in, 292–297
    historical research into, 265–268, 299
    problem solving framework for, 268–285, 299
    standards and control, 285–291
opportunity costs, economics and, 304
optimal capital structure, 243, 246–249
options market, 228–233
organizational behavior (OB), 123–165
    basic organizational model, 146–156, 165

evolution and revolution in
organizations, 159–160, 165
expectancy model of motivation,
131–132, 165
gig economy and remote work and,
163–164
human talent flow model, 156–157
job design, 132–133
office procedures of MBAs, 139–145
organizational behavior and, 161–163
personality traits of MBAs, 133–139
problem-solving model, 125–128
psychology and APCFB model, 128–
130, 165
systems theory and organizational
analysis, 157–158
organizational structures, 146–156, 165,
342, 345
Ouchi, William, 267–268
owners' equity, on balance sheet, 86–90,
92–93

paradigms, organizational behavior and,
156, 165
partnership, as business structure, 208
pay-per-view (PPV), web sites and,
47–48
payback period
business investment decisions and,
235, 236–237
economics of marketing plan and,
56–57
Pearson Tukey Method, 195
PEG ratio, 226
penetration, pricing and, 50
perceived value, to consumer, 49–50
perceptual mapping, 23–25, 34, 60
performance appraisals, office
procedures and, 136–140
personal selling, promotional decisions
and, 40–41
personality traits, of MBAs, 133–139
PERT Technique, 274
Peters, Thomas J., 340–344
Phillips, A. W., 320–321, 324

Phillips Curve, 321
Phillips, Julien R., 340
place of sale decisions, marketing mix
and, 35–37
planograms, 31
point-of-purchase (POP) displays, 43
Poisson distribution, 192
policies, as element of organizational
behavior, 146
Porter, Michael, 352–356
portfolio strategies, 364–370, 380
positioning, 25–26, 34
postpurchase behavior, marketing and, 8
power
McClelland and need for, 132
organizational behavior and types of,
144–145, 165
preferred stock, 227–228
premiums, sales promotions and, 42
present value, 180, 262, 418. *See also* net
present value (NPV)
price and volume variances, 115–118,
121
price-earnings ratio (PE), 225–226
price elasticity of demand, 51, 307–309
price points, elastic and inelastic, 51
price/quality relationship, 50
price-to-sales ratio, 226
pricing decisions, 49–51, 61
prime rate, government policies and, 321
prisoner's dilemma, 363, 380
probability density function, 184,
187–189, 191–192
probability mass function, 184–185,
187, 192–193
probability theory, 183–196
binomial distribution, 184–186, 205
cumulative distribution function,
192–196, 205
distributions, generally, 184–185, 204,
211
normal distribution (bell curve),
187–192, 205, 287–288
problem definition, organizational
behavior and, 156

problem solving framework, for
    operations, 268–285
    capacity, 268, 269–273
    inventory, 268, 278–285
    scheduling, 268, 273–278
    standards and control, 269, 285–291
problem-solving organizational model,
    125–127
procedural laws, 391
procedures, as element of organizational
    behavior, 146
producer price index (PPI), 314
product decisions, marketing mix and,
    32–35, 60
product life cycle (PLC), 17–20, 34–35,
    50, 60, 360
Production and Operations
    Management (POM) classes,
    264–265
production methods, basic types of,
    270–271
products, organizational structures and,
    148, 149
profitability index (PI), 238–239
profitability ratios, 109, 112–113, 114
promotional decisions, 37–49
    advertising and, 38–40
    buying process and, 38
    direct sales, 45–46
    fulfillments, 48–49
    online marketing, 46
    personal selling and, 40–41
    public relations and publicity, 44–45
    sales promotions, 41–44
    search engines, web marketing, and
        vocabulary, 46–48
property law, 395
proprietorships, as business structure,
    207–208
Ps, of strategy, 377
psychographic segmentation, marketing
    and, 13
psychology, organizational behavior
    and, 128–130
public relations/publicity, 44–45

public speaking tips, 386
pull strategies, promotional decisions
    and, 38
purchase decision, marketing and, 8,
    11–12
purchase price variances, in managerial
    accounting, 117
pure competition market structure, 311
pure monopoly market structure, 310
push strategies, promotional decisions
    and, 38
puts, in options market, 229, 232–233,
    263

quality circles, 268
quality control, gurus of, 286–291,
    299
quality of work life (QWL), 133
Quality Theory Equation, 319–321
quantitative analysis, 166–205
    cash flow analysis, 172–183
    decision tree analysis, 167–172
    future value table, 419
    normal distribution table, 420
    present value table, 418
    probability theory, 183–196
    regression analysis and forecasting,
        196–203, 205
    time series techniques, 203
quantitative easing (QE), Federal
    Reserve and, 322
quantitative tightening (QT), Federal
    Reserve and, 322
queueing theory, scheduling and,
    276–278, 299
Quinn, James Brian, 377

R (Range) Control Charts, 289
R square, in regression analysis,
    200–201
rate of return (ROR), 46
ratios, financial statements and, 108–115
real estate investing, tips for, 403–407
Reengineering the Corporation (Champy
    and Hammer), 372

referent power, organizational behavior and, 144

refunds, sales promotions and, 42

regression analysis and forecasting, 196–203, 205

relationship marketing, 20

relativism, business ethics and, 64–67, 74

relevant markets, marketing and, 16–17, 60

remote work, organizational behavior and, 163–164

reprimands, office procedures and, 140

repurchase agreements (Repos), 243

research
  marketing and, 8–9
  tips and resources for, 381–385

reserve requirements, Federal Reserve and, 322

retained earnings (RE), 92, 97, 98–99, 106

return on assets (ROA), 112–114

return on equity (ROE), 112–113

revenue, recorded as credits on balance sheet, 97

reverse repurchase agreements (Reverse Repos), 243

revising, of marketing plan, 57–58

revolution, organizational behavior and, 159–160, 165

reward power, organizational behavior and, 144

Ricardo, David, 326–327

Ries, Al, 25

risk and return, 8, 210–214

role relativism, 65

Roseman, Ray, 137

sales contracts (in UCC), 395–398

sales promotions, 41–44

samples, sales promotions and, 42

Sarbanes-Oxley Act (2002), 69–72, 74, 119

satisfiers and dissatisfiers, 131

scheduling, operations and, 268, 273–278

Schlesinger, Leonard A., 161

Scholes, Myron, 230

Schumpeter, Joseph, 324

search engine marketing (SEM), 46–47

search engine optimization (SEO), 46–47

search engine results pages (SERP), 46–47

secured transactions (in UCC), 400

Securities and Exchange Commission (SEC), 71

security market line (SML), 215–216

segmentation
  direct mail and, 46
  marketing and, 4–5, 12–15, 17, 60

selective distribution, marketing and, 18, 35

Seven S model, strategy and, 340–345, 380

*7 Habits of Highly Effective People* (Covey), 222

"7 Principle of Supply Chains" (Shih), 284

share of voice, 40

shelf talkers, 43

Shewhart, W.A., 287

Shih, Willy, 284

signaling, as competitive strategy, 361–364, 380

six Ms of capacity, 269–273, 299

Six Sigma, 287–288

skills, in Seven S model, 343, 345

skimming, pricing and, 50

Smith, Adam, 323, 338

social relativism, 65

social responsibility, of businesses, 63–64, 73

sole proprietorships, 207–208

source problems, organizational behavior and, 126–127

span of control, organizational behavior and, 153–154, 165

Special Purpose Acquisition Companies (SPACs), 242–243

spending multiplier, 316, 338
spiffs, 43
stablecoins, 334
staff, in Seven S model, 343, 345
stakeholders, 64, 67–68, 74
standard deviation (σ), in probability
    theory, 188–189, 192, 200–201,
    205, 287
standard error, 200–201
standards and control
    managerial accounting and, 115–118
    operations and, 269, 285–291
*stare decisis,* 390
Statement of Cash Flows. *See* cash flow,
    statement of
statistical process control (SPC), 287–
    288, 299
statistics. *See* quantitative analysis
Stern Stewart & Co., 373
stock keeping unit (SKU), 30–31
stocks and stock market, 224–228
    corporate ownership and, 208
    stock issuance, 242
    stock splits, 251
    *see also* dividends
strategic business unit (SBU) system,
    368–370
strategic skepticism, 377–378
strategy, 339–380
    Chinese warfare and, 378–379
    competitive life cycle and, 370–372,
        380
    competitive strategies, 361–364, 380
    as element of organizational behavior,
        146, 340–345
    environmental analysis, 346, 380
    expansion strategies, 351–352
    fads in, 372–373
    generic strategies, 356–361
    globalization and, 373–375, 380
    implementation of, 379
    industry analysis, 352–356
    levels of, 349–351
    portfolio strategies, 364–370, 380
    skepticism and, 377–378

Seven S model and, 340–345, 380
    synergy and, 375–376, 380
    value chain and integration, 347–349,
        380
style, in Seven S model, 342–343, 345
subchapter S corporations, 209–210
subordinate goals, in Seven S model,
    344, 345
subsystems, organizational analysis and,
    157–158
Sun-Tzu, 378–379
sunk costs, 52, 55, 169, 204
supply and demand, economics and,
    302–303
supplier credit, as business financing
    decision, 239–240
supply chain management, 278, 299
supply-side economics, 325–326
sweepstakes, sales promotions and,
    42–43
SWOT (Strengths, Weaknesses,
    Opportunities, and Threats), 21–22,
    60
synergy, 375–376, 380
systemic risk, 211
systems
    as element of organizational behavior,
        154–155
    in Seven S model, 343–344, 345
systems theory, and organizational
    analysis, 157–158, 165

T accounts, 88
T statistic, regression analysis and, 201
Taguchi, Genichi, 290–291
target volume, economics of marketing
    plan and, 54–55
tax rates and strategies
    accounting for taxes, 96
    after-tax costs of business borrowing
        and, 241–242
    double taxation of corporations,
        209–210
    Laffer Curve and, 325
Taylor, Frederick, 265–266, 267, 299

Taylor Rule, 321
television, advertising and, 40
Theories X, Y, and Z, about operations, 267–268
therblig, 266
Thompson, Chuck, 135–136
time and motion studies, 265–266
time-based competition, 292
time series forecasting, 203
time value of money, 180, 220–221, 237
torts, 393
Total Quality Management (TQM), 287
total rating points (TRPs), 39
total (true) advertising cost of sales, 48
trade-directed sales promotions, 43
triple net lease, 403
Trout, Jack, 25
Type A/Type B behaviors, as personality traits, 136–139

unethical decisions, avoiding rationalization for, 66–67
Uniform Commercial Code (UCC), 391
  commercial paper and, 398–399
  sales contracts and, 395–398
  secured transactions and, 400–401
unique (unsystemic) risk, 211
universalism, as ethical framework, 66
upper and lower control limits, production and, 288
US dollar, stablecoins and, 334
user-generated content (UGC), 44, 47
utilitarianism, as ethical framework, 66

value chain, strategy and, 347, 380
variable costs, 52–53, 403

variances, in managerial accounting, 115–118
VCM leadership model, 134–135, 165
view-through click (VTC), 48
viral marketing, 44
visions statements, in Seven S model, 345
volatility, risk and, 211, 221, 230
volume variances, in managerial accounting, 116

Wanniski, Jude, 326
want got gaps, 125–126, 164
Waterman, Robert H., 340
weighted average cost of capital (WACC), 247–250, 258–259
*What a Great Idea* (Thompson), 135–136
white spaces (areas of opportunity), 24
working capital
  on balance sheet, 91, 121
  on cash flow statement, 104–105, 107
  finance and, 257
  net working capital, 91, 104–105, 121
*World Is Flat, The* (Friedman), 375
writing tips, 402–403

X Bar Control Charts, 289

yield curve, 218–219
yield to maturity (YTM), bond market and, 220

Z value, 190–191
zero coupon bonds, 222

# *About the Author*

STEVEN SILBIGER, MBA, CPA, is the chief marketing officer and cofounder of Top Dog Direct and an expert with a gift for communicating sophisticated financial business issues in the clearest manner possible. More than 650,000 copies of his acclaimed *The Ten-Day MBA* have been sold to date. A top-ten graduate of the Darden Graduate School of Business at the University of Virginia, Silbiger lives in Philadelphia and New York with his family.